# Linux®
# Administrator
# Street Smarts
## A Real World Guide to Linux
## Certification Skills

D1517899

Roderick W. Smith

BICENTENNIAL
1807
WILEY
2007
BICENTENNIAL

Wiley Publishing, Inc.

Acquisitions and Development Editor: Maureen Adams
Technical Editor: Randy Muller
Production Editor: Sarah Groff-Palermo
Copy Editor: Judy Flynn
Production Manager: Tim Tate
Vice President and Executive Group Publisher: Richard Swadley
Vice President and Executive Publisher: Joseph B. Wikert
Vice President and Publisher: Neil Edde
Book Designers: Judy Fung, Bill Gibson
Compositor: Jeffrey Wilson, Happenstance Type-O-Rama
Proofreader: Nancy Riddiough
Indexer: Ted Laux
Cover Designer: Ryan Sneed
Anniversary Logo Design: Richard Pacifico

# Acknowledgments

Although this book bears my name as author, many other people contributed to its creation. Without their help, this book wouldn't exist, or at best it would exist in a lesser form. Maureen Adams, the acquisitions editor, helped get the book started. Sarah Groff-Palermo, the production editor, oversaw the book as it progressed through all its stages. Randy Muller, the technical editor, checked the text for technical errors and omissions—but any mistakes that remain are my own. Judy Flynn, the copy editor, helped keep the text grammatical and understandable. Nancy Riddiough, the proofreader, checked the text for typos. I also thank Neil Salkind and others at Studio B, who helped connect me with Wiley to write this book.

# About the Author

Roderick W. Smith is a consultant and writer on computer technology. He has more than a dozen books to his name, mostly about Linux and other open source software. These titles include *Linux in a Windows World* (O'Reilly, 2005), *LPIC-1: Linux Professional Institute Certification Study Guide* (Sybex, 2005), and *Linux+ Study Guide, Third Edition* (Sybex, 2005). He is also the author of *Linux Magazine's* monthly "Guru Guidance" column. His Web page is http://www.rodsbooks.com. Rod resides in Woonsocket, Rhode Island.

# Contents at a Glance

# Contents

# Introduction

Why should you learn about Linux? It's growing in popularity, and it's inexpensive and flexible. Linux is also a major player in the small and mid-sized server field, and it's an increasingly viable platform for workstation and desktop use as well. By understanding Linux, you'll increase your standing in the job market. Even if you already know Windows or Mac OS and your employer uses these systems exclusively, understanding Linux will give you an edge when you are looking for a new job or if you are looking for a promotion. For instance, this knowledge will help you to make an informed decision about if and when you should deploy Linux.

Several Linux certifications have been developed to help Linux professionals demonstrate their qualifications to work with Linux. These include the Linux Professional Institute's (LPI's) LPIC-1 certification and the Computing Technology Industry Association's (CompTIA's) Linux+ certification. These are both introductory Linux exams that cover the basics of Linux system administration and its underlying hardware.

This book exists as a hands-on introduction to Linux with the goal of helping you pass the LPIC-1 or Linux+ exam. Because these exams cover basic Linux command-line tools, software management, hardware configuration, filesystems, the X Window System, the boot process, scripts, security, documentation, administration, and networking, those are the topics that are emphasized in this book. Unlike many certification books, this one emphasizes a hands-on approach by using goal-oriented tasks to demonstrate Linux tools. This approach to learning about Linux makes it a useful adjunct to more traditional textbooks, such as my *LPIC-1: Linux Professional Institute Certification Study Guide* (Sybex, 2005) and my *Linux+ Study Guide, 3rd Edition* (Sybex, 2005).

## What Is Linux?

Linux is a clone of the Unix operating system (OS) that has been popular in academia and many business environments for years. Formerly used exclusively on large mainframes, Unix and Linux can now run on small computers—which are actually far more powerful than the mainframes of just a few years ago. Because of its mainframe heritage, Unix (and hence also Linux) scales well to perform today's demanding scientific, engineering, and network server tasks.

Linux consists of a kernel, which is the core control software, and many libraries and utilities that rely on the kernel to provide features with which users interact. The OS is available in many different distributions, which are collections of a specific kernel with specific support programs.

## Who Should Buy This Book

Anybody who wants to pass the LPIC-1 or Linux+ exam may benefit from this book. As a hands-on tutorial guide, this book should be considered an adjunct to a more traditional certification textbook; given the size of this book, it can't cover every objective of both the LPIC-1 and Linux+ exams. This book, in conjunction with practice on a Linux system, can help you gain the sort of hands-on experience that will help you pass the exam. You can pick up this book and learn from it even if you've never used Linux before, although you'll find it an easier read if you've at least casually used Linux for a few days. Although this book is geared toward LPIC-1 and Linux+ candidates, it's also a good and quick introduction to Linux for those who want to get up to speed on the OS but who don't intend to take either exam.

This book is written with the assumption that you know at least a little bit about Linux (what it is, and possibly a few Linux commands). I also assume that you know some basics about computers in general, such as how to use a keyboard, how to insert a floppy disk into a floppy drive, and so on. Chances are you have used computers in a substantial way in the past—perhaps even Linux, as an ordinary user, or maybe you have used Windows or Mac OS. I do *not* assume that you have extensive knowledge of Linux system administration, but if you've done some system administration, you can still use this book to fill in gaps in your knowledge.

As a practical matter, you'll need a Linux system with which to practice and learn in a hands-on way. LPIC topic 102 is titled "Linux Installation & Package Management," and Linux+ domain 1.0 is titled "Installation," but neither of the exams nor this book focuses on actually installing Linux on a computer from scratch, although some of the prerequisites (such as disk partitioning) are covered. You may need to refer to your distribution's documentation to learn how to accomplish this task.

## How This Book Is Organized

This book consists of seven phases plus this introduction. The phases are organized as follows:

- Phase 1, "Working on the Command Line," covers the basic tools you need to interact with Linux. These include shells, redirection, pipes, the Vi editor, and basic file manipulation commands.

- Phase 2, "Managing Hardware and the Kernel," describes $x86$ and $x86$-64 hardware and how Linux interacts with it. Specific tasks include setting BIOS options, using Linux tools to identify your hardware, configuring USB and disk devices, compiling a kernel, and managing the X Window System.

- Phase 3, "Managing Software," covers the programs you'll use to manage software. Much of this phase is centered around the RPM and Debian package management systems. Additional tasks cover compiling software from source code, managing processes, and controlling the computer's startup scripts.

- Phase 4, "Documenting the System," covers maintaining your own notes on the system's configuration, using log files created by the computer, and locating documentation on the computer itself and online.

- Phase 5, "Managing Partitions and Filesystems," covers the tools used to manage partitions and the filesystems contained on them. Specific tasks include planning your partitions, creating partitions, creating filesystems, mounting and unmounting filesystems, maintaining filesystem health, and installing a boot loader.

- Phase 6, "Configuring Network Features," is the largest phase in the book. It describes basic network configuration (bringing up a network connection, using a network connection, and so on), configuring routers and servers (routers, super servers, mail servers, Web servers, file sharing servers, and SSH servers), and printing.

- Phase 7, "Managing Security," describes security tasks in Linux, including methods of blocking unwanted external access, setting user security restrictions, setting good passwords, and monitoring the system for security breaches.

Each phase consists of a series of numbered tasks. Each task includes several sections:

**Scenario**   This section outlines a situation that would require use of the commands or features described by the task. It also introduces any fictitious hostnames, IP addresses, or other information that will be used as example data in the remainder of the task. You may need to change such fictitious identifiers for use on your own system or network, of course.

**Scope of Task**   This section describes the probable time requirements; the necessary hardware, software, and preparatory setup steps; and any potential pitfalls or risks associated with the task.

**Procedure**   You'll read what to do to perform the task in this section. It's broken down into subsections that vary with the specific task.

**Criteria for Completion**   This section summarizes the task; you should verify that you've achieved each of the goals.

You should perform each task to acquire hands-on experience with Linux, helping you to understand how Linux works. I recommend you don't stop there, though. This book provides you with the basics you're likely to use most often, but most of the commands and features described by each phase's tasks have greater depth than I can cover in the space allotted. Read the online documentation and, above all, try doing more with the commands. Only by using the commands and features yourself will you truly learn them well.

 A few tasks are highly system specific. For instance, Phase 3 includes tasks for installing software via both RPM Package Manager (RPM) and Debian package systems. Most Linux systems use just one of these two systems (in fact, using both is a bad idea), and a few use other systems entirely. Thus, you won't be able to complete both of these tasks unless you have access to two Linux installations. If you can't complete a task because you lack appropriate hardware or software or for any other reason, you should still read the task and do as much of it as you can do.

## Conventions Used in This Book

This book uses certain typographic styles in order to help you quickly identify important information and to avoid confusion over the meaning of words such as onscreen prompts. In particular, look for the following styles:

- *Italicized text* indicates key terms that are described at length for the first time in a chapter. (Italic is also used for emphasis.)

- A `monospaced font` indicates the contents of configuration files, messages displayed at a text-mode Linux shell prompt, filenames, text-mode command names, and Internet URLs.

- *Italicized monospaced text* indicates a variable—information that differs from one system or command run to another, such as the name of a client computer or a process ID number.

- **Bold monospaced text** is information that you're to type into the computer, usually at a Linux shell prompt. This text can also be italicized to indicate that you should substitute an appropriate value for your system. (When isolated on their own lines, commands are preceded by non-bold monospaced $ or # command prompts.)

In addition to these text conventions, which can apply to individual words or entire paragraphs, a few conventions highlight segments of text:

A note indicates information that's useful or interesting but that's somewhat peripheral to the main text. A note might be relevant to a small number of networks, for instance, or it may refer to an outdated feature.

A tip provides information that can save you time or frustration and that may not be entirely obvious. A tip might describe how to get around a limitation or how to use a feature to perform an unusual task.

Warnings describe potential pitfalls or dangers. If you fail to heed a warning, you may end up spending a lot of time recovering from a bug, or you may even have to restore your entire system from scratch.

# The Exam Objectives

Behind every computer industry exam you can be sure to find exam objectives—the broad topics in which exam developers want to ensure your competency. The LPIC and Linux+ objectives are very similar, which is why this book can cover both exams. They aren't quite identical, though.

## LPIC Objectives

The official LPI objectives for the LPIC 101 and 102 exams are listed here. LPI breaks its certification into two exams, but you're likely to take both exams on the same day. Certain topics are covered, to a different extent, in both the 101 and 102 exams.

Exam objectives are subject to change at any time without prior notice and at LPI's sole discretion. Please visit the LPIC Certification page of LPI's website (http://www.lpi.org/en/lpic.html) for the most current listing of exam objectives.

## Exam 101, Topic 101: Hardware & Architecture

1.101.1 Configure Fundamental BIOS Settings

1.101.3 Configure Modem and Sound cards

1.101.4 Setup SCSI Devices

1.101.5 Setup different PC expansion cards

1.101.6 Configure Communication Devices

1.101.7 Configure USB devices

## Exam 101, Topic 102: Linux Installation & Package Management

1.102.1 Design hard disk layout

1.102.2 Install a boot manager

1.102.3 Make and install programs from source

1.102.4 Manage shared libraries

1.102.5 Use Debian package management

1.102.6 Use Red Hat Package Manager (RPM)

## Exam 101, Topic 103: GNU & Unix Commands

1.103.1 Work on the command line

1.103.2 Process text streams using filters

1.103.3 Perform basic file management

1.103.4 Use streams, pipes, and redirects

1.103.5 Create, monitor, and kill processes

1.103.6 Modify process execution priorities

1.103.7 Search text files using regular expressions

1.103.8 Perform basic file editing operations using vi

## Exam 101, Topic 104: Devices, Linux Filesystems, Filesystem Hierarchy Standard

1.104.1 Create partitions and filesystems

1.104.2 Maintain the integrity of filesystems

1.104.3 Control mounting and unmounting filesystems

1.104.4 Managing disk quota

1.104.5 Use file permissions to control access to files

1.104.6 Manage file ownership

1.104.7 Create and change hard and symbolic links

1.104.8 Find system files and place files in the correct location

## Exam 101, Topic 110: The X Window System

1.110.1 Install & Configure XFree86

1.110.2 Setup a display manager

1.110.4 Install & Customize a Window Manager Environment

## Exam 102, Topic 105: Kernel

1.105.1 Manage/Query kernel and kernel modules at runtime

1.105.2 Reconfigure, build, and install a custom kernel and kernel modules

## Exam 102, Topic 106: Boot, Initialization, Shutdown and Runlevels

1.106.1 Boot the system

1.106.2 Change runlevels and shutdown or reboot system

## Exam 102, Topic 107: Printing

1.107.2 Manage printers and print queues

1.107.3 Print files

1.107.4 Install and configure local and remote printers

## Exam 102, Topic 108: Documentation

1.108.1 Use and manage local system documentation

1.108.2 Find Linux documentation on the Internet

1.108.5 Notify users on system-related issues

## Exam 102, Topic 109: Shells, Scripting, Programming and Compiling

1.109.1 Customize and use the shell environment

1.109.2 Customize or write simple scripts

## Exam 102, Topic 111: Administrative Tasks

1.111.1 Manage users and group accounts and related system files

1.111.2 Tune the user environment and system environment variables

1.111.3 Configure and use system log files to meet administrative and security needs

1.111.4 Automate system administration tasks by scheduling jobs to run in the future

1.111.5 Maintain an effective data backup strategy

1.111.6 Maintain system time

## Exam 102, Topic 112: Networking Fundamentals

1.112.1 Fundamentals of TCP/IP

1.112.3 TCP/IP configuration and troubleshooting

1.112.4 Configure Linux as a PPP client

## Exam 102, Topic 113: Networking Services

1.113.1 Configure and manage `inetd`, `xinetd`, and related services

1.113.2 Operate and perform basic configuration of sendmail

1.113.3 Operate and perform basic configuration of Apache

1.113.4 Properly manage the NFS, smb, and nmb daemons

1.113.5 Setup and configure basic DNS services

1.113.7 Set up secure shell (OpenSSH)

## Exam 102, Topic 114: Security

1.114.1 Perform security administration tasks

1.114.2 Setup host security

1.114.3 Setup user level security

The preceding objective list includes only the basic objective titles. You should consult the complete LPIC exam list to learn what commands, files, and procedures you should be familiar with before taking the exam.

## Linux+ Objectives

CompTIA has released two versions of its Linux+ exam. The first version of the exam is no longer being offered. The official CompTIA objectives for the revised Linux+ exam are listed here.

Exam objectives are subject to change at any time without prior notice and at CompTIA's sole discretion. Please visit the Linux+ Certification page of CompTIA's Web site (http://certification.comptia.org/linux/) for the most current listing of exam objectives.

## Domain 1.0 Installation

1.1 Identify all system hardware required (for example: CPU, memory, drive space, scalability) and check compatibility with Linux Distribution

1.2 Determine appropriate method of installation based on environment (e.g., boot disk, CD-ROM, network (HTTP, FTP, NFS, SMB))

1.3   Install multimedia options (e.g, video, sound, codecs)

1.4   Identify purpose of Linux machine based on predetermined customer requirements (e.g., appliance, desktop system, database, mail server, web server, etc.)

1.5   Determine what software and services should be installed (for example: client applications for workstation, server services for desired task)

1.6   Partition according to pre-installation plan using `fdisk` (for example: /boot, /usr, /var, /home, swap, RAID/volume, hot-spare, lvm)

1.7   Configure file systems (for example: (ext2) or (ext3) or REISER)

1.8   Configure a boot manager (for example: LILO, ELILO, GRUB, multiple boot options)

1.9   Manage packages after installing the operating systems (for example: install, uninstall, update) (for example: RPM, `tar`, `gzip`)

1.10  Select appropriate networking configuration and protocols (for example: `inetd`, `xinetd`, modems, Ethernet)

1.11  Select appropriate parameters for Linux installation (for example: language, time zones, keyboard, mouse)

1.12  Configure peripherals as necessary (for example: printer, scanner, modem)

## Domain 2.0 Management

2.1   Manage local storage devices and file systems (for example: `fsck`, `fdisk`, `mkfs`) using CLI commands

2.2   Mount and unmount varied filesystems (for example: Samba, NFS) using CLI commands

2.3   Create files and directories and modify files using CLI commands

2.4   Execute content and directory searches using `find` and `grep`

2.5   Create linked files using CLI commands

2.6   Modify file and directory permissions and ownership (for example: `chmod`, `chown`, sticky bit, octal permissions, `chgrp`) using CLI commands

2.7   Identify and modify default permissions for files and directories (for example: umask) using CLI commands

2.8   Perform and verify backups and restores (`tar`, `cpio`)

2.9   Access and write data to recordable media (for example: CDRW, hard drive, flash memory devices)

2.10  Manage runlevels and system initialization from the CLI and configuration files (for example: /etc/inittab and `init` command, /etc/rc.d, `rc.local`)

2.11  Identify, execute, manage and kill processes (for example: `ps`, `kill`, `killall`, `bg`, `fg`, `jobs`, `nice`, `renice`, `rc`)

2.12  Differentiate core processes from non-critical services (for example: `init`, [kernel processes], PID, and PPID values)

2.13  Repair packages and scripts (for example: resolving dependencies, repairing, installing, updating applications)

2.14  Monitor and troubleshoot network activity (for example: `ping`, `netstat`, `traceroute`)

2.15  Perform text manipulation (for example: `sed`, `awk`, `vi`)

2.16  Manage print jobs and print queues (for example: `lpd`, `lprm`, `lpq`, CUPS)

2.17  Perform remote management (for example: `rsh`, `ssh`, `rlogin`)

2.18  Perform NIS-related domain management (`yp` commands)

2.19  Create, modify, and use basic shell scripts

2.20  Create, modify, and delete user and group accounts (for example: `useradd`, `groupadd`, `/etc/passwd`, `chgrp`, `quota`, `chown`, `chmod`, `grpmod`) using CLI utilities

2.21  Manage and access mail queues (for example: sendmail, postfix, `mail`, `mutt`) using CLI utilities

2.22  Schedule jobs to execute in the future using "`at`" and "`cron`" daemons

2.23  Redirect output (for example: piping, redirection)

## Domain 3.0 Configuration

3.1  Configure client network services and settings (for example: settings for TCP/IP)

3.2  Configure basic server network services (for example: DNS, DHCP, SAMBA, Apache)

3.3  Implement basic routing and subnetting (for example: `/sbin/route`, IP forward statement)

3.4  Configure the system and perform basic makefile changes to support compiling applications and drivers

3.5  Configure files that are used to mount drives or partitions (for example: `fstab`, `mtab`, SAMBA, nfs, syntax)

3.6  Implement DNS and describe how it works (for example: edit `/etc/hosts`, edit `/etc/host.conf`, edit `/etc/resolv.conf`, `dig`, `host`, `named`)

3.7  Configure a Network Interface Card (NIC) from a command line

3.8  Configure Linux printing (for example: CUPS, BSD LPD, SAMBA)

3.9  Apply basic printer permissions

3.10  Configure log files (for example: syslog, remote logfile storage)

3.11  Configure the X system

3.12  Set up environment variables (for example: $PATH, $DISPLAY, $TERM, $PROMPT, $PS1)

## Domain 4.0 Security

4.1  Configure security environment files (for example: `hosts.allow`, `sudoers`, `ftpusers`, `sshd_config`)

4.2  Delete accounts while maintaining data stored in that user's home directory

4.3   Given security requirements, implement appropriate encryption configuration (for example: blowfish 3DES, MD5)

4.4   Detect symptoms that indicate a machine's security has been compromised (for example: review logfiles for irregularities or intrusion attempts)

4.5   Use appropriate access level for login (for example: `root` level vs user level activities, `su`, `sudo`)

4.6   Set process and special permissions (for example: SUID, GUID)

4.7   Identify different Linux Intrusion Detection Systems (IDS) (for example: Snort, PortSentry)

4.8   Given security requirements, implement basic IP tables/chains (note: requires knowledge of common ports)

4.9   Implement security auditing for files and authentication

4.10  Identify whether a package or file has been corrupted / altered (for example: checksum, Tripwire)

4.11  Given a set of security requirements, set password policies to match (complexity / aging / shadowed passwords) (for example: identify systems not shadow passwords)

4.12  Identify security vulnerabilities within Linux services

4.13  Set up user-level security (i.e., limits on logins, memory usage and processes)

## Domain 5.0 Documentation

5.1   Establish and monitor system performance baseline (for example: `top`, `sar`, `vmstat`, `pstree`)

5.2   Create written procedures for installation, configuration, security and management

5.3   Document installed configuration (for example: installed packages, package options, TCP/IP assignment list, changes—configuration and maintenance)

5.4   Troubleshoot errors using systems logs (for example: `tail`, `head`, `grep`)

5.5   Troubleshoot application errors using application logs (for example: `tail`, `head`, `grep`)

5.6   Access system documentation and help files (for example: `man`, `info`, readme, Web)

## Domain 6.0 Hardware

6.1   Describe common hardware components and resources (for example: connectors, IRQs, DMA, SCSI, memory addresses)

6.2   Diagnose hardware issues using Linux tools (for example: `/proc`, disk utilities, `ifconfig`, `/dev`, live CD rescue disk, `dmesg`)

6.3   Identify and configure removable system hardware (for example: PCMCIA, USB, IEEE1394)

6.4   Configure advanced power management and Advanced Configuration and Power Interface (ACPI)

6.5   Identify and configure mass storage devices and RAID (for example: SCSI, ATAPI, tape, optical recordable)

# Phase
# 1

# Working on the Command Line

Linux's tools for running programs and manipulating files are simple, unglamorous, and powerful. Although you can use GUI tools to drag and drop files, real Linux street smarts requires you to be able to manage your files from the command line by using odd-sounding commands such as ls, cp, ln, and mv. In the first few tasks of this phase, you'll learn to use some of the most basic of these tools. Don't think that the basic nature of these commands is unimportant, though; like the foundation of a house, these commands support more dramatic parts of the structure. Specific tasks described in this phase include using basic command-line features; managing files, directories, and links; finding files; and editing files.

Later tasks in this phase go further, examining streams, pipes, redirection, the shell environment, and shell scripts. You'll also learn about managing accounts. Most of the tasks in this phase assume you have both a normal user account and root access, but you must also be able to create, delete, and otherwise manage normal user accounts for yourself or other users of a Linux system.

 This phase maps to portions of the CompTIA Linux+ objectives 2 and 3 and to portions of the LPIC objectives 103, 104, 109, and 111.

# Task 1.1: Use Basic Command-Line Features

Before delving into the details of commands used to manage, find, and manipulate files, you must be able to use basic command-line features. Linux supports several *shells*, which are programs that accept typed commands and display their output. Some shell commands are built into the shell, but many others are actually external programs. Knowing how to use your shell's features will enable to you to be more productive at the Linux command line. The most common Linux shell is the Bourne Again Shell (bash), and it is the one described here. Other shells, such as tcsh and zsh, support similar features, although some details differ.

## Scenario

A user is experiencing problems with the whatis program, a standard Linux script that the user frequently runs. As the administrator, you must check that this script exists and that it's not obviously corrupt. In the process, you'll use several important Linux command-line features.

Actually correcting a problem such as the one described here is likely to require the use of Linux's package management tools. These are described in Phase 3, "Managing Software."

## Scope of Task

This task is fairly straightforward. It requires little time and effort. You might want to continue experimenting with bash after you've completed this task, though.

### Duration

This task will take about half an hour to complete. Once you're familiar with the commands, using each one takes just seconds.

### Setup

You must have access to a working Linux system. For the specific examples shown in this task, your system should be configured to give you a bash shell by default and the whatis program must be installed. Both of these conditions are usually true. If your Linux computer is not currently turned on, do so now and wait for it to finish booting.

### Caveats

Most Linux systems configure bash as the default shell for all users. If your account is configured to use tcsh or some other shell, some of the commands and procedures described here won't work. Even with bash, a few details differ from one account or computer to another. Most commonly, the form of the command prompt varies from one system to another and sometimes even from one account to another. For simplicity and brevity, this book denotes user shell commands with a leading dollar sign ($), which is often used as part of real bash prompts, as in:

```
$ ls
```

This line means to type **ls** at a user command prompt. Some systems use a prompt that ends in a greater-than sign (>) instead of a dollar sign.

Most Linux systems provide a different prompt (often terminating in a hash mark, #) for the superuser (root) account. When a command must be typed as root, this book shows command lines beginning with this symbol:

```
# ls
```

When short commands appear inside paragraph text, the prompt ($ or #) is omitted.

# Procedure

To complete this task, you must log into your account on the affected workstation and enter several Linux commands. In the process, you'll learn how to type and edit commands, how to use command completion, and how to use command history. You'll also learn a few of the more common Linux commands.

## Logging In

The first task is logging into the Linux system. From the console, there are two ways to log in: using a graphical user interface (GUI) login manager or using a text-mode console. In either case, you type your username and then your password, typically in response to a `login` or `username` prompt and a `password` prompt, respectively.

Upon a successful text-mode login, you'll be greeted by a Linux command prompt and you can begin issuing Linux commands. GUI logins, though, present you with a graphical desktop environment—probably the K Desktop Environment (KDE) or the GNU Network Object Model Environment (GNOME). Although GUI desktop environments are convenient for end users, they don't usually present you with a text shell by default. To access one, you must locate an appropriate option from the menuing system. Look for entries called Shell, Terminal, or `xterm`. If all else fails, look for an option to run a command by name and type **xterm** in the dialog box. This should launch an `xterm` window, as shown in Figure 1.1. Your default shell should be running in this window.

If your computer displays a GUI login prompt but you'd prefer to work in a purely text-mode session, press Ctrl+Alt+F1. This key sequence switches to the first virtual console, which normally holds a text-mode session. You can switch between several (usually six) text-mode consoles by pressing Alt+F1 through Alt+F6 for each of the first six virtual consoles. The X Window System, Linux's GUI environment, normally runs in virtual console 7, so pressing Alt+F7 from a text-mode session switches to X if it's running.

**FIGURE 1.1** An xterm window enables you to type text-mode commands in a GUI session.

For this task, you should log in as an ordinary user. In fact, it's good practice to *always* log in as an ordinary user. You can subsequently acquire superuser privileges from your ordinary user account if you need such access (described shortly in "Obtaining Superuser Privileges"). Logging in as an ordinary user and then obtaining superuser privileges is better than logging in directly as root because this two-step process leaves a trace in the system log file of who acquired root privileges. On systems with multiple administrators, this can make it easier to track down who caused problems if an administrator makes a mistake.

The Linux system administration account is conventionally called root, but it's possible to configure Linux with aliases for this name. Under any name, this account is often referred to as the *superuser* account.

## Verifying the Presence of a File

To verify that a file is present, use the ls command. This command's name stands for *list*; it shows a list of files that match a file specification you provide. (Task 1.2 describes file specifications in more detail.) For now, check for the presence of the whatis file, which is located in the /usr/bin directory:

```
$ ls /usr/bin/whatis
/usr/bin/whatis
```

Used without any extra parameters, ls displays the names of all the matching files. Because this example provides the complete name of a single file, only that filename is displayed, on the line immediately following the command's line.

If you type the name of a directory, ls displays the names of all the files in that directory. Try this with the /usr/bin directory now—but be prepared for copious output! The /usr/bin directory holds the program files associated with many (but not all) Linux commands.

Like many Linux commands, ls accepts options that modify its actions. One of the most important is -l (that's a lowercase *L*, not a number *1*), which generates a "long" listing:

```
$ ls -l /usr/bin/whatis
-rwxr-xr-x  1 root root 2409 Nov 19  2004 /usr/bin/whatis
```

I describe what this output means in more detail in Task 1.2.

## Examining the File

Now that you know the command file is present, you can examine it. Three commands are very handy for examining text files:

**cat**   This command's name is short for *concatenate*, and it's used to merge two or more files together. If it's passed just one filename, though, it copies the file to the screen. This can be a good way to look at a short text file. Try it on the whatis file by typing **cat /usr/bin/**

**whatis**. Unfortunately, the whatis file is too long to fit on a standard 80×25 screen, although it might fit on an extra-large screen or resized xterm.

**more** This command is a simple *pager*—it displays text a page (that is, a screenful) at a time. When you're done reading a page, press the spacebar and more displays the next page.

**less** Unix (and hence Linux) programmers aren't afraid to display their (sometimes quirky) senses of humor. The more program is limited—for instance, it doesn't let you page backward in a file. Thus, when it came time to improve more, the authors of the improved program called it less as a joke. You can use the keyboard's arrow keys and various other options to move back and forth in the file. When you're done, press the Q key to exit from the program. Type **man less** to learn more about less. (The man command is described in more detail shortly, in "Getting Help.")

All of these commands are intended to work on text files. When fed non-text files, such as binary program files, cat is likely to cause a lot of annoying beeping and may leave your screen displaying gibberish when you type new commands. Typing **reset** should restore the screen to usability. Both more and less cope a bit better with binary files, but you're not likely to be able to learn much from them. Recent versions of less are often smart enough to recognize certain common binary file types and pass them through a translator so you can see their contents in text form.

## Working with Directories

Whenever you're running a shell, you're working in a specific directory. When you refer to a file without providing a complete path to the file, the shell works on the file in the current working directory. (Similar rules apply to many programs.) The cd command changes the current working directory. For instance, typing **cd /home/sally** changes the current directory to /home/sally. The tilde (~) character is a useful shortcut; it stands for your home directory, so **cd ~** will have the same effect as **cd /home/sally** if your home directory is /home/sally.

Many Linux systems display the current working directory in their prompts. In Figure 1.1, the current working directory is the home directory (~); that character appears in the command prompt and will be replaced by other directory names if you use cd to change directories. If your prompt doesn't include this information and you want to know what directory you're working in, type **pwd**. This command's name stands for *print working directory*; it displays the current working directory's name.

Unlike DOS and Windows, Linux doesn't use drive identifier letters, such as C:. All directories reside in a single unified directory tree. Removable disks and multiple disk partitions are mounted within that tree, as described in Phase 5, "Managing Partitions and Filesystems." Another important difference between Linux and Windows is that Linux uses a forward slash (/) to separate directories, whereas Windows uses a backslash (\) for this purpose.

## Using Command Completion

Many users find typing commands to be tedious and error prone. For this reason, Linux shells include various tools that can help speed up operations. The first of these is *command completion*: Type part of a command or (as an option to a command) part of a filename and then press the Tab key. The shell tries to fill in the rest of the command or the filename. If just one command or filename matches the characters you've typed so far, the shell fills it in and places a space after it. If the characters you've typed don't uniquely identify a command or filename, the shell fills in what it can and then stops. Depending on the shell and its configuration, it may beep. If you press the Tab key again, the system responds by displaying the possible completions. You can then type another character or two and, if you haven't completed the command or filename, press the Tab key again to have the process repeat.

The most fundamental Linux commands have fairly short names—cd, pwd, and so on. Some other commands are much longer, though, such as traceroute or sane-find-scanner. Filenames can also be quite lengthy—up to 255 characters on many filesystems. Thus, command completion can save a lot of time. It can also help you avoid typos.

To try out command completion, type the preceding ls command to verify the presence of the whatis program, but press the Tab key once or twice after you type the wh portion of the whatis name. Chances are you'll see a list of half a dozen or more possible completions. Add the a from the whatis name and press the Tab key again. Your system might then complete the whatis name or display a shorter list of possible completions, depending upon whether or not other files with names beginning wha appear in your /usr/bin directory.

## Using Command History

Another helpful shell shortcut is the *shell history*. The shell keeps a record of every command you type (stored in ~/.bash_history in the case of bash). If you've typed a long command recently and want to use it again, or use a minor variant of it, you can pull the command out of the history. The simplest way to do this is to press the up arrow key on your keyboard; this brings up the previous command. Pressing the up arrow key repeatedly moves through multiple commands so you can find the one you want. If you overshoot, press the down arrow key to move down the history. The Ctrl+P and Ctrl+N keystrokes double for the up and down arrow keys, respectively.

Another way to use the command history is to search through it. Press Ctrl+R to begin a backward (reverse) search, which is what you probably want, and begin typing characters that should be unique to the command you want to find. The characters you type need not be the ones that begin the command; they can exist anywhere in the command. You can either keep typing until you find the correct command or, after you've typed a few characters, press Ctrl+R repeatedly until you find the one you want. The Ctrl+S keystroke works similarly but searches forward in the command history, which might be handy if you've used a backward search or the up arrow key to look back and have overshot. In either event, if you can't find the command you want or change your mind and want to terminate the search, press Ctrl+G to do so.

Try out these features now; use the up arrow key to recall your previous command, and press Ctrl+R and a portion of that command to search for it.

## Editing Commands

Frequently, after finding a command in the history, you want to edit it. The bash shell, like many shells, provides editing features modeled after those of the Emacs editor:

**Move within the line**    Press Ctrl+A or Ctrl+E to move the cursor to the start or end of the line, respectively. The left and right arrow keys will move within the line a character at a time. Ctrl+B and Ctrl+F will do the same, moving backward and forward within a line. Pressing Ctrl plus the left or right arrow keys will move backward or forward a word at a time, as will pressing Esc and then B or F.

**Delete text**    Pressing Ctrl+D or the Delete key deletes the character under the cursor, while pressing the Backspace key deletes the character to the left of the cursor. Pressing Ctrl+K deletes all text from the cursor to the end of the line. Pressing Ctrl+X and then Backspace deletes all the text from the cursor to the beginning of the line.

**Transpose text**    Pressing Ctrl+T transposes the character before the cursor with the character under the cursor. Pressing Esc and then T transposes the two words immediately before (or under) the cursor.

**Change case**    Pressing Esc and then U converts text from the cursor to the end of the word to uppercase. Pressing Esc and then L converts text from the cursor to the end of the word to lowercase. Pressing Esc and then C converts the letter under the cursor (or the first letter of the next word) to uppercase, leaving the rest of the word unaffected.

**Invoke an editor**    You can launch a full-fledged editor to edit a command by pressing Ctrl+X followed by Ctrl+E. The bash shell attempts to launch the editor defined by the $FCEDIT or $EDITOR environment variable or Emacs as a last resort. (Environment variables are described later in this phase.)

These editing commands are just the most useful ones supported by bash; consult its man page to learn about many more obscure editing features. In practice, you're likely to make heavy use of command and filename completion, command history, and perhaps a few editing features.

Try editing your previous command by pulling it out of the history and then changing it. For instance, you might add the -1 option to the command that did not use it or verify the presence of another file, such as /usr/bin/who.

## Getting Help

Linux provides a text-based help system known as man. This command's name is short for *manual*, and its entries (its man pages) provide succinct summaries of what a command, file, or other feature does. For instance, to learn about man itself, you would type **man man**. The result is a description of the man command.

The man utility uses the less pager to display information. When you're done, press Q to exit from less and the man page it's displaying.

Some programs have moved away from man pages to info pages. The basic purpose of info pages is the same as that for man pages, but info pages use a hypertext format so that you can move from section to section of the documentation for a program. Type **info info** to learn more about this system.

Both man pages and info pages are usually written in a terse style. They're intended as reference tools, not tutorials; they frequently assume basic familiarity with the command, or at least with Linux generally. For more tutorial information, you must look elsewhere, such as this book or the Web. The Linux Documentation Project (http://tldp.org) is a particularly relevant Web-based resource for learning about various Linux topics.

## Obtaining Superuser Privileges

To fully administer a Linux system, you must sometimes use the superuser account, which goes by the name root. Although you can log directly into the root account, it's generally best to instead log into a regular user account and then acquire superuser privileges.

One way to do this is to use the su command, whose name stands for *switch user*. You can actually acquire any user's identify in this way by typing the target username after the command, as in **su hyde** to acquire hyde's privileges. If you omit a username, root is assumed, so typing **su** alone is equivalent to typing **su root**. In any of these cases, you must know the target user's password, so only users who know the root password may acquire superuser privileges via su. Once you're using the root account, though, you can use su to acquire any user's privileges without a password. This can be a helpful problem-solving tool, since you can locate problems that are user specific.

Try using su to acquire root privileges. Depending upon your system configuration, chances are your prompt will change. For instance, a Fedora Core system shows the following prompts:

```
[sally@halrloprillalar ~]$ su
Password:
[root@halrloprillalar sally]#
```

## Logging Out

Once you're done, you should log out. This is a particularly important security measure if your computer is in a public place. If you're using a login shell (that is, if you logged into the shell via a login prompt), you can log out by typing **logout** at the command prompt. If you're using an xterm window or have used su to acquire another user's privileges, though, you should type **exit** to log out. (In fact, exit will also work with login shells.)

If you logged into an X session using a GUI login tool, you should log out from that session. Most desktop environments provide an obvious way to do that via their main menuing systems. Typically, you'll see a power button icon or a menu option titled "log out" or "exit." Some environments give you the option of logging out, rebooting the computer, or shutting down the computer. Be sure to save files and exit from programs that open files before logging out of an X session. You needn't worry about shutting down xterm windows or other programs that don't open disk files, though.

**WARNING**  Don't shut down or reboot Linux by pressing the power or reset buttons on the computer's case. Like most modern OSs, Linux requires a controlled shutdown to avoid damaging the data on its hard disk. If you want to shut down the system, use a shutdown option at a GUI login prompt or type **shutdown -h now** as root. Replace -h with -r if you want to reboot the computer rather than shut it down. As a practical matter, if the computer has completely frozen, you may need to perform an uncontrolled shutdown, but you should try to avoid this practice whenever possible.

## Criteria for Completion

You have completed this task when you've verified the presence of the whatis command in /usr/bin and checked to see that it's a shell script (that is, a program that consists of text-mode commands that a shell executes). In the process, you'll learn about file-examination commands, command completion, command history, the Linux man system, and acquiring superuser access. If a user were really having problems with the whatis command, though, it might be missing or corrupt, in which case you'd be unable to find it in /usr/bin or it might contain gibberish rather than text-mode commands.

# Task 1.2: Manage Files and Directories

Many Linux features are implemented via files and directories. To perform some operations, you may need to move, rename, delete, or otherwise modify files and directories. Thus, an understanding of the commands used to accomplish these jobs is necessary for effective use of Linux. This task gives you practice with these commands.

## Scenario

A new project is starting at your place of work. To prepare, you must create a directory to hold files that are to be accessible to all the members of this project, who are already members of the users group. You must also populate this new directory with a few files (which, for purpose of this exercise, you'll copy from the /etc directory).

## Scope of Task

This task requires creating, copying, and managing the permissions of both files and directories.

### Duration

This task should take about half an hour to complete. Once you've learned the task, you should be able to perform similar tasks in just a few minutes.

## Setup

You need perform no special setup to do this task; just log into your computer and acquire `root` privileges.

## Caveats

Because this task is performed as `root` and uses powerful file-manipulation commands, a potential for devastating errors exists. Certain typos, when entered as `root`, can obliterate an entire Linux installation. Be very careful when performing this task, or any other task that requires `root` privileges. When you type a command, remove your hands from the keyboard, proofread the command, and be sure it's the correct command *before* you press the Enter key to finalize it.

All of these commands can be used by ordinary users, with the partial exception of `chown`; only `root` may use `chown` to change the primary owner of a file, although ordinary users may use `chown` to change the group of a file. These examples show `root` using the commands because the task is an administrative one that requires `root` privileges because of the locations of the files.

# Procedure

To perform this task, you must create a shared directory, copy files to the new directory, remove extraneous files, and set the ownership and permissions on the new directory and the files you've copied. These actions utilize some of the most important Linux file-manipulation commands, such as `mkdir`, `cp`, `rm`, `chown`, and `chmod`.

## Creating a Shared Directory

To create the shared directory, use the `mkdir` command, which creates (makes) a directory (hence the command's name). This command takes the name of the directory you want to create as an argument. For instance, to create a directory called `/home/project7`, you'd type this:

```
# mkdir /home/project7
```

Thereafter, the `/home/project7` directory should exist. By default, this directory is owned by the user who issued the `mkdir` command and has permissions based on the defaults for that user. You can tell `mkdir` to create a directory with specific permissions by adding the -m *mode* option between `mkdir` and the directory name. Another method of adjusting permissions is described shortly, in "Setting File and Directory Permissions."

Ordinarily, `mkdir` doesn't create directories in the path up to the final directory specified; for instance, if `/home` didn't exist, the preceding command would return an error message. Adding the -p or --parents option, though, causes `mkdir` to create intervening directories. This can be handy, but it also means that if you mistype a directory name (say, `/hom` instead of `/home`), `mkdir` will merrily create a new directory tree named after your typo.

## Copying Files

Linux's file-copying command is cp (which is short for *copy*). In its most basic form, cp copies a single file from one location to another:

```
# cp /etc/fstab /home/project7/
```

This command copies the /etc/fstab file to the /home/project7 directory; you'll find the copy there under the same name as the original. You can rename the copy as you make it by specifying a filename along with the target directory:

```
# cp /etc/fstab /home/project7/sample-file
```

For clarity, I've shown the target directory alone with a trailing slash (/) in the first of these examples. This indicates that project7 is a directory, not a file, and will result in an error message if /home/project7 doesn't exist. Linux will accept a directory name as a target without a trailing slash, though. For instance, if /home/project7/sample-file were a directory, the second command would copy /etc/fstab into that directory under the name fstab.

You can copy an entire directory tree by using one of the recursion options (-r and -R):

```
# cp -R /etc/X11/ /home/project7/
```

This command copies the entire contents of the /etc/X11 directory, including all its subdirectories, to /home/project7. Using -r in place of -R is likely to result in the same behavior, but some versions of cp produce subtly different effects for these two commands.

For information on other cp options, consult the man page for the command.

## Removing Extraneous Files

Now that you've created the new project directory and placed some files in it, you may want to do some housecleaning. For this task, you may want to first change into the directory in which you want to operate so that you don't need to type the complete path to each file:

```
# cd /home/project7/X11/
```

If you type ls, you'll see a list of files and directories. Perhaps your project doesn't need access to the xorg.conf file; you can remove it with rm:

```
# rm xorg.conf
```

> **WARNING**    Be sure you type this command from within your copied directory tree (/home/project7/X11). If you type this command from the original /etc/X11 directory, X is unlikely to work the next time you start it!

As with cp, you can use the -r or -R option to recursively delete an entire directory tree:

```
# rm -r mwm/
```

Depending upon your configuration, you might or might not be prompted before rm deletes each individual file. If you're prompted and don't want to be, you can add the -f option; if you're not prompted but you do want to be, you can add the -i option.

> The contents of /etc/X11 vary somewhat from one system to another. Thus, you might need to modify these examples on your system.

## Moving and Renaming Files

Linux uses a single command to handle both the move and rename operations: mv. To use this command, type it followed by the current name of a file and then the new name or location of the file. For instance, to rename the /home/project7/X11/chooser.sh file to /home/project7/X11/chooser, you'd type this:

```
# mv /home/project7/X11/chooser.sh /home/project7/X11/chooser
```

If the target name for the file is a directory, mv moves the file to that directory without renaming the file. If the target name is a file in a directory other than the original directory, mv moves and renames the file. You can specify more than one source file, but in that case the target must be a directory.

If the source and destination locations for the file are on the same partition, mv does its work by rewriting directory entries; thus, it can operate quite quickly, even if it's operating on a large file. If you move a file from one partition or removable disk to another, though, mv must copy the file and then delete the original. This operation is likely to take longer, particularly with large files.

## Setting File and Directory Ownership

In Linux, all files and directories have owners. These owners are Linux accounts, such as your user account or root. Files and directories are also tied to Linux groups, which are collections of accounts. By default, mkdir creates directories that are owned by the user who issued the command and with group ownership by that user's default group. After you create a directory as root, you can adjust the directory's ownership by using the chown command:

```
# chown fred:users /home/project7
```

> This example assumes the presence of the fred account and the users group. You may need to adjust it for your system.

This command gives ownership of the /home/project7 directory to the user fred and the group users. You may separate the username and group name with either a colon (:), as shown in this example, or a dot (.). You may apply the chown command to both directories and files. If you omit the username, chown changes the group of the file or directory without changing the file's main owner. This is effectively the same as the chgrp command, which works much like chown but accepts a group name alone (without a dot or colon). If you omit the colon or dot and the group name, chown changes only the primary owner of the file or directory.

The chown command has several options; consult its man page for details. One of the most useful options, though, is -R, which performs a recursive change to a directory and all the files and subdirectories it contains:

```
# chown -R fred:users /home/project7
```

## Setting File and Directory Permissions

Earlier, in "Verifying the Presence of a File" in Task 1.1, I described the long form of the ls command (ls -l), which shows additional information on a file. Specifically, the output looks like this:

```
$ ls -l /usr/bin/whatis
-rwxr-xr-x  1 root root 2409 Nov 19  2004 /usr/bin/whatis
```

The columns in this output are the permissions, the number of links to the file (described in the next task), the owner, the group, the file size in bytes, the file creation date, and the filename. The permissions string can be perplexing at first. It consists of 10 characters. The first of these characters is a code for the file type. A dash (-) denotes a normal file, while various characters stand for special file types. Most important, d refers to a directory and l refers to a symbolic link. Other codes include c and b for character and block devices, respectively (used to access hardware via device files in /dev).

The remaining nine characters in the permissions string represent permissions for the file's owner, group, and all other users (aka *world* permissions). Each of these three classes of users consumes three characters, which denote the presence or absence of read, write, and execute permissions. If an r, w, or x character is present in the respective position, the class has the relevant permission; if a dash is present, the class lacks that type of permission. Table 1.1 summarizes some possible permissions and their uses; however, as there are 512 possible permissions, Table 1.1 is incomplete. (Most of the 512 possible permissions are bizarre, though; Table 1.1 contains the most common permissions in practice.) Note that the leading character is sometimes omitted from the permission string, as it's not really part of the permissions *per se*. Read and write permissions are fairly self-explanatory. Execute permission identifies executable files—that is, program files. Note that you can remove execute permission for some users to ensure that a program may only be run by certain users (such as the program's owner).

**TABLE 1.1**   Example Permissions and Their Likely Uses

| Permission String | Octal Code | Meaning |
|---|---|---|
| rwxrwxrwx | 777 | Read, write, and execute permissions for all users. |
| rwxr-xr-x | 755 | Read and execute permission for all users. The file's owner also has write permission. |

**TABLE 1.1**    Example Permissions and Their Likely Uses *(continued)*

| Permission String | Octal Code | Meaning |
|---|---|---|
| rwxr-x--- | 750 | Read and execute permission for the owner and group. The file's owner also has write permission. Users who are not the file's owner or members of the group have no access to the file. |
| rwx------ | 700 | Read, write, and execute permissions for the file's owner only; all others have no access. |
| rw-rw-rw- | 666 | Read and write permissions for all users. No execute permissions to anybody. |
| rw-rw-r-- | 664 | Read and write permissions to the owner and group. Read-only permission to all others. |
| rw-rw---- | 660 | Read and write permissions to the owner and group. No world permissions. |
| rw-r--r-- | 644 | Read and write permissions to the owner. Read-only permission to all others. |
| rw-r----- | 640 | Read and write permissions to the owner, and read-only permission to the group. No permission to others. |
| rw------- | 600 | Read and write permissions to the owner. No permission to anybody else. |
| r-------- | 400 | Read permission to the owner. No permission to anybody else. |

The second column in Table 1.1 provides an octal (base-8) code corresponding to the permission string. Each cluster of three permission bits can be represented as a 3-bit number, which in turn can be represented as a single octal number from 0 to 7. Read permission corresponds to 4, write permission corresponds to 2, and execute permission corresponds to 1. Add the permissions you want to obtain the corresponding octal digit.

To change permissions, you use the chmod command. (Permissions are sometimes called the file's *mode*, so chmod is short for *change mode*.) This command takes a mode, expressed either in octal form or as a set of symbolic codes. The octal form is easier to understand, although many newcomers find the octal representation confusing:

```
# chmod 660 /home/project7/xorg.conf
```

This command grants rw-rw---- permissions to the xorg.conf file in /home/project7. The symbolic form of the command represents a series of changes to permissions, using the codes summarized in Table 1.2.

**TABLE 1.2**    Codes Used in Symbolic Modes

| Permission Set Code | Meaning | Change Type Code | Meaning | Permission to Modify Code | Meaning |
|---|---|---|---|---|---|
| u | owner | + | add | r | read |
| g | group | – | remove | w | write |
| o | world | = | set equal to | x | execute |
| a | all | | | X | execute only if file is directory or already has execute permission |
| | | | | s | SUID or SGID |
| | | | | t | sticky bit |
| | | | | u | existing owner's permissions |
| | | | | g | existing group permissions |
| | | | | o | existing world permissions |

Using these codes works best if you know the current mode and want to change it by adding or removing certain specific permissions. Table 1.3 summarizes some examples.

**TABLE 1.3**    Examples of Symbolic Permissions with chmod

| Command | Initial Permissions | End Permissions |
|---|---|---|
| chmod a+x bigprogram | rw-r--r-- | rwxr-xr-x |
| chmod ug=rw report.tex | r-------- | rw-rw---- |

**TABLE 1.3**    Examples of Symbolic Permissions with chmod *(continued)*

| Command | Initial Permissions | End Permissions |
| --- | --- | --- |
| chmod o-rwx  bigprogram | rwxrwxr-x | rwxrwx--- |
| chmod g=u report.tex | rw-r--r-- | rw-rw-r-- |
| chmod g-w,o-rw report.tex | rw-rw-rw- | rw-r----- |

As with many other file-manipulation commands, chmod accepts a -R option to operate recursively on an entire directory tree.

## Criteria for Completion

To complete this task, you should have a new directory, /home/project7, which contains a number of files copied from /etc. The copied files should be owned by an ordinary user on your system (fred in the examples).

# Task 1.3: Manage Links

Native Linux filesystems have always supported a feature known as *links*. A link is a way to refer to a file in one location from another location or to use multiple names for a single file. Linux supports two types of links, which are described shortly. They're created and managed with the ln command. In this task, you'll learn how to create and manage links.

## Scenario

To make it easier for users to access the files in the directory you created in Task 1.2, you want to create links to some of the files it contains. To do so, you'll create both types of links, and in the process you'll learn how to remove and manage links.

## Scope of Task

Links are not difficult to manage, although the differences between the two types of links Linux supports can be confusing to new Linux users and administrators. This task will step you through the two types of links and provide tips on how to manage them.

### Duration

This task should take about half an hour to complete. Once you've learned the task, you should be able to perform similar tasks in just a few minutes.

## Setup

You need perform no special setup to perform this task; just log into your computer as the user who owns the files in the /home/project7 directory and type **cd /home/project7** to change into that directory. Be sure to complete Task 1.2 before starting this task.

## Caveats

If you perform this task as an ordinary user, the risk to the computer is minimal. If you opt to perform this task as root, though, you might accidentally delete or corrupt important system files, particularly if you perform these steps in the wrong directory.

# Procedure

The ln command creates links, so it's the most important command to know when it comes to link management. Other link-related tasks can be performed using ordinary Linux file-manipulation commands, such as mv, cp, and rm.

 Links require support in the underlying filesystem. Although all Linux native filesystems support links, they aren't supported in some non-Linux filesystems, such as the File Allocation Table (FAT) filesystem used by DOS and Windows. Thus, if you use non-Linux filesystems on removable disks or partitions shared across OSs, you may not be able to create links on them.

## Creating Hard Links

The ln command works much like the cp command; type the command name, the name of the current file, and the link filename you wish to use:

```
$ ln sample-file fstab
```

This command creates a *hard link* between the original sample-file and the new fstab. (In Task 1.2, fstab was renamed sample-file.) A hard link is a duplicate filename that refers to the original file. Both filenames are equally valid, and once a hard link is created, either may be used with precisely the same effect. You can tell how many hard links exist by examining the long output of ls:

```
$ ls -l
total 9
drwxr-xr-x 22 fred     users 1184 May 25 12:51 X11
-rw-r--r--  2 fred     users 2260 May 25 12:51 fstab
-rw-r--r--  2 fred     users 2260 May 25 12:51 sample-file
```

The second column of this output shows, for ordinary files, the number of filenames that point to the file. Ordinary files show 1 in this column; files with a single hard link in addition to the original name show 2, and so on. (For directories, the second column's number refers to the number of directories within the specified directory, including pointers to the directory itself and its parent directory.)

 Current versions of Linux forbid making hard links to directories, but this was possible with some earlier versions of Linux.

Hard links to a single file may exist in two or more different directories; however, both directories must exist on the same filesystem (partition or removable disk). Because hard links are created by pointing two filenames at the same file data, it makes no sense to create hard links across filesystems.

## Creating Soft Links

Soft links (aka symbolic links) are an alternative to hard links. Instead of creating a duplicate directory entry that points directly to the same underlying filesystem data, you are creating a new file that contains the filename of the target file. As a consequence, it's possible to point to files across filesystems. To create a soft link, you use the `ln` command, but pass it the `-s` option:

```
$ ln -s sample-file another-link
$ ls -l
total 9
drwxr-xr-x 22 fred     users 1184 May 25 12:51 X11
lrwxrwxrwx  1 fred     users   11 May 26 15:30 another-link -> sample-file
-rw-r--r--  2 fred     users 2260 May 25 12:51 fstab
-rw-r--r--  2 fred     users 2260 May 25 12:51 sample-file
```

This example shows the result, including how soft links appear in directory listings. Note that the link count in the second column of the listing doesn't increase when a soft link is created. The soft link itself, though, includes the l file type code in the permissions string and shows the linked-to file after the filename in a long listing.

Unlike hard links, soft links don't work quite exactly like the original link. The time to access a soft link is minutely longer than the time to access the original file. You can delete the soft link itself without affecting the linked-to file, but if you delete the original file, the soft link will be broken; it will point to nothing. You can create soft links to directories.

In practice, soft links are more common than hard links. The fact that they can be created across filesystems and the fact that they can point to directories makes them more flexible. You should be cautious, though, not to break soft links by deleting, moving, or renaming the original files.

## Managing Links

The `mv`, `rm`, and `cp` commands work on links just as they work on the original files. Thus, link management is just like ordinary file management; for instance, suppose you decide you only want the copied fstab file to be accessible under two names; you can delete either of the two hard links with rm:

```
$ rm fstab
```

This example deletes the second link; if sample-file had been deleted instead, you'd break the symbolic link (another-link).

You should be aware that some file operations will do odd things with links, and particularly with symbolic links. For instance, if you create a CD-R from files on your hard disk, you might find that it contains duplicates of files that are links in the original directory tree. This behavior can result in an unexpected increase in the space required on your CD-R media. Some tools provide options that influence how they treat links, so consult your tool's man page or other documentation if you run into link-handling problems.

## Criteria for Completion

To complete this task, you should create and delete links in the test directory you created in Task 1.2. You should create both hard links, which are duplicate directory entries, and soft links, which are special files that point to other files by name.

# Task 1.4: Find Files

A complete Linux system is likely to contain thousands of files. Although Linux uses a hierarchical directory structure designed to place files in particular locations depending upon their types, sometimes files get lost. You might know that a file is present but be unable to locate it because you've forgotten its location or because it's been accidentally moved. In such cases, knowledge of Linux's file-location commands can be invaluable.

## Scenario

Returning to the scenario from Task 1.1, suppose you didn't find the whatis executable where you expected it, in /usr/bin. Your task now is to see if the file might be located somewhere else on the computer. To do this, you'll use several Linux commands that are designed to help you find files.

## Scope of Task

This task covers three Linux commands for locating files: find, locate, and whereis. Each of these three commands has its own unique strengths and weaknesses, and you should learn the basics of all three of them.

## Duration

This task should take half an hour or an hour to complete. Once you've mastered these commands, you should be able to search for files in a matter of seconds—although some of these commands may take several minutes to execute.

## Setup

No special setup is required. Although the commands used in this task may be used by either root or ordinary users, some of them work better when run as root because root may examine the contents of any directory, whereas ordinary users may not. Thus, you should use su to acquire root privileges for this task.

## Caveats

If you run this task as root, be careful what you type. Although the search commands themselves are non-destructive, you should be sure not to mistype a command and make it something destructive.

# Procedure

To perform this task, you'll search for the whatis program file using each of the three file-location commands in turn. In the process, you'll learn the capabilities and limitations of each of these commands.

### Using *find*

The find utility implements a brute-force approach to finding files. This program finds files by searching through the specified directory tree, checking filenames, file creation dates, and so on to locate the files that match the specified criteria. Because of this method of operation, find tends to be slow, but it's very flexible and is very likely to succeed, assuming the file for which you're searching exists. To search the entire computer for the whatis program file by name, type the following command:

```
# find / -name whatis
```

This command specifies the path to search (/, meaning the entire directory tree) and the criteria to use for the search (-name whatis, to search for a file whose name is whatis). Because this command searches the entire directory tree, it's likely to take a long time to complete—perhaps several minutes. This command is guaranteed to find any file meeting the specified criteria, though, at least assuming you have permission to read the directory in which it resides and don't make a mistake when specifying the criteria. The output of the find command is a list of files that match the specified criteria, one file per line.

If you're not certain of the exact filename, you can use wildcards in the filename specification, as in -name "what*" to search for any file whose name begins with what. Using quotes around the search specification ensures that the shell will pass the wildcards to the find command rather than try to expand the wildcard itself.

In addition to the -name criterion, you can search for files in various other ways, such as by permissions (-perm), file size (-size), and owner (-user). The man page for find details these options; consult it for more information.

## Using *locate*

The locate command is much less flexible than find, but it's also much faster. To use locate, type the command name followed by the name of the file you want to find:

```
# locate whatis
```

The locate command works by searching a database that it maintains. (If this database is out-of-date, typing **updatedb** as root will update it.) The locate command returns the names of all the files in the database whose names contain the string you specify. Thus, this command is likely to return the names of many files that merely contain the string you specify, such as makewhatis and whatis.1.gz. This can be a real problem if you're searching for a file with a short name. The locate database also doesn't include every directory on the computer, but it does include enough directories that it's likely to be a useful tool.

Many Linux distributions actually use a program called slocate rather than locate. The slocate program is a more security-aware version of the program; it checks who's calling the program and adjusts its output to remove references to files to which the user shouldn't have access. Distributions that use slocate typically create a link called locate so that you can call the program using this more common name.

## Using *whereis*

The whereis program searches for files in a restricted set of locations, such as standard binary file directories, library directories, and man page directories. This tool does *not* search user directories or many other locations that are easily searched by find or locate. The whereis utility is a quick way to find program executables and related files like documentation or configuration files.

The whereis program returns filenames that begin with whatever you type as a search criterion, even if those filenames contain extensions. This feature often turns up configuration files in /etc, man pages, and similar files. To use the program, type **whereis** followed by the name of the program you want to locate. For instance, the following command locates whatis:

```
# whereis whatis
whatis: /usr/bin/whatis /usr/X11R6/bin/whatis /usr/bin/X11/whatis
 /usr/man/man1/whatis.1.gz /usr/share/man/man1/whatis.1.gz
```

The result shows the whatis executable (/usr/bin/whatis), links to it in other directories, and the man page for whatis, including a link in a second location. (Your system might find hits in a slightly different set of directories than is shown here. Don't be concerned about this.) The whereis program accepts several parameters that modify its behavior in various ways. These are detailed in the program's man page.

## Criteria for Completion

To complete this task, you should use the three file-location commands to locate the whatis program. Although the output from the locate program is likely to be quite long, you should verify that the three programs all return the same key file, which is likely to be /usr/bin/whatis.

# Task 1.5: Edit Files

A great deal of Linux system administration involves editing files. In Linux, most configuration files are ordinary text files, and changing how the system functions involves editing these files. Thus, you should be proficient with at least one text editor in Linux. Although you can use a fancy GUI text editor if you like, one editor that's particularly important is Vi. This editor is a simple text-mode editor, and it's important because it's a very lightweight editor that's accessible from most basic emergency systems. Thus, even if you prefer another editor, you may be forced to use Vi in certain emergency recovery situations.

## Scenario

An accidental change to the /etc/lilo.conf file has rendered a Linux system unbootable. To recover, you must boot using an emergency disk and edit this file using Vi. For the purpose of this exercise, of course, you won't edit the *real* /etc/lilo.conf file, and you needn't even boot from an emergency disk (although you can if you want to). Instead, you'll make a copy of /etc/lilo.conf and edit the copy.

## Scope of Task

This task involves reviewing the basics of the Vi editor and trying out Vi editing tasks. You will *not* need to know anything about the format of the /etc/lilo.conf file to perform this task; for now, the goal is simply to learn the basics of Vi. You might want to know, though, that lilo.conf controls the way Linux boots, at least on computers that use the Linux Loader (LILO) boot loader. Modifying this file therefore modifies the options that are available when you first boot the computer.

## Duration

This task should take half an hour or an hour to complete. Once you're proficient with Vi, you should be able to perform similar tasks in a matter of minutes.

## Setup

In principle, you could use an emergency boot disk, but you'll probably find it more convenient to use your regular Linux installation. Log into your computer as an ordinary user. You should then copy the /etc/lilo.conf file to a safe temporary location, such as your home directory:

```
$ cp /etc/lilo.conf ~/
```

If your system lacks a lilo.conf file, locate one on the Web or enter the one presented shortly in a GUI text editor and save it in your home directory.

## Caveats

Do not try to perform this task as root and do not attempt to directly edit /etc/lilo.conf. Doing so is likely to damage your system. Of course, in a *real* emergency recovery situation, you'd need to perform these tasks as root, but for practice purposes, learning Vi as an ordinary user is safer.

# Procedure

Vi is a bit strange, particularly if you're used to GUI text editors. To use Vi, you should first understand the three modes in which it operates. Once you understand those modes, you can begin learning about the text-editing procedures Vi implements. You must also know how to save files and exit from Vi.

Most Linux distributions actually ship with a variant of Vi known as Vim, or Vi Improved. As the name implies, Vim supports more features than the original Vi does. The information presented here applies to both Vi and Vim. Most distributions that ship with Vim enable you to launch it by typing **vi**, as if it were the original Vi.

## Vi Modes

At any given moment, Vi is running in one of three modes:

**Command mode**   This mode accepts commands, which are usually entered as single letters. For instance, i and a both enter insert mode, although in somewhat different ways, as described shortly, and o opens a line below the current one.

**Ex mode**   To manipulate files (including saving your current file and running outside programs), you use ex mode. You enter ex mode from command mode by typing a colon (:), typically directly followed by the name of the ex mode command you want to use. After you run the ex mode command, Vi returns automatically to command mode.

**Insert mode**   You enter text in insert mode. Most keystrokes result in text appearing on the screen. One important exception is the Esc key, which exits from insert mode back to command mode.

> If you're not sure what mode Vi is in, press the Esc key. This will return you to command mode, from which you can re-enter insert mode, if necessary.

Unfortunately, terminology surrounding Vi modes is inconsistent at best. Command mode is sometimes referred to as normal mode, and insert mode is sometimes called edit mode or entry mode, for instance. Ex mode is often not described as a mode at all, but as colon commands.

## Basic Text-Editing Procedures

In this task, the `lilo.conf` entry for your kernel has been accidentally deleted, so you must re-create this entry. Listing 1.1 shows the original `lilo.conf` file used in this example. If you're using a `lilo.conf` file from your computer or that you found on the Internet, it isn't likely to be identical, so you may need to adapt some of the details in the following procedure in minor ways. Alternatively, you can type Listing 1.1 using a text editor with which you're already familiar and save it to a file on your disk.

**Listing 1.1:** Sample /etc/lilo.conf File

```
boot=/dev/sda
map=/boot/map
install=/boot/boot.b
prompt
default=linux
timeout=50
image=/boot/vmlinuz
        label=linux
        root=/dev/sda6
        read-only
```

> Don't try editing your *real* /etc/lilo.conf file as a learning exercise; a mistake could render your system unbootable the next time you type `lilo`. You might put your test `lilo.conf` file in your home directory for this exercise.

The first step to using Vi is to launch it and have it load the file. In this example, type **vi lilo.conf** while in the directory holding the file. The result should resemble Figure 1.2, which shows Vi running in a Konsole window. The tildes (~) down the left side of the display indicate the end of the file. The bottom line shows the status of the last command—an implicit file load command because you specified a filename when launching the program.

**FIGURE 1.2**    The last line of a Vi display is a status line that shows messages from the program.

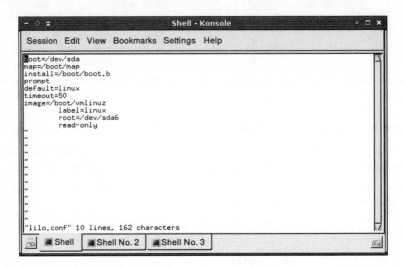

Adding a new entry to `lilo.conf` involves duplicating the lines beginning with the `image=` line and modifying the duplicates. Therefore, the first editing task is to duplicate these four lines. To do this, follow these steps:

1.  Move the cursor to the beginning of the `image=` line by using the down arrow key; you should see the cursor resting on the `i`.

> The h, j, k, and l keys can also be used in place of the left, down, up, and right arrow keys. This is a holdover from the days before all keyboards had arrow keys.

2.  You must now "yank" four lines of text. This term is used much as "copy" is used in most text editors—you copy the text to a buffer from which you can later paste it back into the file. To yank text, you use the yy command, preceded by the number of lines you want to yank. Thus, type **4yy** (*do not* press the Enter key, though). Vi responds with the message `4 lines yanked` on its bottom status line. The dd command works much like yy, but it deletes the lines as well as copying them to a buffer. Both yy and dd are special cases of the y and d commands, respectively, which yank or delete text in amounts specified by the next character, as in dw to delete the next word.

3.  Move the cursor to the last line of the file by using the arrow keys.

4.  Type **p** (again, without pressing the Enter key). Vi pastes the contents of the buffer starting on the line after the cursor. The file should now have two identical `image=` stanzas. The cursor should be resting at the start of the second one. If you want to paste the text into the document starting on the line *before* the cursor, use an uppercase P command.

Now that you've duplicated the necessary lines, you must modify one copy to point to the kernel whose entry was accidentally deleted. To do so, follow these steps:

**1.** Move the cursor to the v in `vmlinuz` on the second `image=` line. You're about to begin customizing this second stanza.

**2.** Up until now, you've operated Vi in command mode. There are several commands that you can use to enter insert mode. At this point, the most appropriate is R, which enters insert mode so that it is configured for text replacement rather than insertion. If you prefer to insert text rather than overwrite it, you could use i or a (the latter advances the cursor one space, which is sometimes useful at the end of a line). For the purpose of these instructions, type **R** to enter insert mode. You should see -- REPLACE -- appear in the status line.

**3.** Type the name of a new Linux kernel. For the purpose of this example, let's say it's called `bzImage-2.6.13`, so that's what you'd type. This entry should replace `vmlinuz`.

**4.** Use the arrow keys to move the cursor to the start of `linux` on the next line. You must replace this label so that your new entry has its own label.

**5.** Type a new label, such as **mykernel**. This label should replace the existing `linux` label.

**6.** Exit from insert mode by pressing the Esc key.

**7.** Save the file and quit by typing **:wq**. This is an ex mode command that writes changes and then exits (quits) from the editor. (The ZZ command is equivalent to :wq.)

Many additional commands are available that you might want to use in some situations. Here are some of the highlights:

**Case changes**   Suppose you need to change the case of a word in a file. Instead of entering insert mode and retyping the word, you can use the tilde (~) key in command mode to change the case. Position the cursor on the first character you want to change and press ~ repeatedly until the task is done.

**Undo**   To undo any change, type **u** in command mode.

**Opening text**   In command mode, typing **o** opens text—that is, it inserts a new line immediately below the current one and enters insert mode on that line.

**Searches**   To search forward for text in a file, type **/** in command mode, followed immediately by the text you want to locate. Typing **?** will search backward rather than forward.

**Changes**   The c command changes text from within command mode. You invoke it much as you do the d or y commands, as in **cw** to change the next word or **cc** to change an entire line.

**Go to a line**   The G key brings you to a line that you specify. The H key "homes" the cursor—that is, it moves the cursor to the top line of the screen. The L key brings the key to the bottom line of the screen.

**Global replacement**   To replace all occurrences of one string by another, type **:%s/** *original*/*replacement*, where *original* is the original string and *replacement* is its replacement. Change % to a starting line number, comma, and ending line number to perform this change on just a small range of lines.

There's a great deal more depth to Vi than is presented here; the editor is quite capable, and some Linux users are very attached to it. Entire books have been written about Vi. Consult one of these, or a Vi Web page like `http://www.vim.org`, for more information.

## Saving Changes

To save changes to a file, type **:w** from command mode. This enters ex mode and runs the w ex-mode command, which writes the file using whatever filename you specified when you launched Vi. Related commands enable other functions:

**Edit new file**   The **:e** command edits a new file. For instance, **:e /etc/inittab** loads /etc/inittab for editing. Vi won't load a new file unless the existing one has been saved since its last change or unless you follow **:e** with an exclamation mark (!).

**Include existing file**   The **:r** command includes the contents of an old file in an existing one.

**Execute an external command**   The ex-mode command **:!** executes the external command that you specify. For instance, typing **:!ls** runs `ls`, enabling you to see what files are present in the current directory.

**Quit**   Use the **:q** command to quit from the program. As with **:e**, this command won't work unless changes have been saved or you append an exclamation mark to the command (as in **:q!**).

You can combine ex commands such as these to perform multiple actions in sequence. For instance, typing **:wq** writes changes and then quits from Vi.

## Criteria for Completion

To complete this task, you must successfully edit a copy of your `lilo.conf` file to add a new kernel. You don't need to test the copy of the file, but you should verify that it's been modified as you desired. To do so, use `cat` or `less`.

# Task 1.6: Manage Accounts

As a multi-user OS, Linux requires that users have accounts. This requirement is part of Linux's security system, so you shouldn't try to bypass account management or give it short shrift—say, by letting many people share an account. Instead, you should learn how to create, delete, and otherwise manage Linux accounts.

Most Linux distributions provide GUI tools for account management. Although these tools are perfectly capable of handling routine account maintenance tasks on small systems, they differ from one distribution to another. The text-based tools described here are much more consistent across distributions and are the tools tested on Linux certification exams.

# Scenario

Personnel changes require you to add an account for a new user (Trevor Brown) and delete an account for an employee who's leaving (Susan Jones). Changes to the amount of free space on two disks also requires you to move another user's (Dale Smith's) files from the /home2 to the /home directory tree.

# Scope of Task

This task involves creating, deleting, and modifying accounts. Each of these operations is fairly straightforward, but you must understand the basics of the relevant commands and you must be aware of the consequences of making mistakes when manipulating user accounts.

## Duration

This task should take about half an hour to complete. Once you're familiar with these tasks, you can create, delete, or modify accounts in a few seconds to a few minutes, depending upon the precise operations you need to perform.

## Setup

You should log into your Linux system and then use su to acquire superuser privileges. Alternatively, you may log in directly as root, although using su is preferable, as described in Task 1.1. You may perform this task from a text-mode login or within an xterm window from a GUI login. For this task, it is assumed that two accounts already exist on the computer—sjones and dsmith. If your computer lacks these accounts (they aren't standard), you can create them yourself by following the instructions for creating the first account, but change the usernames.

## Caveats

Account maintenance operations are potentially risky. You might accidentally delete or modify the wrong account. Even account creation poses risks, particularly when you use advanced options; you might accidentally give two accounts the same user ID (UID) codes, which would make them essentially interchangeable. Thus, you should be particularly cautious when using these commands. Because these commands require root access to work, the usual caveats concerning working as root also apply.

This task assumes that you're working on a Linux system that uses a local account database. Linux systems on LANs often refer to another computer for account management. On such systems, you would ordinarily modify accounts on the password server system instead of on the individual workstations and servers.

# Procedure

Before delving into account management tools, you should understand the fundamentals of how Linux manages its passwords. With a basic understanding in hand, you can proceed to the three parts of this task: adding an account, deleting an account, and modifying an account.

## Understanding the Basics of Account Management

Linux and Unix systems have traditionally stored account information in the /etc/passwd file. This file consists of a series of lines, each of which represents a single account, as in:

```
dsmith:x:512:100:Dale Smith:/home2/dsmith:/bin/bash
```

This line consists of a series of colon-delimited fields that contain the account's username, password, UID number, group ID (GID) number, a free-form comment, home directory, and default shell. Note that in this example the password field contains a single x. This is a code that means the password is encoded in another file, /etc/shadow. Most Linux systems today use this *shadow password* system as a way of increasing security; the /etc/passwd file must be world-readable to enable programs to access information such as the user's default shell and the comment field. Even an encrypted password could be broken if it were readable, so the shadow password system locks this sensitive data, as well as additional account information, in /etc/shadow, which is readable only by root. The format of the /etc/shadow file is similar to that of /etc/passwd in that it consists of colon-delimited fields. The first two fields contain the username and encrypted password, while remaining fields contain account aging and other advanced information.

Account management involves creating, deleting, or modifying the information in /etc/passwd and /etc/shadow. In principle, this can be done with a text editor, and in fact some extraordinarily street-savvy administrators work this way. Most administrators, though, use command-line or GUI tools to help manage the task. These tools obviate the need to remember what fields hold what data and minimize the risk of encountering problems from typos, such as accidentally deleting a colon.

The basic Linux account management tools are useradd, userdel, and usermod. These tools add, delete, and modify existing user accounts, respectively. Linux also provides groupadd, groupdel, and groupmod tools to perform similar tasks with groups, although some of the details of operation differ.

## Adding User Accounts

To add an account, you use the useradd command. At its simplest, you can use this command followed by the username you want to use:

```
# useradd tbrown
```

This command creates an account called tbrown, using defaults for various account parameters. On most systems, the user's home directory will be /home/tbrown, the shell will be /bin/bash, the comment field will be empty, and the UID and GID will be assigned based on the lowest available numbers for both. Most importantly, the account's password will be disabled (more on that shortly).

Some systems give each user a unique GID, and create an appropriate group to go with it, as a default policy. Other systems assign new users to an existing group, typically users, as a default policy.

You can create an account with different defaults by placing appropriate parameters between `useradd` and the account name. Alternatively, you can create an account with the defaults and then use `usermod` to change them. Some features you're particularly likely to want to adjust include:

**Comment**    The `-c` *comment* parameter passes the comment field for the user. Some administrators store public information like a user's office or telephone number in this field. Others store just the user's real name or no information at all.

**Home directory**    You specify the account's home directory with the `-d` *home-dir* parameter. This defaults to /home/*username* on most systems.

**Do or do not create a home directory**    The `-M` option forces the system to *not* automatically create a home directory, while `-m` forces the system to create one. Which behavior is the default varies from one system to another.

**Default group**    You set the name or GID of the user's default group with the `-g` *default-group* option. The default for this value varies from one distribution to another.

**Default shell**    Set the name of the user's default login shell with the `-s` *shell* option. On most systems, this defaults to /bin/bash.

**Specify a UID**    The `-u` *UID* parameter creates an account with the specified user ID value (*UID*). This value must be a positive integer, and it is normally above 500 for user accounts. System accounts typically have numbers below 100. The `-o` option allows the number to be reused so that two usernames are associated with a single UID.

**No user group**    In some distributions, such as Red Hat, the system creates a group with the same name as the specified username. The `-n` parameter disables this behavior.

This list of options isn't complete; consult `useradd`'s man page for more options. As an example of some of these options in action, suppose you want to place Trevor Brown's real name in the comment field and set his home directory to /home2/trevor. You could do so at account creation time by including appropriate parameters:

```
# useradd -c "Trevor Brown" -d /home2/trevor tbrown
```

After typing this command (or the simpler version shown earlier), be sure to check for the existence of the home directory. If it's not present, you must create it yourself and change its ownership (including its group):

```
# mkdir /home2/trevor
# chown tbrown.users /home2/trevor
```

Alternatively (and preferably), you could add the `-m` option to the `useradd` command. This option has the advantage that the system copies a starting set of files from /etc/skel. These files include things such as `bash` configuration files.

The `useradd` command won't ordinarily set a starting password for the account. (There is a `-p` option to do this, but it requires a *pre-encrypted* password.) The best way to deal with this issue is to create new accounts in the presence of their users; you can then, as `root`, use passwd to begin the password-changing process and allow the users to type their own desired passwords:

```
# passwd tbrown
New UNIX password:
Retype new UNIX password:
passwd: password updated successfully
```

You would type **passwd tbrown**, then let the user type a password (twice). The system doesn't echo the password for security reasons.

Alternatively, you can set the password yourself to some random value and find a way to communicate this value to the user. The trouble with this approach is that the communication could be intercepted or copied, leading to an immediate security breach. Users might also leave their passwords set at the value you give them, which is non-optimal but might be acceptable if you choose a unique and good password for each account. (Phase 7 describes passwords in more detail.)

## Deleting User Accounts

You can delete an account with userdel, which works much like useradd:

```
# userdel sjones
```

This command deletes the sjones account. It does not, however, delete the user's home directory or mail spool, much less other files that may be owned by the user elsewhere on the computer. You must manually delete or otherwise deal with these files.

*Before* deleting an account, back it up to tape, CD-R, or some other medium. You can then give the backup to the user, if appropriate, or store it yourself in case another user (such as this individual's replacement in your organization) needs the files.

You can pass the -r option to have userdel delete the user's home directory and mail spool. This option won't delete other files the user may own elsewhere on the computer, though. To locate those files, use find (described in Task 1.4) with its -uid *n* option to search for files owned by UID *n*. If you search for files *before* deleting the account, you can use find's -user *username* option to search by username.

## Modifying User Accounts

What if an account already exists and you want to change it in some way? You can modify the account with usermod, which takes most of the same options as useradd. Another important usermod option is -l *name*, which alters the username associated with the account. To change the home directory of Dale Smith's (dsmith's) account from /home2/dsmith to /home/dsmith, you'd type the following command:

```
# usermod -d /home/dsmith
```

**WARNING**  Don't modify a user account when that user is logged in; certain changes are likely to wreak havoc with work the user is doing. Wait for the user to log out, or if a change must be implemented immediately, ask the user to log out.

Changing the account's home directory won't move the files in the directory. To do that, you must use the `cp` command. In this case, the `-a` option to `cp` will copy the entire directory tree and preserve ownership, permissions, and other file characteristics. You'll then delete the original directory:

```
# cp -a /home2/dsmith /home/dsmith
# rm -r /home2/dsmith
```

To be 100 percent safe, though, you might want to check that the new directory contains all the files it should before deleting the old one. If possible, wait for the user to log in and use the account before deleting the old directory.

## Criteria for Completion

To complete this task, you should have created a new account (`tbrown`), deleted an old account (`sjones`), and changed the home directory location of a third account (`dsmith`), including moving its files. The three commands used to perform this task (`useradd`, `userdel`, and `usermod`) are at the core of Linux account management. The `passwd` command is also critical in that it enables you to set a password on new accounts so that they're usable. File-manipulation commands such as `cp` and `rm` help you manage the files that are associated with accounts.

# Task 1.7: Use Streams, Pipes, and Redirection

The command-line tools introduced earlier enable you to interact with your Linux system at the command line, typing commands and viewing their output. Sometimes, though, you might want to do more with that output than simply view it; for instance, you might want to store it in a file or pass it as input to another program. Fortunately, Linux provides the means to do just that. In Linux, input and output operations are described as *streams*. Standard input and output streams may be *redirected* to send output to or read input from a regular file, or *piped* between two programs. These capabilities provide a great deal of flexibility, as you'll soon learn.

**NOTE**  Part of the Unix philosophy to which Linux adheres is, whenever possible, to do complex things by combining multiple simple tools. Redirection and pipes help in this task by enabling simple programs to be combined together in chains, each link feeding off of the output of the preceding link.

# Scenario

A user of a Linux computer you administer reports problems with network connections from the Mozilla Firefox browser. As part of your diagnosis of this problem, you want to use some diagnostic commands that produce copious output. In order to do this more easily, you will pipe the output streams from these programs into other programs and redirect the output into files that you can peruse later.

This task uses advanced network diagnostic commands. These commands are described in more detail in Phase 6. For now, don't be too concerned with what these commands do; just concentrate on their input and output streams, the redirection of these streams, and piping these streams between programs.

# Scope of Task

This task demonstrates several tools and techniques that you're likely to use quite heavily as a Linux user and system administrator. Each of these commands and techniques is quite powerful and so can take some time to master, but once you've mastered them, they'll become second nature.

## Duration

This task should take half an hour or so to complete. Once you understand streams, pipes, and redirection, you should be able to use these tools and techniques as a matter of course in a wide variety of commands, most of which will take just seconds to type.

## Setup

You need a working Linux computer with a network connection and the Mozilla Firefox Web browser. (You may use another Web browser instead of Firefox, but you must then modify the examples appropriately.) Firefox is an X-based (GUI) Web browser, so you'll need to run it from X; however, the diagnostic commands must be run from the command line—either in an xterm or similar window or from a separate text-mode login.

To prepare for this task, you should log into your Linux system as an ordinary user in GUI mode. Once logged in, launch the Mozilla Firefox Web browser by locating it from the menu system or by typing **firefox** in an xterm window. Once Firefox is running, browse to a Web site (any external Web site will do). You should then launch an xterm or similar window to obtain a command prompt or press Alt+Ctrl+F1 to switch to text mode and log in as an ordinary user to get a command prompt.

## Caveats

If you don't have or don't want to use Firefox, you may use any other Web browser (such as Konqueror, Opera, or even the text-mode lynx). If you do, you must change the references to the browser as appropriate in the following procedure.

This task may be performed as an ordinary user. If you run it as root, you run the usual risks of performing tasks as root.

# Procedure

This task investigates three practical techniques: redirecting output, redirecting input, and piping data between programs. All three techniques rely on the fact that Linux uses input and output *streams*, so you should first understand a bit of theory.

## Understanding Streams

To Linux programs, input and output involve files. A program can read or write data from or to a disk file, but even the keyboard and screen are treated much like files. These devices correspond to three separate streams:

**Standard input**   This stream, often abbreviated *stdin*, corresponds to the keyboard. When a program wants input from the user, it opens standard input and reads data from it as if it were reading data from a disk file.

**Standard output**   This stream is often referred to as *stdout*, and it corresponds to the text-mode display, which can mean a text-mode console, the contents of an xterm or similar window, or a remote login session's display. Programs write data to standard output as if it were a file, and the characters so written then appear on the screen.

**Standard error**   Ordinarily, this stream (often abbreviated *stderr*) is the same physical device as standard output; however, it's used by programs to display error messages rather than ordinary output. The reason it's treated separately is so that it may be redirected separately—so that you can interact normally with a program while sending error message to a file or so that you can redirect normal output to a file while still seeing error messages on the screen.

If you use a Linux computer at the console (that is, using the keyboard and monitor that are attached directly to the computer), these streams correspond to the computer's own keyboard and display. Linux systems can also be used remotely, via logins using protocols such as the Secure Shell (SSH). In such cases, standard input, standard output, and standard error are all directed over the remote login protocol and so ultimately correspond to a keyboard and monitor on the remote computer.

## Redirecting Output

To begin the task, you want to investigate the network connections maintained by Firefox. To do so, you'll use the netstat command, which displays information on all the network connections maintained by the computer. You'll use the -p option to netstat, so as to display the program names:

```
$ netstat -p
```

When you type this command, though, chances are you'll see so much output scroll past that you won't be able to read it all before most of it disappears off the top of the screen. One way around this problem is to redirect standard output to a file. You do this with the redirection operator (>), which you place after the command and before the name of a file that is to receive the output:

```
$ netstat -p > net-connections.txt
```

The file net-connections.txt now contains the output of the netstat -p command, with one exception (described shortly). You can then open net-connections.txt in a text editor or view it with a program such as less in order to study its contents in greater detail. Do so now and search for references to the Firefox browser. (These may be called firefox-bin.) Don't worry about what these references mean, though; the point is to familiarize yourself with redirection, not the output of netstat.

When you ran the netstat -p command with redirection as an ordinary user, chances are you saw a message appear on the screen to the effect that not all processes would be displayed. This message was directed to standard error. It, too, can be redirected, but you must use the standard error redirection (2>) operator rather than the standard output redirection operator:

```
$ netstat -p 2> error-messages.txt
```

If you examine the error-messages.txt file, you'll see that it contains only the warning about not all processes being displayed; standard output appears on the screen. You can redirect both standard output and standard error by using the &> redirection operator:

```
$ netstat -p &> net-connections.txt
```

All of these redirection operators overwrite whatever file you provide as an argument (net-connections.txt or error-messages.txt in these examples). When redirecting standard output or standard error (but not both), you can append to an existing file rather than overwrite it by adding a second greater-than symbol:

```
$ netstat -p >> net-connections.txt
$ netstat -p 2>> error-messages.txt
```

 A common trick is to redirect standard output or standard error to /dev/null. This file is a device that's connected to nothing; it's used when you want to get rid of data. For instance, if the whine program is generating error messages you don't care about, you might type **whine 2> /dev/null** to run it and discard its error messages.

## Redirecting Input

Many Linux programs are designed to accept input from files whose names you specify on the command line. Some programs, though, are designed to accept keyboard input via standard input. What if you want to provide fixed input from a file to such programs, though? The answer is to use standard input redirection via the input redirection operator (<).

As an example, suppose you wanted to convert the error-messages.txt file to a graphics format. You might want to use the text2gif program (part of the giflib package), but it requires you to enter text either as a command-line option or via standard input. Thus, you'd redirect standard input from the `error-messages.txt` file. You'd also have to redirect standard output to save the result in a file:

```
$ text2gif < error-messages.txt > error-graphics.gif
```

You can use a graphics program, such as the GIMP, to view the `error-graphics.gif` file to verify that it contains the correct image.

> When using the redirection operators, you start a command line with the program name and then "point" the operators toward their destinations—the input redirection operator points left, toward the command name, whereas the output redirection operators point right, toward the filename of the file you want to create.

## Piping Data between Programs

The preceding example showed `text2gif` operating on a file that was created by another program. This approach is common in Linux; so common, in fact, that a variant of the redirection operator exists to simplify matters. This tool is known as a *pipe* or a *pipeline*, and it's a way to send standard output from one program directly into another, without using any on-disk file. The symbol for a pipe is a vertical bar (|), located above the Enter key on the same key that holds the backslash (\) character on most keyboards. You place the pipe character between the commands. For instance, instead of saving the output of `netstat -p` in a file and then examining that file with `less`, you can pipe the result directly into `less`:

```
$ netstat -p | less
```

Another common use of a pipe is to send the results of a lengthy command through `grep`, which searches for lines containing a particular string that you specify. For instance, to search for the lines in the `netstat` output that refer to Firefox, you might issue the following command:

```
$ netstat -p | grep firefox
```

You can create a pipeline containing multiple commands and even redirect the output of the final command:

```
$ netstat -p | grep firefox | text2gif > netstat-output.gif
```

## Additional Pipe and Redirection Tricks

Pipes and redirection can be combined in complex ways and obscure variants may be used. For instance, the &1 and &2 strings refer to standard output and standard error, respectively. This fact enables you to pipe standard error without also piping standard output:

```
$ netstat -p 2>&1 > /dev/null | text2gif > error-message.gif
```

This example relies on subtle order effects: On the command line, standard error is redirected to standard output before standard output is redirected to /dev/null; however, bash interprets these redirections in the opposite order. Thus, this command will send nothing as input to text2gif if you reverse the order of the two redirection operators. Also, when redirecting to &1 or &2, you should include no space between the redirection operator and its destination.

## Criteria for Completion

This task demonstrated the use of pipe and redirection operators for standard input, standard output, and standard error. You should now be able to apply these operators in working with Linux commands that generate textual output or expect textual input. (A few commands, such as text2gif, generate binary output on standard output and rely on you to be able to redirect or pipe it appropriately.)

# Task 1.8: Manage the Shell Environment

Linux shells are simply programs, and like many programs, the details of their operation can be customized. You can change the command prompt, set the directories in which the shell searches for program files, and so on. These features are adjusted via *environment variables*, which you can set on the command line or in configuration files. Other programs can also use environment variables, so in some cases, setting an environment variable in a bash configuration file can affect programs launched from bash.

## Scenario

You dislike your current bash prompt and want to change it to something that includes the date and time. You also need to set an environment variable that tells various programs what editor to use when calling an external text editor. You want to test these changes and then make them permanent by modifying your bash configuration file.

## Scope of Task

To perform this task, you'll need to type a few commands at the command line and edit a configuration file. Consult Task 1.5 for information on using Vi for file editing, or use your favorite text-based or GUI editor.

## Duration

This task will take about half an hour to complete. Once you know how to change environment variables, you'll be able to do so in under a minute—but it may take longer than that to determine what environment variable needs changing!

## Setup

To prepare for the task, log into your user account on your Linux system. (You can—and should—perform this task as an ordinary user.) You may perform this task in either a text-mode or a GUI login, but in the latter case, you must launch an xterm or similar command prompt window.

## Caveats

Performing this task as root poses the usual risks of accidentally damaging the installation. If you badly corrupt your own bash configuration files, it's conceivable (but unlikely) that you'll be unable to log in again. If this happens, use a root login to copy /etc/skel/.bashrc to your user home directory and change the ownership of the copied file to your normal user account.

# Procedure

To complete this task, you'll change two environment variables. First you'll do this temporarily so that your changes affect just a single login session. You'll then make your changes permanent by editing a user configuration file. At the end of this procedure, I describe several other important environment variables, which you might choose to change if you so desire.

### Adjusting Your Shell Prompt

The prompt in bash is controlled through the $PS1 variable. You set a variable by specifying the variable name (minus the leading dollar sign, $), an equal sign (=), and the value to which you want to set the variable. In most cases, you should surround the value of the prompt by quotes ("). For instance, you can set your bash prompt to read Your command? by typing the following:

```
$ PS1="Your command? "
```

Pay attention to the spaces (and lack thereof), particularly around the equal sign; adding spaces around the equal sign will cause this command to fail. If you want a space between the prompt and the point at which you begin typing, be sure to include one at the end of the new prompt string.

The scenario presented earlier, though, specified that you want to include the time and date in the command prompt. To do this, you must include special strings that serve as stand-ins for other data. Specifically, the current date can be denoted by \d and the time can be denoted by \@. Thus, you can set your prompt to include the date and time by issuing the following command:

```
$ PS1="\d \@ $ "
```

The result might resemble the following, although of course the date and time shown in the prompt will change with the real date and time:

```
Thu Jun 08 11:44 AM $
```

In most distributions, the system is configured with default prompts that include your username, the computer's hostname, and the current directory, but details differ. You can learn what your shell prompt is by typing **echo $PS1**. This command displays the contents of the $PS1 variable. Consult the man page for bash for more information on common substitution strings, including those found in your distribution's default shell prompt.

Setting the $PS1 variable as just described has one important limitation: The change is restricted to the current running instance of bash. Any program launched from bash will inherit the default value of $PS1. This is true even of bash itself. With your altered prompt displayed, try typing **bash** to launch another shell from the current one. Your command prompt will be replaced by your default prompt. Typing **exit** from the new shell will return you to the original one with the modified prompt.

To make a change that can be inherited by programs launched from your current session, you must use the export command after setting the variable:

```
$ PS1="\d \@ $ "
$ export $PS1
```

A variable that's been exported in this way is referred to as an *environment variable*, as opposed to a simple variable. Alternatively, you can combine these commands on a single line:

```
$ export PS1="\d \@ $ "
```

After typing these commands, if you launch a new instance of bash, it will inherit the changed command prompt. Even this change, though, won't affect new logins or new xterm windows; to make your change truly permanent, you must adjust configuration files, as described shortly in "Making Your Changes Permanent."

## Setting a Program-Specific Environment Variable

Many environment variables affect non-bash programs. One of these that you might want to adjust is $EDITOR. Some Linux programs launch an external text editor for certain operations, and these programs often consult the $EDITOR environment variable to determine what program to use. First, check what program your account is configured to use by default:

```
$ echo $EDITOR
/usr/bin/vi
```

Although the $EDITOR variable is frequently defined, it isn't guaranteed to be. If a variable isn't set, displaying it with echo will show an empty line as output.

Of course, your system might not be configured to use Vi, as shown in this example. Another test is to use a utility that consults the $EDITOR environment variable. One such tool is crontab; type **crontab -e** and you should see a (probably empty) file appear in your default editor. Exit from this editor without making any changes to the file.

Suppose you don't want to use Vi as your default editor, though; perhaps you prefer nano. You can adjust your default editor by changing the environment variable:

`$ export EDITOR="/usr/bin/nano"`

> Check that /usr/bin/nano exists before typing this command. If it doesn't exist, locate the file's true location or substitute another editor, such as /usr/bin/emacs or /usr/bin/jed.

You must use the export command to set the environment variable, not simply a variable for the current bash session, since $EDITOR is used by programs other than bash. Once the environment variable has been set, test it by typing **crontab -e** again. You should see the same (probably empty) file you saw before appear in your new editor.

## Making Your Changes Permanent

Chances are you don't want to type a series of commands to adjust your environment variables every time you log into your Linux system or launch a new xterm window. You can automate the process by modifying bash configuration files. Table 1.4 summarizes the locations and names of these files.

**TABLE 1.4** Common bash Configuration Files

| Type of File | Login File Location | Non-Login File Location |
|---|---|---|
| Global | /etc/profile and files in /etc/profile.d | /etc/bashrc or /etc/bash.bashrc |
| User | ~/.bash_login, ~/.profile, or ~/.bash_profile | ~/.bashrc |

The bash configuration files can be either global (they apply to all users) or user (they apply to individual users), and either login files (they apply to login sessions, such as those initiated from a text-mode login prompt) or non-login files (they apply to non-login sessions, such as those started in xterm windows). The precise names used for these files varies from one distribution to another. The most common user configuration files are ~/.bashrc and ~/.profile, so look for those files. To make your changes permanent, you must locate existing lines that set the environment variables you want to modify or add new lines.

Whatever the name or location, bash configuration files are actually shell scripts, as described in more detail in Task 1.9. For now, you can simply add or modify existing export commands. Type the commands in the shell script just as you'd type them at a command prompt. If you need to add a line rather than modify an existing one, be careful to keep it out of command structures, such as if statements. Your best bet is to add new lines to the very end of the file.

Try modifying an appropriate bash login script to change the shell prompt or default editor. Log out, log in again, and test your changes. If they didn't work, restore the file to its original condition and try again with another file; it may take a bit of trial and error to locate the correct file. If you like, you can change the global configuration file to affect all users, but you must do so as root.

In addition to startup scripts, bash provides shutdown (or logout) scripts. The most common name for this script is ~/.bash_logout, which is a user script. Modifying this or similar scripts can be handy if you want to ensure that certain actions are taken when a user logs out. You might use it to destroy sensitive temporary files, for instance.

## Exploring Other Environment Variables

Linux supports many more environment variables than the $PS1 and $EDITOR variables described earlier. In fact, you can set any environment variable you want—$PHASE1 or $GOBBLEDEGOOK, for instance. To be useful, though, an environment variable must be used by bash or by some other program. Table 1.5 summarizes some common environment variables and their uses. This table is not comprehensive, though; in principle, any program may use its own unique environment variables. If you read in a program's documentation that it uses particular environment variables, you can set them using the techniques described earlier.

**TABLE 1.5**    Common Environment Variables and Their Meanings

| Variable Name | Explanation |
| --- | --- |
| $USER | This is your current username. It's a variable that's maintained by the system. |
| $SHELL | This variable holds the path to the current command shell. |
| $PWD | This is the present working directory. This environment variable is maintained by the system. Programs may use it to search for files when you don't provide a complete pathname. |
| $HOSTNAME | This is the current TCP/IP hostname of the computer. |
| $PATH | This is an unusually important environment variable. It sets the *path* for a session; the path is a colon-delimited list of directories in which Linux searches for executable programs when you type a program name. For instance, if PATH is /bin:/usr/bin and you type ls, Linux looks for an executable program called ls in /bin and then in /usr/bin. If the command you type isn't on the path, Linux responds with a command not found error. The $PATH variable is typically built up in several configuration files, such as /etc/profile and the .bashrc file in the user's home directory. |
| $HOME | This variable points to your home directory. Some programs use it to help them look for configuration files or as a default location in which to store files. |

**TABLE 1.5**    Common Environment Variables and Their Meanings *(continued)*

| Variable Name | Explanation |
|---|---|
| $LD_LIBRARY_PATH | A few programs use this environment variable to indicate directories in which library files may be found. It works much like PATH. |
| $PS1 | This is the default prompt in bash. It generally includes variables of its own, such as \u (for the username), \h (for the hostname), and \W (for the current working directory). This value is frequently set in /etc/profile, but it is often overridden by users. |
| $TERM | This variable is the name of the current terminal type. To move a text-mode cursor and display text effects for programs like text-mode editors, Linux has to know what commands the terminal supports. The $TERM environment variable specifies the terminal in use. This information is combined with data from additional files to provide terminal-specific code information. $TERM is normally set automatically at login, but in some cases you may need to change it. |
| $DISPLAY | This variable identifies the display used by X. It's usually :0.0, which means the first (numbered from 0) display on the current computer. When you use X in a networked environment, though, this value may be preceded by the name of the computer at which you're sitting, as in machine4.example.com:0.0. This value is set automatically when you log in, but you may change it if necessary. You can run multiple X sessions on one computer, in which case each one gets a different DISPLAY number—for instance, :0.0 for the first session and :1.0 for the second. |
| $EDITOR | Some programs launch the program pointed to by this environment variable when they need to call a text editor for you to use. Thus, changing this variable to your favorite editor can help you work in Linux. It's best to set this variable to a text-mode editor, though; GUI editors might cause problems if they're called from a program that was launched from a text-mode login. |

**WARNING**    The PATH variable often includes the current directory indicator (.) so that programs in the current directory can be run. This practice poses a security risk, though, because a miscreant could create a program with the name of some other program (such as ls) and trick another user into running it by simply leaving it in a directory the victim frequents. Even the root user may be victimized in this way. For this reason, it's best to omit the current directory from the PATH variable, especially for the superuser. If it's really needed for ordinary users, put it at the *end* of the path.

To learn what environment variables are set in your particular session, type **env**. This command officially runs a program in a modified environment; however, when typed alone, it displays the values of all the currently set environment variables. The output of this command is likely to be quite long, so you may want to pipe it through less or redirect the output to a file for later examination. Some of the environment variables will have fairly suggestive names, but others are likely to be obscure. You can find the purpose of some in the man page for bash, but others have meaning only to particular programs. If you don't understand the purpose of an environment variable, don't try to change it; ignore it or, if you're curious, try looking it up using a Web search engine.

## Criteria for Completion

To complete this task, you should have successfully tested modifications to at least two environment variables: $PS1 (to set the shell prompt) and $EDITOR (to set the default editor). You should have made both transient changes (by setting the variable and using the export command on a command line) and more permanent changes (by editing a bash configuration file).

# Task 1.9: Write Basic Scripts

The bash and other Linux command-prompt shells are more than simple command-line tools; they're powerful programming languages. You can string together commands to have them execute one after another, add variables to improve flexibility, and use program control statements to have parts of the program execute repeatedly or only upon certain conditions.

Programs written in the bash shell language are often referred to as *scripts*. Compared to programs written in languages such as C, C++, and Pascal, bash scripts are easy to create but slow to execute. This makes them good choices for simple programs and for "throwaway" programs that aren't likely to be used very often. In fact, many of Linux's key startup and system configuration files are actually shell scripts. Thus, understanding how to create and modify scripts will help you administer a Linux system.

## Scenario

You find that you want to simplify or otherwise improve various tasks that you routinely perform, so you want to create scripts to handle these tasks. Specifically, you want a script to launch a few X programs with one command, a way to simplify account creation tasks, a script that reports nothing but the computer's IP address, a script that plays all the .wav audio files in a directory, and a script that copies files only if the destination file doesn't already exist.

## Scope of Task

Script-writing is a very open-ended activity; scripts can perform a wide variety of tasks, and there may be multiple ways of achieving the same goals within a script. This particular task presents a few scripts that illustrate important scripting features.

## Duration

This task will take about an hour to complete. Writing real-world scripts can take anywhere from a minute or so up to several hours or even days, depending on the complexity of the script and your own proficiency at script writing.

## Setup

To perform this task, you must log into your computer as an ordinary user. One of the scripts presented in this task requires root access to run. You'll also need root access if you want to copy any of these scripts to a system directory, but this isn't necessary to complete the task. You may use a text-mode or GUI login, although the first script launches X programs, so you'll need an X session to test it. The scripts themselves are executed from the command line, but you'll edit them in an editor, which may be a purely text-based editor (such as Vi or nano) or a GUI editor (such as KEdit).

## Caveats

As programs, scripts can contain bugs. Although the scripts presented in this task are fairly simple and are likely to be harmless even with typos, bugs in scripts can cause infinite loops (in which the script never terminates), excessive CPU use, accidental file deletions, and other problems. These problems can be more serious if a buggy script is run as root, or even if a bug-free script is used inappropriately by root. Thus, unless a script absolutely requires root access, you should always develop and test scripts as a non-root user.

# Procedure

The first thing to understand about scripts is how to create them: You use a text editor to type commands, then modify the file permissions on the resulting file so that it's executable. Once you know how to perform these basic operations, you can proceed to create scripts that meet the objectives of this task.

## Beginning a Shell Script

Shell scripts are plain-text files, so you create them in text editors. A shell script begins with a line that identifies the shell that's used to run it, such as the following:

```
#!/bin/sh
```

The first two characters are a special code that tells the Linux kernel that this is a script and to use the rest of the line as a pathname to the program that's to interpret the script. Shell scripting languages use a hash mark (#) as a comment character, so the script utility itself ignores this line, although the kernel doesn't. On most systems, /bin/sh is a symbolic link that points to /bin/bash, but it could point to some other shell. Specifying the script as using /bin/sh guarantees that any Linux system will have a shell program to run the script, but if the script uses any features specific to a particular shell, you should specify that shell instead—for instance, use /bin/bash or /bin/tcsh instead of /bin/sh.

When you're done writing the shell script, you should modify it so that it's executable. You do this with the chmod command, as described in Task 1.2. Specifically, you use the +x option to add execute permissions, probably in conjunction with a to add these permissions for all users. For instance, to make a file called my-script executable, you'd issue the following command:

```
$ chmod a+x my-script
```

You'll then be able to execute the script by typing its name, possibly preceded by ./ to tell Linux to search in the current directory for the script. If the script is one you run regularly, you may want to move it to a location on your path, such as /usr/local/bin. When you do that, you won't have to type the complete path or move to the script's directory to execute it; you can just type my-script.

## Using Commands

One of the most basic features of shell scripts is the ability to run commands. You can use both shell internal commands and external commands. Most of the commands you type in a shell prompt are in fact external commands—they're programs located in /bin, /usr/bin, and other directories on your path. You can run such programs, as well as internal commands, by including their names in the script. You can also specify parameters to such programs in a script. For instance, suppose you want to start a script that launches two xterm windows and the KMail mail reader program. Listing 1.2 presents a shell script that accomplishes this goal.

**Listing 1.2:** A Simple Script That Launches Three Programs

```
#!/bin/bash
/usr/bin/xterm &
/usr/bin/xterm &
/usr/bin/kmail &
```

Aside from the first line that identifies it as a script, the script looks just like the commands you might type to accomplish the task manually except for one fact: The script lists the complete paths to each program. (You may need to modify the path to kmail; it's not always stored in /usr/bin.) This is usually not strictly necessary, but listing the complete path ensures that the script will find the programs even if the $PATH environment variable changes. Also, each program-launch line in Listing 1.2 ends in an ampersand (&). This character tells the shell to go on to the next line without waiting for the first to finish. If you omit the ampersands in Listing 1.2, the effect will be that the first xterm will open but the second won't open until the first is closed. Likewise, KMail won't start until the second xterm terminates.

Although launching several programs from one script can save time in startup scripts and some other situations, scripts are also frequently used to run a series of programs that manipulate data in some way. Such scripts typically do *not* include the ampersands at the ends of the commands because one command must run after another or may even rely on output from the first. A comprehensive list of such commands is impossible because you can run any program you can install in Linux as a command—even another script. The following list includes a few commands that are commonly used in scripts:

**Normal file-manipulation commands**    The file-manipulation commands, such as `ls`, `mv`, `cp`, and `rm`, are often used in scripts. You can use these commands to help automate repetitive file maintenance tasks.

**grep**    This command is described earlier, in "Piping Data between Programs" in Task 1.7. It locates files that contain specific strings.

**find**    Where `grep` searches for patterns within the contents of files, `find` does so based on file-names, ownership, and similar characteristics. This command is described earlier, in Task 1.4.

**cut**    This command extracts text from fields in a file. It's frequently used to extract variable information from a file whose contents are highly patterned. To use it, you pass it one or more options that control what it cuts followed by one or more filenames. For instance, users' home directories appear in the sixth colon-delimited field of the `/etc/passwd` file. You could therefore include `cut -f 6 -d ":" /etc/passwd` in a script to extract this information.

**sed**    This program provides many of the capabilities of a conventional text editor but via commands that can be typed at a command prompt or entered in a script.

**echo**    Sometimes a script must provide a message to the user; `echo` is the tool to accomplish this goal. You can pass various options to `echo` or just a string to be shown to the user. For instance, `echo "Press the Enter key"` causes a script to display the specified string.

**mail**    The `mail` command can be used to send email from within a script. Pass it the `-s` *subject* parameter to specify a subject line and give it an email address as the last argument. If it's used at the command line, you would then type a message and terminate it with a Ctrl+D. If it's used from a script, you might omit the message body entirely or pass it an external file as the message using input redirection. You might want to use this command to send mail to the superuser about the actions of a startup script or a script that runs on an automated basis.

> Many of these commands are extremely complex. You can consult their man pages for more information.

Even if you have a full grasp of how to use some key external commands, simply executing commands you might type at a command prompt is of limited utility. Many administrative tasks require you to modify what you type at a command, or even what commands you enter, depending on information from other commands. For this reason, scripting languages include additional features to help you make your scripts useful.

## Using Variables

*Variables* can help you expand the utility of scripts. A variable is a placeholder in a script for a value that will be determined when the script runs. Variables' values can be passed as parameters to scripts, generated internally to the scripts, or extracted from the scripts' environments.

Variables that are passed to the script are frequently called *parameters*. They're represented by a dollar sign ($) followed by a number from 0 up—$0 stands for the name of the script, $1 is the first parameter to the script, $2 is the second parameter, and so on. To understand how this might be useful, consider the task of adding a user. As described earlier, in Task 1.6, creating an account for a new user typically involves running at least two commands—useradd and passwd. You might also need to run additional site-specific commands, such as commands that create unusual user-owned directories aside from the user's home directory.

As an example of how a script with a parameter variable can help in such situations, consider Listing 1.3. This script creates an account and changes the account's password (you'll be prompted to enter the password when you run the script). It creates a directory in the /shared directory tree corresponding to the account, and it sets a symbolic link to that directory from the new user's home directory. It also adjusts ownership and permissions in a way that may be useful, depending on your system's ownership and permissions policies.

**Listing 1.3:** A Script That Reduces Account-Creation Tedium

```
#!/bin/sh
useradd -m $1
passwd $1
mkdir -p /shared/$1
chown $1.users /shared/$1
chmod 775 /shared/$1
ln -s /shared/$1 /home/$1/shared
chown $1.users /home/$1/shared
```

When you use Listing 1.3, you need type only three things: the script name with the desired username and the password (twice). For instance, if the script is called mkuser, you might use it like this:

```
# mkuser sjones
Changing password for user sjones
New password:
Retype new password:
passwd: all authentication tokens updated successfully
```

Most of the scripts' programs operate silently unless they encounter problems, so the interaction (including typing the passwords, which don't echo to the screen) is a result of just the passwd command. In effect, Listing 1.3's script replaces seven lines of commands with one. Every one of those lines uses the username, so by using this script, you also reduce the chance of an error.

Another type of variable is assigned within scripts themselves—for instance, they can be set from the output of a command. These variables are also identified by leading dollar signs, but they're typically given names that at least begin with a letter, such as $Addr or $Name. These variables are the same as variables you can set at the command line (as described earlier, in Task 1.8), but unless you use the export command, they don't become environment variables.

For instance, consider Listing 1.4, which displays the current IP address of the computer on which it runs. This script uses the variable $ip, which is extracted from the output of ifconfig using grep and cut commands. (The trailing backslash on the second line of the script indicates that the following line is a continuation of the preceding line.) When assigning a value to a variable from the output of a command, that command should be enclosed in back-quote characters (`` ` ``), which appear on the same key as the tilde (~) on most keyboards. These are *not* ordinary single quotes, which appear on the same key as the regular quote character (") on most keyboards.

**Listing 1.4:** Script Demonstrating Assignment and Use of Variables

```
#!/bin/sh
ip=`ifconfig eth0 | grep inet | cut -f 2 -d ":" | \
    cut -f 1 -d " "`
echo "Your IP address is $ip"
```

Listing 1.4 relies on the networking command ifconfig, which is described in more detail in Phase 6. You can type **ifconfig** by itself to see what its output includes. The second line of Listing 1.4 uses grep and cut to isolate the IP address from the rest of the ifconfig output.

Scripts like Listing 1.4, which obtain information from running one or more commands, are useful in configuring features that rely on system-specific information or information that varies with time. You might use a similar approach to obtain the current hostname (using the hostname command), the current time (using date), the total time the computer's been running (using uptime), free disk space (using df), and so on. When combined with conditional expressions (described shortly), variables become even more powerful because then your script can perform one action when one condition is met and another in some other case. For instance, a script that installs software could check free disk space and abort the installation if there's not enough disk space available.

One special type of variable was mentioned earlier in this chapter: environment variables. Environment variables are assigned and accessed just like shell script variables. The difference is that the script or command that sets an environment variable uses the export command to make the value of the variable accessible to programs launched from the shell or shell script that made the assignment. Environment variables are most often set in shell startup scripts, but the scripts you use can access them. For instance, if your script calls X programs, it might check for the presence of a valid $DISPLAY environment variable and abort if it finds that this variable isn't set. By convention, environment variable names are all uppercase, whereas non-environment shell script variables are all lowercase or mixed case.

## Using Conditional Expressions

Scripting languages support several types of *conditional expressions*. These enable a script to perform one of several actions contingent on some condition—typically the value of a variable. One common command that uses conditional expressions is if, which allows the system to take one of two actions depending on whether some condition is true. The if keyword's conditional expression appears in brackets after the if keyword and can take many forms. For instance, -f *file* is true if *file* exists and is a regular file; -s *file* is true if *file* exists and has a size greater than 0; and *string1* = *string2* is true if the two strings have the same values.

To better understand the use of conditionals, consider the following code fragment:

```
if [ -s /tmp/tempstuff ]
    then
        echo "/tmp/tempstuff found; aborting!"
        exit
fi
```

This fragment causes the script to exit if the file /tmp/tempstuff is present. The then keyword marks the beginning of a series of lines that execute only if the conditional is true, and fi (if backwards) marks the end of the if block. Such code might be useful if the script creates and then later deletes this file, since its presence indicates that a previous run of the script didn't succeed or is still working.

An alternative form for a conditional expression uses the test keyword rather than square brackets around the conditional:

```
if test -s /tmp/tempstuff
```

You can also test a command's return value by using the command as the condition:

```
if [ command ]
    then
        additional-commands
fi
```

In this example, the additional-commands will be run only if command completes successfully. If command returns an error code, the additional-commands won't be run.

Conditional expressions are sometimes used in *loops* as well. Loops are structures that tell the script to perform the same task repeatedly until some condition is met (or until some condition is no longer met). For instance, Listing 1.5 shows a loop that plays all the .wav audio files in a directory.

**Listing 1.5:** A Script That Executes a Command on Every Matching File in a Directory

```
#!/bin/bash
for d in `ls *.wav` ;
    do play $d ;
done
```

The for loop as used here executes once for every item in the list generated by ls *.wav. Each of those items (filenames) is assigned in turn to the $d variable and so is passed to the play command.

Another type of loop is the while loop, which executes for as long as its condition is true. The basic form of this loop type is like this:

```
while [ condition ]
do
    commands
done
```

The `until` loop is similar in form, but it continues execution for as long as its condition is *false*—that is, until the condition becomes true.

## Using Functions

A *function* is a part of a script that performs a specific sub-task and that can be called by name from other parts of the script. Functions are defined by placing parentheses after the function name and enclosing the lines that make up the function within curly braces:

```
myfn() {
    commands
}
```

The keyword `function` may optionally precede the function name. In either event, the function is called by name as if it were an ordinary internal or external command.

Functions are very useful in helping to create modular scripts. For instance, if your script needs to perform half a dozen distinct computations, you might place each computation in a function and then call them all in sequence. Listing 1.6 demonstrates the use of functions in a simple program that copies a file but aborts with an error message if the target file already exists. This script accepts a target and a destination filename and must pass those filenames to the functions.

**Listing 1.6:**  A Script Demonstrating the Use of Functions

```
#/bin/bash

doit() {
   cp $1 $2
}

function check() {
  if [ -s $2 ]
    then
        echo "Target file exists! Exiting!"
        exit
  fi
}

check $1 $2
doit $1 $2
```

If you enter Listing 1.6 and call it `safercp`, you might use it like this, assuming the file `original.txt` exists and `dest.txt` does not:

```
$ ./safercp original.txt dest.txt
$ ./safercp original.txt dest.txt
Target file exists! Exiting!
```

The first run of the command succeeded because `dest.txt` did not exist. When the command was run a second time, though, the destination file did exist, so the program terminated with the error message.

Note that the functions are not run directly and in the order in which they appear in the script. They're run only when called in the main body of the script (which in Listing 1.6 consists of just two lines, each corresponding to one function call).

## Criteria for Completion

To complete this task, you must have created five scripts to perform the five tasks outlined earlier. I recommend that you try some simple variants on these tasks so that you create scripts that perform other tasks—for instance, you might modify Listing 1.5 so that it displays graphics files in a directory rather than plays audio files.

# Phase

# 2

# Managing Hardware and the Kernel

Linux software requires hardware to be useful, and managing that hardware requires its own set of street smarts. Phase 2 focuses on this topic, beginning with low-level hardware configuration in the Basic Input/Output System (BIOS) and resolving hardware conflicts. This phase then moves on to Linux utilities for identifying and configuring your hardware, and particularly the Universal Serial Bus (USB), hard disk, and power management subsystems. The kernel is a critical part of the hardware equation, so this phase looks at configuring and compiling the kernel. Finally, this phase concludes with three tasks related to the X Window System (or X for short), Linux's GUI environment.

This phase maps to portions of the CompTIA Linux+ objective 6 and to portions of the LPIC objectives 101, 105, and 110.

# Task 2.1: Set BIOS Options

The BIOS is a low-level set of software functions that were designed in the 1980s to simplify the creation of OSs such as Microsoft's original Disk Operating System (DOS). The BIOS would handle functions such as keyboard input, screen output, and even low-level disk input/output. Over the years, as computers and OSs grew in complexity, the BIOS became less and less important in handling these I/O tasks. Nonetheless, the BIOS remains important because it controls the computer's initial boot sequence and hardware initialization. If the BIOS doesn't know your hard disk exists, or if it configures your hard disk incorrectly, the computer won't boot. Improper BIOS settings can also cause unreliable operation, clocks that are set incorrectly, an inability to access on-board hardware devices, and other problems. Thus, care should be taken when setting BIOS options, and checking these options is a wise precaution whenever putting a new computer into operation.

## Scenario

You've just assembled a new computer from parts. Before booting it and attempting to install Linux, you want to check its BIOS options to see that they're sensible. You should pay particular attention to the disk options and to the system clock setting. When assembling a computer from parts, *you* are responsible for setting basic BIOS options. When you buy a pre-assembled computer, in theory the BIOS should be set correctly; however, errors do sometimes appear, so checking the BIOS options is a sensible precaution. The clock is likely to need adjustment even with a store-bought computer.

## Scope of Task

This task is a fairly short one, but you may need to do some research to complete it successfully. You must understand more about your hardware than is necessary for completing most other tasks in this book.

### Duration

This task can be completed in 15 to 30 minutes; however, you must first know a bit about your hardware (as described in the next section, "Setup"). You're unlikely to need to perform this task very often once a computer is up and running, although you may need to do it when you add or remove hardware.

### Setup

You need a minimally functional $x86$ or $x86$-64 computer. This computer needs to be able to start up far enough to enter its BIOS utility, but it doesn't need to have Linux—or any other OS—installed. (You may use a computer with a working OS, but this isn't required.)

> **NOTE**  This task describes $x86$ and $x86$-64 (aka AMD64 or EMT64T) BIOSs, such as Intel's Pentium and Celeron series and AMD's Athlon CPUs. Computers that use PowerPC, SPARC, and other CPUs are likely to have radically different BIOSs. Even among $x86$ and $x86$-64 systems, variations are substantial, and a few exotic systems don't even use BIOSs that closely resemble the ones described here

You must know something about your hardware and, in particular, your disks (both hard disks and floppy disks). You should know the make, model number, and capacity of all your hard disks and know how they're connected. In the case of the more common Advanced Technology Attachment (ATA) drives, you should know if you have the older Parallel ATA (PATA) or the newer Serial ATA (SATA) drives. Some drives are Small Computer System Interface (SCSI) devices, which work on different principles and usually connect via a separate SCSI host adapter. You should know which, if any, of the motherboard's on-board devices (sound, video, Ethernet, etc.) you're using.

If you're assembling a computer from parts, as described in "Scenario," you should know this information because you designed the computer. If you're using an existing Linux computer as a stand-in, you may need to dig out the computer's documentation or skip ahead to Task 2.2 to learn this information.

### Caveats

Adjusting BIOS settings inappropriately can make a computer unbootable. Although you're unlikely to damage the Linux installation, in the sense of the data on the hard disk, you could be in for some frustration if you make changes and can't remember what they were. Thus, you should take careful notes of any changes you make.

Although all mainstream *x*86 and *x*86-64 BIOSs provide similar options, details differ substantially from one computer to another. The examples shown here should therefore be considered rough guidelines only; you may need to consult your motherboard's manual or study the onscreen display, experiment, and apply your intelligence to figure out how to perform the tasks described here.

# Procedure

To perform this task, you must boot (or reboot) your computer, but bypass the Linux boot process to enter the low-level BIOS utilities. There you can check and, if necessary, change a host of settings related to your hardware.

## Entering the BIOS Setup Utility

When you boot an *x*86 or *x*86-64 computer, you'll see a series of text-mode (and sometimes graphical) displays, the details of which vary depending on your computer. Prior to the beginning of the Linux boot process, you're likely to see the name of the motherboard or computer manufacturer, a simple RAM check that counts up the amount of memory installed in the computer, a display of your installed PATA hard disks, and perhaps information on some of the devices built into the motherboard (RS-232 serial ports, parallel printer ports, and so on). Unfortunately for your comprehension of this information, these displays are likely to appear and disappear so quickly that you may have trouble reading them all. A recent trend has been to hide most or all of this information behind a graphical display, but some computers provide BIOS options to do away with the graphics and show the traditional text-mode information.

One of the pieces of information that's likely to be displayed, albeit for just a second or two, is a prompt for how to enter the BIOS setup utility. Typically, you must press one or more keys at some point during the boot process, such as Delete or F12. If your computer is currently running, shut it down, start it up again, and look for a prompt for how to enter the BIOS setup utility in the first few seconds of the boot process. If you don't see such a prompt, consult your computer's or motherboard's manual for the information, or try pressing the Delete key; that's a common method for entering the setup utility.

The BIOS setup utility modifies data stored in complementary metal oxide semiconductor (CMOS) memory, which is a small store of non-volatile on-chip memory on the motherboard. For this reason, this utility is often referred to as the *CMOS setup utility*.

## Touring the BIOS

Upon successfully entering the BIOS setup utility, you'll see a screen that provides a menu of options, as shown in Figure 2.1. (Some BIOS utilities jump directly into option-setting screens, with some way to select other screens among the options.) Take a few moments to peruse the options. In the case of Figure 2.1, most of the main categories, such as Standard CMOS Features and Integrated Peripherals, give some clue as to the functions contained within them, but they aren't entirely clear to the uninitiated.

**FIGURE 2.1**    BIOS setup utilities provide a menu of options from which you can select the features you want to adjust.

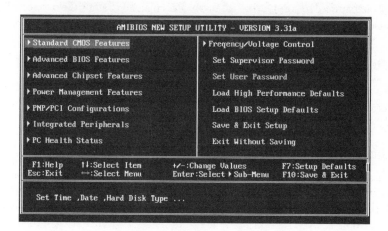

To move among the options, you typically use the keyboard's cursor keys, as prompted in the list of keyboard shortcuts near the bottom of the screen. You can then press the Enter key to enter a submenu or change an option. Once you enter a submenu, press the Esc key to exit from that menu. If these keys don't have the desired effects, though, you may need to use other keys; consult the onscreen prompts or your documentation for details.

Try perusing the options for your system now, but don't change anything. Some of the options should make at least some sense to you, but others will most likely be confusing. Don't try to figure out what every option means; the goal is simply to give you a general idea of what features your motherboard supports and what you can adjust, not for you to learn what *every* option does.

## Setting Disk Options

The first option you should check for this task is your disk settings. In the BIOS depicted in Figure 2.1, these options are accessible from the Standard CMOS Features menu, so select that option from the main screen if your BIOS uses this layout. The result (for this BIOS) is depicted in Figure 2.2. This screen enables adjustment of both disk and time options.

Integrated Device Electronics (IDE), aka PATA, hard disks are auto-detected by most motherboards and so should appear in the list of disks. Figure 2.2 shows two hard disks detected: a Maxtor 91024D4 and a Western Digital (WDC) WD800JB-00ETA0. These are configured as the master and slave drives on the primary PATA controller. If a hard disk you've installed doesn't appear, you can try selecting the drive (by primary/secondary and master/slave location) and selecting the auto-detect option in the menu that appears. If this doesn't work, chances are a cable is loose, the drive isn't connected to the power supply, or its master/slave setting is misconfigured. Shut down the computer, check the connections and settings, and reboot into the BIOS utility.

**FIGURE 2.2**   PC BIOSs enable you to adjust hard disk and system clock settings.

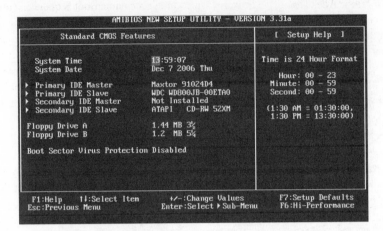

```
           AMIBIOS NEW SETUP UTILITY - VERSION 3.31a
  ┌──────────────────────────────────┬──────────────────────┐
  │   Standard CMOS Features          │  [ Setup Help ]      │
  │                                   │                      │
  │  System Time        13:59:07      │ Time is 24 Hour Format│
  │  System Date        Dec 7 2006 Thu│                      │
  │                                   │  Hour:  00 - 23      │
  │ ▶ Primary IDE Master  Maxtor 91024D4│ Minute: 00 - 59    │
  │ ▶ Primary IDE Slave   WDC WD800JB-00ETA0│ Second: 00 - 59│
  │ ▶ Secondary IDE Master Not Installed│                    │
  │ ▶ Secondary IDE Slave  ATAPI  CD-RW 52XM│ (1:30 AM = 01:30:00,│
  │                                   │  1:30 PM = 13:30:00) │
  │  Floppy Drive A     1.44 MB 3½    │                      │
  │  Floppy Drive B     1.2  MB 5¼    │                      │
  │                                   │                      │
  │  Boot Sector Virus Protection Disabled│                  │
  │                                   │                      │
  │                                   │                      │
  ├───────────────────────────────────┴──────────────────────┤
  │  F1:Help    ↑↓:Select Item   +/-:Change Values  F7:Setup Defaults│
  │  Esc:Previous Menu           Enter:Select ▶ Sub-Menu  F6:Hi-Performance│
  └──────────────────────────────────────────────────────────┘
```

If the computer still doesn't auto-detect a PATA drive, something more serious could be wrong. A few very old drives might not be detected correctly, and the BIOS enables you to move the setting off of Auto onto User or various drive-specific settings. Unless your hard drive is a refugee from the early 1990s or before, though, you shouldn't need to set these options.

> **NOTE**   SATA and SCSI drives aren't detected by the BIOS in the same way PATA drives are. If you have an SATA or SCSI drive, it's normal for the drive to not appear on the IDE drive list.

Figure 2.2 shows a CD-RW drive as the secondary slave device. On rare occasion, CD-ROM, CD-RW, and similar drives aren't detected correctly. If this happens to you, select the device by position and move the selector off of Auto and onto CDROM. This should fix the problem—assuming, of course, that a more fundamental misconfiguration or loose cable isn't the root cause of the problem.

In addition to hard drives, the BIOS enables you to configure your floppy drives. Unlike hard drives, floppy drives aren't auto-detected. To tell your BIOS about your floppy drive (or drives), move the cursor to the text to the right of Floppy Drive A or Floppy Drive B, press the Enter key, and select the appropriate drive type. Figure 2.2 shows one 3.5-inch and one 5.25-inch drive installed, but of course your system may be different.

> **NOTE**   In DOS and Windows, floppy drives are identified as A: and B:. Linux doesn't use these designations; on most systems, floppy drives are mounted as /mnt/floppy, /media/floppy, or something similar. The BIOS doesn't know this, though, and refers to floppy drives as A and B.

Most BIOSs provide some form of boot device option. The BIOS depicted in Figures 2.1 and 2.2 places this option on the Advanced BIOS Features screen under the name Boot Sequence. You can select which device the BIOS attempts to boot first, second, and third and whether or not the BIOS should look on other devices after that. This option is a very useful security feature because it can prevent an intruder from booting a floppy or other removable disk to gain access to the computer. To be a truly useful security feature, though, this option must be combined with a BIOS password. Even then, if the intruder can open the computer, the hard disk could be stolen or modified. Nonetheless, setting the computer to boot only from a hard disk can be part of an overall security strategy.

## Setting the Clock

All $x86$ and $x86$-64 computers include a clock on the motherboard to keep the time while the computer is shut down. You can set your motherboard's clock by moving the cursor to the appropriate items on the System Time and System Date lines and adjusting them. Most BIOSs require you to enter the time in a 24-hour format, so be sure to make the appropriate conversion.

Before you set your clock, though, be aware that Linux keeps time based on Coordinated Universal Time (UTC), which is closely related to Greenwich Mean Time (GMT). If your computer boots *only* Linux, your best bet is to set the motherboard's clock to UTC/GMT. Check `http://wwp.greenwichmeantime.com` for the current time as GMT. If your Linux installation currently works, though, you might do well to not adjust your motherboard's clock, even if it's set for local time; such a change would necessitate a change in your Linux configuration.

If your computer boots both Linux and an OS that keeps its time as local time, you can set your hardware clock to local time and Linux can make the adjustment internally. This feature is normally set at system install time.

It's possible to set the hardware clock from within Linux. To do so, use the `hwclock` command. Typing `hwclock --show` or `hwclock -r` displays the current hardware clock time; `hwclock --hctosys` or `hwclock -w` sets Linux's software clock based on the value of the hardware clock; and `hwclock --systohc` or `hwclock -s` sets the hardware clock based on the software clock. Ordinarily you don't need to use these commands, although they are used in system startup and shutdown scripts to set the software clock from the hardware clock when booting and to set the hardware clock from the software clock when shutting down. If you find your hardware clock has drifted badly off the current time, though, you can type `hwclock --systohc` to correct the problem once you set your software clock appropriately. You can do this with the Network Time Protocol (NTP, `http://www.ntp.org`) for a long-term solution or on a one-time basis via the `date` command.

    With the exception of displaying the current time, you need root privileges to use hwclock or date.

## Enabling and Disabling On-Board Devices

Modern motherboards usually contain a plethora of devices that were, in years past, implemented as separate plug-in cards—sound "cards," network ports, Universal Serial Bus (USB) ports, RS-232 serial ports, parallel ports, and so on. Not everybody wants to use all of these features, though, and some of them offer configuration options that you might want to adjust. To do so, you must access the appropriate BIOS utility screen. In the case of the BIOS depicted in Figure 2.1, you should select the Integrated Peripherals menu. The result is the screen shown in Figure 2.3, in which you can enable or disable the floppy disk (FDC Function), RS-232 serial ports, parallel ports, and more. (This area's options won't fit on one screen; they continue as you move the cursor down the list.)

**FIGURE 2.3** Modern BIOSs enable you to disable on-board devices if you so desire.

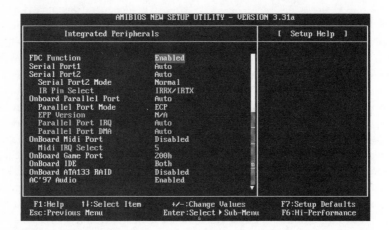

Disabling on-board devices disconnects them electronically from the rest of the motherboard. The result is that Linux won't be able to use those devices. The advantage is that they also won't consume valuable interrupt request (IRQ) lines and other resources.

If you know you won't be using a hardware feature built into your motherboard, either because you don't need it at all or because you intend to use a better plug-in card for that function, disable the feature in the BIOS. This reduces the odds of your encountering IRQ conflicts or other problems related to an unused device consuming resources or otherwise interfering with the hardware you are using.

## Additional BIOS Options

Most BIOSs provide options I don't describe here. Power management, RAM and PCI bus timing options, CPU speed, and more can all be controlled from the BIOS. Most such options are of interest to those who want to tweak the best possible performance from their computers, sometimes at the cost of reliability. If in doubt, leave the options at their factory defaults. Some BIOSs, including the one depicted in Figure 2.1, provide an explicit option to reset the configuration to the factory default (Load BIOS Setup Defaults in Figure 2.1) or to a high-performance state (Load High Performance Defaults in Figure 2.1). Such options can be useful emergency tools; if you tweak some settings, find that they don't work, and can't seem to get the BIOS working as you like it again, use the restore function.

You can also set a BIOS password on most computers. Using one will prevent somebody without the password from accessing the BIOS or perhaps booting the computer. This can be a useful feature in a high-security installation, but it's a bit inconvenient if the computer must be rebooted regularly.

One important option (or set of options) relates to exiting from the BIOS utility. In most cases, at least two exit options exist: One saves your changes and exits, whereas the other discards your changes and exits. These options are the final two in the second column in Figure 2.1. When you're done perusing (and possibly modifying) your BIOS settings, you should select whichever of these options you believe is most appropriate. The computer will then reboot normally—into Linux if it's installed. If you've made any changes to the BIOS, try to verify that they've had the desired effect in Linux.

## Criteria for Completion

To complete this task, you should peruse your BIOS and verify that the computer is configured correctly, particularly with respect to its hard disks, floppy disks, and on-board devices. If necessary, you should change these options and, if Linux is already installed, reboot into Linux and verify that any changes you made had the desired results.

# Task 2.2: Learn about Your Hardware

The $x86$ PC architecture, and therefore the $x86$-64 architecture derived from it, has evolved over a period of more than two decades. For this reason, many parts of the design of these systems are limiting or strange—what seemed a good solution to a problem in the 1980s might be inadequate today. Furthermore, old methods of manually configuring hardware must continue to be supported today, or they may have left behind vestiges of themselves in today's hardware and software.

One consequence of these facts is that configuring PC hardware can be difficult. Adding a new card or other device can sometimes break a working computer, and the many different types of hardware can lead to confusion. This task examines how you can learn about your hardware from within Linux in order to avoid problems when adding new hardware. The next task expands on this topic and looks at troubleshooting procedures

## Scenario

To prepare for planned system upgrades, you must create an inventory of hardware in your computer, including the resources this hardware consumes. This inventory will enable you to decide what additional hardware you can add, as well as any secondary upgrades you might need to support the ones you plan (for instance, whether you need to add a new disk controller to support additional hard drives).

## Scope of Task

This task involves running commands that report on system status, examining configuration and log files, and examining the contents of files in the /proc pseudo-filesystem.

### Duration

This task should take about half an hour to complete. If you need to obtain a specific piece of information in the future, you should be able to do so in a few seconds to a few minutes once you're familiar with the files and utilities in question.

### Setup

To prepare for this task, log into your Linux computer. Because some of these commands require root access, you may want to open two sessions, one as a regular user and one as root; or you can switch back and forth or run all the commands as root (although the latter option increases the risks involved in performing this task). Having a working printer will enable you to easily create a hard copy of some of the configuration files and text output created by the commands described in this task.

### Caveats

The usual caveats concerning root access to the computer apply to the parts of this task that require this access.

Some of the commands and procedures described here don't give a complete accounting of the resources used by your computer unless all the relevant drivers are loaded. Thus, it's possible your hardware inventory will be missing some items. You should have a general idea of what hardware is already installed and be able to activate that hardware before taking your inventory.

## Procedure

This task involves looking up data in two basic ways. First, you'll check system resources used by (optimally) all the hardware installed in your system. Second, you'll check information resources devoted to specific types of devices and for the system generally.

> Each *device*, in the context of this task, is a hardware subsystem. This subsystem may be a physically separate component (such as a scanner or external hard disk), a plug-in component (such as a PCI card), or a device that's integrated on the motherboard (such as the motherboard's built-in audio hardware). The physical form of a device is often impossible to determine from within Linux.

### Checking IRQs

IRQs were mentioned earlier, in Task 2.1. Early PCs supported just eight IRQ lines, numbered 0 to 7. Each device, in the form of motherboard features or plug-in Industry Standard Architecture (ISA) card, used a single IRQ. Later PCs expanded the number of IRQs to 15, numbered 0 to 15 (IRQ 2 serves as an interface to the higher IRQs, with IRQ 9 serving as a substitute for IRQ 2). The latest designs support larger numbers of IRQs—typically 24 or more. Each hardware device, such as a hard disk controller, sound card, or USB port, uses a single interrupt line to signal the CPU when it needs attention. Hardware connected to these devices, such as individual hard disks or USB devices (printers, mice, and so on), don't need IRQs themselves; they communicate with their controllers, which in turn communicate with the CPU.

IRQs are limited in number. Particularly on older computers that use the ISA bus, IRQs shouldn't be shared between devices. Modern computers can usually share IRQs between devices without problems.

IRQs are assigned by jumpers or dip switches on older cards or motherboards or automatically via *Plug and Play (PnP)* technology on newer ISA cards, Peripheral Component Interconnect (PCI) cards, and devices built into modern motherboards. When adding a device, it's best to assign it its own IRQ, either manually or by tweaking the way the motherboard or OS does so.

You can check which IRQs are currently in use by examining the contents of the /proc/interrupts pseudo-file:

```
$ cat /proc/interrupts
           CPU0
   0:  503295414    IO-APIC-edge  timer
   1:     272015    IO-APIC-edge  i8042
   8:          0    IO-APIC-edge  rtc
   9:          0    IO-APIC-level acpi
  14:     767672    IO-APIC-edge  ide0
  15:       4058    IO-APIC-edge  ide1
  16:   33306146    IO-APIC-level eth0, nvidia
  17:     858835    IO-APIC-level libata
  18:        112    IO-APIC-level sym53c8xx
  19:    5491622    IO-APIC-level uhci_hcd:usb1, uhci_hcd:usb2, ehci_hcd:usb3
  20:   48966520    IO-APIC-level VIA8237
 NMI:      58940
 LOC:  503233990
 ERR:          0
 MIS:          0
```

The /proc filesystem is a pseudo-filesystem that contains information on your hardware. The pseudo-files in this directory tree don't exist on disk; they're generated "on-the-fly" by the kernel to provide information to you and to software that needs information on your hardware.

This command's output shows that several devices are consuming IRQs. Some of these, such as `timer` (IRQ 0) and `rtc` (IRQ 8), are motherboard devices. Others, such as `nvidia` (IRQ 16) and `sym53c8xx` (IRQ 18), are plug-in cards. Knowing which is which is a matter of knowing the hardware in your system.

In this example, two IRQs are shared: 16 (`eth0` and `nvidia`) and 19 (three USB controllers). This example system is a fairly modern *x*86-64 system that can handle such IRQ sharing, so this isn't a problem.

Notably absent from this output are IRQs for some standard devices, such as the floppy controller, RS-232 serial ports, and parallel printer port. The reason for their absence is that these devices had not been accessed when the command was issued. If a device is used (say, by mounting a floppy disk), its entry will appear in subsequent accesses of `/proc/interrupts`. Thus, if you don't use a device, its entry might not appear in `/proc/interrupts` but it could still claim its interrupt at some future time. In creating an inventory of used IRQs, you should take this fact into consideration and use every device that your system contains before creating your inventory. Table 2.1 summarizes some of the common IRQs and their uses. This table omits IRQs for some common modern devices, such as USB ports, which are likely to map to different IRQs on different systems.

**TABLE 2.1**     IRQs and Their Common Uses

| IRQ | Typical Use | Notes |
| --- | --- | --- |
| 0 | System timer | Reserved for internal use. |
| 1 | Keyboard | Reserved for keyboard use only. |
| 2 | Cascade for IRQs 8–15 | The original *x*86 IRQ-handling circuit can manage just 8 IRQs; 2 are tied together to handle 16 IRQs, but IRQ 2 must be used to handle IRQs 8–15. |
| 3 | Second RS-232 serial port (`COM2:` in Windows) | May also be shared by a fourth RS-232 serial port. |
| 4 | First RS-232 serial port (`COM1:` in Windows) | May also be shared by a third RS-232 serial port. |
| 5 | Sound card or second parallel port (`LPT2:` in Windows) | |
| 6 | Floppy disk controller | Reserved for the first floppy disk controller. |
| 7 | First parallel port (`LPT1:` in Windows) | |
| 8 | Real-time clock | Reserved for system clock use only. |

**TABLE 2.1**    IRQs and Their Common Uses *(continued)*

| IRQ | Typical Use | Notes |
|-----|-------------|-------|
| 9 | Open interrupt | |
| 10 | Open interrupt | |
| 11 | Open interrupt | |
| 12 | PS/2 mouse | |
| 13 | Math coprocessor | Reserved for internal use. |
| 14 | Primary ATA controller | The controller for ATA devices such as hard drives; typically /dev/hda and /dev/hdb under Linux. |
| 15 | Secondary ATA controller | The controller for more ATA devices; typically /dev/hdc and /dev/hdd under Linux. |

To create an IRQ inventory, copy /proc/interrupts to a file in your home directory or print it. On most systems, typing **cat /proc/interrupts | lpr** will do the trick.

## Checking I/O Addresses

I/O addresses are similar to IRQs in that the PC architecture supports a limited number of them and most devices require an I/O address for communication with the CPU. There are, however, more I/O addresses than IRQs, so conflicts for I/O addresses are rarer than are IRQ conflicts. You can learn about your used I/O addresses by examining the /proc/ioports pseudo-file; so copy it to a file in your home directory or print it:

```
$ cat /proc/ioports | lpr
```

Many of the same caveats that apply to /proc/interrupts also apply to /proc/ioports. In particular, demand for an I/O port might not show up until after a device is used. Table 2.2 summarizes some of the more common I/O ports; however, this table is incomplete, particularly with respect to more modern devices with less fixed I/O port addresses.

**TABLE 2.2**    Common Linux Devices

| Linux Device | Windows Name | Typical IRQ | I/O Address |
|--------------|--------------|-------------|-------------|
| /dev/ttyS0 | COM1 | 4 | 0x03f8 |
| /dev/ttyS1 | COM2 | 3 | 0x02f8 |

**TABLE 2.2**   Common Linux Devices *(continued)*

| Linux Device | Windows Name | Typical IRQ | I/O Address |
|---|---|---|---|
| /dev/ttyS2 | COM3 | 4 | 0x03e8 |
| /dev/ttyS3 | COM4 | 3 | 0x02e8 |
| /dev/lp0 | LPT1 | 7 | 0x0378-0x037f |
| /dev/lp1 | LPT2 | 5 | 0x0278-0x027f |
| /dev/fd0 | A: | 6 | 0x03f0-0x03f7 |
| /dev/fd1 | B: | 10 | 0x0370-0x0377 |

## Checking DMA Channels

*Direct memory addressing (DMA)* is an alternative method of communication to I/O ports. Rather than have the CPU mediate the transfer of data between a device and memory, DMA permits the device to transfer data directly, without the CPU's attention. The result can be lower CPU requirements for I/O activity, which can improve overall system performance.

To support DMA, the *x*86 and *x*86-64 architectures implement several DMA channels, each of which can be used by a particular device. To learn what DMA channels are in use on your system, examine the /proc/dma file:

```
$ cat /proc/dma
 3: parport0
 4: cascade
```

This output indicates that DMA channels 3 and 4 are in use. As with IRQs and I/O ports, DMA channels should not normally be shared. In practice, DMA channel conflicts are rarer than IRQ conflicts, so chances are you won't run into problems. Copy or print the contents of /proc/dma on your system to preserve a record of this information.

## Checking Hard Disk Data

The /proc filesystem provides a way to learn about your PATA hard drives: the /proc/ide directory tree. This directory contains several subdirectories, but the simplest way to get at the data you want is to use the symbolic links that are named after your hard drives, such as /proc/ide/hda for the master drive on the primary controller or /proc/ide/hdd for the slave drive on the secondary controller. These symbolic links point to directories that contain several files each, such as model (the hard drive's model number), settings (many low-level settings), capacity (the drive's size in 512-byte blocks), and driver (the name and version number of the Linux driver that's responsible for the drive). You can examine these files by using `cat` or `less`:

```
$ cat /proc/ide/hda/driver
ide-disk version 1.188
```

 Although most of the pseudo-files in the /proc/ide directory tree are world-readable, some are not; you must be root to access these pseudo-files.

Although the `/proc/ide` directory tree provides useful information, it's not always the best way to learn about your disk devices. One good alternative is the `hdparm` utility, which enables you to read or set various hard disk options. To obtain a summary of information on your drive, use the `-i` option as `root`

```
# hdparm -i /dev/hda

/dev/hda:

 Model=WDC WD600AB-32BVA0, FwRev=21.01H21, SerialNo=WD-WMA7E1272684
 Config={ HardSect NotMFM HdSw>15uSec SpinMotCtl Fixed DTR>5Mbs FmtGapReq }
 RawCHS=16383/16/63, TrkSize=57600, SectSize=600, ECCbytes=40
 BuffType=DualPortCache, BuffSize=2048kB, MaxMultSect=16, MultSect=off
 CurCHS=4047/16/255, CurSects=16511760, LBA=yes, LBAsects=117231408
 IORDY=on/off, tPIO={min:120,w/IORDY:120}, tDMA={min:120,rec:120}
 PIO modes:  pio0 pio1 pio2 pio3 pio4
 DMA modes:  mdma0 mdma1 mdma2
 UDMA modes: udma0 udma1 udma2 udma3 udma4 *udma5
 AdvancedPM=no WriteCache=enabled
 Drive conforms to: Unspecified:  ATA/ATAPI-1 ATA/ATAPI-2 ATA/ATAPI-3
➥ATA/ATAPI-4 ATA/ATAPI-5

 * signifies the current active mode
```

This command returns a wide range of basic information, including the drive's model, firmware revision, serial number, cylinder/head/sector (CHS) counts, buffer size, access modes supported (PIO, DMA, and UDMA), and more. Even if most of this information is like Greek to you, having a record of it should be useful, so save it to a file or print it for future reference.

Unfortunately, both the `/proc/ide` directory tree and `hdparm` are useful only for PATA drives or for SATA drives that are managed by drivers in the PATA section of the Linux kernel. For SCSI drives and SATA drives that are handled by drivers in the SCSI section of the Linux kernel, less information is available through these methods. There is a `/proc/scsi` directory tree, but its contents are more concerned with the SCSI host adapter than with the devices it handles.

For both PATA and SCSI devices (including SCSI-driven SATA drives), you can obtain some basic information and data on drive partitioning by using the fdisk utility's -l option as root, which displays the partition table on the drive:

```
# fdisk -l /dev/sdb

Disk /dev/sdb: 81.9 GB, 81964302336 bytes
16 heads, 63 sectors/track, 158816 cylinders
Units = cylinders of 1008 * 512 = 516096 bytes

   Device Boot      Start         End      Blocks   Id  System
/dev/sdb1              1        9689     4883224+   a5  FreeBSD
/dev/sdb2           9690      158816    75160008    5  Extended
/dev/sdb5           9690       13565     1953472+   c  W95 FAT32 (LBA)
/dev/sdb6          13566       15504      977224+  83  Linux
/dev/sdb7          15505       60073    22462744+  8e  Linux LVM
/dev/sdb8          60074      158816    49766440+  8e  Linux LVM
```

PATA drives have drive identifiers of the form /dev/hdx, where x is a letter from a onward. SCSI drives have identifiers of the form /dev/sdx, where x is a letter from a onward. SATA drive identifiers can take either form, depending on the driver that handles the SATA controller.

The partition information can be useful in certain disaster recovery situations. It can also be helpful if you need to add, remove, or otherwise modify your partitions. For these reasons, you should archive this information to a file or print it. Phase 5 describes Linux partition management in greater detail.

## Checking PCI and USB Data

Modern computers use the PCI bus to connect most devices. Even devices that are built into the motherboard, such as USB controllers, are likely to use the PCI bus internally. You can learn about PCI devices from the /proc/pci pseudo-file. Much of the information retrieved from this pseudo-file will seem meaningless to you unless you're a hardware expert; nonetheless, it can prove useful in debugging problems, once you learn what certain key things mean. Thus, you should copy this pseudo-file or print it out for future reference.

The /proc/bus/usb/devices pseudo-file holds information on USB devices. As with the /proc/pci pseudo-file, much of the information will seem like gibberish, but it's worth saving. With the USB information, though, you may at least be able to spot manufacturer names or device model numbers.

### Checking Kernel Messages

When Linux boots, it displays a large number of messages about the hardware it finds. These messages scroll by so quickly that you're unlikely to be able to read them; however, you can review them by typing **dmesg | less** or print them by typing **dmesg | lpr**. The dmesg command displays the contents of the *kernel ring buffer*, where kernel messages are stored. This buffer is of limited size, and as the system continues to operate, the kernel is likely to place additional messages in this buffer. Thus, your original kernel messages may scroll out of the buffer in time. Some distributions store a copy of the kernel ring buffer as it existed when the computer first booted in a log file, such as /var/log/dmesg.

You should review your kernel ring buffer to familiarize yourself with the messages it contains. You needn't study every detail, but try to spot information on important subsystems, such as your hard disk, so that you know what types of messages to expect from a working system. In the event of hardware problems, the kernel ring buffer can be an invaluable resource. You might find that hardware isn't detected (no mention of it appears in the ring buffer), or you might spot error messages relating to the hardware in the ring buffer.

## Criteria for Completion

To complete this task, you should create a disk file or set of printouts that includes information on several hardware features:

- Used IRQs
- Used I/O addresses
- Used DMA channels
- Low-level hard disk information (for PATA disks)
- Disk formatting information
- PCI summary information
- USB summary information

You should also review your kernel ring buffer messages and be familiar with the basic format of these messages.

# Task 2.3: Resolve Hardware Conflicts

With Tasks 2.1 and 2.2 completed, you now have the knowledge required to identify certain types of hardware conflicts—for instance, if two devices are attempting to use a single interrupt, thus causing problems. What remains is to do something about such conflicts. Several possibilities exist: You can disable one of the offending devices, you can set jumpers on older plug-in cards to change resource use, you can adjust BIOS settings to avoid the conflict, or you can adjust Linux settings to avoid the conflict.

## Scenario

Two devices (a second parallel port and a sound card) are both trying to use IRQ 5 on your computer, and this is causing both devices to malfunction. You must reconfigure the system so that this conflict is avoided.

## Scope of Task

This task involves reviewing jumper settings, BIOS options, and Linux software configuration. As such, it's fairly wide reaching, although each individual part of the task is restricted in scope.

### Duration

This task should take about half an hour to complete. Once you're familiar with hardware reconfiguration, you can perform individual parts of this task in a few minutes.

### Setup

Ideally, you should have a computer with both a second parallel port and a sound card configured to use IRQ 5. In practice, though, you're unlikely to have a computer with this precise configuration, so you should simply follow the descriptions in this task and review your own hardware's capabilities and your own Linux system's software configuration. Start with your Linux system powered down. You'll need to enter the BIOS, and you may want to physically examine the hardware in your computer.

### Caveats

Physically examining or modifying hardware runs the risk of damaging it by accidental static discharge or other mishandling. If possible, you should use an anti-static wrist strap or take other anti-static precautions, such as regularly grounding yourself by touching a radiator while you work. Software adjustments run the risk of rendering your system unbootable if you make a mistake, so be careful not to make inappropriate changes.

## Procedure

To perform this task, you will review several types of settings for your hardware. If you were really fixing a problem, you would adjust one or more of these options to fix the problem. In reality, you'll probably leave these settings alone.

### Adjusting Hardware Jumpers

A hardware jumper is a set of two or more metal pins that stick out of a motherboard, plug-in card, hard disk, or other device and may be shorted together by using a small cap made of metal and plastic. Figure 2.4 shows a typical jumper, shown in the open (unshorted) position. Some jumpers, such as the one shown in Figure 2.4, support only open and closed positions. Others provide three or more pins that may be shorted together in different ways to configure the device.

**FIGURE 2.4**    Hardware jumpers are used on old, and occasionally on new, devices to set options.

Unfortunately, I can't give you any hard-and-fast rules as to when to set jumpers in particular positions. You *must* consult the device's documentation to learn how to set its jumpers to achieve particular goals. (Some devices print basic documentation on the hardware itself, but most require you to read separate documentation.)

Older ISA cards used jumpers as the exclusive means of configuration. You'd use jumpers to set IRQs, I/O ports, and other options and sometimes to disable or enable particular functions of a board. Later ISA cards and PCI cards use PnP technology to enable the computer to set these features, but such cards still sometimes sport a jumper or two. Hard disks also commonly use jumpers to set master/slave status, SCSI ID number, and other features, although hard disk standards are moving toward software-driven configuration as well.

If one or both of the problem devices in this task's scenario uses jumpers, you can avoid the conflict by setting the jumpers of one device so that it uses an unused IRQ rather than the IRQ 5 that's in contention. If the device is part of a multi-function card and you don't need the function in question, you may be able to use a jumper to disable it. For instance, if you don't need the second parallel port, you may be able to disable it on the plug-in card by setting an appropriate jumper while leaving the card's other hardware (such as RS-232 serial ports) working. A still more radical solution is, of course, to completely remove the card, but this will disable *all* of its functions.

## Adjusting BIOS Options

If one or both of the devices in this task's scenario are built into the motherboard or are PCI devices, you may be able to use BIOS settings to resolve the conflict. Review Figure 2.3 and the description earlier of the Integrated Peripherals area of the BIOS configuration utility. The options in this area are similar to the jumpers on older hardware; you can use them to enable or disable motherboard functions and to adjust various hardware options. If you need only one parallel port, you could disable one of them from this screen. Most motherboards provide only a single parallel port, though, so you might need to combine this action with reconfiguring a plug-in parallel port card via its jumpers or PnP settings.

Another way to adjust BIOS options to avoid conflicts is to review its PnP features. These options vary substantially from one BIOS to another, but you might want to review the options provided by your hardware. In Figure 2.1's BIOS, you would select the PNP/PCI Configurations menu option, which produces a screen in which you can set a few features, such as whether you're using a PnP-aware OS (recent versions of Linux qualify, but selecting Yes tells the BIOS to do more PnP configuration itself, which sometimes helps clear up problems) and what IRQs to assign to the devices in particular PCI slots. These options might help you to avoid an IRQ conflict.

### Adjusting Linux PnP Settings

Finally, Linux itself provides several PnP options you can adjust. For older ISA cards, two methods have existed for PnP configuration: the `isapnp` utility and kernel configuration options. The `isapnp` utility is largely outdated, so I don't describe it in detail here.

Both ISA PnP boards and PCI boards can be configured via kernel options. These are passed to the kernel at boot time via your boot loader configuration or to separate kernel modules via lines in the `/etc/modules.conf` file. (Some distributions build this file from files in the `/etc/modules.d` directory tree, so you may need to edit files in that directory instead and then type **modules-update** or a similar command to rebuild `/etc/modules.conf`.) Unfortunately, the details of how to set specific options are highly device specific, so you'll need to consult the documentation for the Linux driver for the device to learn how to do the job. To adjust the IRQ used by a device, you might pass an option such as `irq=10`, or perhaps simply 10, to the driver. When the driver loads, it configures the device to use the requested IRQ instead of the one the kernel or BIOS would otherwise have assigned it.

Sometimes PnP software reconfiguration doesn't work as you'd expect. This can happen because you've specified an option that won't work for the device, because the driver recognizes a conflict that you didn't see, or because of an error in the way you specified the option. Review the driver's documentation and try again if you can't seem to get an option to change.

For devices whose drivers are built into your kernel, you should modify your boot loader configuration. This is typically `/boot/grub/grub.conf` or `/boot/grub/menu.lst` for the Grand Unified Boot Loader (GRUB) or `/etc/lilo.conf` for the Linux Loader (LILO). Phase 5 describes boot loader configuration in more detail.

## Criteria for Completion

To complete this task, you should have reviewed three methods of reconfiguring your hardware: hardware jumpers, BIOS options, and Linux PnP settings (particularly the `/etc/modules.conf` file). Making random changes is inadvisable, but you should have familiarized yourself with the basic form of all these hardware configuration options. If your hardware is particularly modern, though, you might be hard-pressed to find any jumpers at all.

# Task 2.4: Configure USB Devices

USB 1.0, the first incarnation of USB, was finalized in 1996. Since then, USB has played an increasingly important role. Today, mice, printers, scanners, digital cameras, CD-RW drives, and many other devices can interface to computers via USB. Thus, being able to configure USB devices to work with Linux is an important skill.

USB was designed to permit relatively painless *hot-plug* operation, meaning that devices can be plugged into the computer and unplugged while the computer operates. Unfortunately, this type of operation is alien to Linux's basic driver model. Thus, to accommodate USB's hot-plug nature, various special utilities and interfaces have been developed. Configuring USB devices means working with these utilities.

## Scenario

To support efforts to digitize old documents and presentations, your employer has purchased a film scanner. This scanner uses a USB interface and must be configured to work correctly with Linux; however, your default Linux configuration prevents ordinary users from accessing the scanner when it's plugged into the computer and turned on. You must reconfigure Linux to enable ordinary users to work with the scanner.

## Scope of Task

This task involves examining configuration and system status files to learn about your hardware and then modifying configuration files to have the system configure hardware in the way you want. If you're lucky, you won't need to engage in the low-level configuration described here; many distributions provide tools that automatically detect and configure a wide variety of USB devices. These tools fail with obscure or very new hardware, though, necessitating manual configuration.

### Duration

This task will take about half an hour to complete. Once you're familiar with the procedure, you should—in theory—be able to perform similar tasks in half that time. In practice, though, adding hardware often involves overcoming unexpected problems. Thus, when you add your own truly unknown hardware, you could end up taking anywhere from a few minutes to several hours to configure it.

### Setup

To complete this task, you need `root` access to a Linux computer. Ideally, you should have a scanner or other USB device that's not accessible to ordinary users in your default configuration. (For this task, I use a Minolta DiMAGE Scan Elite 5400 film scanner and Fedora Core 5 as the example hardware and software.) This example assumes that your system uses the `udev` filesystem for handling device files, which is common with modern distributions. If you lack appropriate hardware or software, you should still be able to follow along and examine the relevant configuration files on your computer.

Your Linux computer should be booted and your USB device should be ready to be connected to the computer. Although some steps can be completed as an ordinary user, and some testing *must* be completed as an ordinary user, you will have to complete some steps as root.

### Caveats

Modifying the hardware configuration is inherently risky. An error in modifying configuration files could render a wide variety of devices useless. Thus, you should be very cautious when performing this task, above and beyond the usual caution when performing actions as root. Back up any file you plan to change so that you can restore it via an emergency boot system if necessary.

## Procedure

Adding USB hardware involves two basic steps: identifying the hardware and modifying configuration files that tell Linux how to add device files for the hardware. The first step requires examining USB information files, and the second involves modifying udev configuration files.

### Identifying USB Hardware

Before identifying your USB hardware, be sure that the device you want to identify is plugged in and (if applicable) turned on. You can then view the contents of the /proc/bus/usb/devices pseudo-file, say by using less. You'll see several entries for your USB controller hardware on your motherboard or add-on USB cards, as well as entries for USB mice, printers, and other devices. To find the entry for your device, look for the manufacturer's or product's name on the Manufacturer or Product lines. The entry for the Minolta DiMAGE Scan Elite 5400 looks like this:

```
T:  Bus=03 Lev=01 Prnt=01 Port=02 Cnt=01 Dev#=  2 Spd=480 MxCh= 0
D:  Ver= 2.00 Cls=ff(vend.) Sub=ff Prot=ff MxPS=64 #Cfgs=  1
P:  Vendor=0686 ProdID=400e Rev= 0.01
S:  Manufacturer=MINOLTA
S:  Product=DiMAGE Scan Elite 5400
S:  SerialNumber=0000000000000000
C:* #Ifs= 1 Cfg#= 1 Atr=c0 MxPwr=  2mA
I:  If#= 0 Alt= 0 #EPs= 3 Cls=00(>ifc ) Sub=00 Prot=00 Driver=(none)
E:  Ad=01(O) Atr=02(Bulk) MxPS= 512 Ivl=0ms
E:  Ad=82(I) Atr=03(Int.) MxPS=   8 Ivl=125us
E:  Ad=83(I) Atr=02(Bulk) MxPS= 512 Ivl=0ms
```

Most of this information isn't particularly important for configuring the hardware; however, some information is important, either for configuration or for possible troubleshooting:

**Bus number**    The Bus item on the first line identifies number of the bus that handles the device. This corresponds to the physical connector that manages the hardware—03 in this case. You don't need this information for configuration, but it may be helpful in diagnosing problems. For instance, if you suspect bus problems, you could try moving the device to another bus or look up information in the /proc/bus/usb/devices pseudo-file on the configuration of the specified bus.

**Device number**   The Dev# item identifies the number of the USB device on its bus. You don't need this information for configuring the device, but you might need it for debugging purposes.

**Bus speed**   The Spd item, also on the first line, specifies the bus speed in megabits per second—480 in this example. USB 2.0 devices normally communicate at this speed, but USB 1.0 and 1.1 devices communicate at a much more sedate 12Mbps. If you see this value but believe your device should be communicating at a faster speed, you should check that your hardware supports USB 2.0. If it does, look for the presence of an Enhanced Host Controller Interface (EHCI) driver in the Linux kernel, and be sure it's loaded. (Task 2.6, "Configure and Compile a Kernel," describes kernel configuration.)

**Vendor and product IDs**   The Vendor and ProdID codes on the third line identify the device. In this example, Vendor=0686 is reserved for Minolta products, while ProdID=400e uniquely identifies the Minolta DiMAGE Scan Elite 5400. Linux auto-configuration tools look for this information when setting up new devices, and you'll need it to add entries for devices that your distribution doesn't explicitly support.

## Adjusting the USB Hot-Plug Configuration

Once you have the USB vendor and product ID codes, you can begin modifying the udev configuration to support these devices. Most distributions that use the 2.6.x kernel use udev, which dynamically creates entries in the /dev directory tree for your hardware. When udev works well, it's pretty transparent; however, when it fails, it can require modifying some obscure configuration files. These files control the names, ownership, and permissions assigned to device files, among other things. Most distributions place these configuration files in the /etc/udev/rules.d directory. Packages can place udev rules files in this directory to ensure that the devices they use are given suitable device files. For instance, on a Fedora Core 5 system, the udev package installs default rules files, including 50-udev.rules, 50-udev-early.rules, and 51-hotplug.rules. On the same distribution, the sane-backends package installs the 60-libsane.rules file, expanding the set of udev rules. Each udev rules file must have a name that ends in .rules. Most rules files have names that begin with a number; these numbers determine the order in which the rules are implemented.

Before proceeding further, take some time to peruse the udev rules files. They may seem intimidating, but a general familiarity with their forms can be helpful. When creating new rules, you have two choices: modify an existing rules file or create a new rules file. The former option can be a bit simpler, but it runs the risk that your changes may be overwritten by package upgrades. Thus, you may want to create a new rules file. Listing 2.1 shows a sample file, which you might name 61-minolta.rules.

**Listing 2.1:** Sample udev Rules File

```
SUBSYSTEM!="usb_device", ACTION!="add", GOTO="minolta_rules_end"

# Minolta|DiMAGE Scan Elite 5400
SYSFS{idVendor}=="0686", SYSFS{idProduct}=="400e", SYMLINK+="scan-elite" \
```

```
MODE="0664", OWNER="root", GROUP="scanner"

LABEL="minolta_rules_end"
```

This file contains four configuration lines and a comment line (denoted by a leading hash mark, #). The first configuration line is a GOTO statement—it tells udev to go to the line that's labeled minolta_rules_end (via the LABEL statement on the final line) when not configuring USB devices and when not adding entries. Your udev rules file should contain a line like this, although you may want to change the label you use to identify the end of the configuration block, on both this and the final configuration lines.

The second configuration line tells udev to add /dev filesystem entries for a device with a vendor ID of 0686 and a product ID of 400e. The device file created, in the case of USB devices, will be an entry in the /dev/bus/usb directory tree. Specifically, udev creates a numbered subdirectory for each bus and a numbered device file for each device. This is where the bus number and device number from /proc/bus/usb/devices can come in handy—they can point you to your USB device file. The second configuration line in Listing 2.1 also tells udev to create a symbolic link called scan-elite. This symbolic link appears in the /dev directory and points to the real device file. The symbolic link is a handy shortcut for reaching the real device file, which is important for some programs but not for others. Without the symbolic link, you can never be sure what the device filename will be for a USB device since the device number on the bus and even the bus number can change when you unplug a device and plug it back in or when you reboot the computer.

The third configuration line in Listing 2.1 (beginning MODE=) is actually a continuation of the second line, as denoted by the backslash (\) that terminates the second line. This line specifies the mode, owner, and group of the device files that udev creates. This information is particularly important for any device that should be accessible to ordinary users. In the absence of such lines, either in the rules files delivered with your software or in rules files you add, udev will probably create device files with insufficient permissions for ordinary users to access the device. Listing 2.1 causes udev to create a device file with root ownership, scanner group ownership, and 0664 permissions, enabling anybody in the scanner group to read from and write to the device file. Thus, if a user should be able to access the scanner, you can add that user to the scanner group.

## Checking Your Changes

Unfortunately, udev won't pick up your changes immediately upon your making them. To have udev do so, you can stop and restart the udevd daemon process:

```
# ps ax | grep udevd
 2685 ?         S<s    0:00 /sbin/udevd -d
 2747 pts/0     R+     0:00 grep udevd
# kill 2685
# /sbin/udevd -d
```

These three commands locate the udevd process, kill it, and restart it. You should adjust the process ID number in the kill command based on the number output by the ps command. Phase 3 describes Linux process management in more detail.

After restarting udevd, you should attach and (if necessary) turn on your USB device. (If it's already connected, disconnect it first.) You should then check for the presence of a new device file in the /dev/bus/usb directory tree. Remember that the filename will probably change when you disconnect and reconnect the device! Check that the device file has the correct ownership and permissions, and look for a symbolic link, if your rules create one.

Beyond this basic test, you can test the device using appropriate software, such as VueScan (http://www.hamrick.com) for the Minolta film scanner used as an example. Be sure that appropriate users are able to access the hardware and that users who should *not* have access to the hardware are unable to do so.

## Criteria for Completion

This task demonstrates configuration changes to enable access to USB hardware that's not automatically configured by Linux. You should be able to identify a USB device in the /proc/bus/usb/devices file and use the information found there to create a new /etc/udev/rules.d/ file to create suitable device files in the /dev/bus/usb directory tree.

# Task 2.5: Configure Disk Devices

Disk input/output is at the heart of a Linux system. Everyday operations—launching programs, saving files, and so on—entail reading from and writing to disks. Thus, your hard disk configuration is a major factor in your overall system performance and stability.

Task 2.2 described how to learn some of the basics of your hard disk configuration. Phase 5 covers high-level hard disk configuration—partitioning and preparing filesystems. This task covers low-level hard disk identification and tuning procedures.

## Scenario

You're preparing a new computer that's to function as a file server on your local network. In order to provide the best performance, you want to check the hard disk configuration and, if necessary, tweak it to improve its speed.

## Scope of Task

This task involves running a few utilities to verify the presence of particular types of disk hardware and to check your hard disk performance. You may also want to run programs to improve disk performance and modify boot files to make these changes persistent across reboots.

## Duration

This task should take half an hour or so to complete. Once you're familiar with the tools involved, you can check and tune your hard disk configuration in a few minutes.

## Setup

Log into your Linux computer and acquire `root` privileges. Most of the tools you'll use in this task cannot be run as an ordinary user, although one or two can be.

## Caveats

Aside from the usual caveats about using `root` privileges, checking your disk hardware configuration isn't particularly risky; however, tweaking that configuration is dangerous. Setting incorrect disk options can cause a computer to lock up completely, requiring a hard reset, which in turn can sometimes cause data loss. Thus, if you have important data files on your computer, be sure to back them up before proceeding with this task.

# Procedure

This task involves three steps: identifying your disk hardware, testing your disk performance, and adjusting options that influence disk performance. You'll perform the first two tasks no matter what type of disk hardware you have. You might or might not actually do the final part of the task, depending on your disk hardware and the results of your disk performance test.

## Identifying Your Hardware

Linux treats hard disks as belonging to one of two categories:

**ATA disks**   Advanced Technology Attachment (ATA) disks, also known as Integrated Device Electronics (IDE) disks, have long been the most common type on $x86$ hardware. Modern $x86$ motherboards invariably include ATA controllers, and ATA drives have typically been less expensive than other types of drives. In the past few years, ATA has spawned a subtype, Serial ATA (SATA); the older ATA drives are now often referred to as Parallel ATA (PATA).

**SCSI disks**   Small Computer System Interface (SCSI) disks have traditionally been used on high-performance workstations and servers. In the past, they were common on Macintosh computers too, but many modern Macs use ATA disks. SCSI disks tend to be more expensive than ATA disks of similar capacity, but manufacturers often release their best-performing designs as SCSI disks, and SCSI has some inherent design advantages compared to ATA, so you do get better performance for that extra cost.

Several other types of disk devices exist, but Linux tends to treat them as if they belonged to one of these two categories—in most cases, as SCSI disks. In fact, many Linux SATA drivers appear in the SCSI driver category, although this isn't universally true. USB and FireWire drives are also usually treated as SCSI disks. For the remainder of this task, therefore, I will refer to ATA and SCSI disks, but your actual disk hardware might be neither of these things.

If you have an SATA disk, it could be either an ATA disk or a SCSI disk from the Linux driver perspective.

If your Linux system is up and running and if you can use your disk, one easy way to identify it is to use the df command:

```
$ df
Filesystem          1K-blocks       Used Available Use% Mounted on
/dev/sdb6              977180     322112    655068  33% /
udev                  256024        196    255828   1% /dev
/dev/mapper/usr      6291260    5762756    528504  92% /usr
/dev/mapper/home    17825244   11384232   6441012  64% /home
/dev/hda6             101089      35111     61803  37% /boot
```

This command displays disk free space statistics for mounted filesystems. This example output shows four types of filesystem:

**ATA filesystem**    The last entry in the output (/dev/hda6, mounted at /boot) is for an ATA disk. Such disks have device filenames of the form /dev/hd*xn*, where *x* is a letter from a onward and *n* is a number from 1 upward.

**SCSI filesystem**    SCSI disks have device filenames of the form /dev/sd*xn*, where *x* is a letter from a onward and *n* is a number from 1 upward. The first entry in the preceding output, for the root (/) filesystem, is for a SCSI disk.

**LVM filesystems**    The preceding output shows two Logical Volume Management (LVM) filesystems, /usr and /home. These filesystems reside on volumes that constitute one or more physical partitions managed by Linux LVM tools and identified by entries in the /dev/mapper directory tree. LVM is a way to create more flexible partitions, but its configuration is beyond the scope of this task. LVM filesystems can reside on underlying ATA, SCSI, or both types of disk.

**udev filesystem**    Finally, the /dev directory is handled, on this system, by the udev filesystem. As described in Task 2.4, this is a pseudo-filesystem that automatically adds device entries for your hardware. It doesn't correspond to any real disk hardware.

You should be aware that df can only identify hardware that's currently being used in the form of mounted filesystems. If you see LVM filesystems, they could reside on a disk that's not otherwise identified by df output. For instance, in the preceding example, there might be a /dev/sda, /dev/hdb, or other disks that aren't immediately obvious from the df output. One way to track down such additional disks is by using fdisk to display the partition tables of disk devices:

```
# fdisk -l /dev/sdb

Disk /dev/sdb: 81.9 GB, 81964302336 bytes
16 heads, 63 sectors/track, 158816 cylinders
Units = cylinders of 1008 * 512 = 516096 bytes
```

| Device Boot | Start | End | Blocks | Id | System |
|---|---|---|---|---|---|
| /dev/sdb1 | 1 | 9689 | 4883224+ | a5 | FreeBSD |
| /dev/sdb2 | 9690 | 158816 | 75160008 | 5 | Extended |
| /dev/sdb5 | 9690 | 13565 | 1953472+ | c | W95 FAT32 (LBA) |
| /dev/sdb6 | 13566 | 15504 | 977224+ | 83 | Linux |
| /dev/sdb7 | 15505 | 60073 | 22462744+ | 8e | Linux LVM |
| /dev/sdb8 | 60074 | 158816 | 49766440+ | 8e | Linux LVM |

If you see a partition table, or even output with disk size information but no partition information or gibberish for partition information, then a disk is attached. If you see no output, though, then no disk is attached. (Removable disk drives, such as Zip drives and CD-ROM drives, will yield no output unless a disk is inserted in the drive.) You can also obtain a complete list of SCSI devices by examining the /proc/scsi/scsi pseudo-file:

```
$ cat /proc/scsi/scsi
Attached devices:
Host: scsi0 Channel: 00 Id: 05 Lun: 00
  Vendor: IOMEGA    Model: ZIP 100         Rev: D.13
  Type:   Direct-Access                    ANSI SCSI revision: 02
Host: scsi2 Channel: 00 Id: 00 Lun: 00
  Vendor: ATA       Model: Maxtor 6Y080M0  Rev: YAR5
  Type:   Direct-Access                    ANSI SCSI revision: 05
```

This output reveals two SCSI drives: an Iomega Zip 100 removable disk and a Maxtor 6Y080M0 disk. The latter is actually an SATA drive that's handled by an SATA driver in the SCSI section of the Linux kernel, as revealed by the Vendor: ATA part of the output. These devices are on two different SCSI host adapters (scsi0 and scsi2); the second is actually the computer's SATA controller.

## Testing Disk Performance

Now that you know what your hard disks are, you can test their performance. You can do this with the hdparm utility, which includes two performance-testing options: -t tests raw disk input/output speed and -T tests cached disk input/output speed. The latter test is effectively a test of your system's memory (RAM) performance, but if you use both options, hdparm includes a correction factor for memory performance when reporting the non-cached results, improving accuracy. You can test either ATA or SCSI disk performance using this command:

```
# hdparm -tT /dev/hdb

/dev/hdb:
 Timing cached reads:   932 MB in  2.01 seconds = 463.37 MB/sec
 Timing buffered disk reads: 120 MB in  3.03 seconds =  39.60 MB/sec
```

Ideally, you should run this command two or three times to ensure that you're getting consistent results. (Normal disk accesses by background processes can throw off the results of a disk benchmark.) This example shows a disk input speed of 39.60MB/s, with a cached (memory) read speed of 463.37MB/s. If you compare the numbers you obtain to the ones found on your hard disk manufacturer's data sheet, you'll probably be disappointed. Disk manufacturers generally advertise benchmark results taken under ideal circumstances, and it's not unusual to get results showing half the speed the manufacturer claims. Also, manufacturers often advertise their drives' *interface* speed, which will be better than the speed for reading data off the actual disk platters. Be sure to look up the disk's *internal* data transfer rate; this will be the limiting factor for all but short data transfer bursts.

As a general rule, modern hard disks are likely to achieve speeds of at least 30MB/s, and quite possibly well above that level. A speed of 16MB/s or less, at least with a new disk, indicates that the disk is seriously misconfigured.

## Tweaking Disk Performance

If you find that your disk performance is truly sub-par, you may want to attempt to improve it. Linux's ATA drivers provide the ability to tune disk performance in software, but this option doesn't exist for SCSI drivers. Thus, if you have SCSI devices and find that performance is sub-par, you may need to look at your SCSI cabling, SCSI termination, and other issues.

 Both SCSI and ATA have undergone many revisions over the years. If you're using an older or cheap SCSI host adapter or ATA controller with a new hard disk, replacing the host adapter or controller may dramatically improve your disk performance.

To tune an ATA disk's performance, you can use the hdparm utility, but you use the -X *mode* option to set the Direct Memory Access (DMA) transfer mode. Table 2.3 summarizes ATA disk DMA transfer modes and hardware. You can specify modes in several ways, the most mnemonic of which are sd*max* for simple DMA level *x*, md*max* for multiword DMA level *x*, and ud*max* for UltraDMA level *x*.

**TABLE 2.3**    ATA Hardware Types

| Official Name | Unofficial Names | Maximum Speed | Added DMA Modes | Cable Type |
|---|---|---|---|---|
| ATA-1 | IDE | 11.1MB/s | 0, 1, 2, Multiword 0 | 40-wire |
| ATA-2 | EIDE | 16.6MB/s | Multiword 1, Multiword 2 | 40-wire |
| ATA-3 | | 16.6MB/s | | 40-wire |

**TABLE 2.3**    ATA Hardware Types *(continued)*

| Official Name | Unofficial Names | Maximum Speed | Added DMA Modes | Cable Type |
|---|---|---|---|---|
| ATA-4 | UltraDMA/33, ATA/33 | 33.3MB/s | UltraDMA 0, UltraDMA 1, UltraDMA 2 | 40-wire or 80-wire |
| ATA-5 | UltraDMA/66, ATA/66 | 66.6MB/s | UltraDMA 3, UltraDMA 4 | 80-wire |
| ATA-6 | UltraDMA/100, ATA/100 | 100MB/s | UltraDMA 5 | 80-wire |
| ATA-7 | UltraDMA/133, ATA/133 | 133MB/s | UltraDMA 6 | 80-wire |

At the time of this writing, an ATA-8 standard is under discussion, but it has not yet been finalized. In practice, hardware often leads standards, so devices with ATA-8 features will likely become available before the standard is finalized.

If you're certain that your ATA disk *and* its controller both support a particular mode (say, ATA-7), you can activate it as follows:

```
# hdparm -X udma6 /dev/hda
```

Specifying a DMA mode that's too advanced for your hardware can result in the hardware becoming unresponsive. In the case of a hard disk, this can mean that you won't be able to access the disk or cleanly shut down the computer. Thus, you should not use hdparm in this way unless you're willing to take a risk.

Using hdparm to adjust your disk's performance creates a temporary change—once you reboot the computer, your system will revert to its default behavior. In most cases, this is fine, because your computer sets the appropriate mode at boot time. If you find that adjusting your DMA mode improves performance, though, you may want to add your hdparm command to an appropriate system startup script. Appropriate startup scripts vary from one distribution to another. On Red Hat, Fedora Core, Mandrake, and Slackware, the script is /etc/rc.d/rc.local; on openSUSE, edit /etc/rc.d/boot.local; for Debian and its derivatives, create a script in the /etc/rc.boot directory; and on Gentoo, edit /etc/conf.d/local.start.

Another way to tweak disk performance is to change the driver. To do this, you'll need to know about the ATA controller or SCSI host adapter that handles the disk. You may be able to find updated drivers in a newer kernel, on your hardware manufacturer's Web page, or on a third-party Web page. Try doing a Web search, if necessary. Another option, particularly for some SATA disks, is to change from an ATA driver to an SATA driver or vice versa. Drivers for both disk classes are available for some SATA controllers, so you may be able to switch. If you try this, though, be aware that your disk identifiers will change. This means you'll need to edit entries in /etc/fstab, and you may need to adjust your boot loader configuration as well. If something goes wrong in your change, your system may be rendered unbootable, so be ready with an emergency recovery disk.

## Criteria for Completion

To complete this task, you should have correctly identified all your computer's hard disks. (Many computers have a single hard disk, although they may have removable disk devices.) You should also have checked your hard disks' performance with hdparm. If that performance is unacceptably low and if it's an ATA disk, you should try to improve it via hdparm and, if necessary, add an appropriate line to a startup script to make that change persistent when you reboot the computer.

# Task 2.6: Configure and Compile a Kernel

The Linux kernel is the heart of a Linux system. Indeed, in a technical sense, the word *Linux* applies *only* to the kernel; everything else—shells, disk utilities, compilers, and other programs—are programs that happen to run well on the Linux kernel. The kernel itself provides an interface between your hardware and the rest of these programs. It also provides important system services, such as process management. Ideally, if the kernel works well, you never notice it; but if it's misconfigured or buggy, the kernel can cause serious problems indeed.

Kernel configuration is an important system administration task because it enables you to add support for new hardware and to optimize the kernel for your hardware and your needs. A properly tuned kernel can help a system run at its most efficient.

 Most distributions ship with kernels that include support, usually in the form of kernel modules, for a wide variety of hardware. Thus, you probably don't need to recompile your kernel just to add support for a new hardware device you've just bought. You might need to recompile the kernel to support particularly exotic hardware, though, and recompiling the kernel can slightly improve system performance.

## Scenario

You've heard that the latest Linux kernel provides faster and more reliable support for your Ethernet hardware than is available with the Linux kernel you're running. To take advantage of this improvement, you want to compile a new kernel.

## Scope of Task

This task involves configuring a kernel using its configuration tools, compiling the kernel, installing kernel modules, and copying the kernel to a location from which it can be booted. Actually booting and using the new kernel requires modifying your boot loader configuration, which is described in Phase 5.

### Duration

This task will take from one to three hours to complete, depending on how carefully you study your kernel options and the speed of your computer. Once you're familiar with kernel options, you should be able to change one or two options in just a few minutes, but compiling the kernel will still take several minutes to over an hour.

### Setup

To begin, you should download the kernel source code. As I write, the latest version is 2.6.17.7, and it is available from `http://www.kernel.org`. You can use this version or a more recent version, at your discretion. The kernel comes as a bzipped tarball, which ends in a `.tar.bz2` filename extension, or as a gzipped tarball, with a `.tar.gz` filename extension. The former is the more compact file and so is what I describe using.

Before you can configure or compile the kernel, you must uncompress it in a convenient directory. The traditional location for the kernel is in `/usr/src/linux`. This directory is usually a symbolic link to a directory that includes the kernel version number (such as `/usr/src/linux-2.6.17`; the final number is usually omitted). If you want to configure and compile your kernel as an ordinary user, which is best from a safety point of view, you may want to extract the tarball in your home directory and then create a symbolic link to that directory in `/usr/src`, first deleting any existing symbolic link:

```
$ tar xvfj linux-2.6.17.7.tar.bz2
$ su
Password:
# cd /usr/src
# rm linux
# ln -s /home/yourname/linux-2.6.17 linux
```

Of course, you should change *yourname* in the final command to the name of your home directory. At this point, your kernel is ready for configuration.

If you've previously compiled a kernel, or if you want to use the starting configuration for your distribution's default kernel as a starting point, you can copy the `.config` file from your old kernel's directory to the new kernel's directory. You can then type **make oldconfig** to have the kernel configuration utility ask only about changed options, leaving old ones intact.

## Caveats

Kernel configuration can seem quite intimidating to the uninitiated, and making mistakes can result in an unbootable kernel. If you're careful not to overwrite your old kernel, though, and to keep its entry active in your boot loader, compiling a new kernel need not be particularly dangerous, aside from the usual cautions whenever you use `root` privileges.

# Procedure

Creating a custom kernel involves five steps: configuring the kernel, compiling the kernel, installing kernel modules, installing the kernel, and configuring your boot loader. The procedure described here covers the first four of these steps. Boot loader configuration is covered in Phase 5

## Configuring the Kernel

The most tedious part of kernel preparation, and the part that's most likely to lead to confusion and head-scratching, is that of configuring the kernel. In this process, you'll select the drivers, features, and other kernel options that you want to use. To begin the process, type the following commands in an `xterm` window:

```
$ cd /usr/src/linux
$ make xconfig
```

Typing **make xconfig** produces a GUI configuration tool. If you prefer, you can use a text-based configuration tool by typing **make menuconfig**. You'll be able to set the same options, but the user interface isn't as pretty. Typing **make config** produces an even cruder text-based configuration tool. Typing **make oldconfig** to update an old configuration for a new kernel uses this simplest form of configuration prompting.

The result, after a delay of several seconds to a minute or two, is a window similar to the one shown in Figure 2.5. This is the main kernel configuration window, and it's broken into three sections: a set of kernel configuration areas on the left; a set of specific configuration options, and sometimes sub-areas, on the top right; and a pane that holds explanations of specific options on the bottom right.

In the GUI configuration tool, you can add or remove support for an option by clicking the box to its left. Some options have arrows to the left, indicating sub-options, which may be hidden or expanded. Sometimes clicking the sub-option arrow produces an entire menu of new options.

Many kernel features can be compiled directly into the main kernel file, denoted by a check mark (as in the IEEE1284 Transfer Modes option in Figure 2.5), or as a kernel module, denoted by a dot (as in the PC-Style Hardware option in Figure 2.5). Compiling a feature directly into the main kernel file increases the size of this file and means that the option will always be available, including when the system first boots. This may be desirable if you're customizing a kernel for a single system, and it's recommended for boot hardware such as hard disk controllers. Compiling a feature as a module means that it need not be loaded if the hardware isn't present on the computer or at a particular time. This is handy if you're compiling a kernel that will be used for multiple computers or if you just want to keep the size of the kernel to a minimum. Some features can only be compiled directly into the kernel, or they only affect other options and so appear as check-mark options. A few features enable you to select from one of a set of options, such as CPU types.

**FIGURE 2.5**    The Linux kernel provides many configuration options to optimize performance.

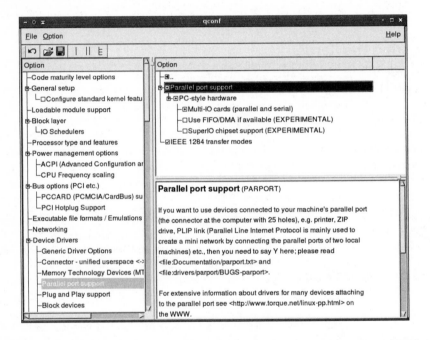

Unfortunately, a complete description of all the kernel options would more than fill this entire book. I recommend you do a quick pass through the kernel to get a feel for the options you're given. If you've copied a working .config file for your computer or from your distribution and then typed **make oldconfig**, that configuration should make a good starting point for further tweaks via **make xconfig** or **make menuconfig**. Pay particular attention, though, to options relating to boot devices. In particular, you should compile in support for your ATA disk controller or SCSI host adapter, as well as for whatever filesystems you use on your hard disk. If you compile these options as modules, the kernel won't have them for accessing the disk, which will bring the boot process to a grinding halt. (Distributions use boot RAM disks to get around this problem, but for a custom kernel, it's easier to compile the drivers directly into the main kernel file.)

As a general rule, you can compile support for hardware that you don't use to boot the kernel and read the initial configuration files—such as Ethernet cards, parallel ports, and sound cards—as kernel modules. Doing so will help keep the kernel file small, which is generally desirable. It also means that you need to be less certain of the hardware you've got installed— if you're not sure what Ethernet card you're using, you can compile support for anything that sounds promising without worrying about bloating your kernel.

Look for options you can safely omit. For instance, if you know you don't have any video capture cards, you can omit those drivers, saving compile time and reducing kernel size. If in doubt, read the description for an option and follow its advice.

Going through all the options is likely to take at least half an hour, and probably an hour or two if you're not already familiar with kernel configuration. When you're done, exit from the kernel configuration tool. You'll be asked if you want to save the configuration; respond Save Changes.

## Compiling the Kernel

Compiling the kernel is remarkably simple; it can be done with one command:

```
$ make
```

Although this command looks simple, it starts a process that can be quite time-consuming. Depending on the speed of your CPU and the number of kernel options you've chosen to compile, this process can take anywhere from a few minutes to over an hour. During this time, you'll see a series of messages appear summarizing the kernel files that are being compiled. You may also see occasional warnings; don't worry about those. If you see an error message and compilation stops, though, it could be you've selected incompatible options or run into a bug. Unfortunately, such problems are tricky to resolve without extensive knowledge of the relevant subsystems. If the message seems to relate to a feature you don't need, though, you could try disabling it. Sometimes compiling an option into the main kernel file rather than as a module will work around a problem.

## Installing Kernel Modules

Once the kernel has finished compiling, you'll see a message to that effect. You can then install kernel modules. This step requires `root` privileges:

```
# make modules_install
```

This command installs the kernel modules in the `/lib/modules/version` directory tree, where `version` is the kernel version number. This process shouldn't take very long; no compilation is involved, just file copies. After you type this command, use `ls` to verify that an appropriate directory has appeared in `/lib/modules`.

## Installing the Kernel

The final step described in this task is kernel installation—copying the kernel file to the `/boot` directory. You can do this as `root` with a single `cp` command:

```
# cp /usr/src/linux/arch/i386/boot/bzImage /boot/bzImage-2.6.17.7
```

This example command assumes you're using a 32-bit *x*86 system and that you're installing a 2.6.17.7 kernel. If you're using a non-*x*86 platform, the source directory will be different. Specifically, i386 will be something else, and bzImage may be another name. You can install the kernel under any name you like; bzImage-2.6.17.7 is a convenient and descriptive name for a kernel of this version number.

 Traditionally, Linux kernels are called vmlinux, vmlinuz, or bzImage, with the last of these being the most common for locally compiled kernels on *x*86 and related platforms.

In addition to the kernel file itself, you may want to copy the System.map file, which appears in the /usr/src/linux directory, to the /boot directory. As with the kernel file, you may want to rename it to include the kernel version number. Once this is done, you can replace the /boot/System.map symbolic link with one that points to the new file you've just copied. The System.map file is not strictly necessary for system operation. It holds the addresses within the kernel of *symbols*—variable names and so on. This information is necessary for some debugging operations, so some tools that report details of system crashes and other problems may not work correctly without this file.

Incidentally, both of these files are copied to /boot simply because this is the most common location for compiled kernels and related files. Some distributions place their kernels in the root (/) directory, but even with these distributions, I recommend using /boot for your own kernels in order to keep the root directory uncluttered.

## Criteria for Completion

To complete this task, you should have successfully configured and compiled your kernel, installed the kernel modules, and copied the kernel file to the /boot directory. Unfortunately, actually testing your kernel's viability will require you to learn how to manage a boot loader, which is a topic that's covered in Phase 5.

# Task 2.7: Use Power Management Features

Computers run on electricity, but this power source isn't infinite. This limitation is particularly relevant on laptop computers, which often run on batteries. Thus, hardware manufacturers provide options to help minimize a computer's use of energy, and Linux provides software tools to help you manage power use. Most of these options enable you to automatically shut down power-hungry devices, such as hard disks and monitors, when they're not in use.

## Scenario

You've installed Linux on a laptop computer, but now you need to check power management options to improve battery life when the computer is taken on the road. To do so, you'll have to determine whether your system is using Advanced Power Management (APM) or the newer Advanced Configuration and Power Interface (ACPI) subsystem.

## Scope of Task

This task requires investigating your system with a few commands. You may then want to edit some configuration files or startup scripts. You'll need to use either APM or ACPI, and in either case you should also investigate options for managing your hard disk's power consumption.

### Duration

This task should take half an hour to an hour to complete. If you need to configure power management on many systems, each one will take just a few minutes—more time if the systems are substantially different from each other, but very little time if they're nearly identical to one another.

### Setup

Log into the computer and acquire root privileges. No special hardware or software configuration is required, although if you're running a particularly old or bare-bones Linux distribution, you might need to install APM or ACPI software. Although the scenario describes a laptop computer, you can investigate power management features even on a desktop computer.

### Caveats

As always, working as root can be dangerous. Power management tools are unlikely to cause catastrophic problems, although you could accidentally set some inconvenient options, such as a too-short hard disk power-down time, which will cause sluggish and erratic performance.

## Procedure

To use power management features, you'll need to activate kernel support and then investigate APM and ACPI options on your system. You'll also want to modify your hard disk options for managing hard disk power consumption.

Distributions and GUI environments are increasingly providing point-and-click interfaces to power management tools. These interfaces can be convenient and useful, but they differ from one distribution or environment to another.

### Activating Kernel Support

Both APM and ACPI rely on kernel features to work. General kernel configuration procedures are described earlier, in Task 2.6, "Configure and Compile a Kernel." The power management features can be compiled into the kernel by activating appropriate options under the Power Management Options menu—both APM and ACPI have their own submenus with options to enable assorted specific features, such as support for fan control, or to enable basic support at system boot time. Generally speaking, enabling an option will do no harm, even if it doesn't apply to your system. You should read the description to see if it applies, though. A few APM options in particular can cause problems. The RTC Stores Time In GMT option can cause your system time to be set strangely after a suspend operation if it's set incorrectly, and a few other options can cause problems with some hardware, as detailed in their descriptions.

When you configure your kernel, keep in mind that Linux will use APM *or* ACPI, but not both. In practice, whichever kernel system loads first will control the computer's power management. The simplest way to deal with this situation is to compile support for one protocol or another, not both. Another approach is to compile both systems as modules and load only the desired modules at boot time. In practice, if you try to use APM or ACPI features, as described in the next couple of sections, and they don't work, the cause could be the presence of support for the other system in the kernel.

If you're using your distribution's stock configuration, chances are it includes a reasonable default APM/ACPI configuration. It may try loading ACPI and then use APM as a fallback, for instance. In any event, you can try using one set of tools and then the other if that doesn't work. You may need to consult distribution-specific documentation to learn the details of how it's configured on your system, though.

## Using APM

To use APM features effectively, you need some way to tell the computer when to enter power-conserving states. This task is accomplished with the apmd package, which ships with most Linux distributions and may be installed automatically. The main apmd program is a daemon, which means that it runs in the background waiting for some event to occur. Most daemons, including apmd, should be started when the computer boots. Once running, apmd monitors the system's battery status, and if the battery's charge gets too low, apmd kicks the system into a suspend mode in which most functions are shut down and only the system's RAM is maintained. The apmd program will also suspend the hard disk if it's gone unused for a long enough time. (You can also use the hdparm utility to control hard disk power management more directly.)

If you want to manually control APM features, you can do so with the apm utility. Typing this command presents basic power management information, such as how much battery power is left. The -s and -S parameters cause the system to go into suspend and standby modes, respectively. Suspend mode shuts off power to most devices, leaving only the CPU and memory operating, and those at minimum power. Standby mode leaves more devices powered up, so the system can recover more quickly, but there's less power savings in this mode. A fully charged laptop can usually last several hours in standby mode and a day or more in suspend mode. Many laptops include a key sequence that will force the system into suspend or standby mode. In most cases, apmd will detect such a keystroke and honor the request. Consult your laptop's documentation for details.

## Using ACPI

Linux's ACPI handling is similar to its APM handling in broad strokes, but of course the details differ. In particular, an ACPI daemon runs instead of an APM daemon. The acpid program is a common ACPI daemon. This daemon is controlled through files in /etc/acpi/events. All the files in this directory whose names do not begin with a dot (.) are parsed and interpreted as sets of events and actions to be taken in response to each event. Each event line begins with the string event=, and each action line begins with action=. The actions point to scripts or Linux commands.

One simple ACPI configuration file contains nothing but comments and a very simple action/event pair, as seen here:

```
event=.*
action=/etc/acpi/default.sh %e
```

This configuration essentially passes all responsibility over to a shell script, /etc/acpi/default.sh. A shell script can be more complex than the simple default ACPI parser, but this approach may be overkill for you.

> Event names are not fully standardized. Thus, you may need to monitor your own system to identify important events' names. Check the /proc/acpi/event file when you perform an ACPI-related event, such as closing the lid of a laptop computer. This file should change to display the event name, which you can then reference in your Linux ACPI configuration file.

You can use files in the /proc/acpi directory to monitor your system and to change defaults. Try using cat to view the contents of some of these files, as in **cat /proc/acpi/event** to view recent ACPI events. Various tools can link into these files to provide you with useful information, such as your CPU's temperature and battery status. The acpi program is one of these tools; type **acpi -V** to have the system display all the information it can.

## Setting Hard Disk Options

You can use the hdparm utility to tell hard disks to enter a low-power suspend mode after a specified period of inactivity. To do so, use the -S option to hdparm, which takes a value from Table 2.4 to specify the idle time before the drive enters suspend mode.

**TABLE 2.4**    hdparm -S Options

| Value | Meaning |
|---|---|
| 0 | Power-saving mode disabled; disk doesn't power down. |
| 1–240 | Suspend mode entered in multiples of 5 seconds; for instance, 12 means to enter suspend mode after 60 seconds of inactivity. |
| 241–251 | Enter suspend mode after 1 to 11 units of 30 minutes of inactivity. |
| 252 | Enter suspend mode after 21 minutes of inactivity. |
| 253 | Enter suspend mode after a vendor-defined time. |
| 255 | Enter suspend mode after 21 minutes and 15 seconds of inactivity. |

Suppose you want to configure the laptop to enter suspend mode after 5 minutes (300 seconds) of disk inactivity. That's 60 5-second units, so you'd pass a value of 60 to hdparm:

```
# hdparm -S 60 /dev/hda
```

```
/dev/hda:
 setting standby to 60 (5 minutes)
```

As with tuning hard disk performance, any change you enter at the command line will be lost once you reboot. To make your change permanent, you should enter an appropriate hdparm command in a local startup script, as described earlier, in "Tweaking Disk Performance" in Task 2.5.

One important caveat regarding hard disk power management is that Linux tends to generate a lot of disk activity on a regular basis. Certain Linux tools check system files very frequently to be sure they've not changed, and other tools generate log file entries on a regular basis—sometimes even when nothing's happened. Thus, it's possible that you won't see much benefit from using hard disk power management features. If your hard disk doesn't seem to be shutting down, or if it comes back to life very frequently, you may want to try to track down the source of the activity. You may be able to modify a program's configuration to keep it from generating so much disk activity.

## Criteria for Completion

To complete this task, you should have investigated your power management options. Your system probably uses APM or ACPI, but not both. In either case, you can also minimize power use by configuring your system's hard disk to power down after an appropriate period of inactivity.

# Task 2.8: Configure X Options

Several implementations of the *X Window System* (X for short) are available, but the most common ones today use identical configuration file formats. The older XFree86 3.3.6 and earlier configuration file differs in some important details, but such old versions of XFree86 are becoming quite rare. The rarer commercial implementations of X use their own configuration file formats, which I don't describe.

## Scenario

As part of ongoing system upgrades at your site, you've replaced the video card, monitor, and mouse on one computer. The new video card is a generic board that uses an nVidia GeForce video chipset; the monitor is a 17-inch liquid crystal display (LCD) device capable of 1280×1024 resolution; and the mouse is a USB model with a scroll wheel. Changing this hardware necessitates making several alterations to the X configuration file.

# Scope of Task

This task describes changing the three specified pieces of hardware; however, you're unlikely to rush out and buy new hardware just to complete this task. In this case, you should read along and review your existing configuration file without changing it. If you happen to have spare hardware, you might try temporarily installing and configuring it, though.

## Duration

This task will take about an hour or two to complete, including installing the new hardware. If you don't actually replace any hardware, it should take only about half an hour to review the configuration file options. In real life, replacing hardware often results in unexpected complications, which can increase the time to perform tasks such as this.

## Setup

If you have an extra video card and want to try actually replacing the hardware, you should shut down the computer and perform the physical replacement. Be sure to follow the usual safety precautions when working inside the computer—unplug the computer from the wall outlet and ground yourself before touching anything inside the computer. Replacing the mouse doesn't require opening the computer, but some older (non-USB) mice should only be plugged in or unplugged when the computer is powered down.

Once you've replaced the hardware, or if you don't have spares and intend to just read along, boot the computer. Some distributions will detect hardware changes and reconfigure themselves automatically, but others won't. Because this task is intended to teach you how to reconfigure the system yourself, you should tell your computer not to make automatic changes if it offers to do so.

If you've changed your video card, chances are you won't see a GUI login screen. Changing the monitor alone might or might not result in a blank screen, and changing the mouse alone might result in a system for which the mouse doesn't work. In any of these cases, press Ctrl+Alt+F1 to get a text-mode login prompt and log in. If you need to make real changes, type **su** to acquire superuser privileges; if not, continue using your regular account.

## Caveats

Swapping hardware runs some risk of damaging it. Be careful not to touch delicate components unnecessarily, and ground yourself by touching a radiator or plumbing before handling the video card or touching any other internal components. (You can also buy anti-static wrist straps or work pads that connect to your building's electrical grounding system.) There's also a chance of your injuring yourself, particularly if you work on a computer that's plugged into a wall outlet. Ordinarily, the 120-volt AC from the wall outlet is reduced to much lower-voltage DC current inside the case, but a fault could expose you to more dangerous current.

As usual, if you make actual changes to your configuration as `root`, you run the risk of damaging your system software. Backing up your X configuration file will enable you to recover if you make an error when editing that file. A backup will also enable you to easily restore your original configuration if you make test changes and then swap your hardware back to its original state.

# Procedure

The X configuration file, like most Linux configuration files, is a text-mode file with options you can alter in a text editor. Before making real changes, you should familiarize yourself with some fundamental X principles and with the basic structure of the configuration file. After that, you can go on to change your mouse, monitor, and video card configurations for the hardware you've installed (or just examine these options if you've not actually changed your hardware).

## X Basics

X is Linux's GUI environment. Like most other Linux tools, X is a separate software component that can be replaced with workalike software and that's configured independently of many other subsystems. Traditionally, XFree86 (`http://www.xfree86.org`) has been the most popular X server for Linux; however, most Linux distributions now use X.org-X11 (`http://www.x.org`) instead.

Technically, X is a server, much like a file server or mail server. Where a file server enables programs to read and write files, though, X enables programs to read from the keyboard and write to the screen. X's server nature gives it certain unusual networking capabilities, some of which are described shortly, in Task 2.9, "Manage X Logins."

To configure X, you edit the X configuration file, which goes by various names. For XFree86, the configuration file is called `XF86Config` or `XF86Config-4` and is located in `/etc/X11` or `/etc`. For X.org-X11, the configuration file is `xorg.conf`, which is normally stored in `/etc/X11`. The configuration files for X.org-X11 and XFree86 4.*x* are identical in format. Before proceeding further, you should change to the `/etc/X11` directory (or possibly just `/etc`), back up the configuration file, and then load the original into your favorite text-mode editor. (Task 1.5 in Phase 1 describes using Vi for this purpose.)

## Familiarizing Yourself with the Configuration File

The X server configuration file is broken down into multi-line sections, one section for each major feature (mouse, keyboard, video card, and so on). Each of these sections begins with a line consisting of the keyword `Section` and the section name in quotes. Each section ends with the keyword `EndSection`:

```
Section "InputDevice"
    Identifier   "Keyboard0"
    Driver       "kbd"
    Option       "XkbModel" "pc105"
    Option       "XkbLayout" "us"
    Option       "AutoRepeat" "500 200"
EndSection
```

This section tells X about the keyboard—its model, layout, and so on. If you examine your X configuration file, you'll find several sections:

**Files**   This section tells X where to find files that it needs. In many cases, this section consists of nothing but `FontPath` entries, which tell X where to find fonts. X font configuration is actually fairly complex, but the font settings in the X configuration file have been falling in importance in recent years. Most X programs now use *Xft fonts*, which are configured via files in the /etc/ fonts/ directory.

**ServerFlags**  You can set miscellaneous server options in this section. Chances are you won't need to adjust it unless you need to alter advanced or obscure options, such as the X server's built-in power-saving options. (Most desktop environments provide other ways to set such options.)

**Module**  Modern X servers are modular, in the sense that they consist of a main program file (such as /usr/X11R6/bin/Xorg) and separate module files that contain drivers for specific video hardware, font-handling routines, and so on. The Module section tells X which of these modules to load. Chances are you won't need to adjust this section.

 Most Linux drivers reside in the Linux kernel; however, X works with the video, mouse, and keyboard hardware at a low enough level that it provides its own drivers.

**InputDevice**  Most X configuration files contain at least two InputDevice sections: one for the mouse and one for the keyboard. You can adjust these sections to better match your hardware, and the upcoming section "Changing the Mouse Configuration" describes how to do this if you change your mouse.

**Monitor**  The Monitor section tells X about your monitor's capabilities. This section is very important for proper X functioning, and the upcoming section "Changing the Monitor Configuration" describes how to adjust it.

**Device**  This section provides information on your video card, including the driver it's to use and hardware-specific options. The upcoming section "Changing the Video Configuration" describes how to adjust it if you change your video card.

**Screen**  In order to work correctly, X needs to know how to combine the monitor and video card information set in the Monitor and Device sections. This is the job of the Screen section. You also set options such as the display resolution in this section.

**ServerLayout**  XFree86 4.*x* and X.org-X11 use the ServerLayout section to combine all the other sections into a coherent whole. This enables you to define multiple mice, use several displays, and so on. Earlier versions of XFree86 lacked this section, the result being less flexibility; these older versions of X could only use a single display and mouse, for instance.

For more information on all of these sections and the options you can set in them, consult the X configuration file man page—type **man XF86Config** if you use XFree86 or **man xorg.conf** if you use X.org-X11.

## Changing the Mouse Configuration

Because you've replaced your mouse, you should first locate the InputDevice section that describes the old mouse. Chances are it begins with an Identifier line with a name such as

Mouse or Mouse1 and a Driver line with a name of mouse. To use a new USB wheel mouse, you must ensure that three Option lines are set:

**Protocol**   The Protocol option tells X how to communicate with the mouse. Several protocols have been used over the years, but modern PS/2 and USB mice all use the PS/2 protocol or variants of it. Wheel mice almost invariably use the IMPS/2 protocol, so you should set this line to that value.

**Device**   The Device option tells X what Linux device file interfaces to the mouse. This could be /dev/mouse, /dev/input/mouse0, or something similar. If you're replacing one USB mouse with another, you shouldn't need to adjust this option. The Linux udev filesystem, used on most modern distributions, should automatically create an appropriate device file, but the name might differ from one distribution to another.

**ZAxisMapping**   This strangely named option tells X about the wheel on the mouse. It should be set to a value of 4  5. Behind the scenes, wheel movements are sent from the mouse to the computer as button presses, and this option tells X to treat the presses of these buttons (numbers 4 and 5) as wheel movements. Note that not all programs recognize wheel movements, but most modern X programs do.

In sum, a proper configuration for a modern USB wheel mouse looks something like this:

```
Section "InputDevice"
    Identifier "Mouse1"
    Driver "mouse"
    Option "Protocol" "IMPS/2"
    Option "Device" "/dev/input/mouse0"
    Option "ZAxisMapping" "4 5"
EndSection
```

As noted earlier, though, the Device file might differ from /dev/input/mouse0. If you're installing something other than a modern USB mouse, you may need to make more radical changes, such as changing the Protocol and omitting or changing the ZAxisMapping line.

## Changing the Monitor Configuration

The Monitor section tells X about your monitor's capabilities. Two options are particularly critical for this section: HorizSync and VertRefresh. These lines tell X about your monitor's horizontal and vertical refresh rates, respectively. Traditional cathode ray tube (CRT) monitors use an electron beam to "paint" a picture on the screen, but the electron beam has a limited scanning speed. The horizontal and vertical refresh rates are the limits on the display's speed for both horizontal scanning (to display a single line of pixels) and vertical scanning (to display an entire screen). The horizontal and vertical refresh rates are measured in megahertz (MHz) and hertz (Hz), respectively. Although LCD monitors don't use electron beams, many of them do have analog interfaces so that they can be used with traditional video cards; thus, these values are important for LCD monitors as well as for CRT monitors.

Unfortunately, you can't tell just by looking at a monitor what its horizontal and vertical refresh limits are; you'll have to crack open the monitor's manual. This information should appear somewhere, probably on a technical specifications page. If you don't have your monitor's manual, try the manufacturer's Web site. Once you have the information, copy it to the Monitor section:

```
HorizSync 30.0-80.0
VertRefresh 55-75
```

You can also examine, and perhaps change, other options in the Monitor section. The Identifier line is used in the Screen section for tying things together. You don't need to change this unless you've copied the whole Monitor section so as to leave the original intact. If you've done this, be sure to change the reference in the Screen section when you get to it. The VendorName and ModelName lines provide model information for human consumption.

One of the most confusing types of lines is the ModeLine. These lines provide timing information to enable X to display screens of different resolutions. In the days of XFree86 3.3.6 and earlier, ModeLine entries were commonplace. With XFree86 4.*x* and X.org-X11, the X server is able to communicate with the monitor to obtain equivalent information from the monitor itself—at least, when using modern video hardware. Thus, you probably don't need to add or adjust any ModeLine entries when you replace a monitor.

## Changing the Video Configuration

The main function of the Device section is to identify your video card's driver. This is done via the Driver line. For most boards with nVidia chipsets, such as the one described in this task's Scenario section, you would specify a driver of nv. The resulting section would look something like this:

```
Section "Device"
    Identifier "mx4000"
    BoardName "EVGA e-GeForce MX4000"
    Driver "nv"
    Option "DPMS"
EndSection
```

 Video card manufacturers are increasingly providing their own X drivers, and in fact nVidia is particularly good in that respect. If you use the video card manufacturer's driver, you would specify it instead of the driver that comes with your X server, such as nvidia rather than nv. Read the documentation that comes with the manufacturer's drivers for detailed installation instructions.

The Identifier option is used to tie things together later in the file; change it only if you copied the entire section to create a new one, and then be sure to change it in the Screen section, too. The BoardName option is for human use, so change it or not, as you see fit. Additional

Option lines set miscellaneous features, some of them driver- or board-specific. Unless you know to do otherwise, it's probably best to leave them as they are.

If you don't know what driver to use, consult your X server's documentation. You may be able to find some clues by examining the X driver module files. These appear in a directory such as /usr/lib/xorg/modules/drivers/ or /usr/lib64/modules/drivers/, depending on your distribution and X server. Drivers have names that end in _drv.o; the part before that string is the driver name that you would enter on the Driver line. You may see a name that seems promising for your card, in which case you can consult the man page for that driver—for instance, type **man trident** if you think the trident_drv.o file might be appropriate for your hardware.

X drivers, like most Linux drivers, are written for chipsets, not cards. The manufacturer of your video card might not be the same as the manufacturer of your video chipset, so you might need to dig a bit to figure out who made the video chipset.

## Putting It All Together

The Screen section ties together the Monitor and Device sections, so be sure you point to the correct sections:

```
Device "mx4000"
Monitor "monitor1"
```

If you didn't change the Identifier lines in the earlier sections, you shouldn't need to make any changes here.

In addition to pointing to the correct Monitor and Device sections, the Screen section tells X what resolution and color depth to use. The DefaultDepth option sets the default color depth, in bits per pixel:

```
DefaultDepth 24
```

As a general rule, 24 is a good value here for modern hardware; however, older hardware might work better with 16-, 15-, or even 8-bit color, at the cost of a reduced number of colors in the display. Occasionally 32-bit color depth works better than 24-bit color. The greater the color depth, the slower the display will be, but this slowdown is generally not a serious problem with even low-end modern video hardware.

Setting the DefaultDepth line tells X which Display subsection to use. These subsections specify what video resolutions to use:

```
Subsection "Display"
   Depth 24
   Modes "1280x1024" "1024x768" "800x600" "640x480"
   Virtual 1280 1024
EndSubsection
```

In this example, X is instructed to try 1280×1024, 1024×768, 800×600, and 640×480 displays, in that order. If X's mode lines (specified by the `ModeLine` entries in the `Monitor` section or as obtained from the monitor itself), `HorizSync`, and `VertRefresh` entries don't permit use of a particular resolution, X ignores it and tries the next one in the list. The `Virtual` line tells X to create a virtual display as large as the specified size. For instance, if X can only manage a 1024×768 display, that display will act like a panning window onto a larger 1280×1024 display. The display will pan when you move your mouse close to the edge of the physical display.

In addition to the `Screen` section, you should examine the `ServerLayout` section. This section ties together one or more `Screen` sections and one or more `InputDevice` sections. Depending upon how you made your changes, you might or might not need to adjust this section.

### Testing Your Changes

Once you've saved the changes to your X configuration file, you can test them. One way to do this is to type **startx** at a text-mode command prompt. (You can do this as an ordinary user.) X should start up and you should be able to use your new mouse, video card, and monitor. If X fails to start, examine the error messages it displays. If you're lucky, you'll immediately spot a typo or other simple error you can fix. If you're less lucky, you might need to spend time fiddling with the `Modes` line in your `Screen` section's `Display` subsection, reading documentation on your video driver, or otherwise troubleshooting the problem.

Starting X via the `startx` command may start up a different window manager or desktop environment than you see when you log in via a GUI login prompt. If this happens, don't worry; just read on....

Once you're sure your new configuration is working, you can begin using it normally. If your system normally presents a GUI login prompt, rebooting will bring it up, or you can read Task 2.9, "Manage X Logins," to learn how to start, stop, and reconfigure the GUI login tool.

## Criteria for Completion

This task involves changing hardware and modifying your X configuration. To complete the entire task, you should have swapped out your computer's video card, monitor, and mouse and gotten a working system using the new hardware. If you don't have access to replacement hardware, you should at least have read the description of what to do and become familiar with the X configuration file generally.

# Task 2.9: Manage X Logins

The X Display Manager Control Protocol (XDMCP) is the tool that Linux uses to provide GUI logins. Most distributions use the X Display Manager (XDM), the KDE Display Manager (KDM), or the GNOME Display Manager (GDM) as XDMCP servers, and the default configurations are reasonable ones for workstations. Sometimes, though, you need to modify these configurations. When this happens, knowing where to look and how to change the options is important.

# Scenario

Your workplace has purchased a powerful Linux computer (called `gandalf`) and installed an expensive commercial software package on this computer. In order to enable users on other systems to use this software, you want to enable remote XDMCP logins; once the system is so configured, users will be able to log into `gandalf` from their own workstations in order to run this software.

 Methods of remote access other than XDMCP exist and are often preferable to XDMCP. Remote XDMCP logins are particularly desirable when a network has X terminals—low-powered computers that consist of a keyboard, a mouse, a monitor, and enough hardware and software to run an X server but not much else. X terminals can provide multiple users with access to a computer running an XDMCP server at minimal cost.

# Scope of Task

This task involves adjusting your XDMCP configuration to permit remote X-based logins. Doing so can be tricky in some ways, so you must pay careful attention to the details of this task.

## Duration

This task should take about an hour to complete. If you were to reconfigure multiple computers along these lines, each one would take just a few minutes once you're familiar with the procedure.

## Setup

Boot the Linux computer you're configuring (and that I'll refer to as `gandalf`). Log in and acquire `root` privileges; like most system configuration tasks, this one requires superuser privileges.

To fully test this configuration, you'll need access to a second computer with an X server. This computer may be, but does not need to be, a Linux system. If you're using a Linux computer for this task, the best approach is to shut down its own XDMCP server; you can then launch X with appropriate options to connect to `gandalf`'s XDMCP server.

## Caveats

As usual, working as `root` poses certain risks. You should back up configuration files before making changes to them so that you can recover from typos or other errors.

Configuring an XDMCP server as described in this task poses security risks because it provides a server through which outsiders might be able to access your computer. This risk is worth taking if you need the functionality and if your network is properly protected by firewalls that block X and XDMCP access; however, if you simply want to learn how to configure an XDMCP server but don't really need the functionality yourself, you should undo your changes once you've tested them.

# Procedure

Unfortunately, the fact that there are three major XDMCP servers for Linux means that configuration of your XDMCP server will vary substantially depending on your existing setup. Before configuring your XDMCP server, you must first figure out which one your system is using. If you're not currently running one, you must choose one to run. Only then can you reconfigure the server to accept remote logins. Once this is done, you can test the configuration using a remote system.

## Identifying Your XDMCP Server

If your computer already boots into GUI mode, it's already running an XDMCP server. To find out which one it's using, type the following command:

```
$ ps ax | grep [gkx]dm
```

The result should be a list of any of the standard XDMCP server processes that are running—gdm, kdm, xdm, or a variant of one of these. (This command may also turn up a few hits on unrelated programs, but these should be obvious.) In most cases, the easiest course of action is to modify the configuration of your default XDMCP server. If necessary, though, you can change which server your system uses. First, of course, you must ensure that it's installed. Search for the files involved, and if you can't find them, install the relevant package for your distribution. How you proceed thereafter depends on your distribution:

**Debian**   Edit the /etc/X11/default-display-manager file, which contains the full path to the XDMCP server you want to run. For instance, enter /usr/bin/X11/xdm in this file to use XDM. This path must match one in the DAEMON variable in the SysV startup script for the server in question.

**Gentoo**   Edit the /etc/rc.conf file. Locate the line that sets the DISPLAYMANAGER environment variable and set it to xdm, gdm, or kdm.

**Mandriva**   Edit the /etc/sysconfig/desktop file, which holds variable assignments. Locate the DISPLAYMANAGER variable and set it to the name of the XDMCP server you want to use, such as gdm to run GDM. Mandriva supports two versions of KDM. Setting DISPLAYMANAGER to KDE uses the mdkkdm XDMCP server, while setting DISPLAYMANAGER to KDM uses the kdm XDMCP server. The mdkkdm server provides a stripped-down appearance compared to the regular kdm server.

**Red Hat and Fedora Core**   Edit the /etc/sysconfig/desktop file, which holds variable assignments. Locate the DISPLAYMANAGER variable and set it to the name of the environment that's associated with the XDMCP server you want to use, such as "GNOME" to use GDM. Use "XDM" to launch XDM.

**Slackware**   The /etc/rc.d/rc.4 file controls starting X, including launching an XDMCP server. This file tests for the presence of the three major servers and launches the first one in the list it finds, using the sequence GDM, KDM, and then XDM. You must remove higher-ranking servers, remove their execute bits, or edit the startup script file to change which one launches.

**OpenSUSE**   The /etc/sysconfig/displaymanager file sets several variables related to XDMCP operation, including the DISPLAYMANAGER variable, which specifies which server to use. Set this variable to the appropriate name, such as "kdm" to use KDM.

In practice, XDM is the simplest of the display managers; it provides only a login prompt. KDM and GDM both support additional user options, such as a choice of which desktop environment to run. They may also provide shutdown options and the like, although these are usually disabled for all but local users. KDM configuration is basically a superset of XDM configuration, but GDM uses its own unique configuration files. GDM lacks a few of XDM's and KDM's IP-based auditing features, so if you use GDM, you should be particularly diligent about setting up your firewall to prevent outside computers from reaching the XDMCP port (UDP port 177).

In some cases, particular servers may be very finicky on certain systems or distributions. If you have problems getting one server to work, try another. It may prove more amenable to modification to accept remote logins than the default server.

In all cases, you must restart the server after you change your XDMCP configuration. In theory, passing a SIGHUP signal to the process should do the job, but in practice this sometimes doesn't work. (Phase 3 describes passing signals to processes via the kill utility.) You may need to log out, switch to a text-mode runlevel (typing **telinit 3** should do this on most distributions; Debian and Gentoo are two exceptions), and then return to the GUI login runlevel (5 for most distributions, but 4 for Slackware). On some distributions, such as Gentoo and Debian, you can restart the XDMCP server via its SysV initialization script, as in **/etc/ init.d/xdm stop** followed by **/etc/init.d/xdm start**. This action will terminate your X session, so shut down all your programs before doing this.

In all cases, XDMCP normally runs only when the system is configured to start X and present a GUI login screen on the console. If you want to configure the system to accept XDMCP logins from remote users but not run X locally, you can do so; however, you must alter the XDMCP configuration, as described in the following sections.

## Configuring XDM

Configuring XDM to accept remote logins begins with the /etc/X11/xdm/xdm-config file. The key change is in the following line, which usually appears near the end of the file:

```
DisplayManager.requestPort:    0
```

This line tells XDMCP not to listen on its usual port. Such a configuration is common on workstations, which normally manage their local X servers more directly. Change the 0 in this line to 177 or comment out the line by placing a hash mark (#) or exclamation mark (!) at the start of the line.

In addition to `xdm-config`, you must edit the `/etc/X11/xdm/Xaccess` file, which controls what XDMCP clients may access the XDMCP server. This file is likely to contain lines such as the following, but they'll probably be commented out:

```
*
* CHOOSER BROADCAST
```

These lines tell the system to accept logins from any host and to provide a *chooser* (a list of available XDMCP servers on the local network) to any client that asks for one. The default commented-out configuration denies access to all computers, so uncommenting the lines enables access. Instead of using an asterisk (*), though, you may want to specify computers by name. An asterisk can stand in for part of a name. For instance, `*.luna.edu` grants access to any computer in the `luna.edu` domain.

The `/etc/X11/xdm/Xservers` file lists the displays that XDM should manage. A typical configuration includes a line like the following:

```
:0 local /bin/nice -n -10 /usr/X11R6/bin/X -deferglyphs 16
```

> This line varies greatly from one system to another. The `:0 local` part is the least likely to vary, and the line will also include a call to your X server program. Other details may differ. If the `-nolisten tcp` option appears on this line, remove it; this option prevents X from accepting remote network connections.

This line tells XDM to run `/usr/X11R6/bin/X` and to display an XDMCP login prompt on this server whenever the XDMCP server itself runs. If you don't want to start X locally but you do want to accept remote XDMCP logins, comment this line out. When you restart runlevel 5, the system should not start X, but it should accept remote XDMCP logins.

## Configuring KDM

KDM's configuration files are the same as those used by XDM, except that some KDM configurations place those files in new locations and under new names. Specifically, `kde-config` may replace `xdm-config`, and it may reside in `/opt/kde/bin/` or `/usr/bin`. `Xaccess` and `Xservers` may reside in `/opt/kde/share/config/kdm`, `/etc/kde/kdm`, `/etc/kde3/kdm`, or some other directory. If you can't find these files, try using your package manager's tools to locate the package from which KDM was installed and then review the package contents. For instance, on a Red Hat or Fedora Core system, you might type the following commands:

```
$ whereis kdm
kdm: /usr/bin/kdm
$ rpm -qlf /usr/bin/kdm | grep Xaccess
/etc/kde/kdm/Xaccess
```

In addition to these configuration files, which you can adjust much as you would XDM's configuration files, KDM provides KDM-specific configuration files. The most important of these files is kdmrc, which may be stored in /etc/kde/kdm, /etc/kde3/kdm, /etc/X11/xdm, or some other location. This file points to other configuration files—possibly including, directly or via links, XDM configuration files. The file also includes a section called [Xdmcp] in which various XDMCP options are set. Be sure that the following lines exist in this file:

```
Enable=true
Port=177
```

## Configuring GDM

GDM uses an entirely unique configuration system. The GDM configuration files usually reside in /etc/X11/gdm, so check that directory first. If you can't find the files there, use your package manager to try to locate them, as described for KDM in the previous section. The main GDM configuration file is called gdm.conf, and the section that's most relevant to XDMCP server operation is called [xdmcp]. To enable remote logins, be sure that this section includes the following lines:

```
Enable=true
Port=177
```

If you want to accept remote XDMCP logins without starting X locally, locate the [servers] section of gdm.conf. This section normally contains a line such as the following:

```
0=Standard vt7
```

Comment out this line by adding a hash mark (#) to the start of the line and GDM won't start X on the local system when it's restarted. (You may need to switch to runlevel 3 and then back to runlevel 5 to restart GDM without X.)

Instead of editing the configuration file in a text editor, you can use a GUI tool. Type **gdmsetup** in an xterm window or select the option for the GDM configuration tool, often called Login Screen, GDM Configurator, or something similar, from a desktop environment menu. The result is the GDM Setup window, shown in Figure 2.6. The XDMCP tab includes several XDMCP options, but the most important XDMCP option is the Enable XDMCP check box on the Security tab. Be sure the program is set to listen on UDP port 177 (set on the XDMCP tab), as well.

## Using an XDMCP Client

Once you've reconfigured and restarted the XDMCP server, it's time to try it with an XDMCP client—that is, an X server. X servers are available for many OSs, not just Linux. For instance, you could use Cygwin/X (http://x.cygwin.com) or XManager (http://www.netsarang .com/products/xmg_detail.html) for Windows if you wanted to access gandalf from Windows clients.

**FIGURE 2.6**    GDM provides a GUI configuration tool in which you can activate XDMCP options.

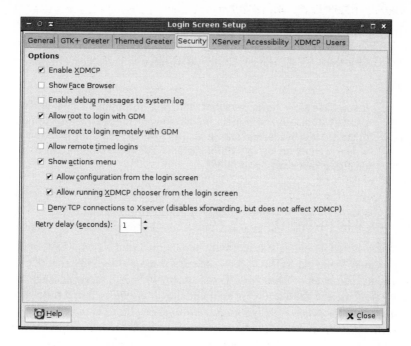

For purposes of this exercise, though, I'll assume you have access to a computer that can run XFree86 or X.org-X11, such as another Linux computer. The trick to using such a system to access another via XDMCP is to not start X in the normal way, which launches a local window manager and may present the system's own XDMCP login prompt. Instead, you launch X from a text-mode login or custom startup script and pass it the `-query host.name`, `-broadcast`, or `-indirect host.name` option, which causes X to try to find and use an XDMCP server in various ways

**Query**    The `-query host.name` option tells the server to connect directly to the specified XDMCP server. If all works well, you'll see the XDMCP login prompt and be able to access the system.

**Broadcast**    The `-broadcast` option tells the local X server to broadcast a query for available XDMCP servers. X connects to the first available server. (Some X servers present a list of XDMCP servers, though, enabling you to select which one you want to use.)

**Indirect**    The `-indirect host.name` option asks the host you specify to display a list of available XDMCP servers on its local network segment. This option is most useful if you're trying to select from machines that reside behind a firewall that blocks broadcasts but not XDMCP logins or other X-related activity.

For instance, with X *not* running, you might type the following command at a text-mode prompt:

```
$ /usr/X11R6/bin/X -query gandalf.luna.edu
```

This command starts X, but rather than launch your local display manager and other software, X connects to gandalf.luna.edu to present a login prompt on that system. When you log in, you'll be using gandalf via the keyboard and display of your local computer.

 If you have slow computers that you want to continue using, one way is to convert them into X terminals. Install Linux on these systems, configure them to start in text mode, and create custom SysV or local startup scripts to launch X. Users can then log into other systems, using the old systems only for their displays, keyboards, and mice.

## Criteria for Completion

To complete this task, you should have successfully reconfigured your XDM, KDM, or GDM software to accept remote logins via XDMCP. You can test for successful completion of this task by using another Linux computer or even a non-Linux system with an X server package installed.

For security reasons, you should reverse your changes after you've tested them, unless you want to use the remote-access features of an XDMCP server. If this is the case, you should review your network security features and employ firewall rules to prevent outside access to your XDMCP server (on UDP port 177) and to the X server (on TCP port 6000).

# Task 2.10: Use X for Day-to-Day Operations

X, like many Linux tools, is highly modular. The X server itself provides networking features but only fairly minimal graphics features: the ability to create windows, draw simple shapes, display text, and so on. X does not, by itself, provide the ability to display dialog boxes, tools for moving or resizing windows via the mouse, program menu bars, and so on. These features are all provided by add-on tools. Some of these tools, known as *widget sets*, are chosen by programmers; you as a user or system administrator have no choice over what widget sets your programs use. Other add-on tools, though, can be chosen by users and system administrators. *Window managers* provide decorative borders around windows and enable users to move and resize windows. They also often provide a few additional features, such as tools for launching programs and the ability to maintain multiple desktops, each with its own set of programs running. *Desktop environments* go further; they provide a collection of useful utilities, including calculators, file browsers, tools to set X options, and so on. Desktop environments are usually built atop particular window managers, but most window managers are independent of desktop environment projects. Some advanced Linux users run "bare" window managers to avoid expending system resources on running a full desktop environment, but novices and other advanced users often prefer to run a complete desktop environment.

The K Desktop Environment (KDE; http://www.kde.org) and the GNU Network Object Model Environment (GNOME; http://www.gnome.org) are the two most popular desktop environments for Linux. Both attempt to provide a wide range of tools but in the process end up consuming vast amounts of memory. A few others, such as XFce (http://www.xfce.org) and XPde (http://www.xpde.com), focus on other goals, such as slimmer resource requirements or a "look and feel" that mimics that of Windows XP, respectively. You can consult http://xwinman.org for information on these and other window managers and desktop environments.

Knowing how to install and select a window manager or desktop environment will enable you to get the most out of your system—you can pick a slim window manager alone if your system is short on memory or a big desktop environment if you've got lots of RAM and want all the creature comforts. As a system administrator, you can choose which options to make available. As a user, you can select which option to use as a personal default or on a per-session basis.

## Scenario

The gandalf computer, which you've just configured for remote access in the previous task, has a dozen users, and they have different preferences concerning their desktop environments. To satisfy these users, you must make several environments available as login options:

- KDE
- GNOME
- XFce
- IceWM (http://www.icewm.org)
- FVWM (http://www.fvwm.org)

The first three of these environments are full desktop environments, but the last two are window managers alone. You must configure gandalf to enable users to select any of these environments at login time.

## Scope of Task

To complete this task, you must modify your system to present certain login-time options. This entails installing software and modifying your KDM or GDM configuration to present the relevant options to users. XDM provides relatively limited login environment selection options—specifically, XDM runs the .xsession script in the user's home directory. This script can launch any window manager or desktop environment that the user desires, but the user cannot select an environment on-the-fly at the moment of login. Thus, I don't describe XDM configuration in detail for this task.

### Duration

This task should take half an hour to an hour to complete. Once you're familiar with the procedure, you should be able to add desktop environments to a system in a few minutes, assuming you don't run into problems installing the software.

## Setup

Begin by logging into the computer and acquiring root privileges. Although the scenario specifies that the computer is configured for remote access, that's not necessary to complete this task—the configuration changes required are identical whether or not the XDMCP server is actually configured for remote access. Because your changes will require restarting your XDMCP server, and therefore terminating any X session, you should work from a text-mode login or at least be prepared to have your X session shut down when you implement the changes. If the computer doesn't display an XDMCP GUI login prompt when it boots, configure it to do so, or at least so that such a server is installed and *can* be run.

## Caveats

As usual, working as root poses the risk of accidentally causing problems on your system. Mistakes in the configurations you implement could conceivably cause X to fail to start, although it's more likely that you simply won't see the options you'd intended to add or that you won't be able to launch those environments.

# Procedure

To add new environments to the options available at login time, you must both install software and configure your XDMCP server. KDM and GDM are configured in similar ways, so you'll follow just one procedure no matter which environment you're using. Once you've made your changes, you should check that you can log in and launch your chosen desktop environment or window manager.

## Installing New Environments

In order to use a window manager or desktop environment, you must install it on your computer. Unfortunately, this task is complex enough that I can't fully describe it here. If you need help, consult Phase 3, "Managing Software."

Fortunately, most Linux distributions install a variety of window managers and desktop environments as default options. Chances are you've got KDE or GNOME (and quite possibly both of them) installed already, along with at least one or two bare window managers. FVWM is often installed by default, and IceWM may be as well. To check for these window managers and desktop environments, look for the following program files: startkde (KDE), gnome-session (GNOME), startxfce4 or xfce4-session (XFce), icewm or icewm-session (IceWM), and fvwm (FVWM).

If a window manager or desktop environment isn't installed, you can install it using your distribution's package system or from the source code provided by the package's developers, as described in Phase 3. Alternatively, you can ignore it or substitute another window manager that is installed in your system.

Many window managers include the letters wm in their names and in their executables' names. Therefore, you can type `ls /usr/bin/*wm* /usr/X11R6/bin/*wm*` to locate likely substitute window managers.

## Configuring KDM and GDM

Modern versions of both KDM and GDM rely on files stored in /usr/share/xsessions to determine what options to present for possible login sessions. This directory holds files with names of the form *environment*.desktop, where *environment* is the environment name (such as KDE or GNOME). The precise names vary from one distribution to another, but you should be able to spot the session file for your environment of choice—if it exists. For this task, look for kde.desktop, gnome.desktop, xfce.desktop, icewm.desktop, and fvwm.desktop or similar files. (Some distributions capitalize parts of certain environment names, and there may be other variations of some of these names.)

If a session file doesn't exist for your environment, you can create one. The simplest way to do this is probably to copy an existing file and make appropriate changes. Listing 2.2 shows a sample file that launches IceWM. You should change the Name and Comment entries if you create a file for another environment. These fields present a name and a comment, both of which are visible to users. Just as important, you should change the Exec and TryExec lines, which point to the program that's used to launch the environment. KDE uses startkde, GNOME uses gnome-session, XFce uses startxfce4 or xfce4-session, and most bare window managers, including fvwm, use their own names. (Listing 2.2's IceWM window manager is an exception; it uses icewm-session, although icewm also works with some IceWM packages.)

**Listing 2.2:**  Sample X Session File for GDM and KDM

```
[Desktop Entry]
Encoding=UTF-8
Name=IceWM
Comment=This session logs you into IceWM
Exec=icewm-session
TryExec=icewm-session
# no icon yet, only the top three are currently used
Icon=
Type=Application
```

Most X session files include a large number of Name and Comment lines, each of which includes a language code, such as Name[fr] for French. You can delete all of these except for the language your system actually uses or even just leave the bare Name and Comment lines, as in Listing 2.2.

Most distributions provide a large number of session files for a wide variety of window managers and desktop environments. Sometimes these come with the GDM and KDM programs; they're likely to be buried in an obscure directory such as /usr/share/apps/kdm/sessions/ or /usr/kde/3.5/share/apps/kdm/sessions/. Sometimes window manager or desktop environment packages ship with a suitable session file; these files may be buried in obscure locations or may be automatically installed in /usr/share/xsessions. In the latter case, you need do nothing special, since the act of installing the environment automatically adds it to your GDM and KDM menus.

### Testing Your Configuration

Once you've added an X session file, you must restart your XDMCP server, as described earlier in "Identifying Your XDMCP Server" in Task 2.9. When KDM or GDM starts up again, you should see your new session in its list of available sessions, such as the Session Type selector in Figure 2.7, which shows a KDM login prompt. The details of where this selector appears varies from one system to another. In GDM, the relevant option is usually called Session rather than Session Type.

**FIGURE 2.7** KDM, like GDM, enables users to select a desktop environment or window manager at login time.

Many distributions remember users' choices for login sessions and use those choices as their defaults or give users the option of changing their defaults when they select a new session. Other distributions, though, including the popular Fedora and Red Hat, require the user to run a special program to make these changes explicit. For Fedora and Red Hat, this program is the Desktop Switching Tool (switchdesk).

## Criteria for Completion

To complete this task, you should have successfully added new window managers and desktop environments to your KDM or GDM login prompt. Doing so requires installing the software and creating X session files in the /usr/share/xsessions directory. Some distributions make this task very easy by placing appropriate files in this directory when you install the relevant desktop environment or window manager.

# Phase
# 3

# Managing Software

An OS is defined largely by its software. The software isn't static, though; once you've installed a package, you may need to remove it, upgrade it, or replace it with something entirely different. Package management software, such as the RPM Package Manager (RPM) and Debian package tools, help you to do this. In addition to understanding package management, to be truly "street smart" in the Linux world, you should know how to install software from source code. This will enable you to tweak the software in various ways and to install unusual software that's not available in a binary package for your distribution. Being able to back up your installed software and user files will help you ensure that your system operates smoothly, with minimal downtime.

Task 3.1 covers RPM and Task 3.2 covers Debian packages. Ordinarily, a single computer runs just one of these two systems, not both, so if you have access to one computer running one Linux distribution, you'll be able to perform only one of these tasks. A few Linux distributions, such as Slackware and Gentoo, use other package management tools, so neither of these tasks applies directly to them.

Even once it's installed, running software needs management—you may need to determine what's running, terminate some running programs, and rein in others that are causing problems. On a bigger scale, you should know how to adjust Linux *runlevels*, which are sets of system software and servers that you can start or stop all at once. Finally, Linux relies heavily on `cron` and similar utilities, which enable you to schedule processes to run at particular times in the future. Doing so lets you schedule routine automated tasks, such as checking for available system software upgrades, at convenient times.

This phase maps to portions of the CompTIA Linux+ objectives 1, 2, and 3 and to portions of the LPIC objectives 102, 103, 106, and 111.

# Task 3.1: Use RPM

RPM is the most popular of the Linux package managers. It enables you to install, upgrade, uninstall, query, and verify the integrity of packages. RPM works on individual package files whose filenames end in `.rpm`. These files are compressed archive files, similar to compressed tarballs or zip files, but they include additional data, such as information on *dependencies*—packages upon which the RPM file depends for normal operation. Managing software via RPMs requires using the rpm utility program, which provides commands for installing, removing, and otherwise manipulating packages. Over the past few years, meta-packaging tools, such as the Yellow Dog Updater, Modified (Yum), have been developed. These tools provide a front-end to download and install or update multiple files from network repositories, which greatly simplifies the task of keeping a system up-to-date.

## Scenario

A Fedora Core 5 system you're administering requires several package changes:

- To minimize security risks, you plan to remove the vsftpd (FTP server) package, which isn't needed on this computer.

- You need to upgrade the yum package to the latest version, 2.6.1-0.fc5.

- You want to install the Z Shell (zsh) package, which isn't currently installed.

- You're not sure what the xpdf package does, so you want to query it.

- You suspect corruption in the samba package and so want to verify its integrity.

- You want to check for, and possibly install, system updates from an archive site.

 In practice, your system is unlikely to be configured with precisely the installed packages specified in this list. Feel free to substitute other packages for those listed here as you follow along on your own system.

## Scope of Task

This task involves using the rpm program to perform five types of operation: removing packages, upgrading packages, installing packages, querying packages, and verifying packages. A sixth sub-task, updating the system, involves using Yum.

### Duration

This task will take about an hour to complete. Individual package operations can take anywhere from a few seconds to a few minutes to perform, so once you're familiar with RPM, you can manage packages quite quickly.

### Setup

You must have a working Fedora Core 5 system to complete the task in precisely the way described. If you're using another RPM-based distribution or another version of Fedora Core, you can still complete this task, but you must locate other packages to install, upgrade, and verify. These packages might be different versions of the ones described here or you might try working with entirely different packages. Package management requires superuser access, so you should log in as an ordinary user and acquire root privileges.

## Caveats

The usual caveats concerning working as root apply. In addition, package management runs the risk that you'll render parts of your system inoperative. In particular, mistakenly removing software that you need is an obvious risk. Upgrading software can cause problems if the new software contains new bugs or if its operation has changed in ways that are detrimental. On rare occasion, packages fail to properly flag configuration files and so upgrading the package can wipe out your configuration files. If you upgrade packages that use configuration files, be sure to back them up first. These risks are all magnified when doing whole-system updates, simply because such updates may upgrade many different packages in a single operation.

# Procedure

This task involves exercising various features of the rpm program, concluding with the network-enabled RPM wrapper Yum. The rpm program takes an operation (denoted by a single dash and a one-letter code or a double dash and a longer operation name), an arbitrary number of options (from zero upward) specified in a similar way, and a package name, a package filename, or an on-disk filename. Generally speaking, when you're working with installed packages, you specify a package name, such as zsh. Package filenames are the names of the files in which uninstalled packages are stored. They can be anything but are conventionally the package name followed by version number and architecture information and the .rpm filename extension, as in zsh-4.2.5-1.2.2.i386.rpm. Sometimes you can use an on-disk filename, typically with the help of the --file (or -f) option. This can be handy if you want to discover what package owns a given file.

## Deleting an Unused Package

To delete a package, you use the --erase (or -e) option to rpm, which takes a package name as an option:

```
# rpm -e vsftpd
```

If the operation completes successfully, you'll see no other messages. If you try to delete a package that's not installed, rpm will tell you so. Similarly, rpm will complain if you try to delete a package that's depended upon by other packages—for instance, if you try to delete a library package upon which program packages rely. If you see such a message, you have three choices:

- Abandon the attempt to delete the package.

- Delete the packages that depend upon the one you're trying to delete. You can add their names to the command line to delete multiple packages at once. You'll need to judge for yourself whether this action is reasonable.

- Use the --nodeps option to tell rpm to ignore dependency problems. This option is not generally recommended because it can result in failures when you try to use the packages that depend upon the one you're trying to remove.

## Upgrading an Existing Package

To upgrade a package, you must either have a package file on your hard disk or have a complete URL to the package file on a server. You can find Fedora Core 5 RPMs at various mirror sites; consult `http://fedora.redhat.com/Download/mirrors.html` for details. The base OS RPMs for *x*86 can be found in the `5/i386/os/Fedora/RPMS` directory under the one listed on the mirrors page, while updated packages are in the `updates/5/i386/` directory. (Substitute your platform's CPU code for `i386` if you're not using the *x*86 distribution.)

To upgrade the `yum` package, you can download the latest version (`yum-2.6.1-0.fc5.noarch.rpm` at the time of this writing) and install it from your hard disk:

```
# rpm -Uvh yum-2.6.1-0.fc5.noarch.rpm
```

The `--upgrade` (`-U`) option specifies an upgrade of an existing package, while the `-vh` (`--verbose --hash`) option tells `rpm` to display a progress bar as a series of hash marks (#). Instead of downloading the package, you can tell `rpm` to install directly from a network repository by placing the complete URL to the package in front of its filename, including an `http://` or `ftp://` specification for a Web or FTP site, respectively. This option can be a handy shortcut, but the extra typing can be tedious.

No matter how you upgrade a package, `rpm` performs dependency checks. If an upgraded package includes additional dependencies, or depends upon newer versions of packages than you've got installed, `rpm` will complain and will refuse to proceed. Although you can overcome this problem with the `--nodeps` option, this is asking for trouble. Instead, you should cancel your upgrade plans or upgrade the dependencies first.

As with deleting a package, you can list multiple packages for upgrade on a single command line. This is particularly handy when performing upgrades of a package and its dependencies; just list them all, in any order, and `rpm` will upgrade them all.

## Installing a New Package

You can install a new package much like you can upgrade an existing one, but you use the `--install` (`-i`) operation rather than `--upgrade` (`-U`):

```
# rpm -ivh zsh-4.2.5-1.2.2.i386.rpm
```

As with upgrades, you can install directly from an FTP or Web site by passing a complete URL in front of the RPM filename.

Many administrators prefer to install software with the `--upgrade` (`-U`) operation; if this operation is fed a package filename for a package that isn't already installed, `rpm` will install it without further comment, aside from its usual dependency checks. This can be handy because you needn't know whether or not a package is already installed and you can mix upgrades and fresh installations on a single command line.

## Querying a Package

If you don't know what a package does, you can use the `--query` (`-q`) operation, which takes a package name as an argument. For the operation to be useful, you're likely to specify the

--info (-i) or --list (-l) options, which display general information on the package and a list of the files it contains, respectively. To find out what xpdf does, you'd use -i:

```
# rpm -qi xpdf
Name        : xpdf                   Relocations: (not relocatable)
Version     : 3.01                        Vendor: Red Hat, Inc.
Release     : 12.1                     Build Date: Sun 12 Feb 2006
➥03:32:24 PM EST
Install Date: Tue 27 Jun 2006 06:57:45 PM EDT  Build Host:
➥ls20-bc1-13.build.redhat.com
Group       : Applications/Publishing  Source RPM: xpdf-3.01-12.1.src.rpm
Size        : 7758073                     License: GPL
Signature   : DSA/SHA1, Mon 06 Mar 2006 04:21:30 PM EST, Key ID
➥b44269d04f2a6fd2
Packager    : Red Hat, Inc. <http://bugzilla.redhat.com/bugzilla>
URL         : http://www.foolabs.com/xpdf/
Summary     : A PDF file viewer for the X Window System.
Description :
Xpdf is an X Window System based viewer for Portable Document Format
(PDF) files. Xpdf is a small and efficient program which uses
standard X fonts.
```

This output indicates that xpdf is a tool for viewing PDF files. It also includes information on when the package was installed, where it was built, and so on. If you'd passed -l instead of or in addition to -i, you'd get a list of files contained in the package.

Instead of passing a package name, you can pass a package filename by using the --package (-p) option, as in **rpm -qpi xpdf-3.01-12.1.i386.rpm**, or you can query the package that owns a specific file on the computer by passing the --file (-f) option, as in **rpm -qfi /usr/bin/xpdf**. You can also query all the packages that are installed on the system by using the --all (-a) option. This action is most useful without the -i or -l options, in order to obtain a simple list of all the installed packages. If you redirect the output to a file or pipe it through less, you can then perform further queries on packages you don't recognize in order to track down packages that may be bloating your system.

## Verifying a Package

RPM maintains a database of all the files it's installed from every package it's installed, along with checksum information on these packages. You can use this information to verify a package's integrity with the --verify (-V) operation:

```
# rpm -V samba
.......T    /usr/bin/smbcontrol
SM5....T    /usr/bin/smbstatus
missing   d /usr/share/doc/samba-3.0.22/htmldocs/using_samba/figs/sam2_0811.gif
```

If the package verifies completely properly, rpm displays no output. If any files don't match what Samba has recorded in its database, it displays an eight-character code summarizing the problem (or missing if the file is missing), an optional code reporting the type of file, and the filename. The preceding example output indicates three potential problems with the package:

- The /usr/bin/smbcontrol file's time stamp doesn't match what RPM has recorded, as indicated by the T as the final character of the eight-character code. This usually isn't a major problem; it can happen because of an accidental use of the touch utility against the file or because the file was accidentally moved and then copied back to its original location.

- The /usr/bin/smbstatus file's time stamp doesn't match what RPM has recorded. Furthermore, the file size (S), mode (M), and MD5 sum (5) don't match. In other words, the file has been changed or replaced. Such problems can be caused by disk corruption, security breaches, or legitimate editing or replacement of individual files. Sometimes these issues appear on configuration files. A properly constructed package should flag configuration files as such, and so an RPM verify operation won't report changes, but not all packages are properly constructed in this way.

- The sam2_0811.gif file in a deep Samba documentation directory is missing. This file is flagged as being a documentation file (the d between the eight-character code and the filename). Missing files usually indicate disk corruption, security breaches, or accidental deletions by root.

If a package doesn't verify properly and you have reason to think that the cause is non-sinister, you might want to uninstall the package and then install it again. This will correct any problems with the package—but be careful to back up your configuration files, just in case they haven't been properly flagged as such by the package maintainer.

You can use the --all (-a) option with --verify (-V) to check all the packages on your system. This operation is likely to take many minutes to complete and will very probably produce rather lengthy output. Redirecting this output to a file for later perusal makes sense. Most of the verification failures in this output will be innocent and related to configuration files that aren't correctly flagged or to packages that do some sort of post-installation modification to their own files. Nonetheless, you may want to verify your whole system from time to time to catch any problems that might develop.

**WARNING**  Packages that don't verify properly can be a sign of a system break-in, but more often such problems are innocent. Pay attention to the type of problem that rpm reports. Time stamp discrepancies are usually innocent and missing files are typically accidents that aren't usually serious, for instance. Changed MD5 checksums on program files are potentially much more serious, though.

## Performing a System Update

The ultimate in package updates is using Yum to update *every* package installed on your system. If your distribution shipped with Yum, chances are it's already configured properly. If not, you can obtain Yum from its home page, http://linux.duke.edu/yum/. Configuring it requires editing /etc/yum.conf or files in /etc/yum.repos.d/ to point to a Yum repository for your distribution. Unfortunately, you'll need to track down distribution-specific instructions on doing this; I can't provide specific instructions. Fortunately, most RPM-based distributions now ship with Yum, so you probably won't have to do this.

 Yum isn't the only network-enabled package updater for RPM-based systems. Mandriva favors a tool called Urpmi and ports of APT that work with RPMs are also available (check http://apt4rpm.sourceforge.net).

Once Yum is installed and configured, you can check for system updates by issuing a single command:

```
# yum check-update
```

Yum will check the repository sites and report on any packages for which updates are available. This operation can take several seconds to several minutes, depending on the speed of your Internet connection and the load on the Yum repositories you end up using. If you want to install all of the available updates, you can do so with another command:

```
# yum -y update
```

 Yum is quirky in that it's designed to automatically locate files on whatever archive site is available. Unfortunately, archive sites aren't updated perfectly simultaneously, which means that a check-update and a subsequent update operation might report that different packages need updating.

 Blindly updating the entire system can be dangerous. Although most package updates work as expected, there's always the possibility of a bug or a change that will break something on your system. Yum could also crash or run into problems at an inopportune time. Thus, you should allow Yum to update your system only under your supervision; don't set it running and walk away for an extended period, and don't let Yum perform unsupervised updates via a cron job (described shortly, in Task 3.8, "Schedule Jobs to Run in the Future").

Alternatively, if you want to update just a few packages (say, tetex and pam), you can specify them on the command line:

```
# yum -y update tetex pam
```

This command will update just those two packages, plus any packages upon which they depend. If you omit the -y option, Yum asks for confirmation before actually installing any updates.

In addition to system updates, you can perform package removals (**yum remove** *packagename*), package installations (**yum install** *packagename*), and more—consult the Yum man page for details. In fact, you can do just about all of your package maintenance using the yum command rather than the rpm command. Yum still relies on RPM to do its "dirty work," though, and sometimes using rpm is necessary. For instance, if you want to install a package that you've obtained from a source other than a Yum repository, you must use rpm or some other derivative tool, such as a GUI front end to rpm.

One potential problem with Yum is that it downloads packages to your hard disk and then installs them, but it doesn't automatically delete packages. To ensure that your hard disk doesn't fill up with package files you no longer need, type **yum clean packages** from time to time. This command removes the package files on a one-time basis.

## Criteria for Completion

To complete this task, you should have performed five types of package maintenance tasks with RPM: removing packages, upgrading packages, installing packages, querying packages, and verifying packages. You should also have used Yum to check for package updates from a Yum repository and optionally to update some or all of your system's packages.

# Task 3.2: Use Debian Packages

Debian packages are conceptually similar to RPM packages, but the two package types aren't interchangeable. You can perform the same basic types of operation with both packaging systems—installing packages, updating packages, uninstalling packages, and so on. To use Debian packages, you'll use the dpkg command to operate on specific package files or packages. The Debian Advanced Package Tools (APT) suite provides network-centric package retrieval and updating features similar to those of Yum.

## Scenario

A Debian system you're administering requires several package changes:

- To minimize security risks, you plan to remove the vsftpd (FTP server) package, which isn't needed on this computer.

- You need to upgrade the apt package to the latest version, 0.6.44.2.

- You want to install the Z Shell (zsh) package, which isn't currently installed.

- You're not sure what the xpdf-reader package does, so you want to query it.

- You want to check for, and possibly install, system updates from an archive site.

In practice, your system is unlikely to be configured with precisely the installed packages implied by this list. Feel free to substitute other packages for those listed here as you follow along on your own system.

## Scope of Task

This task involves using the dpkg program to perform four types of operations: removing packages, upgrading packages, installing packages, and querying packages. A fifth sub-task, updating the system, involves using APT.

 The Debian package system doesn't provide an exact equivalent to the verify operation of the RPM system.

### Duration

This task will take about an hour to complete. Individual package operations can take anywhere from a few seconds to a few minutes to perform, so once you're familiar with Debian package management, you can manage packages quite quickly.

### Setup

You must have a working Debian system to complete the task in precisely the way described. If you're using another Debian-based distribution, you can still complete this task, but you must locate other packages to install, upgrade, and verify. These packages might be different versions of the ones described here or you might try working with entirely different packages. Package management requires superuser access, so you should log in as an ordinary user and acquire root privileges.

### Caveats

The usual caveats concerning working as root apply. In addition, package management runs the risk that you'll render parts of your system inoperative. In particular, mistakenly removing software that you need is an obvious risk. Upgrading software can cause problems if the new software contains new bugs or if its operation has changed in ways that are detrimental. On rare occasion, packages fail to properly flag configuration files and so upgrading the package can wipe out your configuration files. If you upgrade packages that use configuration files, be sure to back them up first. These risks are all magnified when doing whole-system updates, simply because such updates may upgrade many different packages in a single operation.

## Procedure

This task involves exercising various features of the dpkg program, concluding with the network-enabled APT. The dpkg program takes an action (denoted by a single dash and a one-letter code or a double dash and a longer operation name), an arbitrary number of options (from zero upward) specified in a similar way, and a package name, a package filename, or an on-disk filename. Generally speaking, when you're working with installed packages, you specify a package name, such as zsh. Package filenames are the names of the files in which uninstalled packages are stored. They can be anything, but are conventionally the package name followed by version number and architecture information and the `.deb` filename extension, as in `zsh_4.3.2-13_powerpc.deb`. Sometimes you can use an on-disk filename, typically with the help of the `--file` (or `-f`) option. This can be handy if you want to discover what package owns a given file.

## Deleting an Unused Package

To delete a package, you use the `--remove`, `--purge`, `-r`, or `-P` action to `dpkg`, which takes a package name as an option:

```
# dpkg -r vsftpd
(Reading database ... 106705 files and directories currently installed.)
Removing vsftpd ...
Stopping FTP server: vsftpd.
```

If the operation completes successfully, you'll see messages similar to those shown in this example. The `--remove` and `-r` options remove the entire package *except* for configuration files, which are left intact; the `--purge` and `-P` options remove configuration files as well as all other package files. If you try to delete a package that's not installed, `dpkg` will tell you so. Similarly, `dpkg` will complain if you try to delete a package that's depended upon by other packages—for instance, if you try to delete a library package upon which program packages rely. If you see such a message, you have three choices:

- Abandon the attempt to delete the package.

- Delete the packages that depend upon the one you're trying to delete. You can add their names to the command line to delete multiple packages at once. You'll need to judge for yourself whether this action is reasonable.

- Use the `--force-depends` option to tell `dpkg` to ignore dependency problems. This option is not generally recommended because it can result in failures when you try to use the packages that depend upon the one you're trying to remove.

## Upgrading an Existing Package

To upgrade a package, you must have a package file on your hard disk. You can find Debian packages at various mirror sites, and the Debian package database at `http://www.debian.org/distrib/packages` is a very useful resource for locating packages.

To upgrade the `apt` package, you can download the latest version (`apt_0.6.44.2_powerpc.deb` at the time of this writing—note that this is a PowerPC package; make appropriate changes for your CPU architecture) and install it directly from your hard disk:

```
# dpkg -i apt_0.6.44.2_powerpc.deb
(Reading database ... 106653 files and directories currently installed.)
Preparing to replace apt 0.5.28.6 (using apt_0.6.44.2_powerpc.deb) ...
Unpacking replacement apt ...
Setting up apt (0.6.44.2) ...
```

The `--install` (`-i`) action specifies an installation of a new package or an upgrade of an existing package. The output of the program summarizes its actions, as shown here. If you like, you can specify multiple package files on a single command line and **dpkg** installs or upgrades them all.

No matter how you upgrade a package, **dpkg** performs dependency checks. If an upgraded package includes additional dependencies, or depends upon newer versions of packages than you've got installed, **dpkg** will complain and will refuse to proceed. Although you can overcome this problem with the `--force-depends` option, this is asking for trouble. Instead, you should cancel your upgrade plans or upgrade the dependencies first.

## Installing a New Package

With **dpkg**, package installs and upgrades are performed in precisely the same way, using the `--install` (`-i`) action. The output differs slightly when you install a fresh package:

```
# dpkg -i zsh_4.3.2-13_powerpc.deb
Selecting previously deselected package zsh.
(Reading database ... 106653 files and directories currently installed.)
Unpacking zsh (from zsh_4.3.2-13_powerpc.deb) ...
Setting up zsh (4.3.2-13) ...
```

Note that, compared to the upgrade output, the installation output omits the words `replace` and `replacement`. Other than this subtle difference, you'd be hard-pressed to tell the difference between an upgrade and a fresh installation based on the **dpkg** command or output.

## Querying a Package

If you don't know what a package does, you can use the `--status` (`-s`) action, which takes a package name as an argument. This action displays general information on the package:

```
# dpkg -s xpdf-reader
Package: xpdf-reader
Status: install ok installed
Priority: optional
Section: text
Installed-Size: 1792
Maintainer: Hamish Moffatt <hamish@debian.org>
Source: xpdf
Version: 3.00-12
Provides: pdf-viewer, postscript-preview
Depends: lesstif2, libc6 (>= 2.3.2.ds1-4), libfreetype6 (>= 2.1.5-1),
➥libgcc1 (>= 1:3.4.1-3), libice6 | xlibs (>> 4.1.0), libpaper1, libsm6 |
➥xlibs (>> 4.1.0), libstdc++5 (>= 1:3.3.4-1), libt1-5 (>= 5.0.2), libx11-6
➥| xlibs (>> 4.1.0), libxext6 | xlibs (>> 4.1.0), libxp6 | xlibs (>> 4.1.0),
➥libxpm4 | xlibs (>> 4.1.0), libxt6 | xlibs (>> 4.1.0), zlib1g (>= 1:1.2.1),
➥gsfonts (>= 6.0-1), xpdf-common (= 3.00-12)
```

```
Suggests: www-browser
Conflicts: xpdf-i (<= 0.90-8), xpdf (<= 0.93-6)
Description: Portable Document Format (PDF) suite -- viewer for X11
 xpdf is a suite of tools for Portable Document Format (PDF) files. (These are
 sometimes called 'Acrobat' files after the name of Adobe's PDF software.)
 .
 This package contains xpdf itself, a PDF viewer for X11.
 xpdf is designed to be small and efficient. xpdf supports encrypted
 PDF files. Standard X fonts, Truetype fonts and Type 1 fonts are supported.
 .
 This package also contains pdftoppm, a utility for converting
 PDF files to PBM, PGM and PPM formats.
 .
 See also the xpdf-utils package for conversion utilities and the
 other xpdf-* packages for additional language support.
```

This output indicates that **xpdf-reader** is a tool for viewing PDF files. It also includes information on dependencies, conflicts, and so on. If you want to learn similar information about an uninstalled package file, use the --info (-I) option and pass it the package filename.

Another Debian package information tool is the --listfiles (-L) option, which lists the files contained in a package. For instance, typing **dpkg -L xpdf-reader** will show you the files installed from the xpdf-reader package.

If you want to learn the name of a package that owns a file, you can use the --search (-S) option, which takes a filename (or partial filename) as an option:

```
# dpkg -S /usr/bin/xpdf
xpdf-reader: /usr/bin/xpdf
```

## Performing a System Update

The ultimate in package updates is using APT to update *every* package installed on your system. Debian-based systems include a file, /etc/apt/sources.list, that specifies locations from which important packages can be obtained. If you installed the OS from a CD-ROM drive, this file will initially list directories on the installation CD-ROM in which packages can be found. There are also likely to be a few lines near the top, commented out with hash marks (#), indicating directories on an FTP or Web site from which you can obtain updated packages. (These lines may be uncommented if you did a network install initially.)

**WARNING**    Don't add a site to /etc/apt/sources.list unless you're sure it can be trusted. The apt-get utility does automatic and semiautomatic upgrades, so if you add a network source to sources.list and that source contains unreliable programs or programs with security holes, your system will become vulnerable after upgrading via apt-get.

The apt-get utility works by obtaining information on available packages from the sources listed in /etc/apt/sources.list and then using that information to upgrade or install packages. One particularly common use of this utility is to keep your system up-to-date with any new packages. The following two commands will accomplish this goal, if /etc/apt/sources.list includes pointers to up-to-date file archive FTP sites:

```
# apt-get update
# apt-get dist-upgrade
```

In addition to system updates, you can perform package installations (**apt-get install** **packagename**) and more—consult the man page for apt-get for details. APT still relies on dpkg to do its "dirty work," though, and sometimes using dpkg is necessary. For instance, if you want to install a package that you've obtained from a source other than a Debian repository, you must use dpkg or some other derivative tool.

One potential problem with APT is that it downloads packages to your hard disk and then installs them but it doesn't automatically delete packages. To ensure that your hard disk doesn't fill up with package files you no longer need, type **apt-get clean** from time to time. This command removes the package files on a one-time basis.

## Criteria for Completion

To complete this task, you should have performed four types of package maintenance tasks with dpkg: removing packages, upgrading packages, installing packages, and querying packages. You should also have used APT to check for package updates from an APT repository and optionally to update some or all of your system's packages.

# Task 3.3: Install Programs from Source

Although most Linux distributions provide handy binary package systems, such as RPM and Debian packages, truly "street-smart" Linux administrators are just as comfortable compiling and installing programs from source code as they are installing binary packages. The reasons for this are varied. All open-source programs are, by definition, available in source code form, so the ability to handle source code frees you from any omissions that might be made by your distribution maintainer. Compiling and installing source code guarantees that you're using *pristine* code—that is, code as delivered by the developers rather than modified (and perhaps made buggier) by distribution maintainers. Installing from source code also enables you to tweak the code yourself, either by making changes to the code or by just altering compile-time options to better suit your system's needs. On the downside, compiling programs from source code is time-consuming, distribution maintainers often make improvements to better integrate packages with their systems, and bypassing the package system means that you lose features such as dependency tracking and easy software deletion.

Gentoo Linux is unusual in that it employs a source-based package system, known as *Portage*. When you install a package in Gentoo, the package system downloads the source code, applies patches, and compiles the code automatically. This gives you some, but not all, of the advantages of installing from source code on other platforms along with the advantages of easy deletes and upgrades of binary package systems. The RPM and Debian package systems also both offer source packages, which can be useful—you can compile the source package to overcome weird dependency problems, use software on a platform that's not supported by its developers, and so on.

# Scenario

Your distribution lacks oftpd (http://www.time-travellers.org/oftpd/), which is an anonymous-only File Transfer Protocol (FTP) server program. You want to install this program for use on an Internet server that's intended to deliver files to the public at large, so you plan to install it by compiling the source code from the server's Web page.

# Scope of Task

Compiling software from source code requires obtaining the package, unpacking the package, configuring the compile scripts, compiling the software, and installing the software. Unfortunately, each of these tasks can be performed in various different ways, depending upon the package in question. Therefore, I can only present an overview that's likely to apply to most packages. Ultimately, you should read the documentation that comes with any software to learn about its own unique quirks and requirements.

## Duration

This task should take about half an hour or an hour to complete. Compiling software from source code can take anywhere from a minute or two to many hours, depending on the complexity of the software and whether you run into any problems, such as missing development libraries.

## Setup

You need a working Linux computer and root access to that computer to complete this task. You can complete most of the task as an ordinary user, but you must be root to install the software.

## Caveats

The tasks you perform before acquiring root privileges are fairly safe. Once you take on the superuser identity to install the software, the usual caveats apply. In addition, installing software runs the risk of overwriting other software files—perhaps even files from other packages, if an unfortunate naming conflict exists.

# Procedure

Installing software from source requires several steps: obtaining and unpacking the software, preparing to compile the software, compiling the software, installing the software, and testing the software.

## Obtaining and Unpacking the Software

The easiest way to obtain software is usually to check the program's main Web site. In the case of oftpd, download links appear on the main page. The latest version as I write is 0.3.7.

Most packages ship as tarballs that are compressed with gzip (with a .gz or .tgz filename extension) or bzip2 (with a .bz2 or .tbz filename extension). To unpack the software, you should change into a directory in which you want to extract the source code and use tar:

```
$ tar xvfz ~/oftpd-0.3.7.tar.gz
```

For bzip2-compressed packages, change xvfz to xvfj. You should also, of course, provide a correct path to the location of the tarball. If all goes well, the source code will be uncompressed, with tar displaying the files' names as they're extracted from the archive. Most, but not all, packages place their files in a subdirectory named after the package, such as oftpd-0.3.7 for the oftpd package. Change into that subdirectory.

## Preparing the Software for Compilation

Before compiling the software, most non-trivial programs give you the chance to configure them for your system, and many require such configuration. Precisely how you do this varies from one package to another, and this is the step that really requires you to read the package's documentation. Look for a file called README, INSTALL, FAQ, or something similar and read it. (Many packages provide several such documentation files.)

Although not universal, many packages provide a script called configure. To configure the software for your system, run that script:

```
$ ./configure
```

A few packages provide a configure script that's run in another way, via the make utility:

```
$ make config
```

The README, INSTALL, or other documentation file should describe how to configure the package if it's done differently than one of these methods. In addition, you can sometimes pass options to the configuration script. These *compile-time options* can permanently enable or disable certain program features, change program defaults, or otherwise customize the software for your system. For instance, some programs enable you to tweak compiler options for a particular CPU, add or remove support for particular GUI libraries (particularly for X-based programs), change the installation directories, and so on. The oftpd package is simple enough that it doesn't support many such options. (You can change the installation directory by passing the --prefix=*dir* option, but you're unlikely to need to do even that much.)

The configuration process sometimes fails. When this happens, the result is usually a fairly obvious message about a missing library. If you run into such a message, check to see if the library in question is installed. If it's not, install it. Even if the package is installed, you may need to install a separate *development* library package. Such packages usually have names that end in `-dev` or `-devel`, so check your distribution's installation media or use `yum` or `apt-get` to try to install them.

A few packages are so simple that they don't provide any configuration tools; you skip straight ahead to the compilation phase.

## Compiling the Software

Most programs can be compiled with a single command:

```
$ make
```

The `make` program loads the `Makefile` configuration file, which is generated by the configuration tool or provided with the package, to figure out how to compile the software. It then runs the compilers and other programs that are responsible for generating a final executable program.

In the case of `oftpd`, the make process should take just a few seconds, even on a slow computer. Large programs, such as the GIMP or Apache, are likely to take many minutes or even hours to compile, even on a fast computer.

The compile step is the one that's most likely to cause problems, with the possible exception of missing libraries detected by a configuration script. Problems can include program bugs, mismatches between versions of support libraries, and missing development libraries. Unfortunately, there's no easy recipe for tracking down and fixing compile-time problems. Try tracing backward in the error messages until you find the first one—frequently, one error is found and that error then spawns dozens more errors, which might give no clues to the real source of the problem. With any luck, the first error message will provide a helpful clue, such as a complaint about a missing development library.

 Try performing a Web search on part or all of the first error message you encounter. You may find a Web page or post that will provide a fix, or at least additional clues to help you fix your compilation problem.

A few packages require you to issue multiple `make` commands to compile a program suite. Each command specifies a separate make *target*—that is, an action you can specify on the command line. Typically, packages that require multiple commands are large program suites that provide optional functionality in multiple program files. Consult the package's documentation to learn if yours requires multiple compile targets.

## Installing the Software

Once the software is compiled, you can install it. In most cases, you do this by passing the `install` target to `make`; however, you must do this as `root`:

```
# make install
```

This action copies the program files, man pages, sample configuration files, and any other files provided by the package to appropriate locations. Most packages default to installing software in the /usr/local/ directory tree, which is intended to hold locally compiled software. This location keeps such software from accidentally overwriting software installed via your distribution's package manager—precompiled software should never be installed in /usr/local.

You should scan the output of the installation command to be sure no errors were reported. (One common cause of errors is attempting to install software as a non-root user.) If errors were reported, try to track them down.

If you install software from source code but later decide you don't want it, you can use an uninstall target for make that many packages provide. Typing **make uninstall** will remove the software from your system.

## Testing the Software

To test the software, you should run it in the usual way. For ordinary user programs, you should log in as an ordinary user and type the program's name. In the case of servers, such as oftpd, you must either add them to your super server configuration (described in Phase 6) or run them as stand-alone servers. The oftpd server should be run stand alone as root:

```
# oftpd ftpuser /home/ftp
```

This command line runs the server, which changes its permissions to those of ftpuser (this user should exist on your system, or you can use another one). The server delivers files stored in the /home/ftp/ directory—change this directory name as you see fit, but be sure that the user you specify can read files in the directory you use.

You can check that oftpd is working correctly by using an FTP client on the same or another computer to log in and issue normal FTP commands:

```
$ ftp ftpserver
Connected to ftpserver.
220 Service ready for new user.
Name (ftpserver:rodsmith): anonymous
331 Send e-mail address as password.
Password:
230 User logged in, proceed.
Remote system type is UNIX.
ftp> ls
200 Command okay.
150 About to send file list.
total 0
drwxr-xr-x   7 500      100            184 Dec 24  2002 testdir
-rw-r--r--   1 500      100        8646599 Feb 27  2003 testfile.tgz
226 Transfer complete.
ftp> exit
```

This exchange shows that oftpd is working. If it doesn't work for you, you should check to see that the oftpd process appears on the server system, as described shortly, in Task 3.5, "Manage Running Processes." If it's running, it could be that a firewall or network problem is preventing the connection. If you can connect but can't log in or access files, perhaps your specified user doesn't exist or lacks permissions to read data from the directory you specified.

To make a server run whenever you restart your computer, add a reference to that server to a local startup file, such as /etc/init.d/boot.local or /etc/rc.d/rc.local.

**WARNING** For security reasons, you shouldn't leave oftpd running indefinitely unless you have a valid reason to run an anonymous FTP server on your computer. Disable it and, ideally, uninstall the software when you're done with this task.

## Criteria for Completion

This task requires you to install a program from source code. To do this, you must download, uncompress, prepare, compile, install, and test the software. A failure to accomplish any of these sub-goals will prevent ultimate completion of the task. As a small program, oftpd is less likely to cause problems than some other packages. Nonetheless, it's possible that a system-specific incompatibility on your computer will cause a problem. Resolving such problems can be frustrating, particularly if you're new to the software-compilation task.

# Task 3.4: Perform System Backups

To keep your system running well, you must master the techniques of software installation, upgrading, and management described in the preceding tasks. Even with those and other system administration tools at your disposal, though, your system can fail in minor or major ways. For instance, you or a user can accidentally delete files, hard disks can fail, or your system can be compromised and damaged by an intruder. To protect against such problems, you should regularly back up your computer and be prepared to recover part or all of your system from your backup when this becomes necessary. Note my use of the word *when*; Murphy's Law ensures that, sooner or later, you *will* encounter a situation that will require a backup for proper recovery. Without that backup, you will lose data.

## Scenario

Your company's file server is a critical piece of infrastructure that holds hundreds of hours of employees' work. It therefore requires backup, and you've been tasked with planning a backup strategy for that server. To do so, you must select backup hardware, plan a backup schedule, decide what software to use with that hardware, determine what Linux commands and utilities to use to implement the backup plan, and plan how to restore data when it becomes necessary.

## Scope of Task

This task is more about planning and preparing than actually doing. It's therefore less hands-on than most other tasks in this book. You'll need to research hardware and software options and plan a backup strategy for your critical file server computer.

### Duration

This task should take about 1 to 3 hours to complete. Actual system backups typically take anywhere from a few minutes to many hours, depending on the amount of data to be backed up and the speed of the hardware. Fortunately, backups can be performed with little or no user intervention, so the time you actually spend tending to backups, once your strategy is in place, will be minimal.

### Setup

Much of this task involves researching current hardware and planning your backup strategy. You can do this by using any computer with Internet access. You'll also need to log into your Linux computer as an ordinary user in order to read documentation and perhaps write scripts.

### Caveats

Actually planning a backup strategy is fairly risk free; however, implementing the strategy does pose risks. You'll need root privileges to install software and probably to back up the computer, and this presents the usual dangers. The riskiest part of a backup is restoring data; it's possible to overwrite important files on a partially working system, making whatever problem it's experiencing worse.

## Procedure

This task involves a great deal of planning: You must pick your backup hardware, plan a backup schedule, choose the software to be used with the hardware, prepare backup commands, and plan how to restore data.

### Selecting Backup Hardware

Just about any device that can store data and read it back can be used as a backup medium. The best backup devices are inexpensive, fast, high in capacity, and reliable. They don't usually need to be *random access* devices, though. Random access devices are capable of quickly accessing any piece of data. Hard disks, floppy disks, and CD-ROMs are all random access devices. These devices contrast with *sequential access* devices, which must read through all intervening data before accessing the sought-after component. Tapes are the most common sequential-access devices.

Traditionally, tapes have been the backup medium of choice. Although they're sequential-access devices, they're inexpensive on a per-gigabyte basis, and tapes have usually had capacities that match or exceed the capacities of typical computer hard disks. In the past few years, though, the price gap between tapes and other media—particularly recordable DVDs and hard disks—has been narrowing. Thus, these devices are now often used for backups. Typically, recordable DVDs (or the lower-capacity CD-R or CD-RW media) are used for backing up basic system installations or particular projects, while hard disks mounted in special removable drive bays are used for complete system backups. Tapes can fill either role.

If you decide to use a tape drive, your choices aren't over. Several competing tape formats are in common use. These include Travan, which dominates the low end of the spectrum; digital audio tape (DAT), which is generally considered a step up; digital linear tape (DLT) and Super DLT, which are well respected for use on servers and networks; 8mm, which is similar to DAT but has higher capacities; and Advanced Intelligent Tape (AIT), which is a high-end tape medium. Each of these competes at least partially with some of the others. Travan drives tend to be quite inexpensive (typically $200–$500), but the media are pricey. The other formats feature more costly drives ($500–$4,000 for a single drive), but the media cost less. Maximum capacities vary: under 1GB for obsolete forms of Travan, 20GB for top-of-the-line Travan, and 160GB for the largest Super DLT drives. Overall, Travan is a good solution for low-end workstations; DAT is best used on high-end workstations, small servers, and small networks; and the other formats are all good for high-end workstations, servers, and networks.

If you decide to use hard disks in removable mounts as a backup medium, you'll need ordinary internal drives and mounting hardware. The hardware comes in two parts: a mounting bay that fits in the computer and a frame in which you mount the hard drive. To use the system, you slide the frame with hard drive into the mounting bay. You can get by with one of each component, but it's best to buy one frame for each hard drive, which effectively raises the media cost. A similar alternative is to use external hard disks with FireWire or USB connectors. These can be convenient, but the external housings add to the cost. From a Linux software point of view, removable hard disk systems work like regular hard disks or other removable disk systems, like Zip disks. Most of these systems use Advanced Technology Attachment (ATA) disks, which you'll access as /dev/hdb, /dev/hdc or some other ATA device identifier. External hard disks are usually accessed as if they were Small Computer System Interface (SCSI) devices. In either case, the disks are likely to be partitioned, and the partitions are likely to hold ordinary Linux filesystems.

Optical media (recordable DVDs, CD-Rs, and CD-RWs) are odd from a software interface perspective: You must use tools such as cdrecord to write to them rather than accessing their device files directly. CD-R and CD-RW drives and media are very well standardized, from both a software and a hardware perspective, so buy these based on price and features. Several competing recordable DVD formats exist, though, and the market is constantly changing. If you need the higher capacity of a recordable DVD, you should research the current market and formats before buying. (You should be able to use cdrecord or similar Linux programs to write to any recordable DVD drive, though.)

You should go online and check backup hardware options from computer retailers. Decide what basic format to use based on your needs. For a departmental file server, a high-capacity tape or removable disk option is probably best. Check current prices for both the drives (or removable mounts) and their media. Look up data transfer speeds and capacities and decide which options are most appealing and why.

## Planning a Backup Schedule

Regular computer backup is important, but precisely *how* regular is a matter that varies from one system to another. If a computer's contents almost never change (as might be true of a dedicated router or a workstation whose user files reside on a file server), backups once a month or even less often might be in order. For critical file servers, once a day is not too often. You'll have to decide for yourself just how frequently your systems require backup.

Even the most zealous backup advocate must admit that creating a full backup of a big system on a regular basis can be a tedious chore. A backup can easily take several hours, depending on backup size and hardware speed. For this reason, most backup packages support *incremental backups.* An incremental backup scheme involves creating a full backup first. On subsequent backups, only those files that have changed since the last full or incremental backup are backed up. This scheme saves backup time and reduces the need for backup capacity, but at a cost: Data restoration becomes more complex because you may need to use multiple backup media to restore your data.

Despite these problems, incremental backups can be an extremely useful tool for helping make backups manageable. They can also reduce wear and tear on backup devices and media, and they can minimize the time it takes to restore files if you know that the files you need to restore were backed up on an incremental tape.

**WARNING**   Whether you perform incremental backups or nothing but complete backups, you should maintain multiple backups. Murphy's Law guarantees that your backup will fail when you need it most, so having a backup for your backup (even if it's from a week or a month earlier) can help immensely. A typical backup plan includes a rotating set of backup tapes. For instance, you might have two tapes per week—one for a full backup on one day and one to hold several incremental backups. Eight tapes will then hold backups for four weeks.

You should also consider how much data to back up. Sometimes, backing up an entire computer is the best approach. A full backup like this enables you to quickly recover the entire system if it should fail. Often, though, a partial backup is tempting because it can save backup time and media. You might back up just the /home directory on a workstation or whatever directory holds a file server's files. Such a backup enables you to recover lost user files easily, but if the entire system goes south, you'll need to re-install the base OS from scratch and then recover user files from the backup.

**TIP**   If you decide to do a partial backup, be sure to include your system configuration files. Backing up /etc should do this job. You might not want to restore the entire /etc directory over whatever you re-install, but if you back it up you'll at least be able to restore changes to important configuration files with relative ease.

At this point, you should plan your backup schedule. How often do you want to create full backups? What about incremental backups? Bear in mind that there are no completely right or wrong answers to these questions, although some backup plans will become unwieldy or will prove to be inadequate when ultimately tested.

## Choosing Backup Software

You can back up a Linux system, or a portion thereof, using any of many different programs. Some of the more popular programs for creating backups include the following:

**AMANDA**   The Advanced Maryland Automatic Network Disk Archiver (AMANDA) is a powerful network-based backup tool. It builds on `dump` or `tar` to enable one computer to serve as a backup station for potentially dozens of other computers. The project's home page is `http://www.amanda.org`.

**BRU**   The Backup and Restore Utility (BRU) is a commercial backup package for Linux and other Unix-like systems. It creates an archive of backup files at the start of the backup, so you can easily view a list of backed-up files and select those you want to restore from the list. It can be used to back up individual systems or an entire network. The core utility is text based, but BRU also comes with a unique GUI front end. You can read more at `http://www.bru.com`.

**cp**   The standard Linux `cp` command can be used to create backups on disk media but not on tapes. Ordinarily, `cp` modifies file characteristics, such as the owner; however, if you add certain options, such as `-a`, `cp` does a better job of preserving this information.

**cpio**   This program is a popular archiving tool for Linux. You can use it to create an archive directly on a tape, or you can pipe its output through `cdrecord` to create a `cpio`-format optical disc.

**tar**   The `tar` program has long been a staple in the Linux world. It's conceptually very similar to `cpio`, but `tar` has become the standard archive format for exchanging file collections on the Internet. Its name stands for *tape archiver*, so as you might expect, it can be used to archive a filesystem directly to tape. You can also use it with `cdrecord` to create a `tar`-format optical disc.

**dump**   This program has traditionally been a popular Unix and Linux backup tool; however, it has several limitations. Most importantly, it can't be counted upon for 100 percent reliable operation with modern kernels. For this reason, Linus Torvalds himself recommends against its use, and it's hard to argue with such a recommendation!

As a general rule, `tar` is the most popular and lowest-common-denominator backup tool, but it's not always the best choice. AMANDA and BRU are particularly worthy of note for backing up a network. AMANDA includes automatic backup scheduling tools that can greatly simplify the backup and restore procedures. The cost is that it takes a great deal of effort to configure AMANDA on both the backup server and its clients.

**WARNING**   Most backup programs don't encrypt their data. An unauthorized individual who obtains your backup can read sensitive data even if the files have restrictive permissions on the original hard disk. Therefore, you should treat backup media as you would other sensitive documents. If you deal in unusually sensitive data, you may want to consider adding encryption to your backups to protect them in the event they're stolen or "borrowed."

## Preparing Backup Commands

Once you've decided on your hardware, backup schedule, and software, you can begin preparing the commands you'll need to back up your software. To do this, you should peruse the man pages or other documentation for your backup software. The approach you take can vary greatly depending on the decisions you've made to date. Therefore, your solution might be very different from another person's solution.

As an example, consider using tar to back up a computer. Specifically, suppose you want to back up the root directory (/), /home, and /usr. These directories are backed up to a SCSI tape drive (/dev/st0) with the following command:

```
# tar --create --verbose --one-file-system --file /dev/st0 / /home /usr
```

The --create option tells tar to create a backup; --verbose causes it to display a list of files as they're backed up; --one-file-system tells tar to not descend into filesystems mounted on those specified for backup; --file /dev/st0 specifies /dev/st0 as the backup device; and the remaining options list the directories that are to be backed up. This command can be abbreviated as follows:

```
# tar cvlf /dev/st0 / /home /usr
```

 **WARNING**   Using --one-file-system and backing up each partition explicitly is generally a good idea. If you try to simply back up the root partition and all mounted partitions, your backup will include the contents of /proc, any removable media that happen to be mounted, and perhaps other undesirable directories. The extra data will consume space on your backup media and may cause problems when you restore the data.

Studying tar's man page will give you information on additional tar options. One that deserves explicit mention is the method of creating incremental backups:

```
# tar cvplf /dev/st0 --listed-incremental /var/log/incr.dat / /home /usr
```

This command backs up all three partitions to /dev/st0. The --listed-incremental /var/log/incr.dat option tells tar to use /var/log/incr.dat as an index of previously backed-up files. When you run this command to create a full backup, this file should be empty or nonexistent; tar then populates it with a date code and information about each directory that's been backed up. If you later add files to a directory, tar can determine which files are new and back them up.

 **TIP**   You may want to use output redirection (>) to store the verbose output of tar in a file when backing up. This procedure will create a file that lists the contents of the backup, which can make it easier to locate files for restore. When you perform an incremental backup, store the data to different files or use the appending output redirection operator (>>) so that you don't wipe out the full backup's file list.

In many cases, you can use cron to schedule automatic backups on a regular basis. (The upcoming Task 3.8, "Schedule Jobs to Run in the Future," describes cron in more detail.) To do so, you would create one or more backup scripts (Phase 1 describes scripting) and enter them as cron jobs to be run at regular times, such as once a day. When cron is so configured, all you need to do to perform a backup is to swap backup media.

If you've opted to use recordable optical media (CD-R, CD-RW, or recordable DVD drives), you should be aware that you can't write directly to these media using tar or similar tools. Instead, you must create a tarball on disk and then either write that tarball or wrap the tarball in an ISO-9660 filesystem and write it to disc. The tool for writing to optical media is cdrecord; consult its man page for details of its operation.

## Planning a Restore Strategy

Creating backups is advisable, but doing this isn't enough. You must also have some way to restore backups in case of disaster. This task involves two aspects: partial restores and emergency recovery.

Partial restores involve recovering just a few noncritical files. For instance, users might come to you and ask you to restore files from their home directories. You can do so fairly easily by using the --extract (x) tar command, as in the following lines:

```
# cd /
# tar xvlpf /dev/st0 home/username/filename
```

This sequence involves changing to the root directory and issuing a relative path to the file or directory that must be restored. This is required because tar normally strips away the leading / in the names of files it backs up, so the files are recorded in the archive with relative filenames. If you try to restore a file with an absolute filename, it won't work.

With most backup programs, you'll need to know the exact name of the file or directory you want to restore in order to do this. If you don't know the exact filename, you may need to use the --list (t) command to tar (or its equivalent in other programs) to examine the entire contents of the tape, or at least everything until you see the file you want to restore.

If you use incremental backups, you can use the incremental file list to locate the name of the file you want to restore.

A much more serious problem is that of recovering a system that's badly damaged. If your hard disk has crashed or your system has been invaded by crackers, you must restore the entire system from scratch, without the benefit of your normal installation. You can take any of several approaches to this problem, including the following:

**Distribution's installation disk**  Most Linux distributions' installation disks have some sort of emergency recovery system. These may come as separate boot floppy images or as options to type during the boot process. In any event, these images are typically small but functional Linux systems with a handful of vital tools, such as `fdisk`, `mkfs`, Vi, and `tar`. Check your distribution's documentation or boot its boot media and study its options to learn more.

**CD-based Linux system**    Several Linux systems are now available that boot from CD-ROM. One example is Knoppix (`http://www.knoppix.com`); another is a demo version of open-SUSE (`http://www.novell.com/linux/`). Both of these systems can be used to help recover or restore a corrupted Linux installation.

**Emergency system on removable disk**    You can create your own emergency system on a removable disk. If you have a moderately high-capacity removable disk, like a Zip or LS-120 disk, you can create a moderately comfortable Linux system on this disk. The ZipSlack distribution (a variant of Slackware, `http://www.slackware.com`) is particularly handy for this purpose because it's designed to fit on a 100MB Zip disk. You can use this even if your regular installation is of another version of Linux.

**Emergency recovery partition**    If you plan ahead, you might create a small emergency installation of your preferred distribution alongside the regular installation. You should *not* automatically mount this system in `/etc/fstab`. This system can be useful for recovering from some problems, like software filesystem corruption, but it's not useful for others, like a total hard disk failure.

**Partial reinstallation**    You can reinstall a minimal Linux system and then use it to recover your original installation. This approach is much like the emergency recovery partition approach, but it takes more time at disaster recovery. On the other hand, it will work even if your hard disk is completely destroyed.

Whatever approach you choose to use, you should test it before you need it. Learn at least the basics of the tools available in any system you plan to use. If you use unusual backup tools (such as commercial backup software), be sure to copy those tools to your emergency system or have them available on a separate floppy disk. If you'll need to recover clients via network links, test those setups as well.

You may not be able to *completely* test your emergency restore tools. Ideally, you should boot the tools, restore a system, and test that the system works. This may be possible if you have spare hardware on which to experiment, but if you lack this luxury, you may have to make do with performing a test restore of a few files and testing an emergency boot procedure—say, using LOADLIN (a DOS-based boot loader that can boot a Linux system when LILO or GRUB isn't installed or working). Note that a freshly restored system will not be bootable; you'll need a kernel on a DOS boot floppy and LOADLIN, or some other emergency boot system, to boot the first time. You can then reinstall LILO or GRUB to restore the system's ability to boot from the hard disk.

## Criteria for Completion

This task is about planning a backup strategy. To complete it, you should have a complete plan for backing up a departmental file server. This plan should include specifics on the hardware you plan to use, your backup schedule, the software you intend to use, commands or procedures to perform backups (perhaps including scripts to be called by `cron`), and a plan for restoring data (both partial and full restores). If possible, you should implement and test your backup plan. If this isn't possible and you're administering a true production Linux system, make it possible. Murphy's Law applies to backups, and if you don't plan for disaster, it will strike.

# Task 3.5: Manage Running Processes

Running processes must sometimes be monitored and even terminated. You might want to monitor a process if you have reason to believe it might consume undue amounts of CPU time or if the process is taking a long time to do its job. If you conclude that the process is *hung* (that is, unresponsive to input), is working but is consuming too much CPU time, or is otherwise misbehaving, you may want to terminate it.

## Scenario

Users of a multi-user Linux system are reporting sluggish performance. You must trouble-shoot this problem and, if appropriate, terminate any program that's misbehaving or simply consuming too much CPU time.

## Scope of Task

This task involves checking running processes in various ways and terminating those processes. Most of the commands are fairly simple, but some of them have many options.

### Duration

This task should take about half an hour to complete, although you can spend more time studying all the `ps` options if you like. Performing simple checks of processes can take just a few seconds, but you may want to do this job multiple times each day on a working system. In fact, for critical systems, you might want to set up a `cron` job (described in Task 3.8) to perform checks of system load on a regular basis.

### Setup

You need access to a working Linux system with an X server installed. You should log into your Linux system as an ordinary user; `root` access is not required to complete this task, although in real situations it often is needed. In order to simulate an out-of-control process, you should launch `glxgears` from X. The `glxgears` program is a simple program to test the speed of OpenGL 3D extensions to X; it produces a window in which three simulated 3D gears spin continuously. Every few seconds, it displays benchmark data in frames per second (FPS). The point of using `glxgears` is that it tends to hog CPU time, similar to the way many out-of-control programs do, enabling you to practice tracking excessive CPU use.

## Caveats

This task presents few risks, although when performing real-life process management as root, the usual root caveats apply. It's possible that you'll terminate the wrong process if you enter a typo, and this risk can have more serious consequences when you work as root—you could accidentally terminate a critical server, for instance.

# Procedure

To perform this task, you'll use three process-monitoring tools. First, you'll check the overall system load—that is, how much of the system's available CPU time all the running programs are demanding. Second, you'll obtain static process listings. Third, you'll use a dynamic tool that's particularly helpful for spotting processes that are out of control. Once you've identified an out-of-control process, you can terminate it.

## Checking System Load

The system load is most often measured as a *load average*, which is a number from 0 upward. A load average of 0.0 means that no processes are demanding CPU time. A load average of 1.0 means that programs are demanding exactly as much CPU time as the CPU has to offer. A load average greater than 1.0 means that programs are demanding more CPU time than is available, requiring the kernel to ration CPU time. Typically, load averages are measured over some period of time, such as the last minute or the last 5 minutes.

Lightly loaded systems often have load averages between 0.0 and 1.0. Such systems perform as well as they can, given the efficiency of the code they run and the speed of the CPU. (Such systems could be sluggish because of poor disk performance or other reasons, though; load averages only tell you about demands on CPU time.) When the load average climbs above 1.0, efficiency drops—programs become sluggish because they must compete with other programs for CPU time. Thus, ideally your system's load average shouldn't rise above 1.0.

In practice, though, load averages do often exceed 1.0, particularly for short periods of time. If you run a CPU-intensive program in the background and also do something else, the load average will rise above 1.0, although perhaps not by much—it might reach 1.3 or so. Systems that are intended as multi-user computers often have load averages well over 1.0, and this isn't necessarily a problem if the CPU is fast enough. For instance, if System A has a CPU load of 2.0 and a CPU that's three times as fast as System B, System A may be faster than System B.

The easiest way to check your system load is to use the uptime command, which displays the amount of time the system has been running, the number of users who are logged in, and the load averages over the past 1, 5, and 15 minutes:

```
$ uptime
 13:24:49 up 31 days, 17:24,  6 users,  load average: 2.34, 2.28, 1.79
```

The number of users reported by uptime is the number of simultaneous logins of various types. All of these logins could be by the same user.

This example shows load averages of 2.34, 2.28, and 1.79, meaning that programs are demanding roughly twice as much CPU time as is available. This could indicate that two programs are trying to run full out and other programs are making lesser demands or that more than two programs are requesting something less than full CPU time. You'll need to perform additional tests to find out precisely what's happening. The fact that the CPU load is higher for the shorter intervals (1 and 5 minutes) than for the longer one (15 minutes) is a clue that the CPU hogging began in the last few minutes.

## Obtaining Static Process Listings

The main process-monitoring tool in Linux is ps. This program supports a huge number of options, which fall into three broad classes:

**Unix98 options**    These single-character options may be grouped together and are preceded by a single dash (-).

**BSD options**    These single-character options may be grouped together and must *not* be preceded by a dash.

**GNU long options**    These multi-character options are never grouped together. They're preceded by two dashes (--).

For a complete list of ps options, consult the program's man page. Some of the more useful ps features include the following:

**Display help**    The --help option presents a summary of some of the more common ps options.

**Display all processes**    By default, ps displays only processes that were run from its own terminal (xterm, text-mode login, or remote login). The -A and -e options cause it to display all the processes on the system, and x displays all processes owned by the user who gives the command. The x option also increases the amount of information that's displayed about each process.

**Display one user's processes**    You can display processes owned by a given user with the -u *user*, U *user*, and --User *user* options. The *user* variable may be a username or a user ID.

**Display extra information**    The -f, -l, j, l, u, and v options all expand the information provided in the ps output. Most ps output formats include one line per process, but ps can display enough information that it's impossible to fit it all on one 80-character line. Therefore, these options provide various mixes of information.

**Display process hierarchy**    The -H, -f, and --forest options group processes and use indentation to show the hierarchy of relationships between processes. These options are useful if you're trying to trace the parentage of a process.

**Display wide output**    The ps command output can be more than 80 columns wide. Normally, ps truncates its output so that it will fit on your screen or xterm. The -w and w options tell ps not to do this, which can be useful if you direct the output to a file, as in **ps w >** **ps.txt**. You can then examine the output file in a text editor that supports wide lines.

As an example, consider a command to display all of a particular user's processes:

```
$ ps U jennie
  PID TTY       STAT    TIME COMMAND
12172 pts/15    S       0:00 bash
12182 pts/15    S+      0:00 xterm
12184 pts/21    Ss      0:00 bash
12189 pts/21    S+      0:00 xv geese.jpg
```

This output indicates that the user jennie is running four processes: two instances of bash, an xterm, and the xv program, which was passed geese.jpg as a command-line option. You should note the output column that's labeled PID. This acronym stands for *process ID*, and it's a unique way to identify a particular process. Certain methods of terminating processes or changing their priorities require you to know the PID, so if you plan to terminate a process or change its priority, you should note and remember the PID.

This output isn't particularly helpful in finding runaway processes; however, you can use the u option to generate a display that includes a column (marked %CPU) that shows the percentage of total CPU time that goes to particular processes. This option is particularly helpful with the a option, which display all running processes rather than just those associated with the current login session:

```
$ ps au
```

If you try this command, though, you'll find that the output is quite lengthy; you may need to pipe it through less to peruse the output and spot the CPU hogs. If you try this, you should find that glxgears is consuming a great deal of CPU time. Another trick that's useful is to use grep to locate specific processes by name:

```
$ ps au | grep glxgears
rodsmith 12049 30.0 0.9 23292 5116 pts/4  RL+ 13:07 12:09 glxgears
rodsmith 12248  0.0 0.1  2612  532 pts/15 S+  13:47  0:00 grep glxgears
```

This approach isn't really very helpful for locating CPU hogs unless you already suspect a particular program and merely want to confirm that suspicion. This method is helpful if you suspect a process is acting up in some way, even if it's not CPU related. For instance, a process might not have terminated correctly, in which case you can use this method to quickly locate its PID number (which is in the second column in this output format).

## Locating Processes Dynamically

Although ps is the basic Linux process-identification tool, another tool is more helpful in many cases. This program is known as top, and it's a dynamic variant of ps—by default, top enters an interactive mode in which it updates its display on a regular basis (every 3 seconds, by default). Furthermore, top sorts its process listing according to criteria you select, with the default being CPU time. This makes top particularly helpful for locating CPU hogs. Figure 3.1 shows typical top output.

**FIGURE 3.1**    The top utility displays a sorted process listing, which helps in locating misbehaving programs.

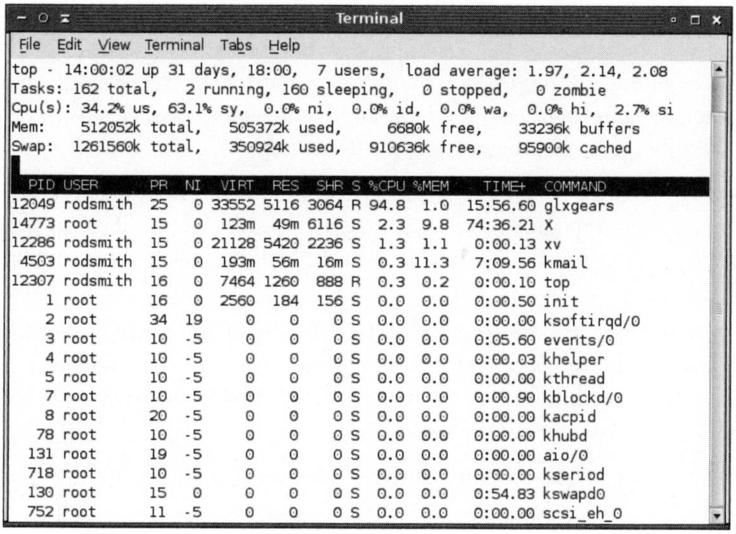

```
 - o z                              Terminal                        o □ x
 File  Edit  View  Terminal  Tabs  Help
top - 14:00:02 up 31 days, 18:00,  7 users,  load average: 1.97, 2.14, 2.08
Tasks: 162 total,   2 running, 160 sleeping,   0 stopped,   0 zombie
Cpu(s): 34.2% us, 63.1% sy,  0.0% ni,  0.0% id,  0.0% wa,  0.0% hi,  2.7% si
Mem:    512052k total,   505372k used,    6680k free,    33236k buffers
Swap:  1261560k total,   350924k used,  910636k free,    95900k cached

  PID USER      PR  NI  VIRT  RES  SHR S %CPU %MEM   TIME+   COMMAND
12049 rodsmith  25   0 33552 5116 3064 R 94.8  1.0  15:56.60 glxgears
14773 root      15   0  123m  49m 6116 S  2.3  9.8  74:36.21 X
12286 rodsmith  15   0 21128 5420 2236 S  1.3  1.1   0:00.13 xv
 4503 rodsmith  15   0  193m  56m  16m S  0.3 11.3   7:09.56 kmail
12307 rodsmith  16   0  7464 1260  888 R  0.3  0.2   0:00.10 top
    1 root      16   0  2560  184  156 S  0.0  0.0   0:00.50 init
    2 root      34  19     0    0    0 S  0.0  0.0   0:00.00 ksoftirqd/0
    3 root      10  -5     0    0    0 S  0.0  0.0   0:05.60 events/0
    4 root      10  -5     0    0    0 S  0.0  0.0   0:00.03 khelper
    5 root      10  -5     0    0    0 S  0.0  0.0   0:00.00 kthread
    7 root      10  -5     0    0    0 S  0.0  0.0   0:00.90 kblockd/0
    8 root      20  -5     0    0    0 S  0.0  0.0   0:00.00 kacpid
   78 root      10  -5     0    0    0 S  0.0  0.0   0:00.00 khubd
  131 root      19  -5     0    0    0 S  0.0  0.0   0:00.00 aio/0
  718 root      10  -5     0    0    0 S  0.0  0.0   0:00.00 kseriod
  130 root      15   0     0    0    0 S  0.0  0.0   0:54.83 kswapd0
  752 root      11  -5     0    0    0 S  0.0  0.0   0:00.00 scsi_eh_0
```

Figure 3.1 shows that the biggest CPU user is glxgears, with a PID of 12049. This process is consuming 94.8 percent of the available CPU time. If you watch the top output for a while, particularly if you run it in an xterm and work in other X windows, you'll see the top display change over time. If you type in a word processor, for instance, its process will probably rise to the top of the list while you type, even with a CPU hog like glxgears running.

You can tell top to sort its list by criteria other than CPU use, too. One of the most helpful of these options is to sort by memory use. Type **M** (without pressing the Enter key) to have top sort by the %MEM (memory use) field. Typing **N** sorts by PID number, **T** sorts by cumulative CPU time, and **P** returns to the default of percentage CPU time. (Cumulative CPU time is the total CPU time the process has used. This value can climb quite high even for programs that aren't CPU hogs if they run for long enough.)

When you're done with top, type **q**. This command terminates the program.

## Terminating Processes

Now that you've identified the CPU-hogging program as glxgears, you must decide what to do about it. Several possibilities exist:

**Do nothing**    You might decide to do nothing. Some processes legitimately consume a lot of CPU time. Knowing what's a legitimate CPU user requires knowledge of your local system. Perhaps a user is running a legitimate CPU-intensive simulation or data analysis and you wouldn't want to terminate such processes.

**Investigate further**    If you don't recognize the process's name, you might try consulting its man page or otherwise investigating the process. This should give you information that will help you make a decision.

**Contact the process's owner**   If you think the process may be out of control but you're not positive of that, you might try contacting the owner of the process. For instance, most word processors consume CPU time in brief bursts. If a word processor is consuming 90 percent or more of the system's CPU time on a continuous basis, that fact is suspicious and could indicate that the process has *hung*—that is, that it's stopped responding to input but is still consuming CPU time. Before terminating the process, though, you should contact the user who owns it to be sure that the program isn't being used for something legitimate. Perhaps the user is running a lengthy mail merge or printing a book-length document.

**Reduce the process's priority**   If the process has a legitimate reason for being run but is interfering with other users, you might consider reducing its priority. This will let the process run, but other processes will get more CPU time. Task 3.6, "Adjust Process Priorities," describes this approach.

**Terminate the process**   Finally, you might decide to terminate the process. This action is something of a last resort, and you normally take it only when processes are misbehaving. (You can use the same command to shut down servers, but most distributions provide startup and shutdown scripts that are better for this task.)

The basic command for process termination is `kill`, and it takes a PID number as an argument:

```
$ kill 12049
```

Users may kill their own processes, but they may not kill other users' processes. Only root may kill arbitrary users' processes.

After killing a process, you should check to be sure that it's been terminated. Some processes don't respond when you kill them in this way; you may need to add an option to have `kill` send a more forceful signal to the process:

```
$ kill -9 12049
```

When used without an argument, `kill` sends a TERM signal (signal number 15) to the process, which is a polite way to ask a process to shut down. The -9 parameter passes a KILL signal to the process, which terminates all but the most badly behaved processes. You can usually substitute -KILL or -SIGKILL for -9, but details vary from one shell and implementation to another.

Signals 9 and 15 are the ones you're most likely to use when terminating processes. Other signals exist, though. Type **man 7 signal** to read about them all.

Another way to kill processes is to use `top`. If you type **k** from within `top`, the program displays the prompt `PID to kill:` just above the process list. You can then type the PID of the offending process, whereupon `top` asks for the signal number to pass to the process. Type **15** or press the Enter key to pass a TERM signal to the process, or type **9** to deliver a KILL signal. You can send other signals in the same way.

In addition to `kill` and `top`, another tool for killing processes is `killall`. This program works much like `kill`, but it accepts a process name, rather than a PID number, as a way to identify the process to be killed. Although `killall` can be a quick and easy way to kill a process if you know its name, it can be dangerous because it kills all instances of that process. For instance, if **root** were to type **killall bash**, all `bash` shells would be terminated. Thus, you should be sure you want to terminate all instances of a process before using `killall`.

**WARNING**    Some Unix-like systems implement a `killall` program that kills all running processes, not just all running processes of a particular name. Thus, you should never use `killall` on an unfamiliar system unless you're sure that the program works in the way you expect!

After killing the `glxgears` process, wait a short time and then use `uptime` and `top` again. You should find that your load average has dropped, although it will take a few minutes for the longer-term load average figure to change significantly.

## Criteria for Completion

To complete this task, you should have determined your system's CPU load, identified running processes with `ps`, used `top` to identify CPU-hogging programs, and terminated processes with `kill`, `killall`, or `top`. These tools will help you manage your Linux system, keeping misbehaving processes from causing too many problems. Running `uptime` every now and then on critical systems will help you keep the systems working well by enabling you to spot runaway processes before they cause too much damage.

# Task 3.6: Adjust Process Priorities

Sometimes a program has a legitimate need to consume a lot of CPU time but you don't want it to consume that CPU time at the expense of other processes. For such situations, the ability to downgrade a process's priority is useful, and of course Linux provides that ability. You can also increase a process's priority if it should have precedence when the kernel doles out CPU time. Knowing how to make these adjustments will enable you to keep your system running smoothly without going to the extreme measure of terminating processes.

## Scenario

A computer is functioning as a multipurpose system with several important processes running. Some of these processes consume a lot of CPU time, but you want to keep them from interfering with other processes. Thus, you want to adjust their process priorities. You'll both adjust the priorities of existing processes and run new processes with modified priorities.

# Scope of Task

This task involves learning to use the `nice` and `renice` commands, which enable you to adjust process priorities. To do this, you'll need multiple test processes on which to experiment so that you can judge the effect of the commands.

## Duration

This task should take about half an hour to complete. In day-to-day practice, adjusting the priority of a process takes just a few seconds once you're familiar with the relevant commands.

## Setup

To begin this task, you should log in as an ordinary user. (Real-world applications of this task's principles often require `root` access, though. As with killing processes, ordinary users may adjust their own process priorities, but only `root` may adjust the priorities of other users' processes.) Either log in using a GUI login prompt or log in using text mode and start an X session by typing **startx**. I recommend using X simply because it lets you launch and easily control multiple programs. If necessary, you could use text-mode processes and multiple virtual terminals instead, but you'll need to find another CPU-intensive program to use for experimentation.

## Caveats

This task can be performed as an ordinary user, although you won't be able to increase the priority of your tasks except as `root`. Thus, if you want to experiment with this ability, you'll need to perform some parts of the task as `root`, with all the usual caveats that entails. Even as an ordinary user, if you mistype a command, you could conceivably cause a program to begin behaving very sluggishly. Recovering from such problems should be possible, but you'll need to either exit from and restart the affected process or increase its priority as `root`.

# Procedure

To perform this task, you'll use the `nice` command to launch programs with priorities that you specify and you'll use the `renice` command to alter the priorities of existing processes. Before you jump into these details, though, you should understand the meaning of the numbers you'll be setting.

## Understanding Process Priorities

Every Linux process has an associated priority number, which ranges from –20 to 19. The default priority value is 0. Confusingly, negative priority numbers correspond to *increased* priority, whereas positive numbers correspond to *decreased* priority.

The Linux kernel is responsible for doling out CPU time; the kernel decides for how long a given process will run before giving CPU time to a competing process. When no programs are making major demands on CPU time, even a low-priority process will get plenty of CPU time; it's only when CPU time becomes scarce (that is, when the load average climbs above 1) that process priorities become important.

Ordinarily, if two processes are competing for CPU time and both have the same priority, the kernel divides CPU time equally between them. The effect of changing the priority of one process is to alter the proportion of CPU time given to the two processes. If the process priorities differ by just 1 (say, nice values of 0 and 1), they'll still get close to equal amounts of time, but the process with a higher nice value will get slightly less CPU time. As the difference in nice values increases, so does the proportion of CPU time given to the two processes. A process with a nice value of 19 is given so little priority that it runs only when no other process is demanding CPU time. This makes a nice value of 19 appealing for processes that are CPU intensive but not critical to overall system operation, such as distributed computing projects like Folding@Home (`http://folding.stanford.edu`).

Intermediate nice values, such as 10, are useful when you want a job to run at a reasonable pace but not interfere *too* much with other processes. For instance, you might run a program compilation at a nice value of 10 if you or other users are doing work on the system while the compile is running.

Most user programs, such as Web browsers, word processors, and shells, spend most of their time idling, waiting for keyboard input. Even if you're typing furiously, the program takes far less time to process your keystrokes than you take making them. Thus, if you're running, say, a word processor and a CPU-intensive ray-tracing program, running the ray-tracing program with a reduced priority won't rob it of much CPU time; however, when your finger does hit a key in the word processor, that action will take priority, so you'll see less of a performance drop in the word processor than you'd see if you ran the ray tracer at normal priority.

## Launching Programs with Specified Priorities

To launch a program with reduced priority, type **nice** followed by the name of the program:

```
$ nice glxgears
```

This command launches the glxgears program with a nice value of 10 (the default). Alternatively, you can specify a particular value by using the -n *value*, --adjustment=*value*, or -*value* options *before* the command you're running with nice. For instance, the following three commands are all equivalent to the previous one:

```
$ nice -n 10 glxgears
$ nice --adjustment=10 glxgears
$ nice -10 glxgears
```

**WARNING**   The -*value* form of adjustment makes a confusing situation worse; it looks like you're specifying a negative value, but in fact the dash just indicates that the following number is an option to nice.

For the purpose of this task, launch two instances of glxgears, one with normal priority and one with a nice value of 10. Try monitoring both processes using top (described earlier, in Task 3.5). This utility displays the nice values of processes under its NI column, so identifying the two processes should be easy. You'll find that the nice-launched process will have a lower %CPU value and will rack up total CPU time (in the TIME+ column) more slowly. You'll probably also notice the difference in the rate of the gears' spinning in the two windows.

You can use nice in scripts, including system startup scripts, if you want to regularly run a program with reduced priority.

### Adjusting Existing Processes' Priorities

With your two instances of glxgears running, it's time to look at how to adjust running processes' priorities. You can do this with the renice command; however, with renice you need a way to tell the program what processes' priorities to adjust. You can do so by username (via the -u option), by group ID (GID, via the -g option), or by PID (via the -p option). Only the final option is possible when you run renice as an ordinary user; the other methods may only be used by root. You pass renice an absolute priority value prior to any methods used to identify processes.

For instance, suppose you want to equalize the two glxgears instances so that they both run at a nice value of 10. If the PID of the higher-priority instance is 2562, you'd use the following command to do the job:

```
$ renice 10 -p 2562
```

This command sets the priority of PID 2562 to a nice value of 10. This will only work if you own PID 2562 and if it currently has a higher priority (that is, a lower nice value). If you run the command as root, these last two restrictions don't apply.

If you continue to monitor the processes with top, you'll see their CPU use equalize. The speed of the spinning of the gears in their windows will also equalize. Both sets of gears may spin slowly, though, particularly if your system is running other CPU-intensive tasks. If you like, you can experiment with different nice values to see the effect. You can even increase processes' priorities by giving them negative values, but only if you do so as root.

## Criteria for Completion

To complete this task, you should have launched processes with varying priorities by using the nice command. You should also have successfully adjusted the priorities of processes you've already run. Using nice and renice can be an effective way to minimize the impact of programs that legitimately consume a lot of CPU time on a system that serves functions in addition to being a platform for the CPU-intensive program.

# Task 3.7: Manage Runlevels

When a Linux system boots, it enters one of seven *runlevels*, which are numbered from 0 to 6. Each runlevel corresponds to a specific set of running processes—servers, system loggers, hardware-monitoring utilities, and so on. Certain runlevels have particular meanings, but you can define others as you see fit. Even if you don't redefine your runlevels, you should know how to switch between them because most distributions configure runlevels in such a way that switching between them can sometimes be useful.

## Scenario

You've installed Linux on a system that's to function as a mail server computer. The basic installation for Linux on this computer starts it in runlevel 5, in which X runs; however, as X is unnecessary for a mail server that will seldom or never be used from the console, you want to change the system's runlevel to 3, in which X does not run. You also want to review the sub-systems that are started in runlevel 3 and adjust them to suit your purposes.

## Scope of Task

This task requires you to manage runlevels in various ways—to change runlevels both tempo-rarily and permanently as well as to change what software is run in your chosen runlevel. Doing so requires you to understand how Linux manages runlevels and how to change these runlevels.

**NOTE**  Most Linux distributions start X in runlevel 5 but not in runlevel 3. A few dis-tributions start X in other ways, though. Debian, for instance, doesn't work in quite this way, although you can configure it to do so by adding the xdm, kdm, or gdm service to runlevel 5. Gentoo uses named runlevels rather than num-bered runlevels and requires you to add the xdm service to your current run-level (probably named default) in order to start X when the system boots.

## Duration

This task should take about half an hour to complete. Once you're familiar with the tools involved, changing the current runlevel or changing the programs that are launched in a given runlevel should take just a few seconds.

## Setup

Ideally, the computer should be configured to start in runlevel 5, but if your system starts in runlevel 3 or some other runlevel, you can reconfigure your system to run in runlevel 5 by changing the appropriate numbers in the following procedure; this will cause most distributions to start X when they boot.

To prepare for this task, log into your Linux system. Because your changes will shut down X, *do not* use a GUI login. If X is running, close all your X programs and log out of your X session. You should acquire `root` privileges in your text-mode login.

## Caveats

As always, working with `root` presents certain risks. Changing runlevels can start up or shut down programs—after all, that's the point of changing runlevels. If your understanding of the services offered in various runlevels is imperfect, the result can be unexpected changes in programs that are running on your computer. Some runlevels are used to shut down or reboot the computer, so a mistake in changing runlevels can result in an unexpected system shutdown or reboot. Changing the software that runs in particular runlevels can cause odd problems if you mistakenly remove a critical item or add something inappropriate.

# Procedure

You can change the current runlevel on either a temporary or a permanent basis. Temporary changes remain in effect until you reboot the computer or manually change the runlevel again. Permanent changes take effect the next time you reboot the computer or when you type a command to explicitly enable them. Although the predefined runlevels that ship with most Linux distributions are good starting points, you may need to change what services are provided by one or more runlevels for various reasons. For instance, you might need to add a server to your default runlevel if you want the server to run by default, or remove a server from a runlevel if you don't want it to run or if you intend to run it from a super server. (Phase 6 describes super server configuration.)

## Temporarily Changing the Runlevel

To change the runlevel on a one-time basis, you use the `telinit` command:

```
# telinit 3
```

On most systems, this command shuts down X. Be sure you don't have any X programs running with unsaved data before you type this command!

This command shifts the system into runlevel 3, where it remains until you enter another `telinit` command or reboot the computer. Most Linux systems run in runlevel 3 or 5, but others are available; Table 3.1 summarizes their purposes on most systems. Some runlevels have conventional purposes across distributions, but other runlevels have distribution- or system-specific functions.

**TABLE 3.1**     Linux Runlevels and their Functions

| Runlevel Number | Purpose |
| --- | --- |
| 0 | Shuts down the computer |
| 1 | Single user mode |
| 2 | Multi-user mode without Network File System (NFS) support or X |
| 3 | Multi-user mode with NFS support but without X |
| 4 | User-defined |
| 5 | Multi-user mode with NFS support and X |
| 6 | Reboots the computer |

Do not use `telinit` to change to runlevels 0 or 6 unless you intend to shut down or reboot the computer. For these purposes, most administrators prefer to use the shutdown command, as in **shutdown -h now** to shut down or **shutdown -r now** to reboot.

You can switch to runlevel 1 by passing 1 or S as the runlevel number. This runlevel is useful for performing certain types of low-level maintenance and recovery tasks that might be difficult or impossible with regular multiuser services running. For instance, you're more likely to be able to unmount filesystems for checking, repair, and other changes from single-user mode than from multi-user mode.

## Permanently Changing the Runlevel

When the Linux kernel boots, it launches the `init` program, which is in charge of handling startup tasks. This program has a PID number of 1 and is at the root of the process tree—all other processes are started by `init`, either directly or indirectly. To control `init`, you edit its configuration file, `/etc/inittab`. This file specifies the default runlevel and provides other options that enable you to control the system startup process.

The `telinit` command is normally a symbolic link to `init`. On most systems, you can use `init` instead of `telinit` to change runlevels, although `telinit` is the preferred name for this function.

To change the runlevel, one line in /etc/inittab is important:

```
id:5:initdefault:
```

This line, like others in /etc/inittab, is a colon-delimited set of options. The id and initdefault options identify this line as specifying the default runlevel, and the number in the field between these two options denotes the default runlevel. Thus, to permanently change a system to use runlevel 3 rather than runlevel 5 when it boots, you must edit this line and change 5 to 3. Making this change will have no immediate effect, although you can implement any changes by typing **telinit Q** or **telinit q**.

The /etc/inittab file holds various other options, including those that launch programs that present text-mode login prompts (getty, mingetty, or similar programs). Some distributions include a line that launches the GUI login prompt:

```
x:5:once:/etc/X11/prefdm -nodaemon
```

This line launches the prefdm program, which chooses which of several X Display Manager Control Protocol (XDMCP) programs to use depending on settings in other configuration files. You shouldn't need to adjust this option unless you want to disable X or change the way it works in runlevel 5. Not all distributions use this method to start X in runlevel 5, though; some use startup scripts, such as those described next, to do the job. These scripts are active only in runlevel 5.

## Changing the Services in a Runlevel

Changing runlevels enables you to switch between sets of standard running servers and other programs; however, most systems support just a limited number of runlevels, so if your desired set of services isn't specified in any runlevel, changing runlevels alone won't let you select the services you want. To do this, you'll need to edit the runlevels in another way.

Linux uses a variant of the Unix System V (or *SysV*) initialization (or *init* for short) script system. As implemented in Linux, SysV init scripts, or links to them, are stored in a series of directories named after the runlevels they control. Typical locations include /etc/rc.d/ rc?.d, /etc/init.d/rc?.d, and /etc/rc?.d, where *?* is a runlevel number. Some distributions provide symbolic links so that you can use two or more paths to reach these directories.

Within each runlevel directory, init scripts have names of the form *A##name*, where *A* is either S or K, *##* is a two-digit number, and *name* is the name of the service (typically it's the name of the script to which a symbolic link in the runlevel directory points). Programs that control the process pass start or stop options to the init scripts depending on the lead letter of the filename: S to start or K (for *kill*) to stop the service.

Thus, in principle the task of managing the services that run in a given runlevel boils down to changing the filenames of the init script symbolic links in the runlevel directories: Change the lead S to a K to stop a service or vice versa to start it. Unfortunately, in practice it's a bit more complex than this because of service dependencies—some services depend on another already being running before they can be started. That's where the numbers come in; they denote the sequence in which services are started and stopped. Unfortunately, there's no standardization across distributions in terms of the SysV startup script sequence numbers, so manually editing them is inadvisable unless you're intimately familiar with your distribution's startup script sequence. Fortunately, tools to do the job exist, although the precise tools you'll find vary from one distribution to another:

**chkconfig**   This command-line utility is most common on Red Hat and related distributions; some don't include it. Pass it the --list parameter to see a summary of services and whether or not they're enabled in each runlevel. You can add or delete a service in a given runlevel by using the --level parameter, as in **chkconfig --level 5 smb on**, which enables Samba in runlevel 5. (Pass it off rather than on to disable a service.)

**rc-update**   This tool is Gentoo's equivalent of chkconfig. To add a script to a runlevel, type **rc-update add *script runlevels***, where *script* is the name of the SysV startup script and *runlevels* is one or more runlevel names. Replace add with del to remove a script from a runlevel. For instance, typing **rc-update add samba default** adds the samba startup script to the default runlevel, causing Samba to run when the system boots.

 As mentioned earlier, Gentoo uses named runlevels rather than numbered runlevels for most purposes.

**ntsysv**   This is a text-mode utility that, like chkconfig, is most common on Red Hat and related distributions. It presents a menu of services run at the runlevel specified with the --level parameter. You can enable or disable a service by moving the cursor to the runlevel and pressing the spacebar.

**ksysv**   This GUI tool supports enabling or disabling services in any runlevel from 1 through 6. Locate and select the service in the Start or Stop section of the given runlevel, right-click the entry, and then select Cut from the pop-up menu. This removes its start or stop entry. You can then drag the service from the Available Services list to the runlevel's Start or Stop list. The system will create an entry in that runlevel and give it a sequence number based on the location to which you dropped it.

**Distribution-specific tools**   Many distributions' general system administration tools, such as Red Hat's Service Configuration tool and SuSE's YaST, provide the means to start and stop SysV services in specific runlevels. Details vary from one distribution to another, so consult your distribution's documentation to learn more.

All of these tools except ksysv handle changes to the SysV sequence numbers automatically, so you shouldn't need to worry about that detail. Changes made with these tools (or by manually editing the runlevel scripts) won't take effect immediately; they'll occur only when you switch into or out of the relevant runlevel or when you reboot the computer. If you want to start or stop a service immediately, you can do so by locating the startup script (either the script itself or a link in a runlevel directory) and pass it the start or stop option. For instance, if you want to stop the sendmail server, on most systems you'd type something like this:

```
# /etc/init.d/sendmail stop
```

Unless your system is already functioning as a mail server computer, temporarily stopping (and subsequently restarting) the mail server should pose no problems. The precise location of the `sendmail` script varies from one distribution to another, and in fact the scripts to start a single service might have different names on different systems. For instance, some systems start Samba with a script called `samba`, others use `smb`, and still others use separate `smb` and `nmb` scripts. Sometimes alternative servers exist to fill the same role; for instance, some distributions use Postfix or Exim rather than sendmail to handle mail delivery, and their SysV startup scripts are likely to reflect this fact. Thus, you may need to do some digging to find the correct startup script.

In addition to starting (with `start`) and stopping (with `stop`) services, most SysV startup scripts include options to perform additional actions. The most common of these is `restart`, which typically calls the `stop` and `start` actions in sequence, resulting in a restart of the service. This can be handy if you've made changes to configuration files and want to implement them; however, restarting a service can be disruptive, since it can disconnect remote users or otherwise interrupt ongoing work. Sometimes a `reload` action will cause programs to re-examine their configuration files and implement changes without causing much disruption.

## Criteria for Completion

To complete this task, you should have changed your system's runlevel on a temporary basis by using `telinit`; changed it permanently by editing `/etc/inittab`; used `chkconfig`, `ntsysv`, or similar tools to change services that are automatically started in a runlevel; and used SysV startup scripts to temporarily start, stop, or restart services. Mastering these commands will enable you to control what software your system runs when it boots, as well as change what servers and other background services your system provides without rebooting it.

# Task 3.8: Schedule Jobs to Run in the Future

Sometimes routine tasks need to be performed at specific times in the future or even at regular intervals in the future. For instance, Linux maintains log files in the `/var/log` directory. Left unchecked, these files will grow to enormous size and eventually fill your hard disk. To prevent this from happening, all Linux distributions run a program that temporarily suspends logging; deletes, renames, or compresses existing log files; and then resumes logging. The result is that log files don't overrun the system. To do this, though, Linux uses a utility, known as `cron`, that runs programs at specified times in the future. You can create your own `cron` jobs to do the same. In fact, you can create both system `cron` jobs and user `cron` jobs; the former usually run as `root` and perform system maintenance, whereas the latter run as an ordinary user to perform tasks for that user. (You can create user `cron` jobs as `root` or run system `cron` jobs as a non-`root` user, though.) An additional tool for running programs in the future is `at`; this utility runs a program on a one-time basis in the future. You might use it to schedule a CPU-intensive job to run in off hours, to remind yourself of something you've got to do at a particular time, or for various other reasons.

# Scenario

You have need to perform three tasks on an automated basis in the future. First, you want to have your system automatically check the CPU load average once an hour during business hours and email the results to you so that you can monitor the system's performance over time. Second, you want the system to automatically use the Advanced Package Tools (APT) to check for (but not automatically install) new packages for your distribution on a daily basis, again emailing the results to your account. Finally, you want the computer to email you a reminder about a dentist's appointment next week.

# Scope of Task

This task involves using both `cron` and `at` to schedule jobs to run in the future. System and user `cron` jobs are very similar to each other, but `at` is used in an entirely different way.

## Duration

This task should take half an hour to an hour to complete. Once you know the techniques, you can modify or create new `cron` jobs in a minute or two, although in practice you might need to write scripts to handle certain tasks, and this can take anywhere from a few seconds to several hours, depending on the complexity of the scripts. You can schedule a single task to run in the future with `at` in a matter of a minute or less, although once again, if you need to write a support script, this can extend the time requirements.

## Setup

You need a working Linux system to complete this task. The scenario specifies using APT, so you'll need a Debian system or a non-Debian system with APT installed; however, you can substitute Yum or other network package utilities for APT if necessary. Most of this task can be performed as an ordinary user, but the second part requires `root` privileges. You might also need `root` access to configure the system to permit ordinary users to use `cron` or `at`.

## Caveats

Whether you run them as an ordinary user or as `root`, `cron` and `at` jobs pose a special risk because if you make a mistake in setting them up, they can wreak havoc unattended. For user `cron` jobs, the potential for havoc is limited to things like filling up certain disk partitions with useless files or consuming inordinate amounts of CPU time. A misconfigured system `cron` job is potentially more damaging, though. For this reason, you should always test scripts you intend to run from `cron` manually before running them unattended. If possible, you should also monitor the first automatic run of `cron` jobs so that you can step in if something seems to be going wrong.

# Procedure

Performing this task requires creating two `cron` jobs and one `at` job. The procedures for the two `cron` jobs are similar, but the `at` job requires using different tools and techniques.

## Creating User *cron* Jobs

The cron (or crond on some systems) utility runs continuously in the background on most Linux systems, having been started by a SysV startup script. (Try using ps to locate cron, and check for its SysV startup script.) Once a minute, cron looks for the presence of user *crontab files*, which are usually stored in /var/spool/cron/crontabs or /var/spool/cron/tabs. (System crontab files also exist but are stored elsewhere, as described later.) Rather than directly editing user crontab files, the usual procedure is to use the crontab utility to install them. To begin, though, you should check for the presence of an existing user crontab file:

```
$ crontab -l
```

This command uses a lowercase -L as an option, not a number -1.

If you have no user crontab file, the utility replies no crontab for *user*, where *user* is your username. If you've already got a crontab file, the utility displays it. In that case, you can edit it by typing **crontab -e**, which loads your crontab file into the editor specified by the $EDITOR or $VISUAL environment variable. Alternatively, you can create a new crontab file or edit a copy you've already got and install it as described shortly. If you want to delete your crontab file, type **crontab -r**.

The superuser may examine any user's crontab file by using the -u *username* option, as in **crontab -u sally -l** to examine sally's crontab file. This same technique can be used to edit or delete a user's crontab file.

Listing 3.1 shows a crontab file that achieves the goal specified in the Scenario section: Create this file in your home directory under any name that you like (perhaps my-crontab). It runs uptime once an hour and emails the result to the username sally. (You should change all three instances of sally to your own username, of course.) The file consists of a number of variable specifications (for SHELL, PATH, and so on). These aren't always necessary, and you can add more if they would be helpful. The MAILTO variable specifies the user who's to receive a report of activity, including any output produced by the commands that cron runs. It's not actually used in this example, but I've included it because it's a common sight in crontab files. Likewise, the HOME variable isn't strictly required in this example but is typically included in crontab files.

**Listing 3.1:** Sample User Crontab File

```
SHELL=/bin/bash
PATH=/sbin:/bin:/usr/sbin:/usr/bin
MAILTO=sally
HOME=/home/sally

0 8-17 * * 1-5 uptime | mail -s "uptime report" sally
```

The final line of Listing 3.1 specifies the commands that are to be run and the times at which this should occur. This line begins with five fields that specify the time. The fields are, in order, the minute (0–59), the hour (0–23), the day of the month (1–31), the month (1–12), and the day of the week (0–7; both 0 and 7 correspond to Sunday). For the month and day of the week values, you can use the first three letters of the name rather than a number if you like. In Listing 3.1, the command is to run Monday through Friday (`1-5` in the final time field) on the hour (0 in the first time field) from 8:00 AM through 5:00 PM (`8-17` in the second time field). The asterisks in the day of the month and month time fields indicate that the `cron` job should run in every month and every day of the month, except when other restrictions exist (such as in the day of the week field).

The actual command to be run follows the time specification. In this case, it's the `uptime` command, which is piped through `mail`, which is a simple text-mode mail utility. The `-s` option to `mail` specifies a subject line, and a username follows this.

> Omitting the pipe character ( | ) and the entire `mail` command would work for this task since `cron` would email the output of the `uptime` command to the user specified by the `MAILTO` variable, but the email with the `uptime` output would lack a Subject: header.

You may find that you want to specify the times at which `cron` jobs run in various ways. For instance, you might want to run a `cron` job every other hour or twice a day. You can specify multiple values in several ways:

- An asterisk (`*`) matches all possible values.

- A list separated by commas (such as `0,6,12,18`) matches any of the specified values.

- Two values separated by a dash (`-`) indicate a range, inclusive of the end points. For instance, `8-17` in the hour field specifies a time of from 8:00 AM to 5:00 PM.

- A slash, when used in conjunction with some other multi-value option, specifies stepped values—a range in which some members are skipped. For instance, `*/10` in the minute field indicates a job that's run every 10 minutes.

With this information in hand, you should be able to create your own `cron` jobs. You're not restricted to using system utilities such as `uptime`, either—you can create your own custom scripts to perform complex actions. You can create a single crontab file with multiple `cron` jobs, one per line. Once you type in Listing 3.1 and save it, you can enter it as your user crontab file by passing it to the `crontab` command:

```
$ crontab my-crontab
```

Once it's installed, you can wait until the hour rolls around to be sure that it's working as expected—check your email inbox to see if a message with uptime output appears.

> For testing purposes, try entering a value in the minute time field that's just a minute or two in the future. (Change the hour and day-of-week fields, too, if you're doing this test outside of the range shown in Listing 3.1.) This way you won't have to wait until the hour ends to see if your `cron` job is working as you expect.

Access to user `cron` jobs may be restricted in various ways:

- The `crontab` or `cron` executable programs may have permissions that prevent certain users from using these programs.

- The `/etc/cron.allow` file may contain names of users who may use the facility, with all others being denied access.

- The `/etc/cron.deny` file may contain names of users who may not use the facility, with all others being granted access.

If none of these access control mechanisms is in use, any user with login (shell) access may create user `cron` jobs.

## Creating System *cron* Jobs

System `cron` jobs are just like user `cron` jobs, but with a couple of important exceptions:

- System `cron` jobs are specified in `/etc/crontab`. This file typically tells `cron` to run all the scripts in the `/etc/cron.hourly`, `/etc/cron.daily`, `/etc/cron.weekly`, and `/etc/cron.monthly` directories at the specified intervals.

- The `/etc/crontab` file is just like a user crontab file, with one exception: A username specification appears between the time specification and the command. When `cron` runs the job, it runs it as the specified user.

The easiest way to create a system `cron` job is to drop a script to do the task into an appropriate `/etc/cron.`*`interval`* directory. For instance, to update your APT package listing once every day, you could put a file with the contents of Listing 3.2 in your `/etc/cron.daily` directory. Be sure the script is executable! If you do this, the script will execute on a daily basis at whatever time `/etc/crontab` specifies for its daily system `cron` jobs. (This time varies from one distribution to another.)

**Listing 3.2:** Sample Script to Update Your APT Database

```
#!/bin/bash
(apt-get update ; apt-get -s upgrade) | mail -s "APT update" sally
```

If your system doesn't use APT, you can substitute another command, such as yum check-update, for the two apt-get commands in parentheses in Listing 3.2. Note that APT requires two commands to retrieve the updated package listing and check it for new packages, whereas yum takes just one command to do this job.

If the default system `cron` jobs don't run at times that are convenient for you or if you want to run a system `cron` job as a non-`root` user, you can edit the `/etc/crontab` file. Treat it just like a user crontab file, except that you *must* include a username between the time specification and the command that's to be run. Alternatively, you could create a user `cron` job; even `root` can have user `cron` jobs, and you can use the `root` account to create user `cron` jobs even for accounts that lack login access, such as accounts that exist for the benefit of servers.

## Running a Single Future Job

Sometimes cron is overkill. You might simply want to run a single command at a specific point in the future on a one-time basis rather than on an ongoing basis. For this task, Linux provides another command: at. In ordinary use, this command takes a single option: a time. (Options to fine-tune at's behavior are also available.) The program then prompts you to enter commands that it will execute at the specified time. When you're done entering commands, press Ctrl+D to terminate input. Alternatively, you can pass a file with commands by using the -f parameter to at, as in **at -f commands.txt noon** to use the contents of commands.txt as the commands you want to run at noon.

The scenario requires that you email yourself a reminder about a dentist's appointment. If that appointment is seven days and a few hours in the future, you might do the job like this:

```
$ at now + 7 days
warning: commands will be executed using /bin/sh
at> echo "Dentist's appointment at 3:00" | mail -s "Reminder" sally
```

This sequence will cause an email message with a subject of "Reminder" and the specified text to be emailed to the sally account in precisely seven days. If specifying the time in precisely this way is inconvenient or impossible, you can use any of several other ways:

**Time of day**    You can specify the time of day as *HH:MM*, optionally followed by AM or PM if you use a 12-hour format. If the specified time has already passed, the operation is scheduled for the next day at that time.

**noon, midnight, or teatime**    These three keywords stand for what you'd expect (teatime is 4:00 PM).

**Day specification**    To schedule an at job more than 24 hours in advance, you must add a day specification after the time of day specification. This can be done in numeric form, using the formats *MMDDYY*, *MM/DD/YY*, or *DD.MM.YY*. Alternatively, you can specify the date as *month-name day* or *month-name day year*.

**A specified period in the future**    You can specify a time using the keyword now, a plus sign (+), and a time period, as in now + 2 hours to run a job in 2 hours.

The at command has several support tools. The most important of these is atd, the at daemon. This program must be running for at to do its work. Check for its presence using ps. If it's not running, look for a SysV startup script and ensure that it's enabled, as described Task 3.7, "Manage Runlevels."

Other at support programs include atq, which lists pending at jobs; atrm, which removes an at job from the queue; and batch, which works much like at but executes jobs when the system load level drops below 0.8. These utilities are all fairly simple. To use **atq**, simply type its name. (The program does support a couple of options, but chances are you won't need them; consult atq's man page for details.) To use atrm, type the program name and the number of the at job, as returned by atq. For instance, you might type **atrm 12** to remove at job number 12.

The at facility supports access restrictions similar to those of cron. Specifically, the /etc/at.allow and /etc/at.deny files work analogously to the /etc/cron.allow and /etc/cron.deny files. There are a few wrinkles with at, though. Specifically, if neither at.allow nor at.deny exists, only root may use at. If at.allow exists, the users it lists are granted access to at; if at.deny exists, everybody *except* those mentioned in this file is granted access to at. This differs from cron, in which everybody is granted access if neither access-control file is present. This tighter default security on at means that the program is seldom installed with restrictive execute permissions, but of course you could use program file permissions to deny ordinary users the ability to run at if you want an extra layer of security.

## Criteria for Completion

To complete this task, you must have created a user cron job, a system cron job, and an at job. The user cron job should use uptime to deliver a report of the system load to your user account on an hourly basis during business hours. The system cron job should update your APT (or other package management) database and issue a report on available updated packages. The at job should deliver a reminder of a dentist's appointment you've scheduled in a week. Each of these methods of scheduling jobs to run in the future is very useful in helping to maintain your system and for performing other tasks.

# Phase

# 4

# Documenting the System

Your ability to use, maintain, and improve a Linux computer is only as good as your knowledge of that computer. For this reason, you should take care to document the system's operation. Part of this task involves keeping records yourself, such as information on major configuration options you've set. You should also keep data on the system's baseline performance so that you can know whether, for instance, your hard disk speed has really dropped or whether it's just your imagination. The computer maintains log files of its own, and knowing how to configure and use them is as important as creating and maintaining your own documentation. In addition to system-specific forms of documentation, more generic Linux documentation is available and can be helpful. This includes system documentation tools such as man and info pages, as well as online resources. Knowing how to use these tools will help you manage your Linux computer.

This task maps to portions of the CompTIA Linux+ objective 5 and to portions of the LPIC objectives 108 and 111.

# Task 4.1: Maintain a System Log Book

A system log book is a physical paper book in which you record notes about your computer. You should begin the system log book when you first install Linux; that way, you can record the name and version number of the Linux distribution you install along with the installation options you select. As you maintain, upgrade, and otherwise modify the system, you can write about your changes in the log book. This will give you an invaluable record in case of problems or when you need a reminder about how something is configured.

## Scenario

To improve system documentation, you want to start a system log book for the Linux computer you're managing. Ideally, you should do this when you install Linux on the computer, but if Linux is already pre-installed, you can still begin a log book, record what you know, and keep it updated as time goes on.

## Scope of Task

Unlike most tasks in this book, this one is open-ended. The point of a log book is to record changes as they occur, so you'll pull it out and add to it whenever you make important changes to your system.

### Duration

Starting a log book and recording the basic information you need for it will take about half an hour or an hour. Because this is an ongoing task, though, it's never really completed. Every time you make a major change to your system, you should take a few seconds to record details in your log book.

### Setup

Obtain a suitable book for use as a log book. It can be a spiral-bound notebook, a lab book, a three-ring binder, a legal notepad, or whatever other type of book you find convenient. A three-ring binder has the advantage that you can insert printouts in it, but you can staple or otherwise attach printouts to other types of log books.

 A system log book should be recorded on a physical medium such as paper, not on a disk file. Part of the purpose of a log book is to aid in disaster recovery, when disk files will be inaccessible.

Most of the information you record in your notebook requires root access to obtain, so when you begin the notebook, you should log in and acquire root access.

### Caveats

Writing on paper obviously poses no risks to your Linux installation, so maintaining a log book is a fairly low-risk endeavor. There are a couple of caveats, though. First, you should not record any extremely sensitive data in the log book, such as the root password or (if you use one) your Basic Input/Output System (BIOS) password. Second, if you type any extra commands as root to obtain information or printouts for the log book, the usual risks of running any command as root apply.

## Procedure

To perform this task, you must decide what sorts of entries belong in your log book. The key is to determine what sorts of information is likely to be useful as log book entries in the future. Remember that actually locating information in a log book will become important; you don't want to record too much information or the important parts may become difficult to find.

## Starting the Log Book

You should begin the log book with basic identifying information on the computer—where it was bought, where it resides, what hardware it includes, and so on. You may be able to use some of the hardware identification commands described in Phase 2, "Managing Hardware and the Kernel," to fill in some of this information.

You should also include basic software information, such as the Linux distribution you've installed, the kernel you're running (including whether it's a kernel delivered with the distribution or one you compiled yourself), and any important nonstandard software packages you've installed (such as commercial programs or programs developed in-house).

One type of hardware and software information that may become vital is partition information. You may want to print the output of the partition tables for your hard disks, as revealed by **fdisk -l /dev/hda** and similar commands for other disks, and include those printouts in the log book. Writing the mount points for these partitions next to their printout entries can be a handy addition. This information can become critical if your partition table is ever overwritten; if you're lucky, you can re-create your existing partition tables based on the printouts.

You may want to include notes about intended uses for the machine, perhaps including descriptions of particular files and directories. For instance, you might make a note of the fact that /var/html contains the Web pages served by a Web server computer. Likewise, the fact that the computer uses Apache to serve these Web pages may be a useful addition. Such information may be very well known to you, but if somebody else needs to administer the computer, its presence in the log book could be useful.

Ask yourself if information you record might be helpful in recovering the system in an emergency situation. This could be an attempt to recover an existing system (such as restoring an accidentally wiped partition table) or an attempt to re-create the system from scratch (such as installing Linux from scratch on a new computer if the original was stolen). If information would be helpful, record it. If not, omit it.

## Adding Log Book Entries

As you administer the system, you should add log book entries. You don't need to record every trivial thing you do, but you should record information that affects how the computer works in a basic way. For instance, you should probably mention alterations to configuration files, security-related software upgrades, and changes to the hardware installed in the computer.

Rather than record line-by-line changes to configuration files, back up your configuration files to a convenient medium, such as a Zip disk or CD-R. You should have no problem backing up the entire /etc directory tree to such media. You can store this configuration backup with your log book so that you can access it easily if the need arises.

## Using the Log Books

System log books can be helpful in various situations. Some of these are emergency situations, but others involve more mundane and routine operations:

**Disaster recovery**    Most dramatically, if your system is damaged in some way, the log book can be invaluable for learning how it was configured before it was damaged. This can help you bring the system back to a working state by reproducing partition tables, directory layouts, installed software sets, major configuration options, and so on. Of course, proper backups (described in Phase 3) are even more important for disaster recovery, but sometimes log book data can enable you to recover more quickly than restoring a backup would require or can help you determine how to recover the backup (such as how large to make various partitions).

**System checks**    Log books can help you verify that your system is (or is not) working correctly. Recording benchmarks, such as those described in Task 4.2, "Monitor System Performance," in a log book will enable you to spot when your system begins operating sluggishly. You can also verify that the correct packages are installed. Keeping backups of configuration files can help you spot accidental or malicious changes to those files.

**System reproduction**    Sometimes it's desirable to reproduce a system without copying it file-by-file. For instance, you might want to give workstations to new employees and configure them in the way that existing workstations are configured. A system log book will help you in this task.

**Personnel training**    When new administrators are hired, system log books can help them become familiar with existing systems and administrative policies.

## Criteria for Completion

To complete this task, you should create a system log book for your Linux computer. Be sure it includes basic identifying information and major system options. Keeping a disk with the /etc directory tree on it with the log book is also helpful. In a real-world situation, the log book will never be complete; it will change as the system changes.

# Task 4.2: Monitor System Performance

"The computer is slow!" This complaint is a common one in offices and computer centers around the world. Frequently, users aren't more specific than this, so it becomes your job to figure out precisely where the bottleneck exists—does the computer have too little RAM, are runaway processes sapping CPU speed, has the disk kicked itself into a low-performance mode, or is something else wrong? Keeping track of basic system benchmarks will help you quickly identify the cause of problems when they occur.

## Scenario

To help you identify problems in the future, you want to record baseline information on your system's overall performance. You also want to set up a procedure to perform similar tests on a regular basis so you can track system performance and, perhaps, spot trends that might lead to trouble down the road if left uncorrected.

## Scope of Task

This task involves running several benchmark programs and system information utilities and recording the results in your system log book. You'll also need to set up a procedure to help you run these tasks on a regular basis in the future.

### Duration

This task should take about half an hour or an hour to complete. Ongoing performance testing will take a few minutes per test, but you can use cron to help automate this task.

### Setup

Some of the commands described in this task can be performed as an ordinary user, but others require root access. Thus, you should log in and acquire root privileges. You should have your system log book, which you prepared in Task 4.1, "Maintain a System Log Book," ready. You may want to print some of these test results rather than copy them by hand, in which case having a working printer will be necessary.

### Caveats

The usual caveats about working as root apply to the commands that require this level of access. Performance tests, although useful, can sometimes be misleading, so you should be alert to results that seem weird—they might indicate a mistyped command or a failure of the utility to produce meaningful results.

## Procedure

To monitor your system performance, you should be prepared to run a number of different types of tests. Broadly speaking, system performance is determined by three types of hardware: your CPU, your memory (RAM), and your disks (particularly your hard disks). After you perform these tests, you should devise a system to help you perform new tests on a regular basis.

### Testing Your CPU

Two factors influence your CPU performance: the overall CPU speed and system load. The CPU's speed is determined by its hardware design and, to a lesser extent, motherboard BIOS settings. Although it's a poor CPU benchmark, the Linux kernel includes a test of CPU speed, which it calls *BogoMIPS*. You can find it by searching for that string in the dmesg output:

```
$ dmesg | grep Bogo
Calibrating delay using timer specific routine.. 4005.24 BogoMIPS (lpj=2002621)
```

If this command produces no results, the relevant line may have scrolled out of the kernel ring buffer. You may be able to find it in a log file, such as /var/log/dmesg, if it exists on your system.

The BogoMIPS value isn't very useful for comparisons from one system to another; it's used mainly in some internal kernel timing loops. Nonetheless, it could clue you in if BIOS options related to CPU performance have been altered, so it's worth looking for this information and recording it in your system log file.

Task 3.5 in Phase 3 included a description of the system load average, which is a measure of how much of your available CPU time is being used by running programs. If your load average, as reported by uptime or top, climbs above 1, this means that programs are demanding more CPU time than your system can provide. Although a load average above 1 is not necessarily a sign of trouble (some systems are supposed to operate with load averages at or above this level), a change in the load average may be cause for concern. Thus, you should record a baseline load average for your system in your system log book—in fact, you should take *several* baseline readings. It's not uncommon for the load average to vary substantially over the course of a day, a week, or even longer periods. (An academic system's load average might spike near the end of the term, for instance.) Understanding these cycles will help you determine whether or not your system's load average is out of line.

For purposes of this task, set aside a page or two in your log book for load averages and record your current load average as the first entry. You will make additional recordings of this data in the future for comparison purposes.

## Testing Your Memory

Memory performance per se doesn't really vary much unless your RAM goes bad, which tends to produce program crashes and other very serious problems. Testing memory therefore focuses on another factor: memory *used*. The free command displays overall memory use:

```
$ free
                total      used       free     shared    buffers     cached
Mem:           512052    485200      26852          0      63388      92680
-/+ buffers/cache:       329132     182920
Swap:         1261560    225724    1035836
```

This output shows the total memory, the amount of that total that's been used, and the amount of the total that's free. (For the moment, ignore the shared, buffers, and cached columns.)

Each line of the output shows the values for a different type of memory. The first line, Mem, shows the RAM use. In this example, 485,200MB of 512,052MB are in use, leaving 25,852MB free. This may seem like a dire situation; however, these numbers include the amount of memory devoted to buffers and caches (that's where the buffers and cached columns come in). Linux uses every last byte of memory it can for disk caches and buffers, which improves disk performance, so the free memory value of the free output is almost always a very low number. The -/+ buffers/cache line shows a more realistic view of the amount of memory that's being used by programs: 329,132MB, leaving 182,920MB available.

The final line of the `free` output, `Swap`, shows swap space use. This is disk space that's treated like memory. When memory demands grow too large, swap space is used to hold currently inactive programs and data, freeing real RAM for active processes. Phase 5, "Managing Partitions and Filesystems," describes creating and activating swap space. The problem with swap space is that it's slow. When your system uses swap space, the whole computer can seem sluggish. To be sure, some swap space use is normal, and the 225,724MB of swap space use shown in the preceding example is not excessive. If your RAM is fully used and the amount of swap space in use on your system is very large, though, this may be a sign that you need to increase the RAM installed in the computer. Alternatively, you can take steps to reduce your RAM demands, such as shutting down running programs that you're not actively using or switching from a memory-intensive desktop environment to a slimmer bare window manager system. (Phase 2 describes some of these options.)

Just as with CPU use, memory use can fluctuate over time. Thus, to truly evaluate memory use, you should monitor it over hours, days, weeks, and perhaps even longer periods. If you notice a spike in memory use, it could be a legitimate normal operation or a sign of something amiss.

To track down the source of a sudden (or slow) increase in memory use, use `top`. Phase 3, "Managing Software," described this utility, with an emphasis on its ability to track CPU use. By typing **M** once `top` is running, you can track the leading users of memory. If your system is running out of memory, you may find that some program is chewing up ridiculous amounts. Shutting down that program may solve the problem, at least temporarily.

Some programs suffer from *memory leaks*, in which memory is allocated but never returned to the available memory pool. When this happens, the program's memory demands grow continuously. A small memory leak in a program that's started and stopped quickly may not be a serious problem, but a bigger memory leak or one in a program that's run for long periods can lead to huge memory demands. Shutting down and restarting the program usually returns memory to the system, but the problem will recur. Notify a program's developers if you think it's got a memory leak that's causing you serious problems.

## Testing Your Disks

Phase 2 described the `hdparm` utility, and in particular its `-t` and `-T` options. This utility, used with these options, tests basic disk input speed:

```
# hdparm -tT /dev/sdb

/dev/sdb:
 Timing cached reads:    2672 MB in  2.00 seconds = 1334.87 MB/sec
 Timing buffered disk reads:  144 MB in  3.02 seconds =   47.66 MB/sec
```

The `Timing cached reads` line reveals disk input from Linux's own cache and so is more of a measure of RAM performance than disk performance. The `Timing buffered disk reads` line, though, is a reasonable low-level measure of disk performance.

Disk performance, at least as measured by `hdparm`, is unlikely to change over time. It could change if you compile a new kernel and you use a different driver or driver options or if the new kernel's driver includes changes that affect performance. Disk performance can also vary with configuration changes made with `hdparm`'s performance-tuning options, as described in Phase 2. Such changes could be incorporated in updated system startup scripts provided in a package update. Thus, you might want to record a baseline for disk performance and check your performance whenever you upgrade your kernel or key boot files. (Boot file changes will only show their effects after a reboot, though.)

Another disk performance issue relates to disk capacity. The `df` command displays information on how much disk space is available in each of the computer's mounted partitions:

```
$ df
Filesystem         1K-blocks     Used Available Use% Mounted on
/dev/sdb6             977180   362972    614208  38% /
udev                  256024      188    255836   1% /dev
/dev/mapper/usr      6291260  4814944   1476316  77% /usr
/dev/mapper/var      2097084   163504   1933580   8% /var
/dev/mapper/home    17825244 11687504   6137740  66% /home
/dev/hda6             101089    35111     61803  37% /boot
```

Pay particular attention to the `Use%` column of this output; this reveals how much of the space on a disk is in use, expressed as a percentage. As a general rule, if used disk space climbs above 80 percent, you should consider cleaning unnecessary files from that partition, increasing the size of the partition, or adding a new hard disk and moving some or all of that partition's files to it.

## Performing Ongoing Tests

How you test your system's performance over time depends on your own needs, abilities, and preferences. If the system isn't a mission-critical computer, you might just perform manual tests every now and then, or perhaps only if you suspect problems. This approach might be reasonable for a Linux computer you run only as an X terminal, for instance.

A more complex monitoring system might use `cron` to run a script that automatically calls some performance-testing commands. Listing 4.1 shows an example of such a script. If you type this script into a file and run it, you'll see that it simply prints the output of each command. To actually use the script in Listing 4.1 for performance monitoring, you might create a `cron` job to run it at a regular time—perhaps every hour or two. You could email the output of the script to yourself or redirect it to a log file—say, `/var/log/performance`. If you do the latter, though, you should take care to delete it occasionally. In fact, you could create another `cron` job to do this task as well. The two `cron` jobs together might look something like Listing 4.2, which is for a user `cron` job, although it would have to be run as `root` to create a file in the `/var/log` directory. Listing 4.2

would run the monitoring script (called `/usr/local/bin/perftest`) every half hour, appending the results to `/var/log/performance`. On the first of each month at 3:20 AM, the second entry in Listing 4.2 renames this file to `/var/log/performance.old`, overwriting any existing file by that name. A more elegant approach would be to add the file to your system's log rotation queue, which is usually handled by a program called `logrotate`, as described in Task 4.3.

**Listing 4.1:** A Script to Run a Series of System Health Tests

```
#!/bin/bash
echo ""
echo "System performance test for " `date`
echo ""

echo "CPU load test:"
uptime
echo ""

echo "Memory test:"
free
echo ""

echo "Disk space test:"
df
echo ""

echo "End of test"
echo "---------------------------"
```

**Listing 4.2:** A cron Job to Run a System-Monitoring Script

```
SHELL=/bin/bash
PATH=/sbin:/bin:/usr/sbin:/usr/bin
MAILTO=steve

30 * * * * /usr/local/bin/perftest >> /var/log/performance
20 3 1 * * mv -f /var/log/performance /var/log/performance.old
```

Listings 4.1 and 4.2 provide a fairly crude way to monitor your system's performance. Gleaning specific information from the log file requires scrolling through it to search for the desired data. You can create more sophisticated scripts, if you like. Perhaps you could extract the data that interests you and summarize it in columns or even convert this summary to graphical form. Such a sophisticated tool can be convenient to use, but it will require considerably more work to design and implement. If you want to give it a try, you can start with Listing 4.1, but you should review Phase 1's coverage of scripting and read the man pages for grep and cut. These two commands will enable you to extract any data you like from the system summary commands; you can then recombine your extracted data into convenient columns.

## Criteria for Completion

To complete this task, you should have obtained baseline performance data on your CPU load average, free memory, disk speed, and disk free space. With this information recorded in your system log book, you can begin planning how to monitor such data over the long term. Such monitoring will enable you to spot trouble before it occurs.

# Task 4.3: Use System Log Files

You're not the only one who should be creating logs concerning system activities: Your computer should, too. Linux systems run a *log daemon* or *system logger*, which is a tool that copies messages from other processes (mostly servers, but also the kernel and occasionally non-server processes) to log files. These log files typically reside in the /var/log directory. Log file street smarts entails the ability to do three things with log files: configure the log daemon to log data in appropriate files, rotate the log files so they don't fill your hard disk, and interpret the data found in your log files.

## Scenario

You need to make several changes to your system's logging facility. Specifically, you want to display emergency log entries on the consoles of logged-in users, log all kernel activities to the /var/log/kernel file, and send non-trivial kernel events to a second system (logger.pangaea.edu). You also want to modify your system's log rotation schedule to keep old compressed log files for longer than it currently does and to rotate the /var/log/kernel file. Once these tasks are completed, you need to examine current log files to check on your mail server's activities over the past day or so because several messages that should have arrived on the system have not appeared in users' inboxes.

## Scope of Task

This task involves three distinct subtasks, each of which is fairly complex in and of itself: modifying system logging, modifying log file rotation, and examining current log files.

### Duration

This task should take about an hour to complete. Once you're familiar with the procedures involved, you can perform individual log file tasks in considerably less time. Examining log files is particularly speedy, although if you need to trace activity over time, you can spend hours perusing log files.

## Setup

This task requires no special setup. You need `root` access to your computer, though. To redirect logging to another system, you need working network access and the other computer must be configured to accept system logs from remote computers.

## Caveats

As usual, working as `root` is potentially risky. For security reasons, most log files can only be read by `root`, so you need `root` access even if you don't intend to change your configuration. Misconfiguring your log files can result in system logs disappearing or being sent to inappropriate files or remote systems.

# Procedure

Before actually configuring your system logging options, you should know a bit about the programs that manage it—particularly `syslogd` and related tools. With the basics under your belt, you can adjust the syslog configuration files as well as the files that manage log file rotation. You can examine log files using tools with which you're already familiar, such as `grep` and `less`, although a few twists are particularly handy when studying log files.

### Understanding *syslogd*

The traditional Linux system logger is `syslogd`, which is often installed from a package called `sysklogd`. The `syslogd` daemon handles messages from servers and other user-mode programs. It's usually paired with a daemon called `klogd`, which is usually installed from the same `sysklogd` package as `syslogd`. The `klogd` daemon manages logging of kernel messages.

 Other choices for system loggers exist. For instance, `syslog-ng` is a replacement that supports advanced filtering options, and `metalog` is another option. This chapter describes the traditional `syslogd` logger. Others are similar in principle, and even in some specific features, but differ in many details.

The basic idea behind a system logger is to provide a unified means of handling log files. The daemon runs in the background and accepts data delivered from servers and other programs that are configured to use it. The daemon can then use information provided by the server to classify the message and direct it to an appropriate log file. This configuration enables you to consolidate messages from various servers in a handful of standard log files, which can be much easier to use and manage than potentially dozens of log files from the various servers running on the system.

In order to work, of course, the log daemon must be configured. In the case of `syslogd`, this is done through the `/etc/syslog.conf` file. The next section describes this file's format in more detail.

## Setting Logging Options

The format of the /etc/syslog.conf file is conceptually simple but provides a great deal of power. Comment lines, as in many Linux configuration files, are denoted by hash marks (#). Noncomment lines take the following form:

```
facility.priority    action
```

In this line, the *facility* is a code word for the type of program or tool that has generated the message to be logged; the *priority* is a code word for the importance of this message; and the *action* is a file, remote computer, or other location that's to accept the message. The *facility* and *priority* are often referred to collectively as the *selector*.

Valid codes for the *facility* are auth, authpriv, cron, daemon, kern, lpr, mail, mark, news, security, syslog, user, uucp, and local0 through local7. Many of these names refer to specific servers or program classes. For instance, mail servers and other mail-processing tools typically log using the mail facility. Most servers that aren't covered by more specific codes use the daemon facility. The security facility is identical to auth, but auth is the preferred name. The mark facility is reserved for internal use. An asterisk (*) refers to all facilities. You can specify multiple facilities in one selector by separating the facilities with commas (,).

Valid codes for the *priority* are debug, info, notice, warning, warn, error, err, crit, alert, emerg, and panic. The warning priority is identical to warn, error is identical to err, and emerg is identical to panic. The error, warn, and panic priority names are deprecated; you should use their equivalents instead. Other than these identical pairs, these priorities represent ascending levels of importance. The debug level logs the most information; it's intended, as the name implies, for debugging programs that are misbehaving. The emerg priority logs the most important messages, which indicate very serious problems.

When a program sends a message to the system logger, it includes a facility code and a priority code; the logger logs the message to a file if you've configured it to log messages with the specified combination. Ordinarily, the system logs messages that arrive with the specified *priority* or higher. Thus, if you specify a *priority* code of alert, the system will log messages that are classified as alert or emerg but not messages of crit or below. An exception to this rule is if you precede the priority code by an equal sign (=), as in =crit, which describes what to do with messages of crit priority *only*. An exclamation mark (!) reverses the meaning of a match. For instance, !crit causes messages *below* crit priority to be logged. A *priority* of * refers to all priorities.

You can specify multiple selectors for a single action by separating the selectors by a semicolon (;). Note that commas are used to separate multiple facilities within a single selector, whereas semicolons are used to separate multiple selectors as a whole. Examples of complete selectors appear shortly.

Most commonly, the *action* is a filename, typically of a file in the /var/log directory tree. Other possibilities include a device filename for a console (such as /dev/console) to display data on the screen, a remote machine name preceded by an at sign (@), and a list of usernames of individuals who should see the message if they're logged in. For the last of these options, an asterisk (*) means all logged-in users.

The Scenario, presented earlier, specifies that emergency log events should be displayed to all currently logged-in users and that kernel messages should be logged in `/var/log/kernel` and non-trivial kernel events should be sent to a second system (`logger.pangaea.edu`). To begin with the first requirement, you should create this entry in `/etc/syslog.conf`:

```
*.emerg          *
```

This line sends all `emerg`-level messages to the consoles of all users who are logged into the computer using text-mode tools. If a message matches both this specification and another one (probably an existing rule), such events will be logged in the way specified by the existing rule *and* displayed on users' consoles.

The second Scenario requirement is to log kernel messages to `/var/log/kernel` and non-trivial kernel events to a second system, `logger.pangaea.edu`. To do so, you'd create entries like this:

```
kern.*                /var/log/kernel
kern.err              @logger.pangaea.edu
```

The specification in the Scenario was a bit vague: What constitutes a "non-trivial" kernel message? For purposes of this task, I've used `err` as the cutoff point, but you could legitimately use just about any other priority code.

The first of these rules logs all kernel messages to `/var/log/kernel`. (It's possible that your configuration already sends kernel messages to this or some other file, so check to see if you're duplicating functionality before making changes.) The next line sends `err`-level messages to `logger.pangaea.edu`. (This system must be configured to accept remote logs, which is a topic not covered in this book.)

Most distributions ship with reasonable system logger settings, but you may want to examine these settings and perhaps adjust them. If you change them, though, be aware that you may need to change some other tools. For instance, all major distributions ship with tools that help rotate log files. If you change the files to which `syslogd` logs messages, you may need to change your log file rotation scripts as well. This topic is covered in the next section.

In addition to the system logger's options, you may be able to set logging options in individual programs. For instance, you might tell programs to record more or less information or to log routine information at varying priorities. Some programs also provide the means to log via the system log daemon or via their own mechanisms. Details vary greatly from one program to another, so you should consult the program's documentation for details.

Most programs that use the system log daemons are servers and other system tools. Programs that individuals run locally seldom log data via the system log daemon, although there are some exceptions to this rule, such as the Fetchmail program for retrieving email from remote servers.

## Rotating Log Files

Log files are intended to retain information on system activities for a reasonable period of time; however, system logging daemons provide no means to control the size of log files. Left unchecked, log files can therefore grow to consume all the available space on the partition on which they reside. To avoid this problem, Linux systems employ *log file rotation* tools. These tools rename and optionally compress the current log files, delete old log files, and force the logging system to begin using new log files.

The most common log rotation tool is a package called logrotate. This program is typically called on a regular basis via a cron job. (This tool is described in Phase 3.) The logrotate program consults a configuration file called /etc/logrotate.conf, which includes several default settings and typically refers to files in /etc/logrotate.d to handle specific log files. A typical /etc/logrotate.conf file includes several comment lines, denoted by hash marks (#), as well as lines to set various options, as illustrated by Listing 4.3.

**Listing 4.3**: Sample /etc/logrotate.conf File

```
# Rotate logs weekly
weekly

# Keep 4 weeks of old logs
rotate 4

# Create new log files after rotation
create

# Compress old log files
compress

# Refer to files for individual packages
include /etc/logrotate.d

# Set miscellaneous options
notifempty
nomail
noolddir

# Rotate wtmp, which isn't handled by a specific program
/var/log/wtmp {
    monthly
    create 0664 root utmp
    rotate 1
}
```

> Because log file rotation is handled by cron jobs that typically run late at night, it won't happen if a computer is routinely turned off at the end of the day. This practice is common with Windows workstations but is uncommon with servers. Either Linux workstations should be left running overnight as a general practice or some explicit steps should be taken to ensure that log rotation occurs despite routine shutdowns.

Most of the lines in Listing 4.3 set options that are fairly self-explanatory or that are well explained by the comments that immediately precede them—for instance, the weekly line sets the default log rotation interval to once a week. If you see an option in your file that you don't understand, consult the man page for logrotate.

The Scenario for this task specifies that you want to keep log files for longer than is the current setting. As just noted, Listing 4.3 specifies a four-week log file rotation, so log files are deleted after this period. To keep log files longer, change the rotate option from 4 to a higher value—6, 8, 10, or whatever you deem appropriate.

The last few lines of Listing 4.3 demonstrate the format for the definition for a specific log file. These definitions begin with the filename for the file (multiple filenames may be listed, separated by spaces) followed by an open curly brace ({). They end in a close curly brace (}). Intervening lines set options that may override the defaults. For instance, the /var/log/wtmp definition in Listing 4.3 sets the monthly option, which tells the system to rotate this log file once a month, overriding the default weekly option. Such definitions are common in the individual files in /etc/logrotate.d, which are typically owned by the packages whose log files they rotate.

To rotate the /var/log/kernel file, you can either add a definition such as the one for wtmp directly to /etc/logrotate.d or create a new file in /etc/logrotate.d for your new log file. Listing 4.4 shows a file that will do the trick for /var/log/kernel.

**Listing 4.4:** A Sample File for /etc/logrotate.d

```
/var/log/kernel {
   rotate 6
   size=100k
}
```

This file tells logrotate that it must handle the /var/log/kernel file. It also includes the size option, which tells logrotate to rotate the log file if it exceeds the specified size. This is a very useful option to keep your log files from growing out of control.

In most cases, servers and other programs that log data either do so via the system logging daemon or ship with a configuration file that goes in /etc/logrotate.d to handle the server's log files. These files usually do a reasonable job; however, you might want to double-check them. You should also check the /var/log directory and its subdirectories every now and then. If you see huge numbers of files accumulating, or if files are growing to unacceptable size, you may want to check the corresponding logrotate configuration files. If an appropriate file doesn't exist, create one. Use a working file as a template, modifying it for the new file. Pay particular attention to the prerotate or postrotate scripts, which tell logrotate how to tell syslogd to temporarily suspend and then resume logging. You may need to consult the documentation for the program that's creating the log file to learn how to force that program to begin using a new log file.

## Reviewing Log File Contents

Log files do no good if they simply accumulate on the system. Their purpose is to be used as a means of identifying problems. When a server isn't responding as you expect, when a computer refuses logins it should be accepting (or accepts logins it should be refusing), or when a system's network interface isn't coming up (to name just three types of problems), you should check your log files as part of your troubleshooting procedures. Several procedures, many of which involve tools described elsewhere in this book, can help you do so:

**Paging through whole log files**    You can use a pager program, such as less (described in Phase 1), to view the entire contents of a log file. A text editor can fill the same role.

**Searching for keywords**    You can use grep (described in Phase 1) to pull lines that contain keywords out of log files. This can be particularly handy when you don't know which log file is likely to hold an entry. For instance, typing **grep mail /var/log/\*** locates all lines in all files in the /var/log directory that contain the string mail.

**Examining the start or end of a file**    You can use the head or tail command to examine the first or last several lines of a log file. The tail command is particularly handy; you can use it to look at the last few entries just after you take some action that you expect to produce some diagnostic log file entries.

**Monitoring log files**    In addition to checking the last few lines of a log file, tail can monitor a file on an ongoing basis, echoing lines to the screen as they're added to the file. You do this with the -f option to tail, as in **tail -f /var/log/messages**.

**Advanced log analysis tools**    Various packages exist expressly for the purpose of analyzing log files. For instance, there's Logcheck, which is part of the Sentry Tools package (http://sourceforge.net/projects/sentrytools/). This package comes with some distributions, such as Mandriva and Debian. Unfortunately, it requires a fair amount of customization for your own system, so it's most easily implemented if it comes with your distribution, preconfigured for its log file format.

Log file analysis is a skill that's best learned through experience. Many log file messages are cryptic, and they can be cryptic in different ways for different programs. Consider the requirement outlined in this task's Scenario: You must examine your log files for mail server activity. Using grep to search for mail should turn up such activity, but the results are likely to be copious. In practice, most logging configurations store mail-related activities in /var/log/mail, so you might want to use tail or less to peruse the last lines of that file. You're likely to see lines like these:

```
Jul 16 23:59:01 speaker postfix/pickup[1047]: 1B67873C3: uid=500 from=<sally>
Jul 16 23:59:01 speaker postfix/cleanup[2269]: 1B67873C3:
    ➥message-id=<44BB0B04.mail1QP11S3EX@mail.example.com>
```

Actually interpreting these lines requires some knowledge of the software involved. Log file entries begin with time stamps and typically identify the computer (`speaker`) and software (`postfix`) that generated the entries. Beyond that, information is likely to be software specific. In the case of this example, mail was picked up at 23:59:01 from `sally` and a subsequent cleanup operation was performed on what was presumably the same message, now given a message ID code. If your missing email matches these times and username, these log file entries indicate that the mail was received on the system you're checking, so the problem could be in mail server configuration or in the mail client used to read the mail. If you can't find mail server entries for the missing messages, it could be that the problem is on the sending system, or perhaps your mail server software has crashed or is otherwise unable to respond.

Overall, you should examine your log files from time to time to become familiar with their contents. This will help you spot abnormalities when the system begins misbehaving or when you want to use log files to help track down an unwelcome visitor.

> Log file entries can be conspicuous by their absence as well as by suspicious content within them. Intruders often try to cover their tracks by editing log files to remove the entries that betray their unauthorized accesses. Sometimes, though, they're sloppy about this and they just delete all the log entries from the time in question. If you notice unusual gaps in your log files, such as a gap of an hour with no entries on a system that normally logs a couple dozen entries in that period, you may want to investigate further.

## Criteria for Completion

To complete this task, you should have performed two system logging configuration changes: You should have added new system logging for certain kernel-related and emergency messages, and you should have configured the log rotation to keep more system log files and to add log file rotation for your new log file. You should also have examined the `/var/log/mail` (or other appropriate) log file to try to track down recent email activity.

# Task 4.4: Use System Documentation

When you maintain a system log book or configure your system to create log files, you're creating documentation for your own or other administrators' use. Fortunately, you're not the only one to do this; Linux ships with a wide variety of documentation, which you can read to learn how standard programs work, what options go in configuration files, and so on. Chances are you've already used some of these types of documentation, but you might not fully understand them or know where to look to find the information you need. This task will help you learn to use the system's existing documentation.

# Scenario

You don't fully understand the Linux printing system, but you want to be able to use a printer you've attached to your computer. You do know that the lpr command is involved in printing. Using this information as a starting point, you want to learn as much as possible about the Linux printing tools.

Phase 6 includes two tasks devoted to printing.

# Scope of Task

This task requires you to learn about Linux's printing tools using documentation installed on your system. As such, you must have appropriate software installed and you must be able to use the basics of the Linux information commands.

## Duration

This task is somewhat open-ended; you can read as little or as much from each information source as you see fit. If you read minimally, you can complete the task in just a few minutes. If you read thoroughly and follow all the links to additional information that you'll find, you can easily spend hours reading about most topics. Chances are you'll spend between half an hour and an hour on this task, though.

## Setup

To begin this task, log into your computer as an ordinary user. You don't need root access to perform this task. Some information sources are in Hypertext Markup Language (HTML; the format used for Web pages), PostScript, or Portable Document Format (PDF). Such documents are most easily read from GUI programs such as Web browsers and PDF viewers, so you might want to log into your system in GUI mode.

## Caveats

There are few risks involved in accessing online documentation, unless of course you do so as root and mistype a command. Linux's system documentation is somewhat spotty, though; some packages come with extremely complete and well-written documentation, whereas others come with documentation that's next to useless. This situation has improved over time, though, and today you're more likely than not to find documentation that will be helpful. Occasionally, documentation lags the software it describes, so it may omit mention of important new features or changes to options. Be aware of this fact, and if something doesn't work the way the documentation suggests, try using online information sources, as described in the next task.

# Procedure

To learn about Linux printing, you'll begin with the man system and the one printing command you know: lpr. This starting point will be enough to provide you with some basic information and pointers to additional documentation. You can also search the system for extra information. Finally, you'll check GUI programs for their own built-in documentation.

## Start with *man*

Earlier phases of this book have referred to man pages for utilities, configuration files, and so on. Linux's man system provides documentation that can be considered a reference manual on various Linux topics. That is, man pages aren't intended to teach you how to use a tool in a tutorial fashion but to document the tool's major features, command-line options, and so on. To be sure, if you're familiar with Linux generally, you can learn about a subject by reading relevant man pages, but you'll probably find the style terse and the entries may be confusing if you lack relevant background information.

Nonetheless, a man page is a good place to start if you know the name of a program or configuration file but don't have much more information. Try typing **man lpr** now. You'll see lpr's man page appear in the less pager. The man page for lpr, like most man pages, is broken down into several sections, with titles like Synopsis, Description, Options, and See Also. The man page for lpr is only about three screens long, so you should take the time to read it before going further with this task.

The Synopsis section specifies how the command may be used in terms of the options it can take. The style for this specification can be confusing if you're not used to it, but it's fairly simple. The most important point is that anything enclosed in square brackets ([]) is an option; you may omit these options if you don't want to use them. The specific options are described in more detail later in the man page, in the Options section. This section, like most others, is written in plain English.

If all you wanted to do was to print a single file, lpr's man page provides the information you need to do so. From the Synopsis and Options, you should be able to figure out that you can type the command name followed by the name of the file you want to print, with optional additional parameters between these two elements. For instance, you might try the following command:

```
$ lpr sample.html
```

This command prints the sample.html file on your default printer. One fact about lpr that's not well described in its man page, though, is that it applies various *filters* to input files. These filters attempt to convert files of various types into formats that may be printed. Unfortunately, these filters don't always do what you expect or want. For instance, because it's an HTML file, you might have expected sample.html to print as the Web page that it is. Unless your system is configured with an HTML filter, though, the preceding command will result in a printout of the raw HTML file. The system I'm using for testing lacks such a filter—but it includes filters for many graphics formats, so printing a graphics file results in a printout of the image.

Although most programs provide man pages, some developers have begun to favor info pages. The info page system closely resembles the man page system, but info pages use a hypertext format so that you can more easily move from one topic to another. Type **info info** to learn more about the info page system. Most projects that favor info pages provide a man page "stub" that points you to the info page.

## Additional *man*-Related Tools

One of the problems with man pages is that it can be hard to locate help on a topic unless you know the name of the command, system call, or file you want to use. Fortunately, methods of searching the manual database exist and can help lead you to an appropriate man page:

**Summary search**    The whatis command searches summary information contained in man pages for the keyword you specify. The command returns a one-line summary (the Name section of the man page, in fact) for every matching man page. You can then use this information to locate and read the man page you need. This command is most useful for locating all the man pages on a topic. For instance, typing **whatis lpr** returns lines confirming the existence of the man page entries for lpr. If you didn't know that command to use for printing, though, whatis might not help you as much—on my test system, at least, **whatis printing** and **whatis print** both return no results.

**Thorough search**    The apropos command performs a more thorough search, of both the Name and Description sections of man pages. The result looks much like the result of a whatis search except that it's likely to contain many more items. In fact, doing an apropos search on a very common word, such as the, is likely to return so many hits as to make the search useless. Even **apropos printing** returns 83 hits on my system. A search on a less common word is likely to be more useful. (The exact number of hits returned by apropos will vary from system to system, depending on the packages installed.)

## Using the CUPS HTML Documentation

Toward the end of most man pages, including that of lpr, you'll find a section entitled See Also. This section contains pointers to additional system documentation. Many of these pointers are to other man pages. You can identify these by the number in parentheses following a name, such as lpstat(1). You can use man to call up these other man pages, as in **man lpstat**.

Linux man pages are classified in sections. Each section holds entries for a particular type of tool, such as commands, configuration files, or system calls. Sometimes the same name is used in multiple sections—say, when a configuration file has exactly the same name as the command it configures. In such cases, you can add the section number before the name, as in **man 1 lpstat**, to disambiguate the reference.

In the case of lpr's man page, the See Also documentation includes a pointer to a useful piece of non-man documentation: http://localhost:631/documentation.html. The localhost hostname refers to your own computer, so this URL isn't network documentation; instead, it's documentation hosted on your own system and accessible via the Common Unix Printing System (CUPS) server, which handles printing, and your Web browser. Enter the URL in a Web browser and you should see the CUPS links to various documentation files on your own computer, as shown in Figure 4.1. You can click the links to view the documentation in HTML or PDF forms.

Most Linux systems today use CUPS for printing; however, older Linux distributions used other printing systems, which didn't make documentation available in quite this way.

**FIGURE 4.1**    The CUPS package includes extensive local documentation that's accessible via a Web browser.

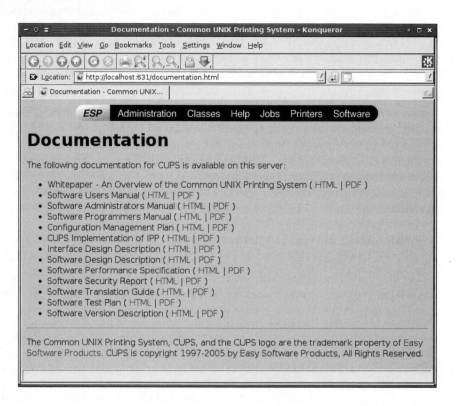

## Looking for Additional Documentation

At this point, you've found most of the CUPS-specific documentation that's available on a typical Linux system. Sometimes, though, man pages aren't informative and they may not reference additional documentation. In such cases, you can try using your Linux package system to track down additional documentation. To do this, you can obtain a listing of all the files in the package that holds any of the program files, man pages, or other files associated with the software you're investigating. You'll first need to locate a relevant file:

```
$ whereis lpr
lpr: /usr/bin/lpr /usr/share/man/man1/lpr.1.gz
```

With an RPM Package Manager system, you can then pass the -qfl option, along with a filename, to the rpm utility:

```
$ rpm -qfl /usr/bin/lpr
```

This command produces a list of all the files installed from the package to which /usr/bin/lpr belongs. You can pipe the output through less to peruse it or use grep to search on key strings, such as doc to locate miscellaneous documentation, man to locate man pages, or pdf to locate documentation in PDF format. (Non-man page documentation usually goes in a directory called documentation, docs, doc, or something similar, and man pages always reside in directories called man.)

If your distribution uses Debian packages rather than RPMs, you can use dpkg -S to locate the package that holds a file, followed by dpkg -L to display the files installed by that package. Similar commands exist for other package systems, such as Gentoo's emerge utility.

If you try searching for extra documentation for lpr in this way, chances are you won't find much. In fact, you might not even find the HTML documentation described earlier. The reason is that, on some systems, this documentation is installed from the cups package whereas lpr is often installed from the cups-client package. Other distributions place both files in a single package, though. The splitting of package-relevant files is not uncommon, and it does sometimes complicate searching for documentation.

Even if you find copious amounts of documentation, some of it may not be very helpful. Distribution maintainers sometimes provide program compilation instructions and other files that are important for developers but not for administrators or users.

## Using GUI Programs' Documentation

Many users are more comfortable with GUI programs and their help systems than with man pages and other types of text-based documentation. With the increasing availability of complex GUI programs in Linux, documentation tools for such users are becoming more accessible. For the most part, they're restricted to large programs and desktop environments. Figure 4.2 shows the result of having searched on the keyword *print* in the OpenOffice.org help system. Using this resource, you can learn a lot about OpenOffice.org's printing system and how to send documents to your OS's main printing system (such as CUPS). You'll learn relatively little about CUPS itself, though.

**FIGURE 4.2**    Large GUI programs frequently include extensive help systems.

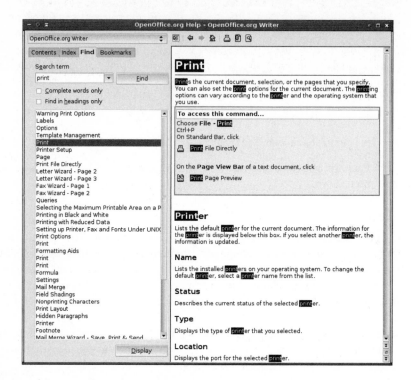

 The xman program provides a GUI interface on the Linux man page system. The xman program is primitive by modern GUI standards and it doesn't support many man features. You can't even pass the name of a command you want to look up directly on the command line; you've got to search for it within xman. Nonetheless, it may be useful if you or your users are more comfortable with GUI tools than with command-line programs.

## Criteria for Completion

To complete this task, you should have used several system documentation resources, starting with the man system and related tools, moving on to non-man documentation provided with a package, and continuing with searching for documentation using package tools and GUI programs' help systems. None of these methods of obtaining information is guaranteed to give you the information you desire, but chances are one of them will do the job, or at least provide you with clues you'll be able to use in an online documentation search.

# Task 4.5: Use Online Documentation

Most Linux systems install large amounts of documentation, but even more information is available on the Internet at large. Knowing what online sites are useful and how to search for documentation online will help you maintain your reputation as a street-smart Linux administrator.

## Scenario

You're configuring a Linux workstation to be used primarily for word processing. The individual who will be using this system wants to have a wide variety of fonts available, and you've bought a commercial font CD-ROM with a suitable selection. You have no idea how to install these fonts, though. To learn, you must consult online documentation.

## Scope of Task

To perform this task, you must locate and read online documentation concerning font installation in Linux. This task is fairly open-ended, but a small number of resources will probably net a good deal of information in a short period of time.

### Duration

You should be able to complete this task in half an hour or an hour; however, as just noted, this task is fairly open-ended. You can spend hours reading about Linux fonts (or most other Linux topics) on the Internet. On the other end of the scale, if you're lucky or have a specific enough query with a well-known answer, you may find that answer in a matter of just a few minutes.

### Setup

This task requires that you have access to a computer with Internet access. If you use a Linux computer, you can log in as an ordinary user; `root` access is not required to perform this task. (You might need `root` access to actually install fonts, though.) Chances are you'll want to use a GUI Web browser, so you should log in using a GUI session or type **startx** once you've logged into a text-mode session.

### Caveats

Reading online documentation poses few risks aside from the risk that you might find incorrect information on the Internet. Internet information resources vary in quality even more than does Linux system documentation.

## Procedure

To begin this task, you'll look at one of the most important online Linux documentation sources, the Linux Documentation Project (LDP; `http://tldp.org`). The LDP isn't the only source of online information, though, so I describe several others as well.

## The Linux Documentation Project

The LDP is dedicated to providing more tutorial information than is commonly provided by man pages. You'll find several types of information at this site:

**HOWTOs**   Linux HOWTO documents are short and medium-length tutorial pieces intended to get you up to speed with a topic or technology. In the past, smaller HOWTOs were classified separately, as mini-HOWTOs; however, the distinction between the two types of document has diminished greatly in recent years. HOWTOs have varying focus—some describe particular programs, whereas others are more task oriented and cover a variety of tools in service to the task. As the name implies, they're generally designed to tell you how to accomplish some task. Perusing the HOWTO index reveals that the Linux Font HOWTO (`http://tldp.org/HOWTO/Font-HOWTO/index.html`) is likely to be relevant to your goal.

**Guides**   Guides are longer documents, often described as book length. (In fact, some of them are available in printed form.) Guides are intended as thorough tutorial or reference works on large programs or general technologies, such as Linux networking as a whole. As I write this, no guides directly address the issue of fonts in Linux.

**FAQs**   A *frequently asked question (FAQ)* is, as the name implies, a question that comes up often—or more precisely, in the sense of the LDP category, a question and an answer to it. LDP FAQs are organized into categories, such as the Ftape FAQ or the WordPerfect on Linux FAQ. Each contains multiple questions and their answers, often grouped in subcategories. If you have a specific question about a program or technology, an appropriate FAQ can be a good place to look first for an answer. As I write this, no FAQ is devoted exclusively to fonts; however, some FAQs, such as the WordPerfect on Linux FAQ and the WINE FAQ, provide at least some information on fonts within the FAQs' topic areas.

LDP documents vary greatly in their thoroughness and quality. Some (particularly some of the guides) are incomplete; you can click on a section heading and see an empty page or a comment that the text has yet to be written. Some LDP documents are very recent, but others are outdated, so be sure to check the date of any document before you begin reading—if you don't, you might end up doing something the hard way, or in a way that no longer works. Despite these flaws, the LDP can be an excellent resource for learning about specific programs or about Linux generally. The better LDP documents are excellent, and even those of marginal quality often present information that's not obvious from man pages, info pages, or official program documentation.

Most Linux distributions include the LDP documents in one or more special documentation packages. Check your distribution's package list to locate them. If you have fast always-up Internet access, though, you might want to use the online versions of LDP documents because you can be sure they're the latest available. Those that ship with a distribution can be weeks or months out-of-date by the time you read them.

## Additional Online Help Resources

Several additional online resources exist to provide documentation and help. Each of these sources has its own unique strengths and weaknesses:

**Program Web pages**    Most Linux programs have associated Web pages, and these Web pages frequently include documentation. This resource is particularly helpful if you want to evaluate competing products or read up on one before installing it. Program information included in package files often points you to a program's Web page. For instance, type `rpm -qpi` *`packagename`*`.rpm` to find information on *packagename* in an RPM system. Because fonts aren't programs and most font foundries barely know that Linux exists, you're unlikely to find font information in this way; however, you might locate a Linux fonts Web page in a Web search, as described shortly.

**Vendor Web pages**    Companies often provide Linux information on their Web pages. These are usually identical to the program Web pages just described in the case of commercial programs, but sometimes they're not. For instance, you might be able to locate Linux information relating to a video card or printer on the manufacturer's Web site. Also, don't forget your distribution maintainer's Web site. These are particularly useful when dealing with distribution-specific issues.

**Web searches**    Random Web sites often host useful information, but the trick is in locating them. You can use search engines such as Google (`http://www.google.com`) and Yahoo! (`http://www.yahoo.com`) to search the Web for keywords you specify. With luck, this will turn up a helpful Web site. Searching on *Linux fonts* on Google turns up over 27 million hits. The first page of hits alone includes several tutorials and informational articles, including the Linux Font HOWTO.

**Web forums**    A Web forum is a Web site that enables people to post messages to it. Many distributions support Web forums in which users discuss issues related to the distribution. These forums can be very useful resources and are often the first place you'll see new problems discussed, as well as fixes for those problems. If you don't know of any Web forums for your program or topic, you might locate one via a Web search or another resource, such as a vendor's Web page.

**Usenet newsgroups**    Usenet news is a forum that's similar in concept to a Web forum, but Usenet was around long before Web forums. Usenet posts are similar to email messages in many ways except that they're public. Most ISPs and organizations such as universities maintain Usenet news servers, and you as an individual can access these using Linux programs like `tin` (`http://www.tin.org`) or Pan (`http://pan.rebelbase.com`). The Google Groups Web site (`http://groups.google.com`) maintains a database of newsgroup postings, so you can search for help in the form of previous queries about your problem. You should probably do this before posting a new cry for help; a quick search often turns up an answer much more quickly than does a new posting. Usenet is the most open of the major forum systems, which unfortunately means that it attracts more in the way of verbally abusive posts and off-topic discussions. Although there's no Linux fonts group, queries about Linux fonts would be reasonable in the `comp.fonts` newsgroup or in some Linux-specific groups, such as `comp.os.linux.setup` or `comp.os.linux.x`.

**Mailing lists**   Mailing lists are similar to Web forums and Usenet newsgroups except that discussions are carried out via email messages. (In fact, some forums are carried in multiple forms, so you can choose which you prefer.) Check vendor Web sites, distribution Web sites, and the Web sites for specific programs for information on mailing lists related to the product in question.

**IRC**   *Internet Relay Chat (IRC)* is a system for real-time interactions with other users. It's similar to the instant messaging systems that are also quite popular, but IRC involves public discussions. To use IRC, you must install an IRC client, such as Xchat (`http://www.xchat.org`). You then point the client to an IRC server, which links with other servers in an IRC network, and join an IRC channel (which is a specific discussion forum, similar to a Usenet newsgroup). Check `http://www.irchelp.org/irchelp/networks/` for information on IRC networks.

By taking advantage of any or all of these resources, you can learn a great deal about Linux in a short period of time or solve almost any Linux problem. Not all resources are appropriate for solving all problems, though.

Even if you don't make extensive use of any given information resource, you should at least take some time to familiarize yourself with the *type* of information to be found in each of these sources. Knowing what information a resource can provide can be very valuable if and when you need to locate that type of information.

## Criteria for Completion

To complete this task, you should read some online documentation concerning Linux fonts. The Font HOWTO document is particularly likely to be helpful, but you might also obtain useful information via a Web search or by other means. The open-ended nature of this task means that there's no fixed stopping point; you can read for a few minutes or a few days.

# Phase

# 5

# Managing Partitions and Filesystems

Phase 1 described commands used to manipulate files—cp, mv, rm, and so on. The files these commands manipulate aren't just thrown onto blank hard disks like so many spoons and forks in a drawer. Linux, like any OS, needs a set of data structures on the disk in order to help it find files on the disk, something like partitions or plastic organizers to help you keep your spoons and forks separate in your drawers. These data structures fall into two broad categories: *partitions*, which split a disk into a few distinct parts, and *filesystems*, which are data structures within partitions that enable Linux to organize and find files. This phase is devoted to creating and otherwise manipulating partitions and filesystems. Along the way you'll learn everything you need to know if you want to add a new hard disk to your system or perform basic maintenance on your partitions and filesystems.

This task maps to portions of the CompTIA Linux+ objectives 1, 2, and 3 and to portions of the LPIC objectives 102 and 104.

# Task 5.1: Plan a Partition Scheme

Before you can use a disk, you must partition it, and before you partition it you must decide how you want to partition it. To do so you must understand the basics of how your computer's partitioning system works and what function partitions serve in your computer. This task addresses these issues and enables you to plan a partitioning scheme for a disk.

## Scenario

You've just purchased or built a new computer and you want to install Linux on it. To do so, you must decide how to partition the computer to hold Linux, including space for system files, user files, a swap partition, and so on. The computer has a single 120GB hard disk on which you'll be storing Linux and all the system's data files.

You must also plan a partitioning scheme if you add a disk to an existing computer. Typically, in that situation you'll move some data from the old disk to the new one and recycle cleared partitions from the old disk to some new purpose. For instance, you might move the contents of /home from the old disk to the new one and then reuse the old /home partition as /usr/local.

# Scope of Task

This task is a paper-and-pencil exercise that involves planning for future activities. As such, it poses no risks and requires no special access to any computer. You might, however, want to check current systems' configurations to estimate how much space they require.

## Duration

You should be able to complete this task, including obtaining estimates of existing systems' disk use, in half an hour or so. Once you're familiar with typical disk use patterns, you should be able to plan a partitioning scheme in 5 minutes or less.

## Setup

In theory, you can perform this task with nothing but paper and a pen or pencil. In practice, you'll find it helpful to review the configurations of one or more existing computers. Ideally, your review systems should run the same Linux distribution you plan to install on the new one and should be used in similar ways. Having user (non-**root**) access to any computers you plan to review will be necessary, and occasionally **root** access to these systems can be helpful.

## Caveats

Planning disk partitioning poses no risks per se, unless you damage systems whose existing layouts you check. The biggest risk is with making incorrect choices. If you make a partition too small, correcting that mistake can be tedious and time-consuming and, depending on how you make the correction, can require system downtime. With today's big hard disks, it's usually better to err on the side of making a partition too large instead of too small. Another risk-avoidance strategy is to use Logical Volume Management (LVM), which is a way to create partitions that can be easily resized. LVM is more complex than traditional partitioning, though, and I don't describe it in this book.

# Procedure

You should do three things to complete this task: review existing systems' configurations, use those configurations and knowledge of your new system's needs to estimate its disk space requirements, and design a layout that suits your purposes. If you have no existing systems whose layouts you can review, you'll have to go by more general guidelines. Before you do these things, though, you should understand some background information on disk partitioning.

## Understanding *x*86 Disk Partitioning

A disk partition is just a way to carve up disk space so that multiple OSs can use a single computer or so that a single OS can treat parts of the disk in different ways. Partitioning requires writing data to the disk to define the partitions, but as usual in the computer world, multiple disk partitioning schemes exist. The most common is the *x*86 partitioning system that's used by most *x*86 and *x*86-64 (aka AMD64) computers. This partitioning scheme traces its history back to the mid-1980s, when a big hard disk was 10MB in size (about one-sixtieth the size of a modern CD-R).

Given the small size of hard disks and the number and nature of the OSs that ran on *x*86 hardware at the time, the designers of the original *x*86 partitioning scheme saw no need to support more than four partitions per disk. This limit was therefore hard-coded into the data structures. As OSs became more plentiful and flexible, the four-partition limit became a problem and a scheme to expand the limit was retrofitted onto the *x*86 partitioning system: One of the four original-style (*primary*) partitions became a placeholder (*extended*) partition for additional (*logical*) partitions. In practice, the number of logical partitions is limited by OS addressing issues, such as the number of Linux device nodes that can refer to them. The end result, therefore, is that you can have up to three primary partitions and an arbitrary number of logical partitions on a disk (with a single extended partition holding the logical partitions) or up to four primary partitions.

Primary partitions are defined in the *Master Boot Record (MBR)*, which is the first sector on the hard disk. The MBR also holds the *boot loader*, which is the software that the computer loads when it boots the computer. Task 5.7 describes how to install a boot loader. Logical partitions are defined in the extended partition's space.

> Most non-*x*86 systems use other partitioning schemes, and most of these partitioning systems don't distinguish between primary, extended, and logical partitions.

Linux is a clone of Unix systems, which developed independently of the *x*86 computer hardware during the 1980s. Unix, and hence Linux, has traditionally used partitions as a way to split up logical parts of the OS. In principle, you can drop Linux into a single partition, which will hold the root (/) directory and all its subdirectories; however, this approach has limitations. You can't use different filesystem types (ext3fs, ReiserFS, and so on) for different directories, a disk error in the one filesystem will affect everything, you can't use filesystem options as a security tool (say, to prevent writing to certain directories), disk partitioning can simplify system upgrades by enabling you to wipe some partitions clean while preserving others, you'll need to either do without swap space or create it in a file on your main filesystem, and so on. On the other extreme, if you create too many partitions, judging the appropriate size for each one can become very difficult, and the probability of running out of space on one or more partitions goes up.

A typical Linux system uses between three and a dozen or so distinct partitions, but details differ greatly from one computer to another. With the exception of swap partitions, each partition is assigned a *mount point*—a directory that corresponds to a partition's files. For instance, if you mount a partition at /usr, Linux will look to that partition whenever you try to access files in the /usr directory tree. Much of what you'll do in this task is deciding how many separate partitions to create and how large to make them.

> If your Linux system dual-boots between Linux and another OS, you'll have to remember to include one or more partitions for the other OS. Some OSs are fussy about requiring primary partitions, but Linux is very flexible in this respect.

## Reviewing Existing Systems

If you have access to existing Linux computers that run software similar to what you plan for your new system, you can review their partitions. You can use df to do this job:

```
$ df
Filesystem         1K-blocks      Used Available Use% Mounted on
/dev/sdb6             977180    362768    614412  38% /
udev                 256024       188    255836   1% /dev
/dev/sdb5            6291260   4820608   1470652  77% /usr
/dev/hda7            2564012    346868   2217144  14% /usr/local
/dev/hda8            3145628    832012   2313616  27% /usr/portage
/dev/sdb7            2097084    163748   1933336   8% /var
/dev/sdb12          17825244  11834228   5991016  67% /home
/dev/hda1            101089     35111     61803  37% /boot
```

This example shows seven partitions and one virtual filesystem (udev, mounted at /dev). Pay particular attention to the partitions' sizes (the 1K-blocks column, which shows the filesystem sizes in kilobytes) and to how full each partition is (the Use% column). The partition device names in the first column are unimportant for your purposes, but the mount points in the final column are important. Figure 5.1 shows the filesystems from this example (except for /dev, which isn't a disk filesystem) in graphical form, which should help you visualize how they're organized.

**FIGURE 5.1**    Linux enables you to access partitions as directories in its directory tree.

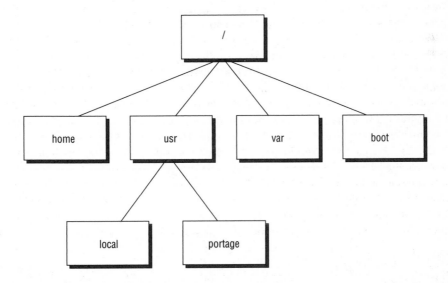

Ideally, you should review at least two or three computers that will be similar to the one you're building. This should give you an idea of the range of partitioning schemes and the sizes of the partitions. One complication is the fact that partition layouts can differ substantially from one computer to another. For instance, you might find a layout like the one shown here on one computer but another computer might not split /usr off from the root partition. This can make estimating the amount of space in each directory tree difficult. The du command, used in conjunction with its -s option, can be a handy stand-in:

```
# du -s /usr
6032044 /usr
```

This command displays the disk space consumed in the /usr directory tree (5.8GB), including all partitions mounted in that tree (such as /usr/portage and /usr/local in the preceding example). Although you can issue this command as an ordinary user, doing so is likely to produce an underestimate for some directory trees since ordinary users may not be able to read all the directories in a given directory tree. Because du scans every file in the directory tree to arrive at its estimate of disk use, the command can take several minutes to execute if the directory tree you specify holds lots of files.

Using du in this way is most likely to be helpful if you've already got an idea about how you want to partition a disk—for instance, if you know you want to split /usr off into its own partition.

## Estimating Disk Space Requirements

To estimate disk space requirements, I recommend you begin with a fundamental split between system data and user data. System data includes program files, system configuration files, the package system database, and so on. Most system data is installed via your package management system, although it also includes locally compiled programs (typically stored in /usr/local) and a few other odds and ends. This contrasts with user data, most of which resides in the /home directory. Some systems place a great deal of user data in other locations, though. For instance, a system that functions as a mail server is likely to have significant user data in the form of mail spools, which might reside in /var/spool/mail. To proceed, you'll need to know where most of your user data will reside and how much user data the system will hold.

If the system you're creating should be similar to one you've reviewed as an example, you could use the example system's partition layout and sizes as a model. You might need to make adjustments if a partition seems squeezed for size or if you know you'll have need for more or less disk space. Your estimate of user data needs may require a change, particularly if the two systems will be dissimilar in this respect but similar in terms of installed software, and hence system data needs.

Once you've estimated your user and system data needs, you can begin planning how much disk space to allocate to each. In the preceding example, the root partition, /usr, and /boot hold system data, while /home and /var hold user data. This gives estimates of about 6.1GB required for system data and 11.4GB for user data. The 120GB disk specified in the Scenario is more than big enough to hold all of this data. Of course, you're not reproducing this example system exactly, so you should adjust your estimates accordingly. For instance, if the new system will have software similar to the first one, but if users will be storing huge multimedia files, you might plan to devote huge portions of the disk to user data.

## Planning Your Partitions

At this point, you can begin planning how to create specific partitions. You can create partitions to hold files at any location in the directory tree you like, with a few exceptions. The /etc, /bin, /sbin, and /lib directories should never be split off onto their own partitions; they should always reside on the root partition. The /dev and /proc filesystems are usually handled by their own special virtual filesystem drivers, although until recently /dev was usually an ordinary directory on the root partition. These filesystems are normally set up when you install Linux, so you shouldn't need to deal with them explicitly.

If you're new to Linux administration and have no compelling reason to do otherwise, I recommend using a simple partitioning scheme:

**The root (/) partition**    This partition is an absolute necessity.

**/home**    This partition is worth splitting off because it's relatively easy for new administrators to estimate its size and because it's often helpful to keep user data separate from system data.

**/usr**    This partition is one of two system data partitions that might reasonably be split off by new administrators. It holds most program files and so should be the largest of the system data partitions—much larger even than the root filesystem in most cases. (Some distributions place significant files in /opt, though, so be aware of that fact.)

**/boot**    On older computers, a separate /boot partition can be handy because you can place that partition where the boot loader will be able to access it using the old Basic Input/Output System (BIOS) calls. Newer BIOSs are less restrictive, though.

Further subdivisions are generally inadvisable because your experience might not be sufficient to tell you how much disk space needs will fluctuate. Installing new software, upgrading existing software, temporary disk space requirements associated with building software, temporary and permanent disk space demands by users, and so on all place demands for space in specific directories. If you create many partitions, each one will have less free space than would be the case with fewer partitions, so you'll be more likely to run out of disk space.

If you're a more experienced administrator or if you have a compelling reason to do so, you can further subdivide your system. Popular additional partition splits include the following:

**/tmp**    This directory holds temporary files. Some administrators like to keep it as a separate partition so that if a runaway process creates ridiculously large temporary files, this fact won't cause disk space problems in more critical directories.

**/var**    This directory holds miscellaneous temporary and user files, including spool directories and package databases. It's most often split off as a separate partition on systems that function as servers in which /var holds significant quantities of files.

**/usr/local**    If you build significant numbers of programs locally and install them in this directory, keeping it as a separate filesystem can be beneficial. You can wipe out your regular system partitions and re-install Linux from scratch while leaving your locally compiled software untouched.

**/usr/portage**    This directory is important on Gentoo systems but not on others. It holds files related to the Gentoo package system, and keeping it as a separate partition enables you to more easily monitor its disk use, but at the cost of an increased risk of running out of disk space.

**/opt**    Commercial packages often install in /opt, and some distributions place KDE or other big open source packages there as well. Using a separate partition is useful for the same reason that keeping /usr/local separate is useful.

**Site-specific partitions**    You may create site-specific directories. For instance, you might create a directory tree to hold Web pages on a Web server. If such a directory holds a significant number of files, separating the partition may be worth considering.

Once you have a list of partitions, you should go back to your disk space estimates and assign each one a size. If you know how much disk space each will take, double each estimate. This will give you room for growth and slack space in case you underestimate your disk space.

You can now add up your disk space estimates and see how they compare to your available disk space (120GB). If your estimates exceed your available disk space, you can either cut back on your estimates or plan to buy a second disk or a bigger disk. Buying more disk space is almost always the better idea, although if you went overboard on your disk space estimates, revising them may be reasonable.

 Disk manufacturers define *gigabyte* as 1,000,000,000 ($10^9$) bytes, but most disk utilities define it as 1,073,741,824 ($2^{30}$) bytes. Between this fact and the overhead required when creating partitions and filesystems, you can find a rude shock when you discover that your disk holds less data than you anticipated. Be sure to take these differences into consideration when computing disk space.

Before proceeding further, add another partition for swap space. A good size for a Linux swap partition is about twice the size of your computer's RAM. If you're adding a second disk and the first one already has an adequate swap partition, you needn't add another. You should also remember space for non-Linux partitions if your system dual-boots between Linux and another OS.

If your disk space estimates are significantly below your available disk space, you can begin increasing your allocations to match available disk space. (You can safely exclude your swap partition from this procedure.) One approach is simply to increase each partition's size proportionately. This approach is simple, but you'll likely end up with huge amounts of space you'll never use in partitions such as /boot (if you use this partition). Another approach is to increase partitions' sizes based on your estimate of which ones are most likely to hold more or bigger files in the future. As a general rule, /home is a good candidate for big increases in size. Others depend on the use to which the computer is put—/var might be a good candidate in some cases, /usr/local in others, and so on. A third approach, and one that's the most flexible, is to leave some or all of the extra space unallocated. If you run into problems with a partition being too small in the future, you can then allocate some or all of the extra space to a new partition, move files from a single directory tree in the affected partition to the new partition, and then mount the new partition at the appropriate location. You might end up with an odd separate partition, such as /usr/lib or /var/www, but at least your partitions will be reasonably sized.

For *x*86 systems, you should decide which partitions will be primary partitions and which ones will be logical partitions. As a general rule, it's best to keep as few primary partitions as possible. Typically, either the root filesystem or /**boot** as a primary partition and everything else as logical partitions in a single extended partition works well. This approach gives you the option of more easily creating primary partitions in the future, if this becomes necessary—say, to support a dual-boot between Linux and Windows or FreeBSD.

## Criteria for Completion

To complete this task, you should have a plan for how to partition your disk, including partition sizes and planned mount points for each partition. Your plan should include the Linux filesystems, Linux swap space, and possibly space for non-Linux OSs. If your disk is big enough, you might include some unallocated space. With your written partitioning scheme in hand, you can proceed to actually creating these partitions using fdisk or your Linux distribution's installation program.

# Task 5.2: Use *fdisk* to Create Partitions

Linux's traditional tool for creating, deleting, and otherwise manipulating hard disk partitions is known as fdisk. This program is named after the DOS and Windows FDISK tool, but Linux's fdisk isn't a clone of the DOS/Windows FDISK. Being able to manipulate your disk partitions with fdisk (or a similar tool) is necessary when you add a disk to a system, and perhaps when you install Linux. (Most distributions provide other tools for partitioning the disk during installation.)

GNU Parted (http://www.gnu.org/software/parted/) is an alternative disk partitioning program that's growing in popularity. It includes support for operations such as moving and resizing partitions, which fdisk lacks.

Hard disks are ordinarily partitioned, as are many removable disks, such as Zip disks. Floppy disks, CD-R discs, and some other removable disks (such as magneto-optical disks) are not normally partitioned.

## Scenario

You need to expand the disk space in two computers. You've replaced the disk in one computer with a larger disk, and now you want to use the first computer's disk to expand the second computer's disk space. You plan to use the new disk to house the /home2 partition (which will hold new users' home directories) and to expand the computer's swap space. Therefore, you need to delete the existing partitions from this disk and create two new partitions, one to hold the new filesystem and one for the swap space.

## Scope of Task

This task covers using fdisk to view an existing partition table, delete existing partitions, and create new partitions. These tasks are potentially dangerous, but they can be performed quickly.

### Duration

This task should take about half an hour to complete. Once you're familiar with the operation of fdisk, making changes should take just a minute or two. The operations surrounding such changes are likely to take far more time, though. Physically installing hard disks, creating filesystems, backing up or moving data, and so on are likely to require several minutes to over an hour. This task is focused simply on the partition manipulations, though.

### Setup

Prior to performing this task, you should install a hard disk whose existing partitions you can safely delete—perhaps an old disk that you no longer use. You must have **root** access to your computer to perform this task, so you should log in and acquire **root** privileges. Check that you can access the new disk.

 This example uses a 100MB Zip disk as the sample disk. This is ridiculously small to hold a computer's home directories and unbearably slow for a swap partition, but a spare Zip disk makes an excellent disk for experimentation and learning because accidentally damaging its data isn't a problem.

### Caveats

Modifying partition tables is extremely dangerous. If you make a mistake, you can easily wipe out your entire Linux installation. Thus, you should exercise extreme care in performing this task. Check, double-check, and triple-check every action. If you're in any doubt, back out of the operation. Once you're using fdisk, type **q** to quit from the program without writing your changes.

## Procedure

This task involves three main sub-tasks: examining existing partitions, deleting existing partitions, and creating a new partition. I also briefly describe some of the other fdisk options.

## Examining the Partition Table

Before modifying any disk's partitions, you should first examine the existing partition table. The quickest way to do this, particularly if you don't need to perform other fdisk actions, is to use the -l option to the command along with the device filename for the disk:

```
# fdisk -l /dev/sda

Disk /dev/sda: 100 MB, 100663296 bytes
4 heads, 48 sectors/track, 1024 cylinders
Units = cylinders of 192 * 512 = 98304 bytes

    Device Boot      Start         End      Blocks   Id  System
/dev/sda1               1         510       48936   83  Linux
/dev/sda2             511        1024       49344    5  Extended
/dev/sda5             511        1024       49320   83  Linux
```

This example shows that the disk is 100MB in size and contains three partitions, /dev/sda1, /dev/sda2, and /dev/sda5. The second partition, though, is marked as an extended partition; it serves only as a placeholder for logical partitions, and only one logical partition exists: /dev/sda5. In other words, there are really only two partitions on which you might store data: /dev/sda1 and /dev/sda5.

Linux numbers primary (including extended) partitions from 1 to 4 and logical partitions from 5 upward. The primary partitions can have discontinuous numbers; for instance, a disk could have /dev/sda1 and /dev/sda3 but not /dev/sda2 or /dev/sda4. Logical partitions are numbered sequentially, though, so if there's a /dev/sda6 there should also be a /dev/sda5.

If you intend to operate on the disk, as you must for this task, you should enter fdisk's interactive mode by passing the device filename without options, as in **fdisk /dev/sda** to modify the first SCSI disk. The program displays a prompt that reads Command (m for help):. You can then verify the disk's contents by typing **p**. The output should resemble that shown earlier.

**WARNING** Always check a disk's current partitions before modifying them. Checking the partitions may alert you to a careless mistake or typo made when you entered the disk device. If you fail to verify that you're working on the correct disk on a multi-disk system, you could easily wipe out your Linux installation.

If you modify a brand-new disk or a disk that has previously been used in a non-*x*86 system, it could show nothing at all or gibberish for the partition table. In the latter case, you might be able to delete the nonsense partitions using the commands described next, or you can type **o** in fdisk to write a fresh MBR:

```
Command (m for help): o
Building a new DOS disklabel. Changes will remain in memory only,
```

until you decide to write them. After that, of course, the previous
content won't be recoverable.

Command (m for help): **p**

## Deleting Existing Partitions

To delete partitions, you use the d command within fdisk. If you're still within the fdisk command you launched earlier, you could delete the logical, extended, and primary partitions as follows:

Command (m for help): **d**
Partition number (1-5): **5**

Command (m for help): **d**
Partition number (1-5): **2**

Command (m for help): **d**
Selected partition 1

Instead of deleting partitions one by one, you can use the o command, as just described. This command wipes out all the partitions, which is what's needed for this task. If you only wanted to delete some of the partitions, o would be inappropriate.

Note that fdisk didn't prompt for a partition number for the final deletion; only one partition was left, so there was no need. You should delete logical partitions before you delete the extended partition that carries them. You can delete primary partitions before or after deleting extended and logical partitions, though.

At this point, you should have no partitions on the disk. Verify this fact by using the p command:

Command (m for help): **p**

Disk /dev/sda: 100 MB, 100663296 bytes
4 heads, 48 sectors/track, 1024 cylinders
Units = cylinders of 192 * 512 = 98304 bytes

   Device Boot     Start      End     Blocks   Id  System

When no partitions are left, p displays the usual partition list header but no data after that point.

## Creating New Partitions

Now that the disk is cleared of its existing partitions, you can create new ones and save your changes. You can begin by creating a new Linux data partition. Make it somewhat smaller than the available disk space—say, 80MB on the 100MB Zip disk:

```
Command (m for help): n
Command action
   e   extended
   p   primary partition (1-4)
p
Partition number (1-4): 1
First cylinder (1-1024, default 1): 1
Last cylinder or +size or +sizeM or +sizeK (1-1024, default 1024): +80M
```

With the first partition created, it's time to create the second one, for swap space. You could do this by creating a second primary partition; however, so you can see how it's done, try first creating an extended partition and then creating a logical partition within it:

```
Command (m for help): n
Command action
   e   extended
   p   primary partition (1-4)
e
Partition number (1-4): 2
First cylinder (816-1024, default 816):
Using default value 816
Last cylinder or +size or +sizeM or +sizeK (816-1024, default 1024):
Using default value 1024

Command (m for help): n
Command action
   l   logical (5 or over)
   p   primary partition (1-4)
l
First cylinder (816-1024, default 816):
Using default value 816
Last cylinder or +size or +sizeM or +sizeK (816-1024, default 1024): 1024
```

At this point, your partitions exist but the Linux swap partition has a type code of 0x83 (hexadecimal 83, or decimal 131), which denotes a Linux filesystem partition. To avoid confusion, you should set the partition type of 0x82, which denotes a Linux swap partition:

```
Command (m for help): t
```

```
Partition number (1-5): 5
Hex code (type L to list codes): 82
Changed system type of partition 5 to 82 (Linux swap / Solaris)
```

Finally, you should review your changes to be sure they're correct and then save the partition table:

```
Command (m for help): p

Disk /dev/sda: 100 MB, 100663296 bytes
4 heads, 48 sectors/track, 1024 cylinders
Units = cylinders of 192 * 512 = 98304 bytes

   Device Boot    Start       End    Blocks   Id  System
/dev/sda1             1       815     78216   83  Linux
/dev/sda2           816      1024     20064    5  Extended
/dev/sda5           816      1024     20040   82  Linux swap / Solaris

Command (m for help): w
The partition table has been altered!

Calling ioctl() to re-read partition table.
Syncing disks.
```

 You may want to type **p** after every major change to be sure it was correct. I didn't do so in this example to keep it brief.

When specifying the partition's position and size, you give fdisk a starting cylinder number and either an ending cylinder number or a size in bytes, kilobytes (+nK), megabytes (+nM), or gigabytes (+nG). This example used both methods of specifying a size. Typically, you'll give a size in megabytes or gigabytes for most partitions, but use an end cylinder number for the final partition on the disk.

By default, fdisk creates partitions with a type code of 0x83, which denotes a Linux filesystem. Many other partition type codes exist, most of them corresponding to non-Linux filesystems. You can see a list of the most common codes by typing **L** when Linux prompts you for a type code or by typing **l** from the main fdisk prompt.

The preceding sequence ends with the w command, which writes the changes to disk and exits from the program. If your examination of the disk's partition reveals problems, you should instead type **q** to quit from fdisk without saving changes. Like most text editors, fdisk doesn't actually write the changes you enter until you tell it to do so.

In most cases, the Linux kernel won't be aware of the changes you've made until you reboot the computer. If this is true, fdisk will warn you with a message to that effect when you exit.

The filesystem type code is part of the partition table but doesn't actually create a filesystem. Linux ignores the filesystem type code for most purposes, but many OSs use these codes to determine what partitions to mount. A few type codes are used by multiple OSs for different purposes. This is true of the Linux swap partition type code, 0x83, which is also used by Solaris to mark its native filesystems. Such collisions can be confusing and potentially dangerous in certain dual-boot scenarios but are harmless if your computer doesn't dual-boot between the OSs in question.

## Using Advanced Options

You can do much more with fdisk than examine, delete, and add partitions, although those are the three primary functions of the utility. Typing m at the fdisk command prompt reveals a list of supported commands. In fact, fdisk supports *two* sets of commands. The second menu, for experts, is accessible by typing x from the main menu. Here are some of the highlights from both menus:

**Disk verification**    You can perform a basic sanity check on the disk by typing v from either menu. Ideally, you'll see a message to the effect that there are a certain number of unallocated sectors. Because the *x*86 partition table allocates space by cylinders rather than sectors, there are likely to be a few unallocated sectors even when all available space has been used.

**Toggle the bootable flag**    Typing a from the main menu enables you to toggle the bootable flag for a partition. This flag tells a standard DOS MBR boot loader which partition to boot. If you use a Linux boot loader in the MBR, this flag is unimportant.

**Change CHS geometry**    The *x*86 partition table uses a cylinder/head/sector (CHS) system for identifying each sector. This system necessitates the use of fictitious CHS relationships for modern disks, though. You can change the way the system maps these values by using the c, h, and s options in the experts menu. Ordinarily you wouldn't do this with a disk that's already got partitions on it. The main reason to use this option would be if a disk's CHS geometry is being incorrectly detected by the kernel and fdisk.

**Change partition order**    If you delete and create logical partitions, their numbering and on-disk order might not match. This situation shouldn't cause problems with Linux, but it can be confusing and can cause problems for some OSs. You can type f from the expert menu to synchronize partition numbers and on-disk order. If you do this, you may need to adjust entries in /etc/fstab, as described shortly in Task 5.5, "Use /etc/fstab."

Additional options are available but are extremely obscure or require extremely advanced knowledge to use. If you're interested, type m to see the options.

## Criteria for Completion

To complete this task, you should have successfully deleted existing partitions from a disk you intend to reuse in a new computer and created two new partitions in the resulting empty space.

One of these partitions should be for Linux filesystems and the other should be marked as Linux swap space. To do this, you can use the Linux fdisk utility, which is powerful but not the most user-friendly tool around. When using fdisk—or any other disk partitioning software—you should exercise extreme care to be sure you don't accidentally wipe out important partitions.

# Task 5.3: Create Filesystems

Creating partitions alone won't make a disk usable. A *filesystem* does this job: A filesystem is a set of data structures that enable the computer to write files to the disk and to find those files at a later date. Linux supports many different filesystems, so you'll have to decide which ones you want to use. You can then create them and, as described later in Tasks 5.4 and 5.5, actually access them.

The word *filesystem* has two meanings. As used in this phase, the term refers to the data structures that enable an OS to store data on a disk. Another meaning of the word is more or less synonymous with the term *directory tree*. Which meaning is meant is usually clear from context. When there is ambiguity, I use additional words, such as *low-level filesystem*, to disambiguate the meaning.

## Scenario

This task's scenario is a continuation of the one in Task 5.2, "Use fdisk to Create Partitions." Using the partitions you created in that task, you want to create a filesystem and prepare the swap space for use. To do so, you'll use Linux's filesystem creation tools as well as a specialized tool for preparing swap space for use.

Creating a filesystem is sometimes called *formatting a disk*. This phrase is a bit imprecise, though, as it can refer to either *low-level formatting* or *high-level formatting*. Low-level formatting of hard disks is done at the factory, but you can low-level-format a floppy disk using the Linux fdformat utility. Creating a filesystem is synonymous with high-level-formatting a disk.

## Scope of Task

This task is fairly simple and straightforward, although it's a potentially very dangerous task—specifying the wrong partition when you create a filesystem can destroy a lot of data!

### Duration

This task will take about 15 or 30 minutes to complete. You'll spend much of that time mulling over the Linux filesystem options. Once you're familiar with the tools used to create filesystems, you'll be able to do the job in a few seconds.

## Setup

To perform this task, you must have a disk with partitions you're not currently using so that you can create new filesystems on the partitions. The disk you prepared in Task 5.2 is ideal, but in a pinch you can use a floppy disk (accessed as /dev/fd0) to practice. You must also have root access to your computer, so you should log in and acquire superuser privileges.

## Caveats

Creating a new filesystem writes low-level data structures to the disk. This act renders it nearly impossible to recover old filesystem data. Thus, if you mistakenly create a new filesystem on a disk that holds important data, you will effectively destroy that data. In theory, most or all of the data can be recovered, but such recovery requires specialized skills. Acquiring such skills is impractical in the short term, and hiring somebody who possesses those skills is expensive. Thus, you should be extremely cautious when you create a new filesystem. Check, double-check, and triple-check your command before you press the Enter key.

# Procedure

This task involves three sub-tasks. First, you must decide what filesystem to use. Different file-systems have different strengths and weaknesses, so you should spend some time learning about their differences. Second, you must create a data filesystem. Third, you must prepare your swap partition for use. These final two parts of the task take very little time to actually execute.

## Deciding What Filesystem to Use

Filesystems consist of data structures along with rules for how to access them, including details such as what characters are legal in filenames, how long filenames may be, and what sort of ancillary information (creation dates, permissions, and so on) are stored with files. Some of the data structures, and the algorithms that interact with them, influence a filesystem's speed and reliability. For these reasons, selecting the correct filesystem for the job is an important decision for any computer.

Over the past few years, Linux has seen the transition to *journaling* filesystems from older non-journaling filesystems. A journaling filesystem records a *journal* of disk activity *before* data structures are changed. The idea is that, in the event of a power failure or system crash, the journal will hold information on all the disk's data structures that could possibly be in need of repair. The journal therefore speeds up recovery after power failures or system crashes—with a non-journaling filesystem, the disk check utility (fsck in Linux) must check all the file-system's data structures, which can be quite time-consuming on large disks. For this reason, use of a journaling filesystem is advisable in Linux, particularly for large disks. The journal consumes disk space, though, and with some journaling filesystems, the disk space require-ments can be significant on small media. Thus, you might want to use a non-journaling file-system for small removable media such as floppies and Zip disks, and even for some small disk partitions, such as /boot, if it's a separate partition.

Linux native filesystems (that is, those that Linux can use for its root filesystem and other critical directories, such as /usr) all provide more or less the same set of features in terms of filenames, permissions, and so on. Thus, non-administrative users may not know or care what filesystem you use so long as it works. The different Linux filesystems do offer different performance features and advanced options, though:

**Ext2fs** The *Second Extended File System* (*ext2fs* or *ext2*) is the traditional Linux native filesystem. It was created for Linux and was the dominant Linux filesystem throughout the late 1990s. Ext2fs has a reputation as a reliable non-journaling filesystem. Ext2fs has since been eclipsed by journaling filesystems, but it still has its uses. In particular, ext2fs can be a good choice for a small /boot partition, if you choose to use one, and for small (sub-gigabyte) removable disks. On such small partitions, the size of the journal used by more advanced filesystems can be a real problem, so the non-journaling ext2fs is a better choice. The ext2 filesystem type code is ext2.

**Ext3fs** The *Third Extended File System* (*ext3fs* or *ext3*) is basically ext2fs with a journal added. The result is a filesystem that's as reliable as ext2fs but that recovers from power outages and system crashes much more quickly. The ext3 filesystem type code is ext3.

**ReiserFS** This filesystem was designed from scratch as a journaling filesystem for Linux and is a popular choice in this role. It's particularly good at handling partitions with large numbers of small files (say, smaller than about 32KB) because ReiserFS uses various tricks to squeeze the ends of files into each other's unused spaces. This small savings can add up to a large percentage of file sizes when files are small. You can use reiserfs as the type code for this filesystem.

**JFS** IBM developed the *Journaled File System (JFS)* for its AIX OS and later re-implemented it on OS/2. The OS/2 version was subsequently donated to Linux. JFS is a technically sophisticated journaling filesystem that might be of particular interest if you're familiar with AIX or OS/2 or want an advanced filesystem to use on a dual-boot system with one of these OSs. As you might expect, this filesystem's type code is jfs.

**XFS** Silicon Graphics (SGI) created its *Extents File System (XFS)* for its IRIX OS and, like IBM, later donated the code to Linux. Like JFS, XFS is a very technically sophisticated filesystem. XFS has gained a reputation for robustness, speed, and flexibility on IRIX, but some of the XFS features that make it so flexible on IRIX aren't supported very well under Linux. Use xfs as the type code for this filesystem.

In practice, most administrators seem to choose ext3fs or ReiserFS as their primary filesystems; however, JFS and XFS also work well, and some administrators prefer them. Hard data on the merits and problems with each filesystem are difficult to come by, and even when they do exist, they're suspect because filesystem performance interacts with so many other factors. For instance, as just noted, ReiserFS can cram more small files into a small space than can other filesystems, but this advantage is not very important if you'll be storing mostly larger files.

 If you're using a non-*x*86 platform, be sure to check filesystem development on that platform. A filesystem might be speedy and reliable on one CPU but sluggish and unreliable on another.

When choosing a filesystem, be sure to check on your distribution's filesystem support. Although you can compile support for any Linux native filesystem yourself and install its support tools, not all distributions support all Linux native filesystems in their default configurations. JFS and XFS are the most often omitted filesystems, but sometimes even ReiserFS isn't supported. Ext3fs is supported by all but very old Linux distributions, and ext2fs is supported by everything but truly ancient (early 1990s) distributions.

You can use multiple filesystems on a single Linux system. For instance, you might use ext2fs on a small /boot partition and ReiserFS on other partitions. Using multiple filesystems enables you to tune the filesystem to the needs of the partition, but it does add some overhead in kernel memory requirements.

In addition to its native filesystems, Linux supports a large number of non-native and specialized filesystems. These filesystems lack certain features that Linux requires in its native filesystems, such as support for Unix-style ownership and permissions, or they don't perform reliably enough to be used as native filesystems. Examples of these filesystems appear in Table 5.1. Although you won't create and use any of these filesystems for Linux-only use on your hard disk, you should be aware of their existence in case you need to install Linux on a dual-boot system or create or read removable media that should be readable on non-Linux systems.

**TABLE 5.1**   Common Non-Linux Filesystems

| Filesystem Name | Linux Filesystem Type Code | Native OS or Use |
| --- | --- | --- |
| File Allocation Table (FAT) | msdos, umsdos, or vfat, depending on feature set | DOS, Windows, and OS/2; useful for cross-platform removable disks. |
| New Technology File System (NTFS) | ntfs | Windows NT/200*x*/XP. |
| High-Performance File System (HPFS) | hpfs | OS/2 and early versions of Windows NT. |
| Hierarchical File System (HFS) | hfs | MacOS. |
| Extended Hierarchical File System (HFS+) | hfsplus | MacOS. |
| Minix Filesystem | minix | Minix; early versions of Linux (but too limited for serious modern Linux use except on floppies). |
| Unix File System (UFS) | ufs | Several Unix and Unix-like OSs; limited in Linux mainly by poor write support. |

**TABLE 5.1** Common Non-Linux Filesystems *(continued)*

| Filesystem Name | Linux Filesystem Type Code | Native OS or Use |
| --- | --- | --- |
| ISO-9660 | iso9660 | CD-ROMs and similar media; Linux includes Joliet and Rock Ridge support for long file-names and Unix-style permissions and ownership. |
| Universal Disc Format (UDF) | udf | DVDs and read/write optical media. |

Linux can create many, but not all, of the filesystems described in Table 5.1. To create an ISO-9660 or UDF filesystem, you'd ordinarily use the mkisofs utility, which creates a disk file that holds an image of the filesystem and all the files it's to contain. You can then write that image file to a CD-R or similar disc using cdrecord. Various GUI tools, such as X-CD-Roast and ERoaster, provide point-and-click interfaces to this process.

In addition to disk-based filesystems, Linux supports various filesystems that provide access to files on other computers. The most important of these are the Network File System (NFS) and the Server Message Block/Common Internet File System (SMB/CIFS). NFS is most often used between Linux and Unix systems, whereas SMB/CIFS is used on DOS and Windows networks. You don't create an NFS or SMB/CIFS filesystem on your disk, though; instead, these filesystems are network protocols that give remote access to ext2fs, ReiserFS, FAT, ISO-9660, or any other disk filesystem. You can use the nfs filesystem type code with a mount command to mount an NFS export or use the smbfs or cifs type code to mount an SMB/CIFS share.

## Creating a Filesystem

To create a filesystem, you use the mkfs tool, to which you pass the filesystem type code using the -t option and the device file for the partition or disk that should hold the filesystem:

```
# mkfs -t ext3 /dev/sda1
```

Remember to check, double-check, and triple-check your command! You do *not* want to enter the wrong device filename! If you accidentally omit the partition number (as in /dev/sda rather than /dev/sda1), you'll create a filesystem on the entire disk, wiping out all the disk's partitions.

The output of the mkfs command varies depending on the filesystem you've selected. The filesystem creation process typically takes just a few seconds, although this varies depending on the size and speed of the disk, the filesystem in question, and other factors.

In reality, mkfs is just a front end to filesystem-specific tools, most of which use the name mkfs.*filesystem*, where *filesystem* is the filesystem name, such as ext3 or jfs. The mke2fs, mke3fs, mkreiserfs, and mkdosfs programs are additional names for creating ext2fs, ext3fs, ReiserFS, and FAT filesystems, respectively.

Once you've created a filesystem, you should check it by mounting it, as described in Task 5.4. You can then verify its size using df and be sure that you can write files to the disk and read them back.

## Creating Swap Space

Swap space enables your computer to treat disk space as if it were RAM—slow RAM, but memory in which active data can reside when real RAM is insufficient. For it to do so, though, you must first prepare a disk file or partition to be used as swap space. You do this with the mkswap command:

```
# mkswap /dev/sda5
```

 **WARNING** As with the mkfs command, mkswap is potentially extremely destructive. Review the command carefully to be sure you've specified the correct disk and partition.

Another option for swap space is to use an ordinary disk file. You can create a disk file of any size using dd:

```
# dd if=/dev/zero of=/swap bs=1048576 count=500
```

This example creates a file in the root directory, called /swap, that's 500MB in size (500 units of 1,048,576 bytes each). Of course, in practice you'd put the file wherever you have available disk space. In any event, you can then prepare it much as you'd prepare a swap partition:

```
# mkswap /swap
```

To verify that your swap space is properly configured, you can test it by first using free to examine the amount of available swap space, then using swapon to activate the swap space, and then using free again:

```
# free
              total      used      free    shared    buffers     cached
Mem:         512052    505548      6504         0      63064     106176
-/+ buffers/cache:     336308    175744
Swap:       1261560    276004    985556
# swapon /dev/sda5
```

```
# swapon /swap
# free
                total     used     free    shared    buffers    cached
Mem:           512052   505672     6380         0     63180    106176
-/+ buffers/cache:      336316   175736
Swap:         1793584   282792  15107928
```

Note that the total swap space increased from 1,261,560 to 1,793,584 after the swap space was activated. This indicates that your swap space was successfully activated. This activation is temporary, though; to make it permanent, you must add an /etc/fstab entry for each new swap partition or swap file, as described in the upcoming Task 5.5.

If you want to manually deactivate swap space, you can do so with the swapoff command, as in **swapoff /dev/sda5**. This command can take several seconds or even longer to execute if the swap space you're deactivating currently holds data; Linux must read the data back into memory and may even transfer it to another swap area.

## Criteria for Completion

To complete this task, you should decide on a filesystem to use for the new partition you created in Task 5.2. You must also create that filesystem and prepare swap space in the swap partition you also created in Task 5.2. To actually use your new filesystem, though, you must mount it, as described in the next task.

# Task 5.4: Manually Mount and Unmount Filesystems

Preparing partitions and creating filesystems on them are necessary prerequisites to using a hard disk in Linux. To actually make the disk space available for use, though, you must take the final step: You must *mount* the filesystem—that is, associate it with a directory so that users can write files to the disk and read them back. You can perform this task manually on a one-time basis, as described in this task, or in a way that makes filesystems available whenever the computer boots, as described in the next task, "Use /etc/fstab." You should also know how to undo a mount operation so that the disk is no longer accessible. This is most often done with removable media, but some system maintenance tasks require you to unmount partitions that are normally mounted.

## Scenario

Having created a new partition to store new users' home directories in Task 5.2, and having created an ext3 filesystem on it in Task 5.3, you're now ready to mount the partition. As specified in Task 5.2's Scenario section, this new filesystem should be available as /home2. You intend to mount the partition manually at first, in order to test that the filesystem works as intended. In Task 5.5, you'll mount the partition permanently.

# Scope of Task

This task explores the `mount` and `umount` commands, which mount and unmount a partition, respectively. (The `umount` command is spelled correctly; it contains just one `n`.) The basics of these commands are fairly simple, but `mount`, in particular, supports important options you should understand.

## Duration

This task should take about half an hour to complete. Once you're familiar with these commands, you'll be able to use them in a matter of seconds.

## Setup

You need `root` access to your computer to perform this task. This task is written with the assumption that you've completed the previous two tasks and so have a partition you can mount and unmount at will. If not, you should create an appropriate partition. In a pinch, you can create a filesystem on a floppy disk (`/dev/fd0`) and use it.

## Caveats

Because you need `root` access to perform this task, the usual caveats concerning superuser status apply. In addition, you should be aware of the risks of mounting and unmounting filesystems. If you accidentally mount a filesystem over a populated directory tree (say, `/home`), the files in that directory tree will become inaccessible. You can restore the original files by unmounting the filesystem, but in the meantime you may run into any of many different problems, depending on the directory tree you've blocked. Linux prevents unmounting filesystems on which files are open, so you're unlikely to be able to accidentally unmount a truly critical filesystem. You could accidentally unmount a filesystem that's important but not currently in use, though. Fortunately, these mount-specific problems are all easily corrected. In a worst-case scenario, rebooting should restore the system to normal.

# Procedure

This task involves mounting a filesystem and then unmounting it. Between these two fairly basic operations, I describe additional capabilities of the `mount` command. These extra features are handy when you want to give ordinary users the ability to mount a filesystem or when you need to fine-tune the mount operation.

## Mounting a Filesystem

Before you can mount your new filesystem, you must prepare a mount point for it. You already know how to do this, although you may not realize it because a mount point is nothing but an ordinary directory. Thus, the command to create a mount point is the same as the command to create a directory: mkdir. To create the /home2 mount point, type this command:

```
# mkdir /home2
```

The basic form of the mount command is fairly simple: Type the command name followed by the device file for the filesystem and the mount point:

```
# mount /dev/sda1 /home2
```

Once this is done, you can verify that it's been mounted in several ways. One is to check the mount point for files:

```
# ls /home2
lost+found
```

Of course, a freshly minted filesystem will contain no files. This example shows one file (actually, a directory): lost+found. Ext2fs and ext3fs use this directory to store files that have been recovered in disk maintenance operations. Most other filesystems don't use this directory or create it only when it's needed. Of course, if you mount a filesystem that you know already contains files, you should see them.

Another check of the filesystem's presence is to use df. You can specify the mount point or device filename to limit the output of this command:

```
# df /home2
Filesystem        1K-blocks      Used Available Use% Mounted on
/dev/sda1            75733       4127     67696   6% /home2
```

This output reveals that the filesystem has been successfully mounted. You might consider it odd that df claims that 6 percent of the filesystem is in use. Most of this space is consumed by the filesystem's journal—recall that in Task 4.4, a journaling ext3 filesystem was specified. Some journaling filesystems consume even more space. For instance, using ReiserFS on this partition would result in 42 percent use at mount time. These figures are a consequence of the small size of the sample partition, though; on partitions of reasonable size (measured in the gigabytes), the journal size isn't a major concern.

If a filesystem is described in /etc/fstab, you can use a shorthand notation in which you specify only the mount point or only the device filename, not both:

```
# mount /home2
```

Even ordinary users can issue this form of the mount command under certain circumstances, as described in the next task.

## Additional *mount* Options

The mount command supports a number of options that modify its behavior. The most important of these is -t, which accepts a filesystem type code:

```
# mount -t ext3 /dev/sda1 /home2
```

Normally, mount can correctly identify the filesystem type, but on occasion it needs an extra nudge. You might use this option when mounting a FAT filesystem, since Linux supports three FAT filesystem codes: msdos mounts the partition with short DOS filenames, vfat supports long Windows filenames, and umsdos provides a Linux-only method of encoding long filenames and Unix-style ownership and permission information on the disk. You can also mount an ext3 filesystem using the ext2 type code if you don't want to use the journal. On rare occasion, this approach can help you get around filesystem corruption on an ext3 filesystem. Occasionally Linux fails to identify the filesystem type, in which case you must supply it.

Another useful mount option is -a, which causes mount to examine the /etc/fstab file and mount all the filesystems described there (except for those that use the noauto option, as described in Task 5.5). This is particularly useful if you've temporarily unmounted filesystems for maintenance or if you've just made changes to /etc/fstab. You don't pass any device filename or mount point when you use this option; just type **mount -a**.

Still more mount options can be passed with the -o parameter, which accepts an option name. These are summarized in Table 5.2.

**TABLE 5.2**    Important Filesystem Options for the mount Command

| Option | Supported Filesystems | Description |
|---|---|---|
| loop | All | Causes the loopback device to be used for this mount. Allows you to mount a file as if it were a disk partition. For instance, **mount -o loop image.img /mnt/image** mounts the file image.img as if it were a disk. |
| remount | All | Changes one or more mount options without explicitly unmounting a partition. To use this option, you issue a mount command on an already-mounted filesystem but with remount along with any options you want to change. This feature can be used to enable or disable write access to a partition, for example. |
| ro | All | Specifies a read-only mount of the filesystem. This is the default for filesystems that include no write access and for some with particularly unreliable write support. |
| rw | All read/write filesystems | Specifies a read/write mount of the filesystem. This is the default for most read/write filesystems. |
| uid=value | Most filesystems that don't support Unix-style permissions, such as vfat, hpfs, ntfs, and hfs | Sets the owner of all files. For instance, uid=500 sets the owner to whoever has Linux user ID 500. (Check Linux user IDs in the /etc/passwd file.) |

**TABLE 5.2**    Important Filesystem Options for the mount Command *(continued)*

| Option | Supported Filesystems | Description |
|---|---|---|
| gid=*value* | Most filesystems that don't support Unix-style permissions, such as vfat, hpfs, ntfs, and hfs | Works like uid=*value*, but sets the group of all files on the filesystem. You can find group IDs in the /etc/group file. |
| umask=*value* | Most filesystems that don't support Unix-style permissions, such as vfat, hpfs, ntfs, and hfs | Sets the umask for the permissions on files. *value* is interpreted in binary as bits to be removed from permissions on files. For instance, umask=027 yields permissions of 750, or –rwxr-x---. Used in conjunction with uid=*value* and gid=*value*, this option lets you control who can access files on FAT, HPFS, and many other foreign filesystems. |
| conv=*code* | Most filesystems used on Microsoft and Apple OSs: msdos, umsdos, vfat, hpfs, hfs | If *code* is b or binary, Linux doesn't modify the files' contents. If *code* is t or text, Linux auto-converts files between Linux-style and DOS- or Macintosh-style end-of-line characters. If *code* is a or auto, Linux applies the conversion unless the file is a known binary file format. It's usually best to leave this at its default value of binary because file conversions can cause serious problems for some applications and file types. |
| norock | iso9660 | Disables Rock Ridge extensions for ISO-9660 CD-ROMs. |
| nojoliet | iso9660 | Disables Joliet extensions for ISO-9660 CD-ROMs. |

Some filesystems support additional options that aren't described here. The man page for mount covers some of these, but you may need to look to the filesystem's documentation for some filesystems and options. This documentation may appear in /usr/src/linux/Documentation/filesystems or /usr/src/linux/fs/*fsname*, where *fsname* is the name of the filesystem.

## Unmounting a Filesystem

Sometimes you don't want to leave a filesystem mounted permanently. This is most often the case for removable media, but if you need to perform maintenance or alter your partition layout, you need to unmount even a filesystem that's normally mounted. In either case, the tool to use is umount:

```
# umount /home2
```

You can specify either the mount point or the device filename to unmount a filesystem, so you could substitute /dev/sda1 for /home2 in the preceding example. You're unlikely to use options, aside from the mount point or device filename; however, umount does support several. You should check its man page for details, but a few options you might want to use on occasion are listed here:

**Remount read-only on failure**   The umount command fails if files are open on the filesystem. The -r option causes the command to attempt to switch the mount to read-only mode if this happens. This can be helpful because it can limit damage if you're about to do something that could damage filesystems, say by crashing the computer.

**Unmount all filesystems**   The -a option causes umount to unmount all filesystems that are recorded in /etc/mtab (a file that the system uses to track mounted filesystems). You wouldn't ordinarily use this option, but you can combine it with the next one to unmount all filesystems of a particular type.

**Operate on specific filesystem types**   The -t *fstype* option tells umount to operate only on filesystems of the specified type.

**Force unmount**   The -f option forces an unmount of an NFS mount even if it doesn't respond. This option has no effect with most filesystem types, though; it's intended to enable you to unmount an NFS mount if the server goes down or becomes unreachable.

## Criteria for Completion

To complete this task, you should have mounted a filesystem (such as the one created in Task 5.3), verified that it's mounted, and unmounted it. This task also presents a number of filesystem options. You might use these in the future, but you don't need to use them to complete this task.

# Task 5.5: Use */etc/fstab*

The mount command is useful for enabling access to a filesystem on a one-time basis. If you want to make a filesystem permanently accessible, though, you must modify the /etc/fstab file, which describes all the filesystems that Linux mounts at boot time. You can also tell your system about swap space in /etc/fstab.

## Scenario

You want to permanently add the filesystem and swap space you created in Task 5.3 to the computer. In addition, you want to add an NFS export (/optexp on the nfsserver computer, to be mounted at /opt) in read-only mode and an entry for a Zip drive you've added to the system. The Zip drive entry should enable ordinary users to mount and unmount disks.

## Scope of Task

This task requires editing a single configuration file, /etc/fstab. To test that your changes work, you'll need to use the mount command both as root and as an ordinary user.

### Duration

This task should take about half an hour to complete. Once you're familiar with it, making simple changes to the /etc/fstab file will take just a few seconds, and testing them will take a few seconds more. If you need to gather data such as filesystem type codes or add hardware, though, total modification times can stretch into several minutes.

### Setup

You'll need access to the disk you used in Task 5.3, so be sure it's installed and ready. To add the NFS server and Zip disk entries, you'll need access to an NFS server and a Zip disk. If you don't have these things, you should simply read the relevant descriptions. Most of this task requires root access, so you should log in and acquire superuser privileges.

### Caveats

The usual cautions concerning working as root apply to this task. Furthermore, the /etc/fstab file is a critical system configuration file. If you accidentally delete or change a line, you could cause problems ranging from subtle and minor problems on relatively unimportant filesystems to rendering your system unbootable.

Make a backup of your /etc/fstab file before proceeding further. You can then restore your backup copy once you're done, which should minimize the risk of problems cropping up because of mistakes in your configuration.

## Procedure

To perform this task, you must add four lines to your /etc/fstab file, one for each of the three filesystems and one swap partition you want to configure. Before you begin, though, you should familiarize yourself with the file format used by /etc/fstab.

### Understanding the */etc/fstab* File Format

The /etc/fstab file consists of a series of lines that contain six fields each; the fields are separated by one or more spaces or tabs. A line that begins with a hash mark (#) is a comment and is ignored. Listing 5.1 shows a sample /etc/fstab file.

**Listing 5.1:** Sample /etc/fstab File

```
#device        mount point   filesystem options    dump fsck
/dev/hda1      /             ext3       defaults      1 1
```

```
LABEL=/home    /home        reiserfs    defaults           0 0
/dev/hdb5      /windows     vfat        uid=500,umask=0 0 0
/dev/hdc       /mnt/cdrom   iso9660     users,noauto       0 0
/dev/fd0       /mnt/floppy  auto        users,noauto       0 0
/dev/hda4      swap         swap        defaults           0 0
```

The meaning of each field in this file is as follows:

**Device**    The first column specifies the mount device. These are usually device filenames that reference hard disks, floppy drives, and so on. Some distributions, such as Red Hat, have taken to specifying partitions by their labels, as in the LABEL=/home entry in Listing 5.1. When Linux encounters such an entry, it tries to find the partition whose filesystem has the specified name and mount it. This practice can help reduce problems if partition numbers change, but many filesystems lack these labels. It's also possible to list a network drive, as described shortly in "Adding Network Mounts."

**Mount point**    The second column specifies the mount point. This should usually be an empty directory in another filesystem. The root (/) filesystem is an exception. So is swap space, which is indicated by an entry of swap.

**Filesystem type**    The filesystem type code is the same as the type code used to mount a filesystem with the mount command. You can use any filesystem type code you can use directly with the mount command. A filesystem type code of auto lets the kernel auto-detect the filesystem type, which can be a convenient option for removable media devices. Auto-detection doesn't work with all filesystems, though.

**Mount options**    Table 5.2 describes several common mount options, which are passed using the -o command-line option to mount. You may specify multiple mount options, separated by commas. For instance, uid=500,umask=0 for /windows in Listing 5.1 sets the user ID (owner) of all files to 500 and sets the umask to 0. Type **man mount** or consult filesystem-specific documentation to learn more.

**Backup operation**    The next-to-last field contains a 1 if the dump utility should back up a partition or a 0 if it should not. If you never use the dump backup program, this option is essentially meaningless. The dump program is no longer a recommended backup tool for Linux, making this field unimportant in most cases.

**Filesystem check order**    At boot time, Linux uses the fsck program to check filesystem integrity. The final column specifies the order in which this check occurs. A 0 means that fsck should *not* check a filesystem. Higher numbers represent the check order. The root partition should have a value of 1, and all others that should be checked should have a value of 2. Some filesystems, such as ReiserFS, should not be automatically checked and so should have values of 0.

## Adding a Local Filesystem

To add a new filesystem, you must add an entry to /etc/fstab describing that filesystem—its device filename, mount point, filesystem type code, and so on. Entries for permanently mounted filesystems resemble the first two or three noncomment lines in Listing 5.1, but of course you'll set the specifics according to the filesystem you want to add. For the filesystem created in Task 5.3, the entry would look like this:

```
/dev/sda1    /home2      ext3        defaults        0 2
```

This line tells Linux to mount /dev/sda1 at /home2, treating the filesystem as using ext3fs and using the default options. The entry tells the system not to use dump to back up the filesystem but to check it at boot time after checking the root filesystem.

Most Linux native filesystem entries will closely resemble this one or one of the first two entries shown in Listing 5.1. If you add non-Linux filesystems, they're likely to deviate more from this mold. The entry for the /windows directory in Listing 5.1 is an example. Consult Table 5.2, mount's man page, and any filesystem-specific documentation you can find to learn how to achieve any specific results you need when mounting filesystems.

## Adding Swap Space

The final line in Listing 5.1 tells Linux about swap space. To add more swap space, you'd create a similar listing. For instance, to add the swap space you created in Task 5.3, you'd add a line that resembles the following:

```
/dev/sda5    swap        swap        defaults        0 0
```

Swap space entries shouldn't ordinarily deviate far from this example, aside from changing the device file specification in the first column. If you created swap space as an ordinary file rather than a partition, you should provide the complete path to the swap file in place of a partition identifier. You can define multiple swap space entries in /etc/fstab. If you do so, Linux will attempt to use all the swap space.

If you mistakenly specify a non-swap partition, Linux should recognize that fact and ignore the entry. Thus, you're unlikely to wipe out valuable data if you make a typo when entering the device file specification. Nonetheless, you should be cautious with that field, just to be on the safe side.

## Adding Network Mounts

Network mounts work much like local filesystem specifications. The main difference is that you must enter a server name and the name of the resource you want to access instead of a device filename. For instance, to mount the /optexp export from the NFS server known as nfsserver, you might create an entry that looks like this:

```
nfsserver:/optexp /opt   nfs         ro              0 0
```

In the case of NFS servers, the export is identified by the server hostname, a colon, and the path to the directory to be accessed. The rest of the /etc/fstab entries on the client computer are similar to those for local mounts. This example specified ro rather than defaults as a mount option because the Scenario specified a read-only mount. (Presumably you want to share software, fonts, or other data that ordinary users won't be modifying via the /opt directory tree and have no need for machine-specific data in /opt on any of the clients.)

If you want to mount an SMB/CIFS share, the procedure is similar, but you specify the server and share as //*server*/*share* rather than *server*:/*export*. (NFS uses the term *export* for its shared directories, whereas SMB/CIFS uses the term *share*.) SMB/CIFS also uses user-names and passwords to control access, which complicates matters. The best way to pass this information is to include a `credentials=`*filename* option in `/etc/fstab` and place the user-name and password in the specified file:

```
username=george
password=somepassword
```

A configuration such as the one shown here also requires configuring the NFS server computer. This is done by editing the /etc/exports file on the server. The server computer must be told to enable specific clients (or groups of clients) to access its exports. This topic is covered in Phase 6.

## Adding User-Controlled Mounts

Linux requires filesystems to be mounted in order to access them in an ordinary way, but Linux doesn't permit ordinary users to mount and unmount arbitrary filesystems. This can lead to a problem: How can an ordinary user access a floppy disk, CD-ROM, or other removable media? This problem can even extend to network mounts, if keeping them permanently mounted is unnecessary or undesirable. One solution to these problems is to use an *automounter*, which is a software tool that checks for accesses to particular directories and automatically mounts a file-system when it detects such accesses. Many Linux distributions that are intended for use on desk-top computers ship with automounter support. Another approach is to enable ordinary users to mount and unmount filesystems that are specified in `/etc/fstab`. This is done by adding options to the `/etc/fstab` entry for a file:

**users**   This option enables ordinary users to mount and unmount the filesystem using a sim-plified syntax, as described shortly.

**user**   This option works just like `users` except that the system remembers who mounted the filesystem. Only that user (or `root`) may unmount the filesystem.

**owner**   This option works very much like `user` except that only the user who owns the mount point (or `root`) may mount the filesystem. This is handy if you want to give just one user the right to mount a filesystem.

**noauto**   This option tells Linux to not automatically mount the filesystem when it boots or when you type **mount -a**. This is most helpful for removable media, but you can use it with any filesystem except those that are required for system operation.

The Scenario specifies that you want to enable ordinary users to mount and unmount a Zip disk that you've added to the computer. Zip disks are ordinarily partitioned so that the fourth primary partition holds the disk's single partition. (They can be repartitioned in other ways, though.) Thus, assuming your Zip disk is accessible as `/dev/sdb`, you could create an entry like the following to do the job:

```
/dev/sdb4    /mnt/zip    auto    users,noauto    0 0
```

You will, of course, need to create the mount point—/mnt/zip in this example. Because the filesystem type is specified as auto, Linux should auto-detect the filesystem type, whether it's FAT, ext2fs, HFS, or anything else. You could use the user or owner option in place of users, depending on the precise rules you want to use for who may mount and unmount Zip disks. To test this change, you should first type **mount -a** as root. This command is necessary to register the new entry with Linux, even though Linux won't automount the disk. You can then type **mount /mnt/zip** as an ordinary user. The Zip disk should mount and become accessible. Typing **umount /mnt/zip** should unmount it.

## Criteria for Completion

To complete this task, you should have successfully added /etc/fstab entries for four items: a new /home2 filesystem, additional swap space, an NFS export, and a user-mountable Zip disk. Each of these entries takes just one line in /etc/fstab.

# Task 5.6: Check Filesystem Integrity

Unfortunately, computers aren't perfect. Bugs, hardware failures, power outages, and other problems can cause data corruption. If left uncorrected, such problems can cause further data corruption, possibly leading to the loss of all the data on a disk. For this reason, Linux provides a tool, fsck, which checks the integrity of your filesystem's basic data structures. Knowing how to use fsck can help you keep your system healthy and fix problems when they occur.

 The fsck tool checks the *filesystem's* data structures. It won't help you if *individual data files* become garbled unless that problem is directly related to a filesystem issue.

## Scenario

After your /home2 filesystem has been in operation for some time, you begin hearing complaints from users about files vanishing, filenames changing, and other mysterious disk-related issues. You suspect the filesystem may have been damaged, so you want to check and repair it with fsck.

## Scope of Task

This task involves using a single fsck command and a couple of preparatory and clean-up commands, so the task itself is fairly limited. You should understand some of what fsck can and cannot do before you proceed, though.

## Duration

This task should take about half an hour to complete. A single run of fsck can take anywhere from a few seconds to many minutes (perhaps even over an hour), depending on the size of the filesystem, the speed of the disk, the number of files stored on the filesystem, and so on.

## Setup

You should have access to the disk you prepared in Tasks 5.2 and 5.3 or to some other convenient partition that's not required for system operation. (If necessary, you can create a filesystem on a floppy disk and use it to complete this task.) You must have superuser access to check a filesystem, so log in and acquire root privileges.

## Caveats

The usual caveats concerning root access apply to this task. Beyond these cautions, checking a filesystem is theoretically safe, even if you accidentally enter the wrong partition device code. Checking a filesystem that's currently mounted, though, is not safe; changes made by the filesystem check code can cause the kernel to become confused and result in additional corruption. Fortunately, fsck checks to see if you're calling it on a mounted filesystem and warns you about this. Be sure to read all the messages displayed by fsck as it operates. If you see a warning you don't understand or that causes you concern, tell the software to stop and research that message before proceeding.

# Procedure

To perform a disk check, you use the filesystem check (fsck) program. Ordinarily, its use is fairly straightforward. On occasion, though, you might want to use additional tools to give your filesystem a tune-up.

## Basic Disk Checking

To check the integrity of a filesystem and automatically repair any damage, you can pass the device filename to fsck. If necessary, unmount the filesystem first:

```
# umount /dev/sda1
# fsck /dev/sda1
```

**WARNING**    As noted earlier, you should be sure the filesystem is unmounted before using fsck. Failure to unmount the filesystem can, paradoxically, cause filesystem damage.

The fsck program, like mkfs, is actually a front end to other programs, named fsck.*filesystem*, where *filesystem* is the filesystem name. Some filesystem utility packages provide additional links to their filesystem check programs, such as e2fsck for ext2 and ext3 filesystems. Thus, you may have multiple options for how to check a filesystem, but `fsck` should always work—at least if a filesystem check program for your filesystem is installed.

 Filesystem check programs are delivered in packages of support tools for particular filesystems. If you haven't installed the relevant package, the appropriate filesystem check tool won't exist. Linux lacks support entirely for checking some non-Linux filesystems, although filesystem check tools for some common ones, such as FAT, do exist (called `fsck.msdos`).

The details of what happens when you use `fsck` depends on the filesystem and its specific checking program. In some cases, you'll see one or more lines summarizing the actions the program is taking, which in the case of a clean filesystem will be nothing but checks. In other cases you'll be asked to authorize certain actions, even including initiating the check operation. If the filesystem contains errors, you may be asked what to do about them. These prompts can be quite confusing, so taking the default action is usually the best approach unless you have expert knowledge. You can pass the `-a` option to have `fsck` perform filesystem cleaning options without prompting you about them.

Because each filesystem has unique features, filesystem check programs also support unique features. You can pass filesystem-specific options to the check programs by calling them directly or by passing them via `fsck` after a double dash (`--`) option. For instance, the `fsck.ex2` program doesn't ordinarily perform a full check unless it finds that the filesystem hasn't been cleanly unmounted. You can force it to check a filesystem by passing it the `-f` option:

```
# fsck /dev/sda1 -- -f
```

If you prefer, you can call `fsck.ext2` (or `e2fsck`) directly:

```
# fsck.ext2 -f /dev/sda1
```

All filesystem check programs support a wide variety of options. You may want to review the man pages for `fsck` and for the check programs for your most important filesystems.

## Tuning Your Filesystem

Some filesystems provide maintenance tools beyond their `fsck.filesystem` programs. The most notable of these tools is `tune2fs`, which is used to adjust the features of an ext2 or ext3 filesystem. You can change parameters that you ordinarily set at filesystem creation time and you can fine-tune the filesystem in other ways. This tool supports a very large number of options, so you should consult its man page for a complete listing. Some of the more interesting features you can change included the following:

**Adjust maximum mount count**   Ext2fs and ext3fs require a periodic disk check with `fsck`. This check is designed to prevent errors from creeping onto the disk undetected, and it's normally performed automatically at boot time. You can adjust the maximum number of times the disk may be mounted without a check with the `-c` *mounts* option, where *mounts* is the number of mounts. You can trick the system into thinking the filesystem has been mounted a certain number of times with the `-C` *mounts* option; this sets the mount counter to *mounts*.

**Adjust time between checks**   Periodic disk checks are required based on time as well as the number of mounts. You can set the time between checks with the -i *interval* option, where *interval* is the maximum time between checks. Normally, *interval* is a number with the character d, w, or m appended, to specify days, weeks, or months, respectively.

**Add a journal**   The -j option adds a journal to the filesystem, effectively converting an ext2 filesystem into an ext3 filesystem.

**Set the reserved blocks**   The -m *percent* option sets the percentage of disk space that's reserved for use by root. The default value is 5, but this is excessive on large multi-gigabyte hard disks, so you may want to reduce it. You may want to set it to 0 on removable disks intended to store user files. You can also set the reserved space in blocks, rather than by the percentage of disk space, with the -r *blocks* option.

As with most low-level disk utilities, you shouldn't use tune2fs to adjust a mounted filesystem. If you want to adjust a key mounted filesystem, such as your root (/) filesystem, you may need to boot up an emergency disk system, such as the CD-ROM-based Knoppix (http://www.knoppix.org).

## Criteria for Completion

To complete this task you should have performed a disk check on one or more filesystems. You should be sure to unmount any filesystem before you check it. If your disk check revealed errors, the check program should have corrected them, possibly with some intervention by you.

The Scenario specified that users reported strange disk-related behavior. Such problems can result from corrupted disk data structures, but they can also occur because of bad RAM, a bad CPU, buggy software, a system intrusion, or other problems. If a filesystem check reveals no errors, or if you correct errors but problems recur, you should investigate other possible sources of such problems.

# Task 5.7: Configure a Boot Loader

Most Linux software is stored in filesystems, which are normally held (on hard disks) in partitions. One critical piece of software, though, resides partly outside of filesystems and perhaps even outside of partitions. This software is the *boot loader*, which is the first program that a computer runs when it boots, outside of the BIOS. The boot loader is responsible for loading the Linux (or other OS's) kernel into memory and running it. Most Linux systems use one of two boot loaders: the Linux Loader (LILO) or the Grand Unified Boot Loader (GRUB). Knowing how to configure these boot loaders will enable you to upgrade your kernel or pass new options to your kernel.

LILO and GRUB both work on *x*86 and *x*86-64 computers. Other platforms, such as PowerPC or SPARC computers, have their own boot loaders. You'll need to consult platform-specific documentation to learn how to configure them.

# Scenario

In Phase 2, "Managing Hardware and the Kernel," you compiled a new kernel for your computer. Now it's time to configure your boot loader to use that new kernel.

# Scope of Task

This task involves editing a configuration file and possibly typing a command to implement your changes. In principle, this is a fairly straightforward operation. In practice, it can be a bit tricky to get it right and debugging problems can be difficult because you must reboot the computer to test your changes.

## Duration

You should be able to complete this task in about 15 to 30 minutes if all goes smoothly. If you encounter problems, it could take longer than that, particularly if you need to tweak your kernel configuration and recompile your kernel again, as described in Phase 2.

## Setup

You must have completed a kernel compilation, as described in Phase 2, or have installed a suitable kernel in some other way. (Installing a kernel package may do the trick on many distributions.) Reconfiguring your boot loader requires `root` access, so you should log in and acquire that access.

## Caveats

The usual `root` access caveats apply. In addition, reconfiguring your boot loader runs the risk of your rendering the computer unbootable. This risk is minimal if you're careful to *add* new entries rather than *change* working entries. Replacing LILO with GRUB or GRUB with LILO greatly increases the risks, so you're advised to modify your working boot loader's configuration rather than change from one boot loader to the other.

# Procedure

Before proceeding, you should understand a few boot loader principles. These will enable you to better understand what your boot loader does, and therefore how you can modify its configuration. LILO and GRUB are both popular boot loaders, but their configuration procedures are entirely different from one another. Therefore, you must start by determining which boot loader your system uses. You can then proceed to modifying your installed boot loader. Whichever one you modify, you'll conclude by rebooting your computer to test the new configuration.

## Boot Loader Principles

The LILO and GRUB boot loaders both consist of several components:

- A small piece of code that resides in the MBR or boot sector of the boot partition. The BIOS runs this code when the system boots, and this code is then responsible for loading your kernel into memory and running it. For simplicity's sake, I refer to this component as *MBR code*, even when it's installed outside of the MBR.

- Support files, including configuration files and ancillary code. The boot loader calls upon these files, either at boot time or when placing the code in the MBR, to perform tasks that are too complex for the simple MBR code to perform.

- Linux utility programs. These programs place code in the MBR and otherwise configure the boot loader.

When you install a LILO or GRUB package, you're really installing the utility programs and at least some support files. Actually installing the MBR code requires running a utility program. In the case of LILO, you must do this every time you make a change to the boot loader configuration. In the case of GRUB, the MBR code doesn't change once it's installed; instead, you change configuration files that the MBR code reads (with the help of additional support files) at boot time.

Boot loaders (that is, their MBR code) can reside either in the MBR or in the boot sector (that is, the first sector) of a disk partition or removable disk. If the MBR code resides in the MBR, it's referred to as a *primary boot loader*. Generally speaking, this is the simplest and best configuration for a Linux-only system. If the MBR code resides outside of the MBR, in the boot sector of a bootable partition, then LILO or GRUB becomes a *secondary boot loader*. Another boot loader must then reside in the MBR. This primary boot loader is most often the simple boot loader that's been used on *x86* systems since the days of DOS. This approach has an advantage in dual-boot scenarios because DOS and Windows have a habit of overwriting the MBR code when they're installed. Thus, if you install Linux and then install or upgrade Windows, LILO or GRUB can be wiped out. Putting your Linux boot loader in a partition keeps it safe and you can begin using it again by using DOS's FDISK to mark the Linux boot partition as being bootable.

The assumption in the rest of this task is that your Linux boot loader configuration works; you just need to add a new kernel to it. If your boot loader has stopped working, you might need to use DOS's FDISK, as just noted, to mark a primary Linux partition as bootable, or you might need to use a Linux emergency disk to re-install LILO's or GRUB's MBR component.

## Identifying Your Boot Loader

Once your OS is booted, no traces remain of which boot loader started the kernel running. To determine which boot loader your system uses, therefore, you'll need to look for clues in the form of options presented by the boot loader at boot time, configuration files on your computer, and so on. Specifically, you should look at the following items:

**Boot-time options**    In its simplest form, LILO presents a boot prompt that reads `lilo:` or `boot:`. You can then press the Tab key to see a list of options or type an option name to boot that kernel or OS. GRUB is more visually interesting; it presents a list of options, which often have multi-word names; you select from them by using the keyboard's arrow keys. Modern LILO configurations often present similar menus, though, so spotting which boot loader your system uses at boot time can be tricky unless it's LILO configured to use a non-menu boot prompt.

**Configuration files**    LILO uses a configuration file called `/etc/lilo.conf`. GRUB uses a configuration file called `/boot/grub/grub.conf` or `/boot/grub/menu.1st`, depending on your distribution. If your system has one of these files but not the others, you can be pretty sure that your system uses the associated boot loader. Some systems have both LILO and GRUB configuration files, though, so this identification method isn't always perfectly reliable.

**Support programs**    Both LILO and GRUB use ordinary program files to install themselves to the MBR. For LILO, this program is called `lilo`, and for GRUB, it's `grub`. Both program files are likely to reside in `/sbin`, but check `/bin`, `/usr/bin`, `/usr/sbin`, `/usr/local/bin`, and `/usr/local/sbin` to be complete.

**Package presence**    Try using your package manager to locate the boot loader's package. LILO is typically installed as `lilo` and GRUB is generally installed as `grub` or `grub-static`. It's conceivable that you'll miss a package if it's installed under some other name, though, so this method of identification isn't perfectly reliable.

The worst-case scenario when you search for evidence of LILO and GRUB is to find indications of both packages' presence. This can happen if your system has undergone upgrades that included a change from one boot loader to another or if a previous administrator experimented with both boot loaders. In this case, you might want to reboot, take notes on the OSs and kernels that are presented as boot options, and compare these options to the ones shown in both boot loader configuration files.

Assuming you can identify the boot loader your system uses, you should proceed to configuring it. You should read the section on the other boot loader for completeness, but don't attempt to use it; if it's improperly configured, the result can be an unbootable system.

## Adding a Kernel to LILO

The LILO configuration file, `/etc/lilo.conf`, consists of a series of lines that set options, mostly by specifying an option name, an equal sign (=), and an option value. Listing 5.2 shows an example. The `boot=` option is a particularly important global option; it identifies where the MBR code will reside. Give it a disk identifier (such as `/dev/hda`) and the code goes in the MBR of the specified disk; give it a partition identifier (such as `/dev/hda3`) and the code goes in the boot sector of the specified partition. In addition to the global options, each Linux kernel configuration begins with an `image=` line, which points to a Linux kernel image file. Subsequent lines are typically (but not always) indented and provide options that are passed to the kernel, that identify the kernel, and so on. Non-Linux OSs may be booted by LILO and typically begin with an `other=` line. An `image=` or `other=` line and all subsequent lines up until the next `image=` or `other=` line are called a *stanza*.

**Listing 5.2:** Sample `lilo.conf` File

```
boot=/dev/hda
prompt
delay=40
map=/boot/map
install=/boot/boot.b
default=linux
lba32
message=/boot/message
image=/boot/bzImage-2.6.10
        label=linux
        root=/dev/hda9
        append="mem=256M"
        read-only
other=/dev/hda3
        label=windows
        table=/dev/hda
```

It's possible to configure LILO to boot either of two or more kernels using the same distribution. This can be very convenient when you want to test a new kernel. Rather than eliminate your old working configuration, you install a new kernel alongside the old one and create a new `lilo.conf` entry for the new kernel. The result is that you can select either the old kernel or the new one at boot time. If the new kernel doesn't work as expected, you can reboot and select the old kernel. This procedure allows you to avoid otherwise ugly situations should a new kernel not boot at all.

Assuming you don't need to change kernel options or other features, one procedure for adding a new kernel to LILO is as follows:

1. Install the new kernel file, typically in /boot. Ensure that you *do not* overwrite the existing kernel file, though. You should have done this as part of the kernel recompilation in Phase 2.

2. Copy the stanza for the existing kernel file in /etc/lilo.conf. The result is two identical stanzas.

3. Modify the name (`label`) of one of the stanzas to reflect the new kernel name. You can use any name you like, even a numeric one, such as 26177 for the 2.6.17.7 kernel.

4. Adjust the `image` line in the new kernel's stanza to point to the new kernel file.

5. If you want to make the new kernel the default, change the `default` line to point to the new kernel.

It's generally best to hold off on making the new kernel the default until you've tested it. If you make this change too early and then can't get around to fixing problems with the new kernel for a while, you might find yourself accidentally booting the bad kernel. This is normally a minor nuisance.

**6.** Save your /etc/lilo.conf changes.

**7.** Type **lilo** to install LILO in the MBR or boot partition's boot sector.

At this point, your new kernel is set up and ready to be tested, as described shortly in "Testing Your Changes."

## Adding a Kernel to GRUB

LILO was designed expressly for Linux, but GRUB was designed with a broader set of OSs in mind. Thus, it does things a bit differently, which can be confusing at times. In particular, GRUB introduces a new way of referring to hard disks and their partitions. Rather than Linux device files, such as /dev/hda and /dev/hda9, GRUB uses strings of the form (hd*x*, *y*), where *x* is a disk number and *y* is a partition number. (The *y* and preceding comma may be omitted to refer to an entire disk or its MBR.) Both the *x* and the *y* are numbered starting from 0, which contrasts with Linux's numbering partitions starting with 1. Thus, Linux's /dev/hda9 is GRUB's (hd0,8). GRUB doesn't distinguish between ATA and SCSI disks; hd0 is the first disk recognized by the BIOS, hd1 is the second disk, and so on.

Listing 5.3 shows a typical GRUB configuration file. Like the LILO configuration file, it consists of a series of global options followed by stanzas (beginning with the keyword **title**) for the OSs or kernels it boots. You should be able to figure out what most of these options mean, even if a few of them remain mysterious.

**Listing 5.3:** Sample GRUB Configuration File

```
default=0
timeout=4
splashimage=(hd0,3)/grub/splash.xpm.gz
title Linux (2.6.10)
    root (hd0,3)
    kernel /bzImage-2.6.10 ro root=/dev/hda9 mem=256M
    boot
title Windows
    rootnoverify (hd0,1)
    chainloader +1
    boot
```

The procedure for adding a kernel to GRUB is very similar to the procedure to add a kernel to LILO:

**1.** Install the new kernel file, typically in /boot. Ensure that you *do not* overwrite the existing kernel file, though. You should have done this as part of the kernel recompilation in Phase 2.

**2.** Copy the stanza for the existing kernel file in your GRUB configuration file. The result is two identical stanzas.

3. Modify the name (`title`) of one of the stanzas to reflect the new kernel name. You can use any name you like, but it's typical to use a moderately long and descriptive name.

4. Adjust the `kernel` line in the new kernel's stanza to point to the new kernel file. Note that the kernel file reference is relative to the GRUB root directory, which is specified by the **root** option. This will be the Linux root (/) directory unless you have a separate /**boot** partition, in which case the GRUB root directory is the Linux /**boot** directory. In Listing 5.3, the kernel is specified without the /**boot** directory name, so the system presumably uses a separate /**boot** partition.

5. If you want to make the new kernel the default, change the `default` line to point to the new kernel. GRUB numbers its stanzas starting with 0.

 It's generally best to hold off on making the new kernel the default until you've tested it. If you make this change too early and then can't get around to fixing problems with the new kernel for a while, you might find yourself accidentally booting the bad kernel. This is normally a minor nuisance.

6. Save your GRUB configuration file changes.

There's no need to re-install your MBR code in the way you do with LILO. The existing GRUB MBR code should find your GRUB configuration file changes and implement them. If your GRUB installation is damaged and you've booted using an emergency disk, however, you can re-install GRUB using the `grub-install` command:

```
# grub-install (hd0)
```

This command installs the GRUB MBR code to the MBR of the first disk, (`hd0`)—normally /dev/hda or /dev/sda. If your setup is odd or complex, you may need to use the interactive `grub` utility instead. Consult its `info` page for details.

## Testing Your Changes

At this point, you should be able to test your changes. Shut down and reboot your computer. You should see your new kernel appear as a menu option (or as an option you can type at a `lilo:` or `boot:` prompt, in the case of simpler LILO configurations). Selecting this option should boot you into your new kernel. Once you've booted and logged in, type **uname -a**. This command produces a line or two of output summarizing various system information, including the kernel version number. Verify that the kernel version number matches what you expect. If it doesn't, review your boot loader configuration to be sure you remembered to change the kernel filename.

If the kernel doesn't boot, or if it begins to boot but then hangs before finishing, it's possible that your boot loader configuration is incorrect. Reboot into your old kernel and check to be sure you didn't introduce any typos, particularly in the LILO root= line or in the GRUB root= option on the `kernel` line. It's also possible that your freshly compiled kernel is lacking a critical driver or filesystem. Remember that the kernel must be able to read your root (/) filesystem, which means it needs drivers for your disk controller and the filesystem you used on your root partition. If necessary, go back to Phase 2, review your kernel configuration, and recompile it.

If you've gotten everything working, then you may want to go back to the boot loader configuration procedures described earlier. For both LILO and GRUB, repeat the steps beginning with step 5 to make your new kernel the default. Thereafter, your system should boot into the new kernel. You might even want to delete or comment out old kernel configurations. This is particularly helpful if you upgrade your kernel regularly, to keep your boot loader configuration uncluttered.

## Criteria for Completion

To complete this task, you should have successfully added a new kernel (the one you compiled in Phase 2) to your boot loader's configuration. This task requires you to identify which boot loader your system uses, modify its configuration file, re-install the MBR code (for LILO only), and test the configuration by rebooting into your new kernel.

# Phase

# 6

# Configuring Network Features

Linux is frequently deployed in a network-centric role—often as a network server, but frequently as a platform for network client programs or as a router. (Network server programs respond to requests from other systems for data transfer, whereas network clients initiate those requests.) For Linux to function in one of these network-centric roles, you must be able to configure it to use a network. Most of this book has assumed that your Linux system is so configured, but this phase looks at actually doing the job, beginning with basic network configuration and monitoring tasks. Next up are several tasks relating to routing and common network servers, including mail servers, Web servers, and file servers. (Clients typically require less configuration and so aren't described in detail.) Finally, this phase examines printer configuration; Linux's printer support is inherently network enabled.

This task maps to portions of the CompTIA Linux+ objectives 2 and 3 and to portions of the LPIC objectives 107, 112, and 113.

# Task 6.1: Understand TCP/IP

Before you delve into the details of network configuration, you should learn something about how the Transmission Control Protocol/Internet Protocol (TCP/IP) works. TCP/IP is the basis of most of Linux's networking tools, including the tools at the core of the Internet and Linux's ability to use the Internet.

## Scenario

You're preparing to configure a computer to use your office's local area network (LAN). In order to do so, you must understand various networking concepts: network hardware, protocol stacks, network addressing, hostname resolution, and ports. This task presents tools and procedures you can use to help learn about these concepts. Subsequent tasks in this phase build on this knowledge, enabling you to configure your system to use a network in a practical way.

## Scope of Task

This task involves using various network tools on a computer that's already configured for basic network connectivity. None of these tools is described in great detail, but each should help you better understand the concept it utilizes.

## Duration

This task should take about an hour to complete. In practical use, each of the tools described in this task requires just a few seconds to a few minutes to use.

## Setup

You must have access to a Linux computer with a working network connection to complete this task. (Ideally, the computer should be connected to the Internet, but this isn't strictly required.) You don't need `root` access to complete this task.

## Caveats

Because `root` access isn't required to complete this task, risks are low. Some of the tools described in this task do have the potential to cause problems on your LAN or on the Internet at large if abused, but you'd need to be extremely careless or malicious to cause problems with these programs.

# Procedure

To perform this task, you'll use a variety of Linux commands and configuration files to learn about network concepts. You've used some of these commands in previous tasks, and some of the others appear in subsequent tasks.

## Understanding Network Hardware

At the core of any computer network is the hardware. Without dedicated network hardware, no network can function. The details of network hardware vary, though, and one LAN can use hardware that's quite different from another LAN. Common network hardware includes:

**Modems**   At the low end of the scale, modulators/demodulators (modems) enable network connections over telephone lines. Modems are typically used in conjunction with the Point-to-Point Protocol (PPP) to initiate a connection between your computer and an Internet service provider's (ISP's) PPP server, which in turn is connected to the Internet. PPP connections are usually transitory in nature; you dial up, perform some Internet tasks, and then log off. Modems can plug into your computer or they can be stand-alone devices that connect via Universal Serial Bus (USB) or RS-232 ports. Modem connections are becoming less important since broadband is taking over the market niche traditionally occupied by modem ISPs.

**Broadband**   A broadband connection provides a high-speed link between your computer and your ISP. Broadband connections are also often always up, which reduces the lead time required when you want to perform network activities. Broadband typically comes in one of two forms: *Digital Subscriber Line (DSL)*, which uses telephone lines, and *cable modems*, which work over cable TV lines. Some broadband providers deliver internal broadband modems (although they're not compatible with conventional modems). Others use external modems, which usually connect to your computer using USB or Ethernet. External Ethernet-based modems are the most likely to work correctly with Linux.

**Ethernet**   Today, Ethernet is the most common type of hardware for LANs in offices, and it's also moderately common in homes. Modern computers often come with Ethernet support built in, and for those that lack this support, it's most easily provided with a plug-in Ethernet card. Ethernet uses cabling that resembles telephone wires, but with somewhat wider plugs. Linux supports most Ethernet cards on the market. Several types of network hardware similar to Ethernet, such as Token Ring, exist; however, Ethernet dominates the wired LAN market.

**Wireless devices**   Wireless networking has become quite common in recent years. This form of networking requires plug-in cards similar to Ethernet cards, but wireless networks use radio transmissions rather than wires. The advantage is obvious: You're not tethered to a wire for your network connection. You may even be able to use wireless connections provided in coffee shops, hotels, and other environments away from your home or office. Wireless networking has two major drawbacks compared to Ethernet: First, it's usually slower than wired networking. Second, because your data are transmitted over radio frequencies, it's easy to intercept your transmissions. Wireless hardware and protocols support encryption, but all too often it's disabled. Even when it's enabled, wireless encryption can often be broken. Thus, if your network transactions are sensitive, you should either use a wired connection or be sure your wireless network is properly configured to provide the best security possible.

You may already know something about your network hardware. You might know you've got a cable modem, for instance, or that your office uses an Ethernet network. If you don't know much about your network hardware, try perusing your dmesg output:

**$ dmesg | less**

Try searching the output for network-related messages, and particularly those that refer to your network hardware. For instance, you might find something like this:

```
r8169 Gigabit Ethernet driver 1.2 loaded
divert: allocating divert_blk for eth0
eth0: Identified chip type is 'RTL8169s/8110s'.
eth0: RTL8169 at 0xffffff000004de00, 00:0c:76:96:a3:73, IRQ 10
eth0: Auto-negotiation Enabled.
eth0: 100Mbps Full-duplex operation.
```

This output describes information related to eth0, the first Ethernet interface. It uses the r8169 Ethernet driver, which supports the RTL8169 (RealTek 8169) chip. The driver has configured the Ethernet port to use 100Mbps full-duplex mode. Much of this information may seem like gibberish to you, but if you want to understand your hardware, it can be a useful starting point. You can perform a Web search to learn more.

Some computers contain two or more network interfaces and are configured to transfer traffic between those two interfaces; these are known as *routers* or *gateways*. For instance, a router in your office might contain both an Ethernet card and a wireless card, enabling laptops with wireless connections to use a print server that has nothing but an Ethernet connection. Routers don't need to link different types of network hardware; they can link together two networks that use similar hardware, such as two Ethernet networks. This can be handy for security reasons and to help segment a network to more easily support disparate groups of network addresses. Routers also tie the Internet together; when you communicate with a distant network, your data travels across multiple routers.

An isolated LAN can function without a router. If your LAN is connected to the Internet, though, it *must* have at least one router. Part of the network configuration is giving each computer on the LAN the address of the router.

## Using Network Protocol Stacks

Networking involves more than just network hardware; to communicate with an arbitrary computer elsewhere on your LAN or on the Internet, your computer must do more than simply blast random data out its network port. To facilitate communication, a network requires at least one *protocol stack*. This is a set of protocols that enable two computers to communicate with one another. Figure 6.1 provides a graphical illustration of the TCP/IP protocol stack, which is the one that's most commonly used today.

**FIGURE 6.1**    The TCP/IP protocol stack enables applications on disparate computers to communicate by providing a series of intervening software layers.

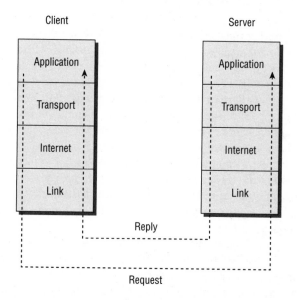

Each layer of the TCP/IP protocol stack communicates with the layers above and below it, with the exception of the top (Application) and bottom (Link) layers. The Application layer consists of network-enabled programs, such as Web browsers, email clients, Web servers, and email servers. The Link layer enables low-level communication with other computers via the network hardware. The intervening layers are responsible for "packing" and "unpacking" the data. An Application-layer program generates and responds to network requests using fairly high-level OS commands, but by the time the data have been sent or received by the Link layer, the data have been transformed into network *packets*, which are data segments of relatively small size (a few hundred bytes).

The key to a protocol stack is *compatibility*. A Linux TCP/IP stack might share no code in common with a stack for, say, Windows or Solaris, but the two stacks must be able to communicate with one another, and that means they must perform the same protocol operations. Without this compatibility, the Internet would not work, and even most LANs would be in trouble.

TCP/IP is the most common protocol stack, and it's the one on which the Internet is based. It's not the only one in existence, though. Linux supports a few other protocol stacks, as you can see if you check your kernel options:

```
# cd /usr/src/linux
# make xconfig
```

Phase 2 describes kernel configuration in more detail, and depending on how you completed Phase 2, you may be able to perform these steps as an ordinary user.

If you check the Networking area of the kernel configuration menus and click the Networking Options submenu, you'll see a wide variety of networking options. Most of these are related to TCP/IP and are in fact grouped under the TCP/IP Networking menu. Additional menus on the same level as TCP/IP Networking include The IPX Protocol and Apple-Talk Protocol Support. These are two alternatives to TCP/IP that are used on some LANs. If you know your LAN uses one or both of these protocols, you can enable it; however, you'll also need a suite of software packages to sit at the top of these protocol stacks (in the equivalent of Figure 6.1's Application layer).

Other kernel and Linux options affect other layers of the protocol stack. For instance, the Network Device Support submenu of the Device Drivers area of the kernel enables you to select network device drivers, which reside at the Link layer of the TCP/IP stack. Changing application programs or servers (for instance, switching from the Mozilla Firefox browser to KDE's Konqueror) alters the Application layer.

TCP/IP supports several Transport-layer protocols. The most important of these are the Transmission Control Protocol (TCP), after which TCP/IP is partially named; the User Datagram Protocol (UDP); and the Internet Control Message Protocol (ICMP). Most Application-layer protocols use TCP, which supports complex connections. Some protocols use UDP, which is less complex and robust than TCP but requires less overhead. A few low-level tools use ICMP, which is the least complex of these three protocols.

## Understanding Network Addressing

In order to work, networks require that computers have methods of addressing one another. Network addresses are something like telephone numbers or street addresses. Several different types of network addresses exist, though.

*Media Access Control (MAC) addresses*, also known as *hardware addresses*, are built into network hardware. They enable Ethernet cards and similar hardware to filter out packets that are addressed to other computers. You don't ordinarily need to deal with MAC addresses, but you can learn your computer's MAC address by using the `ifconfig` command:

```
$ ifconfig eth0
eth0    Link encap:Ethernet  HWaddr 00:0C:76:96:A3:73
        inet addr:192.168.1.3  Bcast:192.168.1.255  Mask:255.255.255.0
        UP BROADCAST NOTRAILERS RUNNING MULTICAST  MTU:1500  Metric:1
        RX packets:2351099 errors:0 dropped:0 overruns:0 frame:0
        TX packets:1668639 errors:0 dropped:0 overruns:0 carrier:0
        collisions:0 txqueuelen:1000
        RX bytes:1515498602 (1445.2 Mb)  TX bytes:262164666 (250.0 Mb)
        Interrupt:16 Base address:0xee00
```

This command reveals some basic information about `eth0`, the computer's first Ethernet interface. If your computer doesn't use Ethernet, omit `eth0` from this command. The result will be information on all of your network interfaces. Ignore the `lo` interface, which is for local functions only. Chances are there'll be only one other entry.

The MAC address appears on the first line of output, labeled `HWaddr`. In the case of Ethernet cards, the MAC address is a 6-byte number, typically expressed in hexadecimal (base 16) with colons between each number. Every hardware manufacturer is assigned a set of partial MAC addresses, and it's responsible for filling out the rest of each address. In theory, no two Ethernet cards should have the same MAC address. In practice, manufacturers sometimes slip up, but MAC addresses are usually unique. MAC addresses may be used only on a single LAN; this information is lost in cross-LAN data transfers using routers.

A second layer of addressing is the *IP address*. This address is a 4-byte number that's usually expressed in *dotted quad* notation: four decimal (base 10) numbers separated by dots. The computer's IP address appears on the second line of `ifconfig` output, labeled `inet addr`. Two related numbers are the *broadcast address*, which enables computers to send packets to all the computers on the network, and the *network mask* (*netmask* for short), which tells the computer which parts of the IP address specify the network and which parts specify the machine on the network. Converted to binary, 1 values in the netmask denote the network portion of the address while 0 values denote the computer portion. A netmask of 255.255.255.0 is common, but not universal, on small networks.

IP addresses are assigned in blocks to individuals or organizations who want a presence on the Internet. If you use a broadband or dial-up ISP, your ISP "owns" its IP addresses and tells you which one you may use. The ISP may do this personally or via a protocol such as the Dynamic Host Configuration Protocol (DHCP), which enables a computer that lacks an IP address to obtain one from a DHCP server. The same protocol is commonly used on LANs, many of which are assigned a block of IP addresses. Part of the job of the network stack is to associate IP addresses to MAC addresses. For cross-LAN transmissions, the router is responsible for keeping MAC addresses on both LANs straight.

Some IP addresses are reserved for private use: 192.168.0.0 to 192.168.255.255, 172.16.0.0 to 172.31.255.255, and 10.0.0.0 to 10.255.255.255. These addresses are not ordinarily routed, and the intent is that they may be used on LANs that aren't directly connected to the Internet. Even some Internet-connected LANs use these addresses, though. The trick is to use Network Address Translation (NAT) technology to enable one computer to function as a *NAT router*. To the rest of the Internet, the NAT router generates all the requests that are actually generated by computers on the protected network. This can be an important part of a network security scheme, but it complicates running servers on the NAT network. It's often used to connect clients at companies and other organizations to the Internet and to enable home and small business users to connect multiple computers to the Internet via a broadband link.

 The 4-byte IP address in common use in 2006 is likely to be supplanted by a new 16-byte addressing scheme, known as *IPv6*. The older (*IPv4*) system provides too few addresses for projected Internet growth and so is being phased out. This process is taking longer than was projected a few years ago, but Linux is capable of using both IPv4 and IPv6 addresses.

The final type of address used on LANs and the Internet is the *hostname*. People are bad at remembering long numbers, so hostnames are used instead. The process of *resolving* hostnames (that is, converting between hostnames and IP addresses) is described in the next section.

## Resolving Hostnames

TCP/IP hostnames are hierarchical. At the top level are the *top-level domains (TLDs)*, which are the short abbreviations at the ends of domain names, such as .com, .net, and .uk. Below this in the hierarchy are domain names that identify the organization (such as sybex in sybex.com) or occasionally an intervening layer (such as .co.uk). TCP/IP hostnames can continue for several levels, ultimately uniquely identifying a single computer, such as www.sybex.com, Sybex's Web server computer.

The conversion between domain names and IP addresses is the responsibility of the *Domain Name System (DNS)*. DNS is, essentially, a global distributed database managed by a series of DNS servers. Each DNS server is responsible for pointing DNS clients (ordinary computers or other DNS servers) to a DNS server that's likely to know more about the domain in question. Suppose you're a computer that's looking up a hostname (say, www.sybex.com). You begin by querying your local DNS server. This server will consult one of the *root servers*, which know the IP addresses of servers that know about the TLDs. Using this information, your local DNS server contacts the server that knows about the .com TLD. This .com DNS server gives your local DNS server the IP address of a server that knows about the sybex.com domain. This server will then be able to deliver the IP address of the www.sybex.com computer.

This process of looking up a hostname may sound convoluted, but given the size of the Internet, it's actually quite efficient. The process can be sped up, too, by the use of caches. If your local DNS server is asked about www.sybex.com, it will probably remember that address for a while. If another query for the same hostname arrives, the local DNS server can deliver an answer immediately.

To investigate DNS lookups, you can use three Linux commands:

**nslookup**   This command is deprecated, meaning that it's still present on many Linux systems but is being phased out. Type **nslookup *host.name***, where *host.name* is the DNS hostname of a computer. The program should respond with a summary of the server it's using to provide an answer and the IP address of the specified computer. You can also perform reverse lookups (giving an IP address to obtain a hostname) and more; consult the program's man page for details. Because it's deprecated, though, you might want to focus on host and dig instead.

**host**   This command does some of the job of nslookup, and in the simplest case, it's used in the same way: Type **host *host.name***. The result should be the IP address of the computer you specified.

**dig**   This command replaces some of the more advanced functions of nslookup. Type **dig *host.name*** to obtain advanced information on the specified host or domain. Unless you understand DNS zone files, which provide mappings between IP addresses and hostnames on DNS server computers, you're unlikely to fully understand dig's output. Nonetheless, you should try it to see what the results look like.

Small networks frequently use a simpler method of name resolution: the /etc/hosts file. This file consists of a series of lines, each of which begins with an IP address and includes one or more names for that IP address:

```
127.0.0.1       localhost
192.168.1.3     hogwartsia.pangaea.edu hogwartsia
```

The /etc/hosts file should always contain an entry for localhost. Additional names are useful for identifying local computers by name if those computers don't have entries on your computer's default DNS server. This method of name resolution is very basic and is easy to configure on a small LAN; however, coordinating changes becomes unwieldy on large networks. You can use both conventional DNS name resolution and the /etc/hosts file; typically you'll use DNS for Internet name resolution and /etc/hosts for local computers.

## Understanding Ports

If IP addresses are like telephone numbers, *port numbers* are like telephone number extensions in large businesses. On a computer that functions as a server, each individual server program links itself to a specific port number, such as port 25 for a Simple Mail Transfer Protocol (SMTP) mail server or port 80 for a Hypertext Transfer Protocol (HTTP, or Web) server. A single computer can then run two or more separate server programs, extending its flexibility. The mappings of port numbers to server types are standardized; except for odd configurations, SMTP servers always run on port 25 and Web servers always run on port 80. This standardization means that users don't need to remember port numbers; the client programs just connect to the standard port unless they're told to do otherwise.

Ports are also used by client programs, but clients don't tie themselves to specific ports. Instead, clients include their port numbers when they make their initial connections to servers. The servers reply to the specified ports.

In Linux, ports below number 1024 may be accessed only by root. Most servers run on these *privileged* ports, whereas clients use the higher-numbered *unprivileged* ports. This distinction used to be an important one and was part of the security procedures for some servers; however, on today's Internet, the distinction isn't very useful. Nonetheless, Linux retains it and a few servers' configuration options refer to it.

You should peruse the /etc/services file on your computer. This file contains a listing of ports, letter codes used to refer to them, and comments describing the function of each port. Some configuration options and program arguments enable you to refer to ports by letter codes, but to do so, the mapping must exist in /etc/services. In most cases, you'll leave your /etc/services file untouched, but on rare occasion you'll want to modify it, usually to add a service name to the file.

## Criteria for Completion

To complete this task you should have used several commands and files:

- dmesg enables you to identify your network hardware drivers.
- The kernel configuration process enables you to add or remove protocol stacks from your kernel.
- ifconfig provides information on your MAC address and IP address.
- nslookup, host, and dig provide mappings between IP addresses and hostnames.
- The /etc/services file identifies which application-level protocols are associated with specific port numbers.

Using these tools and files should help you understand the basics of TCP/IP networking.

# Task 6.2: Bring Up the Network

Most Linux distributions guide you through the process of network configuration at system installation time. A few distributions don't do this, though, and sometimes the install-time configuration doesn't work. You may also need to manually take a computer off the network without shutting it down and then bring it back (for instance, if you think it may have been compromised and you want to investigate the matter without risking other computers). In any of these situations, knowledge of how to bring up a network connection is invaluable.

## Scenario

You must configure two Linux computers to use your LAN. Neither computer is currently configured to work on a network, but both have network hardware installed. One computer must be configured using a static IP address (that is, an IP address that's assigned manually and that doesn't change). The other computer should use DHCP to obtain its IP address automatically when it boots.

## Scope of Task

This task involves configuring networking options on two computers. To do so, you'll need to use the `ifconfig` utility and modify various configuration files on your computer. Unfortunately, Linux distributions vary substantially in how they store network configuration details, so you may need to dig through various files to find the relevant configuration options.

### Duration

This task should take about an hour to complete. Once you're familiar with how to configure networking on a given distribution, you should be able to do the job on new computers in just a few minutes.

### Setup

Bringing up a network connection requires `root` access, so you must have this access on the computers you configure. The scenario specifies configuring two computers, but if you have just one, and if your network includes a DHCP server, you can configure your computer to use a static IP address and then configure it to use a DHCP server. If your network doesn't have a DHCP server, you'll have to forgo actually configuring your system to use one.

### Caveats

The usual caveats concerning working as `root` apply to this task. Because this task requires changing network configurations, you cannot perform this task working from a remote computer; you must work at the console, using either a text-mode or GUI login. Misconfiguring your network can result in subtle or extreme problems, depending on the nature of the misconfiguration. Unlike most other tasks, this one can cause problems for *other* computers if you get it wrong. Specifically, if you misconfigure your computer to use the IP address that's assigned to another computer on your LAN, you can prevent that computer from communicating on the network.

## Procedure

Configuring your computer for network operations requires you to first ensure that your network hardware is ready. Once that's done, you can proceed with either DHCP or static IP address configuration. The DHCP approach is almost always easier—at least if your network has a DHCP server. If you perform manual IP address configuration, you'll also need to perform at least minimal routing configuration. (More sophisticated routing options are described later, in Task 6.4.)

### Network Hardware Configuration

The most fundamental part of network configuration is getting the network hardware up and running. In most cases, this task is fairly automatic—most distributions ship with system startup scripts that auto-detect the network card and load the correct driver module. If you recompile your kernel, building the correct driver into the main kernel file will also ensure that it's loaded at system startup.

If your network hardware isn't correctly detected, though, subsequent configuration (as described in the upcoming sections "DHCP Configuration" and "Static IP Address Configuration") won't work. To correct this problem, you must load your network hardware driver. You can do this with the `modprobe` command:

```
# modprobe tulip
```

You must know the name of your network hardware's kernel module, though (`tulip` in this example). If you're not sure of your network hardware's driver name, consult Task 6.1 and Phase 2.

## DHCP Configuration

One of the easiest ways to configure a computer to use a TCP/IP network is to use DHCP, which enables one computer on a network to manage the settings for many other computers. It works like this: When a computer running a DHCP client boots up, it sends a broadcast in search of a DHCP server. The server replies (using nothing but the client's hardware address) with the configuration information the client needs to enable it to communicate with other computers on the network—most importantly the client's IP address and netmask and the network's gateway and DNS server addresses. The DHCP server may also give the client a hostname. The client then configures itself with these parameters. The IP address is not assigned permanently; it's referred to as a *DHCP lease,* and if it's not renewed, the DHCP server may give the lease to another computer. Therefore, from time to time the client checks back with the DHCP server to renew its lease.

Three DHCP clients are in common use on Linux: `pump`, `dhclient`, and `dhcpcd` (not to be confused with the DHCP server, `dhcpd`). Some Linux distributions ship with just one of these, but others ship with two or even all three. All distributions have a default DHCP client, though—the one that's installed when you tell the system you want to use DHCP at system installation time. Those that ship with multiple DHCP clients typically enable you to swap out one for another simply by removing the old package and installing the new one.

Ideally, the DHCP client runs at system bootup. This is usually handled either by its own SysV startup file, as described in Phase 3, "Managing Software," or as part of the main network configuration startup file (typically a SysV startup file called `network` or `networking`). To enable networking when the computer next boots, use `chkconfig`, `rc-update`, `ntsysv`, or another tool (as described in Phase 3) to activate the network or networking script in your default runlevel:

```
# chkconfig --add network
```

This command adds the `network` script to the current runlevel, if it's not already active. As described in Phase 3, the details of SysV init script configuration vary from one distribution to another, so you may need to adjust this command.

The system often uses a line in a configuration file to determine whether to run a DHCP client. For instance, Red Hat and Fedora Linux set this option in a file called `/etc/sysconfig/network-scripts/ifcfg-eth0` (this filename may differ if you use something other than a single Ethernet interface). The line in question looks like this:

BOOTPROTO=dhcp

If the BOOTPROTO variable is set to something else, changing it as shown here will configure the system to use DHCP. It's usually easier to use a GUI configuration tool to set this option, however. Such tools include Network Configuration (aka system-config-network) in Red Hat and Fedora, and YaST and YaST2 in openSUSE.

 If you don't know where the relevant configuration line is found, try searching the /etc/sysconfig or /etc/conf.d directories, if they're present. Chances are you'll find configuration files with fairly obvious names. You can use grep to search these directories, or all of /etc if necessary, for files that refer to DHCP or your network interface.

Once a DHCP client is configured to run when the system boots, the configuration task is done—at least if everything works as it should. On very rare occasions, you may need to tweak DHCP settings to work around client/server incompatibilities or to have the DHCP client do something unusual. Consult the man page for your DHCP client if you need to make changes. You'll then have to modify its SysV startup script or a file to which it refers in order to change its operation.

If you want to bring the network up without rebooting the computer, you can call the SysV script directly:

```
# /etc/init.d/network start
```

As described in Phase 3, the exact path to the SysV startup scripts vary from one distribution to another. If your network was already working, but didn't use DHCP, you may need to pass the stop parameter to the script before you can pass it the start parameter.

## Static IP Address Configuration

If a network lacks a DHCP server, you must provide basic network configuration options manually. Static IP address configuration is also useful for computers that require a constant IP address, such as servers. You can set these options using interactive commands, as described shortly, but to set them in the long term, you adjust a configuration file such as /etc/sysconfig/network-scripts/ifcfg-eth0. Listing 6.1 shows a typical ifcfg-eth0 file, configured to use a static IP address. (Note that this file's exact location and name may vary from one distribution to another.)

**Listing 6.1:** A Sample Network Configuration File

```
DEVICE=eth0
BOOTPROTO=static
IPADDR=192.168.29.39
NETMASK=255.255.255.0
NETWORK=192.168.29.0
BROADCAST=192.168.29.255
GATEWAY=192.168.29.1
ONBOOT=yes
```

Several specific items are required, or at least helpful, for static IP address configuration:

**IP address**   You can set the IP address manually via the ifconfig command (described in more detail shortly) or via the IPADDR item in the configuration file.

**Network mask**   The netmask can be set manually via the ifconfig command or via the NETMASK item in a configuration file.

**Gateway address**   You can manually set the gateway (that is, your LAN's router) via the route command. To set it permanently, you need to adjust a configuration file, which may be the same configuration file that holds other options or another file, such as /etc/sysconfig/network/routes. In either case, the option is likely to be called GATEWAY. The gateway isn't necessary on a system that isn't connected to a wider network—that is, if the system works *only* on a local network that contains no routers.

**DNS settings**   In order for Linux to use DNS to translate between IP addresses and hostnames, you must specify at least one DNS server in the /etc/resolv.conf file. Precede the IP address of the DNS server by the keyword nameserver, as in nameserver 192.168.29.1. You can include up to three nameserver lines in this file. Adjusting this file is all you need to do to set the name server addresses; you don't have to do anything else to make the setting permanent.

The network configuration script may hold additional options, but most of these are related to others. For instance, Listing 6.1 has an option specifying the interface name (DEVICE=eth0), another that tells the computer to assign a static IP address (BOOTPROTO=static), and a third to bring up the interface when the computer boots (ONBOOT=yes). The NETWORK and BROADCAST items in Listing 6.1 are derived from the IPADDR and NETMASK items, but you can change them if you understand the consequences.

If you aren't sure what to enter for the basic networking values (the IP address, network mask, gateway address, and DNS server addresses), you should consult your network administrator. *Do not* enter random values or values you make up that are similar to those used by other systems on your network. Doing so is unlikely to work at all, and it could conceivably cause a great deal of trouble—say, if you mistakenly use an IP address that's reserved for another computer.

As just mentioned, the ifconfig program is critically important for setting both the IP address and netmask. This program can also display current settings, as described earlier in "Understanding Network Addressing" in Task 6.1. As an example of using ifconfig to bring up a network interface, the following command brings up eth0 (the first Ethernet card) using the address 192.168.29.39 and the netmask 255.255.255.0:

```
# ifconfig eth0 up 192.168.29.39 netmask 255.255.255.0
```

This command links the specified IP address to the card so that the computer will respond to the address and claim to be that address when sending data. It doesn't, though, set up a route for traffic beyond your current network. For that, you need to use the route command:

```
# route add default gw 192.168.29.1
```

Substitute your own gateway address for 192.168.29.1. (Routing and the route command are described in more detail shortly, in Task 6.4, "Configure Routing.") Both ifconfig and route can display information on the current network configuration. For ifconfig, omit up and everything that follows; for route, omit add and everything that follows. To use route for diagnostic purposes, you might try the following:

```
$ route
Kernel IP routing table
Destination  Gateway        Genmask        Flags Metric Ref  Use Iface
192.168.29.0 *              255.255.255.0 U     0      0      0 eth0
127.0.0.0    *              255.0.0.0     U     0      0      0 lo
default      192.168.29.1 0.0.0.0        UG    0      0      0 eth0
```

This shows that data destined for 192.168.29.0 (that is, any computer with an IP address between 192.168.29.1 and 192.168.29.254) goes directly over eth0. The 127.0.0.0 network is a special interface that "loops back" to the originating computer. Linux uses this for some internal networking purposes. The last line shows the *default route*, which describes what to do with everything that doesn't match any other entry in the routing table. This line specifies the default route's gateway system as 192.168.29.1. If it's missing or misconfigured, some or all traffic destined for external networks, such as the Internet, won't make it beyond your local network segment.

As with DHCP configuration, it's almost always easier to use a GUI configuration tool to set up static IP addresses, at least for new administrators. The exact locations of the configuration files differ from one distribution to another, so the examples listed earlier may not apply to your system.

## Criteria for Completion

To complete this task, you should have brought up network connections using both DHCP and static IP address configuration. DHCP is the easier approach if your network supports DHCP, but running a DHCP server for a small network may be more effort than it's worth. Static IP address configuration is useful for servers and other computers that work best with an IP address that remains constant over long periods of time.

# Task 6.3: Monitor Network Connections

Most people who use networks simply rely on them, and when things go wrong, they call their network administrators or ISPs to complain. As a Linux system administrator, though, part of your job is to monitor network connections and diagnose network problems. Even if you're not responsible for your site's network as a whole, you should possess enough knowledge to perform basic tests to determine how your system is interacting with the network.

# Scenario

After bringing up the network connections in Task 6.2, you want to give the computer's network connectivity a quick once-over to ensure that it's working the way it should be working. To do so, you'll use three network diagnostic tools: `ping`, `traceroute`, and `netstat`.

# Scope of Task

You'll use three commands to perform this task. These commands test basic network connectivity and enable you to monitor the network connections that are currently being maintained by the computer.

### Duration

This task should take between half an hour and an hour to complete. Once you're familiar with them, you can use each individual command in just a few seconds. Because these tools are often used to help diagnose problems, though, you're likely to use them in tasks that will take anywhere from a few minutes to many hours to complete, depending on the severity of the problem and your ability to find and correct the cause of the problem.

### Setup

You need a working Linux computer with a network connection to complete this task. You can perform most of this task as an ordinary user, so log on using your ordinary account. (A few `netstat` options require `root` access, though.)

### Caveats

The commands described in this task are fairly innocuous, so you're unlikely to do serious harm by using—or even abusing—them. If you need `root` access to fully utilize `netstat`, though, the usual `root` caveats apply.

# Procedure

The first two diagnostic commands, `ping` and `traceroute`, test for connectivity between your computer and one other computer. You can use these tools to verify that a network link exists between your site and another site. The third diagnostic command, `netstat`, enables you to check on the status of your local network connections. This ability is useful in determining whether or not a program is making a connection, in determining how many and what specific connections a program is making, and so on.

### Testing Basic Connectivity

The most basic network test is the `ping` command, which sends a simple packet to the system you name (via IP address or hostname) and waits for a reply. In Linux, `ping` continues sending packets once every second or so until you interrupt it with a Ctrl+C keystroke. Here's an example of its output:

```
$ ping speaker
PING speaker.rodsbooks.com (192.168.1.1) from 192.168.1.3  : 56(84) bytes of
➥data.
64 bytes from speaker.rodsbooks.com (192.168.1.1): icmp_ seq=0 ttl=255
➥time=149 usec
64 bytes from speaker.rodsbooks.com (192.168.1.1): icmp_ seq=1 ttl=255
➥time=136 usec
64 bytes from speaker.rodsbooks.com (192.168.1.1): icmp_ seq=2 ttl=255
➥time=147 usec
64 bytes from speaker.rodsbooks.com (192.168.1.1): icmp_ seq=3 ttl=255
➥time=128 usec

--- speaker.rodsbooks.com ping statistics ---
4 packets transmitted, 4 packets received, 0% packet loss
round-trip min/avg/max/mdev = 0.128/0.140/0.149/0.008 ms
```

This command sent four packets and waited for their return, which occurred quite quickly (in an average of 0.140 ms) because the target system was on the local network. By pinging systems on both local and remote networks, you can isolate where a network problem occurs. For instance, if you can ping local systems but not remote systems, the problem is most probably in your router configuration. If you can ping by IP address but not by name, the problem is with your DNS configuration.

Try pinging some local and remote systems. You'll need to know the hostnames or IP addresses of local systems. For remote systems, try a few Web sites you frequent. (Pinging a site generates very little network traffic, so a brief ping test isn't abusive, but don't leave ping running indefinitely.) You should also try pinging a system or two that you know won't respond, such as a local computer that's currently turned off.

 Some Web sites and other Internet servers are configured so that they don't respond to pings. Don't be concerned if you run into this behavior; just move on to another site.

## Tracing a Route

A step up from ping is the traceroute command, which sends a series of three test packets to each computer between your system and a specified target system. The result looks something like this:

```
$ traceroute -n 10.1.0.43
traceroute to 68.1.0.43 (68.1.0.43), 30 hops max, 52 byte packets
 1  192.168.1.254  1.021 ms  36.519 ms  0.971 ms
```

```
2   10.10.88.1  17.250 ms   9.959 ms   9.637 ms
3   10.9.8.173  8.799 ms   19.501 ms  10.884 ms
4   10.9.8.133  21.059 ms   9.231 ms  103.068 ms
5   10.9.14.9   8.554 ms   12.982 ms  10.029 ms
6   10.1.0.44   10.273 ms   9.987 ms  11.215 ms
7   10.1.0.43   16.360 ms  *   8.102 ms
```

The -n option to this command tells it to display target computers' IP addresses rather than their hostnames. This can speed up the process a bit, and it can sometimes make the output easier to read—but you might want to know the hostnames of problem systems because that can help you pinpoint who's responsible for a problem.

This sample output shows a great deal of variability in response times. The first hop, to 192.168.1.254, is purely local; this router responded in 1.021, 36.519, and 0.971 milliseconds (ms) to its three probes. (Presumably the second probe caught the system while it was busy with something else.) Probes of most subsequent systems are in the 8–20 ms range, although one is at 103.068 ms. The final system only has two times; the middle probe never returned, as the asterisk (*) on this line indicates.

Using traceroute, you can localize problems in network connectivity. Highly variable times and missing times can indicate a router that's overloaded or that has an unreliable link to the previous system on the list. If you see a dramatic jump in times, it typically means that the physical distance between two routers is great. This is common in intercontinental links. Such jumps don't necessarily signify a problem, though, unless the two systems are close enough that a huge jump isn't expected.

What can you do with the traceroute output? Most immediately, traceroute is helpful in determining whether a problem in network connectivity exists in a network for which you're responsible. For instance, the variability in the first hop of the preceding example could indicate a problem on the local network, but the lost packet associated with the final destination most likely is not a local problem. If the trouble link is within your jurisdiction, you can check the status of the problem system, nearby systems, and the network segment in general.

## Checking Network Status

Another useful diagnostic tool is netstat. This is something of a Swiss Army knife of network tools because it can be used in place of several others, depending on the parameters it is passed. It can also return information that's not easily obtained in other ways. Some examples include the following:

**Interface information**   Pass netstat the --interface or -i parameter to obtain information on your network interfaces similar to what ifconfig returns. (Some versions of netstat return information in the same format, but others display the information differently.)

**Routing information**   You can use the --route or -r parameter to obtain a routing table listing similar to what the route command displays.

**Masquerade information**   Pass netstat the --masquerade or -M parameter to obtain information on connections mediated by Linux's NAT features, which often go by the name "IP masquerading." NAT enables a Linux router to "hide" a network behind a single IP address. This can be a good way to stretch limited IP addresses.

**Program use**    Some versions of netstat support the --program or -p parameter, which attempts to provide information on the programs that are using network connections. This attempt isn't always successful, but it often is, so you can see what programs are making outside connections.

**Listening software**    Using the --listening or -l option to netstat causes it to display a list of programs that are listening for connections—in other words, network servers. This option is particularly handy in tracking down servers that you might not know are installed and working. If you combine this option with -p, you'll also see the name of the software that's doing the listening.

**Open ports**    When used with various other parameters, or without any parameters at all, netstat returns information on open ports and the systems to which they connect.

Keep in mind that netstat is a very powerful tool and its options and output aren't entirely consistent from one distribution to another. You may want to peruse its man page and experiment with it to learn what it can do.

One of the more useful applications of netstat is to check on open connections and the programs that have opened them. To do so, use the -p option, preferably as root:

```
# netstat -p
Active Internet connections (w/o servers)
Proto Recv-Q Send-Q Local Address          Foreign Address
  ➥State        PID/Program name
tcp       0        0 nessus.rodsbooks.:47820 speaker.rodsbooks.c:ftp
  ➥ESTABLISHED 5960/gftp-gtk
```

The netstat output often exceeds 80 columns in width. You might want to widen your xterm window or redirect output to a file that you can examine in a text editor that can display wide lines.

The output shown here is a truncation of real netstat output; a typical Linux computer has so many active network connections at any moment that the output will run to dozens or hundreds of lines. This example shows just one connection, from nessus.rodsbooks.com (the hostname has been truncated) on port 47,820 to speaker.rodsbooks.com on the ftp port (netstat has looked up the server's port number in /etc/services and translated to the port name in that file). You can also see the process ID (PID) number (5960) and the program name (gftp-gtk). You can use this information to kill an errant process if the network connection shouldn't exist or is causing problems such as excessive bandwidth consumption.

## Criteria for Completion

To complete this task, you should have used ping to test basic connectivity between your site and another, traceroute to obtain a detailed diagnostic of the network connectivity path between your site and another, and netstat to obtain information on the network ports that are in use on your computer. These three tools will help you verify proper network functioning and track down a wide variety of network-related problems.

# Task 6.4: Configure Routing

Preceding tasks have referred to routing as something that other computers do—you configure your computer to know about a router on your local network, or you use `traceroute` to determine the path (through routers) a packet takes between your computer and another one. Linux, however, can *be* a router. To configure Linux as a router, you must install two network interfaces in the computer and issue a few commands. This task guides you through the process of configuring your system in this way.

## Scenario

A small business has a LAN that's linked to the Internet via a broadband connection using a dedicated broadband router. This business wants to support wireless connections for its employees' laptop computers, providing those computers with access to the LAN's local servers and to the Internet at large, as illustrated by Figure 6.2. To this end, the business has hired you to configure an old computer as a dedicated router between its Ethernet LAN and its wireless network. The computer is already set up with both Ethernet and wireless hardware, and Linux is installed on the system and can "talk" to machines using both the Ethernet and wireless hardware. Your task is to configure the computer as a router.

**FIGURE 6.2**   A router links two or more networks, which can have different types of network hardware.

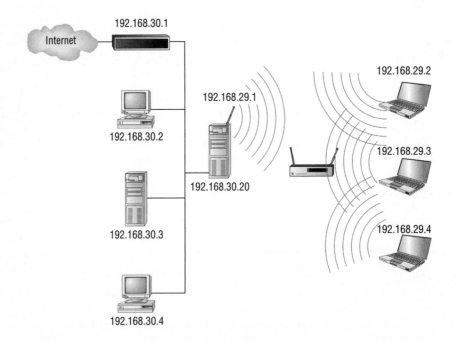

## Scope of Task

This task requires using the `route` command in more advanced ways than have been described previously. You must also use a few other commands to enable routing between the networks.

### Duration

This task should take about half an hour to complete. The individual actions, of course, take less time than this, and once you're familiar with routing configuration, you should be able to do the job in just a few minutes.

### Setup

You must have `root` access to the computer in order to configure routing. Configuring a computer as a router also requires that it have two network interfaces. If you don't have access to such a computer, you should read this task but not attempt to implement its actions.

 It's possible to configure routing on certain types of virtual networks. For example, you can use a network of emulated computers running in virtual environments such as those provided by VMware (http://www.vmware.com). Configuring such software to bring it to the point where you could route traffic for it is a topic that's beyond the scope of this task, though.

### Caveats

The usual caveats concerning `root` access apply to this task. In addition, router configuration poses certain risks and opportunities, most of which are security related. At its simplest, a router provides no security protection for any of the networks it links. More complex routers can block certain types of traffic, protecting one or both networks from certain types of network attacks. Such routers are referred to as *firewalls*. Although firewalls are very useful, firewall configuration is beyond the scope of this task. (Consult Phase 7 for information on basic Linux firewall features.) You should be concerned with your router's security, particularly if you configure it as a firewall; a breach of a router, or especially a firewall, can put the network it protects at risk.

## Procedure

Basic router configuration involves two specific tasks. First, you must use the `route` command to ensure that network routes exist for both the networks to which the computer is connected. Second, you must configure the computer to forward packets between the two networks. An ancillary task, which might not involve Linux at all, is to configure computers on both of the linked networks to recognize the Linux system as a router.

## Using *route*

Earlier, in "Static IP Address Configuration" in Task 6.2, I described the basics of the `route` command to tell an ordinary Linux system about the network's router. Specifically, you used a command like the following one to add a default route to the computer's routing table:

```
# route add default gw 192.168.29.1
```

Configuring a router is a bit more complex because a router has two or more interfaces, so a router has to know where to send data depending on the IP address of the target. Consider the router you're configuring, as depicted in Figure 6.2. The router must know to send data to the 192.168.29.255 network over its wireless connection, to send data to the 192.168.30.255 network over its Ethernet connection, and to send all other data over its Ethernet connection using the 192.168.30.1 system as its gateway. To fully configure the router in this way, you must use the `route` command to define each of these three routes. To do so, you can use some additional `route` options:

```
# route add -net 192.168.29.0 netmask 255.255.255.0 dev ath0
# route add -net 192.168.30.0 netmask 255.255.255.0 dev eth0
# route add default gw 192.168.30.1
```

Chances are, though, that most of these routes are already defined. You can use the `route` command by itself to examine the routing table. On a system that's already configured to use both networks and the gateway to the Internet, you should see entries for all the routes, and perhaps one or two others:

```
# route
Kernel IP routing table
```

| Destination | Gateway | Genmask | Flags | Metric | Ref | Use | Iface |
|---|---|---|---|---|---|---|---|
| 192.168.30.0 | * | 255.255.255.0 | U | 0 | 0 | 0 | ath0 |
| 192.168.29.0 | * | 255.255.255.0 | U | 0 | 0 | 0 | eth0 |
| loopback | * | 255.0.0.0 | U | 0 | 0 | 0 | lo |
| default | 192.168.30.1 | 0.0.0.0 | UG | 0 | 0 | 0 | eth0 |

If the router's routing table is missing any entries, you must add them manually. Unfortunately, typing these commands once isn't sufficient; routing table entries are not stored between boots. Thus, you must find a way to make the changes permanent. One way is to modify configuration files, as described earlier (see "Static IP Address Configuration" in Task 6.2). Another approach is to place the necessary `route` commands in a local startup file, such as `/etc/init.d/boot.local` or `/etc/rc.d/rc.local`.

## Enabling IP Forwarding

One more thing you need to do if you're setting up a router is to enable routing. Ordinarily, a Linux system will not forward packets it receives from one system that are directed at another system. If Linux is to act as a router, though, it must accept these packets and send them on to the destination network (or at least to an appropriate gateway). To enable this feature, you must modify a key file in the /proc filesystem:

```
# echo "1" > /proc/sys/net/ipv4/ip_forward
```

This command enables IP forwarding. Permanently setting this option requires modifying a configuration file. Some distributions set it in /etc/sysctl.conf:

```
net.ipv4.ip_forward = 1
```

Other distributions use other configuration files and options, such as /etc/sysconfig/ sysctl and its IP_FORWARD line. If you can't find it, try using grep to search for ip_forward or IP_FORWARD, or enter the command to perform the change manually in a local startup script.

## Configuring the Routed Networks

Finally, you must know how to configure the computers on both of the networks to use the new routing configuration. In the case of the wireless network (192.168.29.255 in this example), configuration is very conventional: You simply tell these computers that the Linux computer you've just configured (192.168.29.1) is the gateway. To the wireless computers, the Linux router looks just like any other router, and in fact it *is* an ordinary router.

The computers on the existing 192.168.30.255 network are another matter. There are now *two* routers on this network. One is the existing broadband router (192.168.30.1), which the computers are presumably already configured to use. The second router is the new Linux system, which is visible to the subnet's computers as 192.168.30.20. One way to deal with this situation is to explicitly configure all of these computers so that they know about the two routers. If they're Linux computers, you could set up this route to the wireless network with the following command:

```
# route add -net 192.168.29.0 netmask 255.255.255.0 gw 192.168.30.20
```

This command adds a new gateway address (192.168.30.20) and tells the computers to route traffic for the 192.168.29.255 network via that address. This approach is the most efficient way to do the job, but it requires modifying the configurations of all the computers on the Ethernet network. You'd typically do it by adding the appropriate command to local startup scripts.

Another approach is to modify just one computer on the Ethernet network: the broadband router. Once this computer is configured to know about the Linux router, it will redirect traffic for that network back to the Linux router. This greatly simplifies the configuration of the other computers, since they now need no adjustments. There is a cost, though: All the traffic destined for the wireless network that originates from the Ethernet network must traverse the Ethernet network twice. First it goes from the origin to the broadband router and then it goes from the broadband router to the Linux router. Depending on the amount of traffic, the result can be a significant increase in network load. Fortunately, not all traffic is doubled by this approach. Return traffic from the wireless network to the Ethernet network only traverses the Ethernet network once. Similarly, if computers on the wireless network initiate Internet transfers, no additional Ethernet traffic is generated by this approach.

As specified by the scenario, the broadband router is a dedicated appliance—the type you can buy in most computer stores. You should be able to add a secondary route for the wireless network to such devices; however, the details of how you would do this vary greatly from one device to another. Therefore, you should consult your router's documentation to learn how to do the job.

> **NOTE**  An alternative to this configuration is to use a broadband router that can handle both wireless and Ethernet traffic. Such a router has three interfaces: one for the Internet, one for the Ethernet LAN, and one for the wireless network. This approach simplifies local network configuration, since both your Ethernet LAN and your wireless network use just one router. In practice, this configuration is likely to be superior to the one described in this task, but this task's configuration teaches you more about routing.

## Criteria for Completion

To complete this task, you should have successfully configured a Linux computer as a router. The router should pass traffic back and forth between its two network segments, enabling computers on both networks to communicate with one another. This task requires both configuring the two network interfaces on the router and enabling routing functions. You may also need to adjust the routing tables on computers on one or both of the network segments managed by the Linux router.

# Task 6.5: Manage a Super Server

Many Linux computers operate as servers, which respond to data transfer requests initiated by clients. Many server programs run as *daemons* on the server computer, meaning that the server programs run constantly in the background, waiting for connection requests. This isn't the only way to run a server, though. You can also use another program, known as a *super server*, to remain in memory as a daemon and listen for connection requests. When one arrives, the super server launches the server that should handle the request. This approach has certain advantages, such as minimizing memory use by servers that aren't frequently accessed and providing an opportunity to add security controls to limit who may access the server. On the downside, the act of launching the server takes time, so the server's initial response to connection requests increases compared to a stand-alone configuration.

## Scenario

Your network's Web server computer requires a way for users to deploy Web pages. You've opted to use a File Transfer Protocol (FTP) server to enable such transfers. You've installed an FTP package using your system's package maintenance tools (described in Phase 3), but now you must configure the FTP server to run. The server you've chosen can be run from a super server, so you must reconfigure your super server to handle the FTP server.

## Scope of Task

This task requires modifying one or two super server configuration files. As such, the changes required are fairly minor; however, you should be aware of the potential pitfalls of running servers via a super server. Two super servers are common in Linux, and this task covers both of them, although you're likely to be able to modify just one super server's configuration.

This task is focused on the super server side of the task. Configuring an FTP server, or any other server that's launched from a super server, requires attention to server-specific configuration and security details that aren't covered in this task.

### Duration

This task should take about half an hour to complete, although if you have access to computers running both `inetd` and `xinetd`, the total time could approach one hour. Once you're familiar with the details of super server configuration, you should be able to add a new server in just a few minutes.

### Setup

You must have `root` access to a computer that's already running a super server (`inetd` or `xinetd`). As described in the scenario, your FTP server package should already be installed. This task uses the Netkit FTP server (`http://www.hcs.harvard.edu/~dholland/computers/netkit.html`), which is usually called `ftpd` or `in.ftpd`, as an example. Many, but not all, other FTP servers can be used instead, or you can use an entirely different server, such as a Telnet server, if you prefer.

### Caveats

The usual `root`-access caveats apply to this task. In addition, adding servers that run via a super server—or by any other means—opens your computer to potential security problems. Buggy servers or poor server security options can make your system vulnerable to attack. For this reason, you should undo your configuration changes after you're done with this task, unless you have a real need to run an FTP server. If so, you should carefully review the security and other configuration options for your server.

## Procedure

This task requires modifying your super server configuration; however, two super servers are common on Linux: `inetd` and `xinetd`. Thus, you must first determine which super server you have installed. After you've done so, you can modify the configuration for your particular server. (If your system runs xinetd, you may want to read both the inetd and xinetd sections, because xinetd configuration is rather like an expanded version of inetd configuration.) The final part of this task is to test your configuration to be sure it's working correctly.

## Identifying Your Super Server

Linux distributions have traditionally used inetd, but they've been slowly shifting to xinetd. Both super servers offer similar basic features, but xinetd provides *more* features, particularly in the area of access control options. Using xinetd, you can restrict who may access a server based on IP address, network port, time of day, and more. You can use a package called TCP Wrappers in conjunction with inetd to provide similar access controls. An additional advantage of xinetd is that its configuration file can be split into parts. This enables distributions that use xinetd to provide xinetd configuration files with individual servers, simplifying configuration.

Type **ps ax | grep inetd** to see which super server is running on your system—the output should include a line with either the inetd or the xinetd command. Some systems run neither super server, though. If you can't find a trace of either server, use your package manager to search for the inetd and xinetd packages. If one is installed, you might need to modify your SysV configuration to launch the server in your runlevel, as described in Phase 3. If neither package is installed, install one (preferably xinetd) using your distribution's package management tools, as described in Phase 3.

## Configuring *inetd*

You control servers that launch via inetd through the /etc/inetd.conf file. This file consists of a series of lines, one for each server. A typical line resembles the following:

```
ftp stream tcp nowait root /usr/sbin/tcpd /usr/sbin/ftpd -l
```

> If your system doesn't use ftpd, or if it's called in.ftpd or is located in a directory other than /usr/sbin, adjust the command appropriately. The -l option is specific to ftpd and so may also need to be changed for your FTP server.

Each line consists of several fields separated by one or more spaces. The meanings of these fields are as follows:

**Service name**   The first field (ftp in the preceding example) is the name of the service as it appears in the /etc/services file.

**Socket type**   The socket type entry tells the system what type of connection to expect—a reliable two-way connection (stream), a less-reliable connection with less overhead (dgram), a low-level connection to the network (raw), or various others. The differences between these types are highly technical; your main concern in editing this entry should be to correctly type the value specified by the server's documentation.

**Protocol**   This is the TCP/IP Transport-layer protocol used, usually tcp or udp.

**Wait/no wait**    For `dgram` socket types, this entry specifies whether the server connects to its client and frees the socket (`nowait`) or processes all its packets and then times out (`wait`). Servers that use other socket types should specify `nowait` in this field.

**User**    This is the username used to run the server. The `root` and `nobody` users are common choices, but others are possible as well. As a general rule, you should run servers as a low-privilege user whenever possible as a security precaution. Some servers require `root` access, though. Consult the server's documentation for details.

**Server name**    This is the filename of the server. In the preceding example, the server is specified as `/usr/sbin/tcpd`, which is the TCP Wrappers binary. This program provides some security checks, enabling you to restrict access to a server based on the origin and other factors.

**Parameters**    Everything after the server name consists of parameters that are passed to the server. If you use TCP Wrappers, you pass the name of the true target server (such as `/usr/sbin/ftpd`) in this field, along with its parameters.

The hash mark (#) is a comment symbol for `/etc/inetd.conf`. Therefore, if a server is running via `inetd` and you want to disable it, you can place a hash mark at the start of the line. If you want to add a server to `inetd.conf`, you'll need to create an entry for it. Most servers that can be run from `inetd` include sample entries in their documentation. Many distributions ship with `inetd.conf` files that include entries for common servers as well, although many of them are commented out; remove the hash mark at the start of the line to activate the server.

After modifying `inetd.conf`, you must restart the `inetd` super server itself. This super server normally runs as a standard SysV server, so you can restart it by typing something similar to the following:

```
# /etc/rc.d/init.d/inetd restart
```

Alternatively, you can tell `inetd` to reload its configuration by passing the SysV startup script the `reload` parameter rather than `restart`. The `restart` option shuts down the server and then starts it again. When you use `reload`, the server never stops running; it just rereads the configuration file and implements any changes. As a practical matter, the two are quite similar. Using `restart` is more likely to correctly implement changes, but it's also more likely to disrupt existing connections.

Instead of using the SysV startup scripts, you can use `kill` or `killall` (described in Phase 3) to pass the SIGHUP signal to `inetd`. This signal causes many servers, including `inetd`, to reload their configuration files. For instance, you might type **`kill -HUP`** _`pid`_ if you know the process ID (PID) of `inetd` or **`killall -HUP inetd`** to have all instances of `inetd` reload their configuration files. (Ordinarily, only one instance of `inetd` runs on a system.) In practice, this should work very much like the `reload` option to the SysV startup script—in fact, such scripts often use this technique to implement this option.

It's generally wise to disable as many servers as possible in `inetd.conf` (or the `xinetd` configuration files, if you use `xinetd`). As a general rule, if you don't understand what a server does, disable it. This will improve the security of your system by eliminating potentially buggy or misconfigured servers from the equation.

## Configuring *xinetd*

The xinetd program is an extended super server. It provides the functionality of inetd plus security options that are similar to those of TCP Wrappers. Modern versions of Fedora, Mandriva, Red Hat, openSUSE, and a few other distributions use xinetd by default. Other distributions may use it in the future. If you like, you can replace inetd with xinetd on any distribution.

The /etc/xinetd.conf file controls xinetd. On distributions that use xinetd by default, though, this file contains only global default options and a directive to include files stored in /etc/xinetd.d. Each server that should run via xinetd then installs a file in /etc/xinetd.d with its own configuration options. Look for a file called ftp, ftpd, in.ftpd, or something similar in the /etc/xinetd.d directory. If it's present, you can edit this file to activate your FTP server. If not, you can either create this file and add an FTP entry as described shortly or add such an entry to your /etc/xinetd.conf file.

Whether the entry for a service goes in /etc/xinetd.conf or a file in /etc/xinetd.d, it contains information similar to that in the inetd.conf file. The xinetd configuration file, though, spreads the information across multiple lines and labels it more explicitly. Listing 6.2 shows an example that's equivalent to the earlier inetd.conf entry. This entry provides precisely the same information as the inetd.conf entry except that it doesn't include a reference to /usr/sbin/tcpd, the TCP Wrappers binary. Because xinetd includes similar functionality, it's generally not used with TCP Wrappers.

**Listing 6.2:**  Sample xinetd Configuration Entry

```
service ftp
{
        socket_type     = stream
        protocol        = tcp
        wait            = no
        user            = root
        server          = /usr/sbin/in.ftpd
        server_args     = -l
}
```

Your existing xinetd configuration file for your FTP server may not be identical to Listing 6.2. If it's not, it's probably best to leave the configuration as you found it, with the exception of the disable option (described next) and any other options you research and that you know you want to modify.

One additional xinetd.conf parameter is important: disable. If you include the line disable = yes in a service definition, xinetd ignores the entry. Some servers install startup files in /etc/xinetd.d that have this option set by default; you must edit the file and change the entry to read disable = no to enable the server. You can also disable a set of servers by listing their names in the defaults section of the main xinetd.conf file on a line called disabled, as in disabled = ftp shell.

As with inetd, after you make changes to xinetd's configuration, you must restart the super server. You do this by typing a command similar to the one used to restart inetd. As with that command, you can use either reload or restart, with similar effects:

```
# /etc/rc.d/init.d/xinetd restart
```

Also as with inetd, you may pass the SIGHUP signal to xinetd via the kill or killall command to have it reload its configuration file. This approach may be preferable if you're using a distribution, such as Slackware, that doesn't use a conventional SysV startup script to launch xinetd.

## Testing Your Configuration

After making the changes described in the last two sections, your FTP server should now be accessible. You can test it by using the text-mode ftp program or a GUI FTP program such as gftp:

```
$ ftp localhost
Connected to localhost (127.0.0.1).
220 www.example.com FTP server (Version 6.4/OpenBSD/Linux-ftpd-0.17) ready.
Name (localhost:rodsmith): rodsmith
334 AUTH SSL OK.
[SSL Cipher AES256-SHA]
331 Password required for rodsmith.
Password:
230-
230 User rodsmith logged in.
Remote system type is UNIX.
Using binary mode to transfer files.
ftp>
```

You can then type FTP commands, such as ls, cd, get, put, and exit. (If you test using a GUI client, you'd use appropriate point-and-click operations instead.) This example shows connecting to the computer using the localhost interface. If successful, it proves that the server is running and accessible to the local computer; however, super server, TCP Wrappers, or FTP server configuration options could limit accesses from other computers. Thus, you should test in the same way using a remote computer as well. If you have problems with remote access, examine your configuration files for options that restrict access, such as the only_from option in xinetd or any FTP options in /etc/hosts.allow or /etc/hosts.deny if you use TCP Wrappers.

Unless you really want to run an FTP server, remember to disable it by removing its super server configuration and reloading or restarting your super server when you're done. Better yet, remove the FTP server package from your computer; a server that's not installed can't be run!

## Criteria for Completion

To complete this task, you should have configured your super server to enable an FTP server. This task requires first identifying which super server your computer runs and then making appropriate changes to the `/etc/inetd.conf` file or to a file in the `/etc/xinetd.d` directory. You must then verify that the FTP server is running by accessing it with an FTP client program.

# Task 6.6: Operate a Mail Server

Email is a very important Internet feature; it enables users to send messages to one another to be read at the recipient's leisure. This function requires computers that run Simple Mail Transfer Protocol (SMTP) server software such as the popular sendmail (`http://www.sendmail.org`). This software accepts messages that are created in email client programs such as `mutt` or KMail and delivers the messages across the Internet to another mail server. The recipient server then stores the messages in a form that enables their retrieval by local programs or via another server that runs a protocol such as the Post Office Protocol (POP) or the Internet Message Access Protocol (IMAP).

This task focuses upon sendmail configuration, which is the most central and critical part of the email delivery equation. A full email server is likely to support POP or IMAP in addition to SMTP or might support user logins and access via mail client programs. Be aware that SMTP is a complex protocol and SMTP server configuration is correspondingly complex. This task barely scratches the surface. If you have a need to configure a real email server, you should consult a book that's dedicated to the software you choose to run.

Although sendmail is the most popular SMTP server software on the Internet at large, it's not the only option. Postfix (`http://www.postfix.org`), Exim (`http://www.exim.org`), and qmail (`http://www.qmail.org`) are all popular in Linux, and some Linux distributions use one of these as the default mail server rather than sendmail. If your system is configured in this way, you must either replace your current mail server with sendmail (which could render it inoperative until you fix it) or simply read through this task without actually changing your configuration.

## Scenario

You are in charge of setting up the mail server for Pangaea University (`pangaea.edu`), which also manages mail for the Institute for Mesozoic Studies (`mesozoic.edu`). You must configure the server to accept mail addressed to users at either domain name. You must set up several email *aliases*, redirecting mail for certain users (such as `postmaster`) to specific users on the system. You must also configure some Linux workstations' mail server programs to relay mail through the main Pangaea University mail server system (`mail.pangaea.edu`).

## Scope of Task

This task requires changing the sendmail configurations on several computers, the most important being the main mail server computer for the university. Fortunately, the changes to the secondary servers should all be identical, so this part of the task shouldn't take long on a per-computer basis.

### Duration

This task should take about an hour to complete. (In reality, if you had to reconfigure enough computers to relay through `mail.pangaea.edu`, the task could take substantially longer, but this task describes just one such reconfiguration.) Once you're familiar with email configuration, making small changes should take just a few minutes. Unfortunately, sendmail uses one of the more complex Linux configuration files, so learning the basics can take a while.

### Setup

You need `root` access to two computers to complete this task: a system that's configured to accept outside mail (`mail.pangaea.edu` in this example) and another computer that you'll configure to relay mail through the first one.

### Caveats

This task presents the usual risks associated with working as `root`. In addition, mail server configuration poses its own risks. Like any server, sendmail presents security risks in the event of a bug or misconfiguration. Worse yet is the problem of *spam*, which is unsolicited bulk email. Any domain is likely to be inundated with spam, and real mail servers are often configured with add-on software such as SpamAssassin (`http://spamassassin.apache.org`) to deal with the problem. Potentially worse, certain misconfigurations of sendmail can make it easy for spammers to abuse your system and make it part of the spam delivery chain. Such *open relay* configurations can get your mail server listed on various mail blacklists, blocking legitimate email that originates from your site.

 Linux uses sendmail (or another mail server) for handling local mail. All major Linux distributions provide default mail server configurations that make the mail server fairly safe to run. Typically, the servers are configured so that they don't listen to external network ports. You must undo some of these safeguards to configure sendmail as a working Internet mail server.

## Procedure

Before you proceed to configuring your sendmail software, you should understand a few email basics. You can apply this knowledge to setting some basic mail server options. You can then proceed to examining your sendmail configuration files, setting hostname options, configuring the system to accept mail, setting redirection options, and setting relay options.

## Email Basics

Several protocols exist to manage email. The most common of these is SMTP, which is designed as a push mail protocol, meaning that the sending system initiates the transfer. This design is good for sending data, so SMTP is used through most of a mail delivery system. The final stage, though, often employs a pull mail protocol, such as POP or IMAP. With these protocols, the receiving system initiates the transfer. This is useful when the receiving system is an end user's workstation, which might not be powered on at all times or able to receive incoming connections.

SMTP was designed to enable a message to be relayed through an arbitrary number of computers. For instance, an end user might compose a message on a workstation (say, `client.example.com`), which is sent to the local SMTP server (`mail.example.com`). This server looks up a recipient system using DNS and sends the message to that system (for instance, `mail.pangaea.edu`). This system enables the message might be read, either directly or via a POP or IMAP server. In the latter case, the final recipient system would be a fourth computer (such as `wegener.pangaea.edu`). This arrangement is illustrated in Figure 6.3. Bear in mind that the number of links in this chain is variable and depends on how each system is configured. In the simplest case, local email stays on just one system. In theory, an arbitrarily large number of computers can be involved in an email exchange, although in practice it's rare to see email pass through more than half a dozen systems.

**FIGURE 6.3**   Email typically traverses several links between sender and recipient.

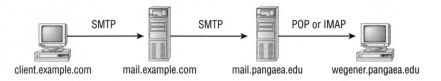

At each step in a relay chain, email is altered. Most importantly, each server adds a *header* to the email, which is a line that provides information about the message. In particular, mail servers add `Received:` headers to document the path the mail has taken. In theory, this enables you to trace the email back to its source. Unfortunately, spammers and other email abusers often forge email headers, which greatly complicates such analysis.

Because an SMTP server can function as both a server (receiving mail from other systems) and a client (sending mail to other systems), you must deal with both sides of the configuration equation. Sometimes a system will never function in one role or the other, which can simplify matters—but you must then be careful not to accidentally configure the system incorrectly. In particular, open relay configurations, in which a mail server relays mail from anybody, should be avoided.

## Sendmail Configuration Files

Sendmail uses a number of configuration files, each with its own unique purpose:

**sendmail.cf**   This file is the official primary sendmail configuration file. It includes information relating to relaying options, the server's hostname, and so on. Unfortunately, its syntax is very difficult for most people to understand, so in practice, it's usually created from another file that's easier to edit. You can usually find `sendmail.cf` in `/etc/mail`.

> If your system lacks a `sendmail.cf` file, it's possible that your computer is running Postfix, Exim, or some other mail server program, or your system might not be running any mail server at all.

**The m4 file**    The file that's used to generate the `sendmail.cf` file is called an m4 file, after the m4 program that does the translation. This file's name varies from one system to another, but it usually ends in `.mc`. Examples include Red Hat's or Fedora's `/etc/mail/sendmail.mc` and Slackware's `/usr/share/sendmail/cf/cf/linux.smtp.mc`. This file is sometimes not installed with the main sendmail package; you may need to install it from its own package, such as `sendmail-cf`.

`aliases`    The `/etc/aliases` file (which sometimes appears in `/etc/mail` instead of `/etc`) holds username translations, as described in "Redirecting Mail" later in this task. Sendmail actually reads a binary version of this file, `aliases.mc`, which is generated via the `newaliases` program, as described later.

`access`    The `access` file (which is usually stored in `/etc` or `/etc/mail`) controls mail relaying, as described in "Configuring Sendmail as a Relay" later in this task.

`local-host-names`    This file contains a list of hostnames that sendmail will treat as local. That is, if the server receives mail addressed to a user at one of these names, the server will attempt to deliver that mail to a local user of that name. If this file isn't used (its use can be disabled in `sendmail.cf`), or if it's empty, sendmail accepts mail addressed only to its own name.

If you check the `/etc/mail` directory, you'll see several additional configuration files. These files are important for more advanced configurations, but for the basic configuration tasks described in this task, you can ignore them.

To configure sendmail, you'll edit an m4 file and then convert it to a `sendmail.cf` file with m4:

```
# m4 < myconfig.mc > sendmail.cf
```

> If you issue this command in the same directory in which the original `sendmail.cf` file resides, the command copies over the existing `sendmail.cf` file. For added safety, back up that file first. You can then restore it from the backup if something goes wrong.

Generally speaking, you'll want to start with the m4 file provided by your distribution but rename it to something appropriate. After you make a change and create a new `sendmail.cf` file, you must pass the `reload` or `restart` parameter to the sendmail SysV startup script, as described in Phase 3:

```
# /etc/init.d/sendmail reload
```

You should be aware that the m4 file uses the dnl string to denote comments. Thus, if a line begins with dnl, it's a comment line. If you want to use that line in your configuration, remove the dnl characters.

## Hostname Options

All mail servers must know their own hostnames. This information is used in a variety of ways, such as when initiating communications with other servers and as identification to be added to usernames for the benefit of clients that don't provide this detail. Ordinarily, sendmail retrieves its hostname from system calls designed for this purpose. (In most cases, these calls deliver the name that was in /etc/HOSTNAME or /etc/hostname at boot time.) Sometimes, though, you might want to override this hostname. For instance, your mail server might be known by multiple names and you want to set one for the system and another for sendmail alone. Sometimes you want outgoing email to omit the machine name, as in alfred@pangaea.edu rather than alfred@wegener.pangaea.edu. To make such a change, look for lines like the following in the m4 file:

```
MASQUERADE_AS(`pangaea.edu')
FEATURE(masquerade_envelope)
```

> The MASQUERADE_AS line includes two types of single-quote marks. The first one (`) is a backtick, which appears to the left of the 1 key on most keyboards. The second (') is an ordinary single quote, which is to the left of the Enter key on most keyboards. Be sure to get these right or your configuration won't work!

If you don't see such lines in your file, add them. You can then change the MASQUERADE_AS address to whatever you like. This change will add the specified hostname to any addresses in the From: header of outgoing mail that lack this information. The FEATURE(masquerade_envelope) line takes things further, substituting the specified address for those that users specify in their mail clients.

## Accepting Mail

Recently, sendmail configurations have begun to include a line like the following in their m4 files:

```
DAEMON_OPTIONS(`Port=SMTP,Addr=127.0.0.1, Name=MTA')dnl
```

This line has the effect of limiting sendmail to listening on the 127.0.0.1 (localhost) address. The result is that the server is available to local programs but not to other computers. This is a desirable configuration for most workstations and even non-mail servers. If you want sendmail to accept incoming mail or to function as a mail relay, though, you should remove this line. Ideally, you should comment it out by adding dnl to the start of the line. You can then rebuild your sendmail.cf file and have the server reload its configuration.

If you want sendmail to accept mail addressed to users of a whole domain or to a hostname other than the one the computer has, you should add those domain names or hostnames to the

/etc/mail/local-host-names file. In the case of the mail.pangaea.edu server, you should add both pangaea.edu and mesozoic.edu to this file in order to have the server accept mail addressed to both domains. You should also ensure that the following line is present in your m4 file:

FEATURE(use_cw_file)

> Accepting mail addressed to a domain requires configuring your domain's DNS records. Specifically, you must add a new or change an existing mail exchanger (MX) record to point to the mail server computer—mail.pangaea.edu in this example. If you don't know how to do this, you should consult with whoever maintains your domain's DNS server.

## Redirecting Mail

Email aliases enable one address to stand in for another one. For instance, all mail servers are supposed to maintain an account called postmaster. Email to this account should be read by somebody who's responsible for maintaining the system. One way to do this is to set up an alias linking the postmaster name to the name of a real account. You can do this by editing the aliases file, which usually resides in /etc or sometimes in /etc/mail.

The aliases file format is fairly straightforward. Comment lines begin with hash marks (#) and other lines take the following form:

name: addr1[,addr2[,...]]

The *name* that leads the line is a local name, such as postmaster. Each address (*addr1*, *addr2*, and so on) can be a local account name to which the messages are forwarded, the name of a local file into which messages are stored (denoted by a leading slash), a command through which messages are piped (denoted by a leading vertical bar character), the name of a file whose contents are treated as a series of addresses (denoted by a leading :include: string), or a full e-mail address (such as fred@example.com).

A typical default configuration includes a few useful aliases for accounts such as postmaster. Most such configurations map most of these aliases to root. Reading mail as root is inadvisable, though—doing so increases the odds of a security breach or other problem because of a typo or bug in the mail reader. Thus, you may want to set up an alias line like the following:

root: *yourusername*

This redirects all of root's mail, including mail directed to root via another alias, to *yourusername*. Once you make this, or any other, change to the aliases file, you must rebuild its binary counterpart, aliases.db. To do so, use the newaliases command:

# **newaliases**

Another approach to redirecting mail is to do so on the user level. In particular, you can edit the ~/.forward file in a user's home directory to have mail for that user sent to another address. Specifically, the ~/.forward file should contain the new address—either a username on the current computer or an entire email address on another computer. This approach has the advantage that it can be employed by individual users—say, to consolidate email from multiple systems into one account without bothering system administrators. A drawback is that it can't be used to set up aliases for nonexistent accounts or for accounts that lack home directories. The ~/.forward file could also be changed or deleted by the account owner, which might not be desirable if you want to enforce a forwarding rule that the user shouldn't be able to override.

## Configuring Sendmail as a Relay

All modern Linux distributions configure themselves so that they do *not* relay mail by default—or at least, they configure themselves so that they relay mail for only a very limited set of computers. The most common type of relay configuration in sendmail uses the following control line (or one similar to it) in the m4 file:

```
FEATURE(`access_db')
```

This line tells the system to read the access file (stored in /etc or /etc/mail) for information on who may relay messages. Listing 6.3 shows a typical access file. This example file enables relaying for the local computer (as localhost.localdomain, localhost, and 127.0.0.1) and for the local network (172.25.98.0/24). Most default configurations omit this last option, which appears in Listing 6.3 to fulfill the requirement in the scenario that the server relay mail for the pangaea.edu domain. The assumption is that pangaea.edu has a rather small network, consisting of that one block of IP addresses. Alternatively, you could specify all the domain's network blocks or use the domain name itself—IP addresses are safer, though, because they're harder to forge. If your system shouldn't be relaying mail, the access file should lack any lines beyond the ones for local relaying.

**Listing 6.3:** A Typical access File for Controlling Mail Relaying

```
# by default we allow relaying from localhost...
localhost.localdomain          RELAY
localhost                      RELAY
127.0.0.1                      RELAY
# Relay for the local network
172.25.98                      RELAY
```

Some other m4 file relaying options are also available in sendmail. Most of these include the word relay in their names, such as relay_entire_domain. Unless you've learned a great deal about email configuration and management, I recommend you avoid using such options. In fact, one of these options, promiscuous_relay, should *never* be used. It tells the computer to indiscriminately relay *all* mail. In the days before spam, such configurations were considered a courtesy. Today, they're madness!

Because open relays are such a threat, you should explicitly check for them. Review your `access` file and look for any option with the word `relay` in the m4 configuration file. You can also use services that will connect to your mail server and attempt to relay mail as a way of testing your system, then give you a report of the results. One of these is hosted at `http://www.abuse.net/relay.html`. Be careful, though—it's conceivable that a spammer somewhere has set up such a service as a way of locating open relays to abuse, so you should only use a trusted service.

## Outgoing Relay Configuration

Many Linux mail servers, particularly on workstations and small networks, should be configured to use an outgoing mail relay, aka a *smart relay*. This is the case for the workstations described in this task's scenario. To configure these systems to use Pangaea University's main mail server for outgoing mail, enable outgoing relaying in the workstations' m4 files:

```
FEATURE(`nullclient', `mail.pangaea.edu')
```

In reality, you would change `mail.pangaea.edu` to the hostname of the computer that should relay the mail. You should also remove or comment out two other lines, if they're present:

```
MAILER(local)dnl
MAILER(smtp)dnl
```

Another way to make similar changes is to use the SMART_HOST feature:

```
define(`SMART_HOST', `mail.pangaea.edu')
```

The difference between the two is that the `nullclient` method is intended for very simple configurations that contain few other options. A workstation that should send *all* its email via the outgoing relay might use this option. SMART_HOST, by contrast, can be used in more complex configurations in which some mail remains local and some is relayed.

When you've made these changes, rebuilt `sendmail.cf`, and restarted or reloaded sendmail, the server should send all non-local mail to the specified mail server. This is handy if your ISP blocks direct outgoing SMTP connections (as many home-oriented ISPs do as an anti-spam measure) or if you want your organization's mail to be filtered through a single powerful mail server system.

## Criteria for Completion

To complete this task, you should have configured one mail server to accept mail for two entire domains (`pangaea.edu` and `mesozoic.edu`). You should also have adjusted the server to redirect mail for `postmaster` (and, perhaps, some other addresses) to specific local users of your choice. Finally, you should have configured at least one other system's sendmail configuration to direct its mail through the first one. These options can be tricky to implement, so be sure to test them by sending and reading mail using local mail clients such as `mutt` or KMail.

# Task 6.7: Run a Web Server

The World Wide Web (WWW or Web for short) is, to many people, synonymous with the Internet, although in reality the Web is just part of the Internet. The Web is, though, an extremely visible and popular part of the Internet. Naturally, Linux can function as a Web server computer. Several programs to handle this job exist, but Apache (`http://httpd.apache.org`) is the most popular by a wide margin. Apache, like sendmail, is a complex and powerful tool. This task can therefore only present the most basic Web server features and options; for more information, you should consult a book on the topic.

## Scenario

In addition to configuring the mail server described in Task 6.6, you must configure the Pangaea University Web server, `www.pangaea.edu`. The Web server should display Web pages housed in the `/var/web/pangaea` directory tree. This system should respond to the `www.mesozoic.edu` address by displaying a different set of Web pages than the ones displayed when accessed as `http://www.pangaea.edu`; the `http://www.mesozoic.edu` pages should be located in the `/var/web/mesozoic` directory. The Web server should also display users' home pages, accessed using the usual user Web page format—`http://www.pangaea.edu/~user/` or `http://www.mesozoic.edu/~user/` for its two addresses. You will use Apache to accomplish these goals.

## Scope of Task

To perform this task, you must install and configure the Apache Web server. Most of the Apache default options are suitable for a simple Web site, but you'll need to tweak or verify a few of them to ensure that the goals laid out in the scenario are met.

### Duration

This task should take half an hour to an hour to complete. Real-world Apache configuration changes can take anywhere from a couple of minutes to many hours, depending on the complexity of the configuration, your experience, and whether or not you run into any unexpected problems.

### Setup

You must have **root** access to a Linux system that runs Apache. If the computer you're using doesn't currently run Apache, you should download and install it. Because Apache ships with all major Linux distributions, check your distribution's package system first; Apache usually ships as a package called `apache` or `httpd`, so look for both of these names. (Phase 3 describes Linux package management.)

In addition to the Linux system on which you're configuring the Web server, you should have access to another computer and its Web browser. You'll use this system to test your Apache configuration changes.

The Linux system you're configuring must be accessible under two different hostnames (www.pangaea.edu and www.mesozoic.edu in this example). This configuration normally requires editing DNS server entries; however, you might be able to achieve the same effect by editing the /etc/hosts file on your client computer.

## Caveats

The usual root-access cautions apply to this task. In addition, Web servers are unusually visible network servers. Crackers frequently attack Web server computers, and if the Web server software (or any other server running on the computer) is buggy or misconfigured, the result can be a serious compromise of the computer. This can lead to defacement of your Web pages, theft of your data, use of your system for further attacks on your own or other networks, and so on. For this reason, you should be very cautious about configuring a Web server. If you don't need to run Web server software on your computer, you should shut it down or, better yet, uninstall the software when you're done with this task. As a general rule, if you're running a Web server on the Internet at large, you should learn more about Apache than you can learn from this task alone. If you want to run Apache on a well-protected computer on a local network (say, behind a NAT router for use by local users), the risks are much less substantial.

# Procedure

To complete this task, you must first prepare directories for storing your Web pages. You should then find and understand the Apache configuration files. You can then configure Apache to use the directories you've created, both for the main domain Web pages and for user Web pages.

## Preparing Your Web Space

The scenario for this task specifies that the /var/web/pangaea and /var/web/mesozoic directories should hold the Web pages for the two main Web sites hosted by your Web server. You can create these directories using ordinary Linux directory-creation commands:

```
# mkdir -p /var/web/pangaea
# mkdir /var/web/mesozoic
```

The -p option on the first command ensures that the /var/web directory will be created if it doesn't already exist. When you create these directories as root, they'll be owned by root and, in all probability, other users won't be able to create files in them. Chances are other users have been tasked with creating the actual Hypertext Markup Language (HTML) files that make up each Web site. Thus, you might want to change the ownership, group ownership, or permissions of these directories to enable other users to write to them. For instance, suppose the computer has a wmaster group and users of this group should be able to modify Web pages. You might enable this access by changing ownership and permissions in this way:

```
# cd /var/web
# chgrp wmaster mesozoic pangaea
# chmod 0775 mesozoic pangaea
```

Alternatively, you could give ownership of these directories to individual users, employ different groups for each directory, or use any other security scheme you see fit. Giving world write access (0777 permissions) is inadvisable, though; this sort of permission gives anybody who has an account on the computer—or who breaks into any user's normal account—the ability to write to the Web space directories.

Actually creating Web pages requires creating or editing HTML files. Traditionally, Apache loads a file called index.html or index.htm as the default page for a site. Listing 6.4 shows a simple HTML file you can use as a placeholder. Change the file's identification lines (the lines beginning <TITLE> and <CENTER>) for each site so that you can verify that Apache is delivering the correct file for each of its hostnames. Creating complex HTML files and Web sites is a topic that's well beyond the scope of this task.

**Listing 6.4:** Sample HTML File

```
<!DOCTYPE HTML PUBLIC "-//W3C//DTD HTML 4.01 Transitional//EN"
 "http://www.w3.org/TR/html4/loose.dtd">
<HTML><HEAD>
<TITLE>Pangaea University</TITLE>
</HEAD>
<CENTER><H1 ALIGN="CENTER">Pangaea University's Web Page</H1></CENTER>

<p>This is a sample Web page. The server is willing, but the Web
site is weak.</p>
</body>
</html>
```

## Touring Apache Configuration Files

Apache's main configuration file takes on various names depending on the distribution. The most common are httpd.conf, httpd2.conf, apache.conf, and apache2.conf. (Apache 2.0 and later packages sometimes use a 2 in the configuration filename.) The location of the Apache configuration file also varies from one system to another, but common places include /etc/apache, /etc/apache2, /etc/httpd, /etc/httpd2, or the conf subdirectory of any of these. The name of the Apache executable can vary, but it is usually httpd.

 If you can't find your Apache configuration file, use your package manager to find it. For instance, if you installed Apache on an RPM-based system as apache, you could type **rpm -ql apache | grep conf**. This command lists all the files in the apache package and narrows the list to those that include the string conf. Phases 3 and 1 describe package management and grep, respectively.

Whatever its name, the Apache configuration file consists of comments, denoted by hash marks (#), and directive lines that take the following form:

*Directive Value*

The *Directive* is simply an option name or command, such as LoadModule, Listen, or MaxClients. In most cases, the *Value* is a filename, number, or other single value that's assigned to the *Directive*. Sometimes the *Value* consists of multiple items; for instance, LoadModule takes a two-part directive that consists of a module name and a module filename. The parts of such a multi-part *Value* are separated by spaces.

Some option lines are grouped together in blocks, which are identified by beginning and ending lines in angle brackets (<>), with the name of the ending angle bracket line beginning with a slash (/):

```
<IfModule perchild.c>
NumServers          5
StartThreads        5
MaxThreadsPerChild  20
</IfModule>
```

Typically, these blocks apply only if a particular condition exists. For instance, the <IfModule perchild.c> block shown here applies only if the perchild.c module is available and loaded. (Modules are described shortly.)

Several servers other than Apache have adopted Apache-like configuration file formats. Thus, familiarizing yourself with this style of configuration file can be helpful even if you don't need to administer Apache.

## Configuring Your Domains

Apache uses the DocumentRoot directive to specify where the server looks for Web pages. You should locate this line and change it to point to whichever directory you want to hold Apache's default Web site:

```
DocumentRoot "/var/web/pangaea"
```

Chances are you'll find a <Directory> reference to the directory that the server used as its default Web space location; you should find this option and change it to point to your new default directory:

```
<Directory "/var/www/html">
```

As described earlier, such lines specify the beginnings of directive blocks. In this case, the Apache configuration file is setting options that apply to the default server directory. If you fail to change the directory specified on this line, Apache will apply its defaults to your new directory. These defaults might or might not be appropriate for your site.

To support http://www.mesozoic.edu addressing, you must use the NameVirtualHost directive and implement a <VirtualHost> directive block for each hostname, with the default name's configuration appearing first:

```
NameVirtualHost *:80

<VirtualHost *:80>
    ServerAdmin webmaster@pangaea.edu
    DocumentRoot /var/web/pangaea
    ServerName www.pangaea.edu
    ErrorLog logs/pangaea-error_log
    CustomLog logs/pangaea-access_log common
</VirtualHost>

<VirtualHost *:80>
    ServerAdmin webmaster@mesozoic.edu
    DocumentRoot /var/web/mesozoic
    ServerName www.mesozoic.edu
    ErrorLog logs/mesozoic-error_log
    CustomLog logs/mesozoic-access_log common
</VirtualHost>
```

Your Apache configuration file may provide a sample <VirtualHost> section that's been commented out, so look for one. If you can't find one, add appropriate lines at the very end of your Apache configuration file.

Apache supports both name-based (as shown here) and IP-address-based virtual hosts. Additional options enable Apache to host multiple domains without the need to explicitly set up each domain, as shown in this example. Such tools are most helpful to large domain hosting companies, which can host hundreds of domains on a single computer.

Once you've implemented your changes, you must restart your Apache server. Typically, you can do this via your SysV startup scripts:

# **/etc/init.d/httpd restart**

As described in Phase 3, the exact path to the SysV startup script may differ from the one shown here. You might also need to use **apache** or some other variant script name rather than **httpd**.

If you had to install Apache for this task, it might not be running, in which case you would pass the script the start option. Phase 3 describes configuring SysV startup scripts to start services automatically when the system boots.

At this point, you should try accessing the Web server computer using each of its two names. You should see the two variants of the Web page described by Listing 6.4 appear depending on the name you used.

## Setting User Web Page Options

To enable ordinary users to create their own Web pages, you must enter or uncomment the following lines:

```
UserDir enable
UserDir public_html
```

Most default Apache configuration files include the first of these options, but set to disable, and a commented-out version of the second option. Look for these options in the existing file and set them in this way. (You can change public_html to another directory, if you like.)

The public HTML options rely on an Apache module called mod_userdir. If this module isn't loaded, these features won't work. Near the start of your Apache configuration file, you should see a series of LoadModule lines. Look for one that loads the mod_userdir module:

```
LoadModule userdir_module modules/mod_userdir.so
```

If you can't find such a line, or if it's commented out, add it or uncomment it. If your line differs slightly from the one shown here, leave it as is.

To prepare user Web pages, first ensure that the public_html directory is present in a user's home directory. You can then copy HTML files into this directory, including one called index.html. (Use a variant of Listing 6.4 if you like.) Finally, ensure that the public_html directory has world read and execute permissions and that the user's home directory has world execute permissions. If these permissions aren't present, Apache won't be able to read the user's Web pages.

Upon restarting Apache, you should now be able to access user Web pages by using a URL of the form http://www.pangaea.edu/~*user*/, where *user* is the username. The same page should appear no matter what hostname you use to access the server. If this process doesn't work, consult your Apache error logs, which are usually located in a subdirectory of the /var/log directory.

# Criteria for Completion

To complete this task, you should have enabled an Apache server and set it up to deliver two different Web sites depending on the hostname used to access the server (www.pangaea.edu or www.mesozoic.edu, for instance). You should also reconfigure the server to enable user Web pages, as maintained by individual users in their own home directories. Once you've finished this task, be sure to disable or (better) uninstall the Apache server unless you have a valid reason for running it. Because of its high profile, Apache is even more of a security risk than most servers and so should not be left running unnecessarily.

# Task 6.8: Manage a File Sharing Server

A *file sharing server* enables users working on separate computers to store their files on one central computer. The same technologies enable users to share files directly with one another from their workstations (using a so-called *peer-to-peer* configuration). File sharing, either using a central server or a peer-to-peer arrangement, is a great boon for many offices because it can simplify sharing of files between users. In the case of centralized servers, backup of the most critical work files is also simplified. As you might expect, Linux can function as a file sharing server, and this task describes how to configure Linux in this way, using either of two protocols.

## Scenario

Your office network includes several types of workstations, which run Linux, Mac OS X, and Windows OSs. You want to enable users of all of these platforms to easily collaborate on projects, and you've determined that a file sharing server will help accomplish this goal. Therefore, you want to configure a Linux system, `sirius.example.com`, as a file sharing server. The Linux and Mac OS X clients, being Unix-like OSs, will use the Network File System (NFS) to access the Linux server. The Windows systems, on the other hand, will use their native Server Message Block/Common Internet File System (SMB/CIFS) protocol.

You want to give users home directories on the server computer, enabling them to read and write their own files. You also want to share two more directories: `/opt/clipart` holds a clip art collection that should be readable, but not writable, to all users; and `/home/xfers` is a directory that's dedicated to file transfers (it should be readable and writable to all users).

## Scope of Task

This task is fairly involved because it requires configuring *two* servers: Linux's native NFS server for NFS and the Samba server for SMB/CIFS. Fortunately, both servers ship with default configurations that should be close to what you need in most ways. The Samba server requires more extensive changes to meet the scenario's requirements.

 Phase 5 includes basic information on configuring Linux as a file sharing client.

## Duration

This task should take one to two hours to complete. Making small changes to each server's configuration should take very little time, but setting a server up from scratch—particularly a Samba server—requires attending to a number of small but important details.

## Setup

You must have root access to the file server computer (sirius.example.com in this example). This task assumes that the NFS server and Samba packages are installed on this computer. If they're not installed, you should attend to this matter using your distribution's package management system (described in Phase 3). NFS is usually installed as part of a package called nfs-utils, while Samba is usually installed as samba, smb, or something similar.

Before proceeding further, you should create the directories you want to export. Presumably /home already exists and holds users' home directories. You should create the /home/xfers subdirectory within this directory and give all users write privileges to this directory by changing its mode to 0777. You should also create /opt/clipart and populate it with some clip art files if this directory and its files don't already exist. Ensure that world read permissions exist on this directory and its files.

## Caveats

The usual root-access caveats apply to this task. In addition, both NFS and Samba are potentially dangerous servers to have installed. Both servers have the potential to hide bugs that can lead to security breaches. In addition, if they are misconfigured, you could give inappropriate access to critical system files or to confidential user files via either server. You should be very careful about the directories that you share and about the security-related options you apply to the directories that you do share.

# Procedure

To perform this task, you must configure both NFS and Samba. NFS configuration is relatively simple. Samba configuration can be quite complex, but most default Samba setups are close to adequate as delivered. Once you've configured both servers, you should test them from appropriate client systems.

 In NFS parlance, directories that are made available to other computers are called *exports*. Such directories are called *shares* in the Samba world. Both words can also be used as verbs to describe the act of making the directory available.

## Configuring NFS

NFS uses a *trusted hosts* security model, meaning that the server trusts the client to do the authentication. This may seem naïve in today's world, but it was the norm in the days when NFS was created. The result of this design is that you must be *very* careful about the clients you trust. In fact, setting up that trust relationship is a large part of NFS configuration.

In Linux, NFS server configuration is handled through a file called /etc/exports. This file contains lines that begin with a directory that's to be shared followed by a list of hostnames or IP addresses that may access it, with their options in parentheses:

```
/home taurus(rw,async) littrow(rw) 192.168.1.0/24(rw)
/opt/clipart taurus(ro,all_squash) 192.168.1.0/24(ro)
```

These examples share two directories: /home and /opt/clipart. The first of these exports gives users access to their home directories and to /home/xfers. Two computers (taurus and littrow), along with the entire 192.168.1.0/24 network block, may access /home, but only taurus and the same network block may access the /opt/clipart export. You can also specify hosts using wildcards (such as *.luna.edu, which matches all systems in the luna.edu domain), using IP addresses (as in 192.168.1.39), or as an NIS netgroup if your network supports NIS (as in @agroup). The options in parentheses specify security restrictions and other server features, such as the following:

**secure and insecure**    The default operation is secure, which denies access requests from port numbers above 1024. On Unix and Linux systems, only root may initiate connections using these secure ports, so this is a security feature—but not a very effective one in today's environment. You can disable this protection by specifying the insecure option.

**ro and rw**    These options specify read-only or read/write access to the export, respectively. The default has changed over time; most current servers use ro as the default, but some older ones used rw. I recommend you set this option explicitly to avoid any potential for confusion.

**sync and async**    Ordinarily, an NFS server is supposed to complete certain operations by writing data to disk before responding to the client. This configuration is denoted by the sync option. You can improve performance by specifying async instead, which allows the server to respond to clients before the disk operation is completed. The drawback is that data loss is more likely in the event of a server crash.

**root_squash and no_root_squash**    By default, NFS treats accesses from the client's root user (UID 0) as if they were coming from a local anonymous user, as set by the anonuid and anongid options, described shortly. This *squashing* is a security measure that can be overridden by specifying the no_root_squash option. Ordinarily, you shouldn't use this option because it opens the door to abuses should a client system be compromised. It might be necessary in some cases, though.

**all_squash and no_all_squash**    Just as root access can be squashed, access by other users can be squashed. Specifying all_squash does so, giving access by all users a low privilege status. This configuration can be useful if you want to share a public directory to which users should be unable to write.

**anonuid and anongid**    You can set the UID and GID of the anonymous account used for squashing operations. To do so, use these options, an equal sign, and the UID or GID number, as in anonuid=703.

In most cases, just a few options are necessary for most exports. You should always specify rw or ro, simply to avoid the possibility of confusion since the default for this option has changed in the past. The `async` option can be a useful one if you want the best possible performance, but it increases the risk of losing data in the event of a server crash. As an added security measure, you might want to use the `all_squash` option on publicly accessible NFS exports, such as the clip art export in this example. (This will render files' groups ineffective in controlling access, though.)

You can specify different options for different computers. For instance, you might give one system full read/write access to the server but deliver read-only access to others. This configuration enables one person or a group of people (the users of the read/write systems) to change the contents of an export—for instance, to update that clip art collection.

Because NFS was designed for Unix-to-Unix file sharing, it supports Unix-style ownership and permissions. Thus, you can use ordinary Linux file ownership and permissions tools, as described in Phase 1, to control access to files in NFS exports. Furthermore, Linux ownership and permission information will be preserved on NFS exports. This fact is most important for the `/home/xfers` directory; given 0777 (`-rwxrwxrwx`) directory permissions, users will be able to create files in this export, but other users might or might not be able to read those files, depending on the files' permissions. You must educate your users about these matters if they're to make effective use of this directory.

## Configuring Samba

Samba was designed to share files with DOS, Windows, and OS/2 systems, and this fact leads to design complications. Specifically, Samba's primary target client OSs support different filesystem features than does Linux, so Samba must somehow find a way to support system bits, hidden bits, case-insensitive filenames, and so on. Samba's task is also complicated by the need to provide security based on usernames and passwords, including a password encryption scheme that's incompatible with the one Linux uses to store its own passwords. SMB/CIFS uses its own naming system, separate from TCP/IP hostnames, as well as dedicated network components to support this naming system and other SMB/CIFS features. For all of these reasons, Samba is a very complex server compared to NFS. To configure it, you must first understand its configuration file. With that knowledge in hand, you can proceed to setting global Samba options for your network and configuring the shares you want to create.

### Understanding the Samba Configuration File

Samba's configuration file, `smb.conf`, is usually stored in the `/etc/samba` or `/etc` directory. Look for yours and load it into a text editor. The file contains comments denoted by hash marks (#) or semicolons (;). Configuration lines consist of an option name, an equal sign (=), and a value:

```
netbios name = SIRIUS
server string = Share and Enjoy
```

These configuration lines are placed in configuration file sections, each of which begins with a name in square brackets:

```
[global]
```

The [global] section sets global options that apply to the server as a whole. It also sets default values for share options. Each share definition begins with a configuration section name, which specifies the name by which the share can be accessed (with a couple of important exceptions, as described shortly). For instance, the [clipart] section creates a share that clients can access as CLIPART.

SMB/CIFS share names are case insensitive. Most smb.conf files use lowercase for share names in section headings. I use uppercase when referring to the shares as referenced from clients because they were historically used in this way beginning with older clients, such as DOS, that used uppercase filenames and share names.

## Setting Global Samba Options

Review the [global] section of your smb.conf file. Chances are most of the options can remain as they are; most distributions provide options that work reasonably well on most networks. The first two options require your attention are netbios name and workgroup:

```
netbios name = SIRIUS
workgroup = OFFICE
```

These options set the *Network Basic Input/Output System (NetBIOS) name* and *workgroup name* for the computer. The NetBIOS name is the SMB/CIFS equivalent of the DNS hostname. If you don't set this option, Samba uses the first part of your DNS hostname, which is usually a reasonable choice.

The workgroup option, though, must be set. The workgroup name is a name that SMB/CIFS applies on top of the NetBIOS name, similar to a domain name that's used in conjunction with a DNS hostname. In most simple configurations, all the computers on a LAN should have the same workgroup name. Thus, you should discover what that name is for your site and set it appropriately in Samba.

Another two or three global options that require attention relate to password authentication:

```
security = User
# password server = 192.168.1.1
encrypt passwords = Yes
```

The security option sets the security model used by Samba: User, Share, Server, or Domain. The first option is the best for a stand-alone server; it tells Samba to authenticate users based on a local password database. The Share option emulates Windows 9*x*/Me security, in which shares have passwords but not usernames. The Server and Domain options both defer authentication to another computer (known as a *domain controller*). You can use Server authentication fairly easily by setting the password server option to point to your domain controller. (The preceding examples show this parameter commented out because it's not needed for user-level security.) Using Domain authentication also requires setting password server, but you must also use external tools to explicitly join the domain—a topic that's beyond the scope of this task.

The `encrypt passwords` option tells Samba whether or not to encrypt passwords. Setting this option to `Yes` is required if you use a domain controller for authentication. If you use encrypted passwords with the `User` or `Share` options for `security`, Samba stores encrypted passwords itself, independently of the Linux passwords. This requires you to set up passwords, which can be a hassle. If you set `encrypt passwords = No`, Samba can use Linux's existing password database, but passwords are sent in unencrypted form. Worse, all modern versions of Windows refuse to use unencrypted passwords by default, as a security precaution. You can reconfigure Windows clients, but this requires effort on all the clients. Thus, it's usually better to encrypt your passwords.

Finally, you should check that the following options are set as shown:

```
local master = No
domain master = No
preferred master = No
```

These options all refer to *master browser* configuration. On an SMB/CIFS network, a master browser is a computer that maintains lists of computers in each workgroup or domain. If you're adding a Linux server to an existing network, you should *not* attempt to configure it as a master browser since incorrect configuration can lead to serious problems.

You'll find many additional global options in your `smb.conf` file. Unless you understand an option, the best course of action is usually to leave it set at its default value. You can consult the `man` page for `smb.conf` to learn more about all of these options.

### Setting Samba Passwords

Because encrypted passwords are the norm, chances are you'll want to set `encrypt passwords = Yes` and set up a Samba encrypted password database. To do this, you'll need to use your Linux shell and issue the `smbpasswd` command:

```
# smbpasswd -a fred
```

This command prompts you to enter a password, then to repeat this entry. It then creates a Samba password for `fred` using the password you entered. You must repeat this process for every user who should have an account. In practice, you might want to have users visit you so that they can type their own passwords.

The first time you use the smbpasswd command, it will complain about the lack of an /etc/samba/smbpasswd file. This complaint looks like an error message, but the utility creates the file, so nothing is wrong or needs your attention.

The `smbpasswd` command will create Samba passwords only for users who already have regular Linux accounts. If the server computer lacks such accounts, you should first create them, as described in Phase 1.

Creating passwords in this way is unnecessary if you set security to Server or Domain. In these cases, you can instead rely on the domain controller for authentication; however, you must still have local Linux accounts for all the system's users. Methods of more tightly integrating the two systems, so that Samba automatically creates local accounts for users with existing domain accounts, do exist. These methods are well beyond the scope of this task, though.

### Sharing Home Directories

The scenario for this task specifies that users should be able to access their home directories. For NFS, this was done by exporting the /home directory. Although creating a share for /home is possible with Samba, a better approach is the [homes] share. This share name is a special case: It enables a share whose name and shared directory vary depending on the user who accesses the server. If fred accesses the server, the share's name is fred and it shares fred's home directory (probably /home/fred). If sally accesses the server, the share's name is sally and it shares sally's home directory (probably /home/sally). Most sample smb.conf files include a [homes] share definition that looks something like this:

```
[homes]
   comment = Home Directories
   browseable = no
   writable = yes
   valid users = %S
   create mode = 0644
   directory mode = 0755
```

The share's options can vary from these, and for the most part you shouldn't adjust them. You should ensure that the writable = yes option (or its synonyms, writeable = yes or read only = no) is present; this ensures that users can write to their own home shares. The create mode and directory mode options set the file permissions for files and directories created via this share. You can adjust these options if you want stricter or looser permissions on users' files.

### Sharing the */opt/clipart* and */home/xfers* Directories

The clip art and data transfer shares both require their own definitions:

```
[clipart]
   comment = Clip Art Files
   path = /opt/clipart
   write list = sally
   writable = No
   create mask = 0644
   directory mask = 0755


[xfers]
   comment = Data transfer directory
```

```
path = /home/xfers
writable = Yes
create mode = 0666
directory mode = 0777
```

These two shares give read-only access to the /opt/clipart directory and read/write access to the /home/xfers directory. The [clipart] share also grants sally write access. This exception to the usual read-only access is a good way to enable one user to maintain an ordinarily read-only share.

The create mode and directory mode options in the [xfers] share give all users full read and write access to all the files and directories created via this share. This configuration is useful for an open data-transfer directory that's used for exchanging files. With this configuration, all users are guaranteed access to all other users' files. When exchanging files transferred via NFS, though, the Unix-style permissions of the NFS client apply, and these might be more restrictive.

## Testing Your Configuration

After making changes to your NFS and Samba configurations, you can test the changes. To begin with, you'll need to tell the server processes about the changes.

In the case of NFS, you should type **exportfs -ra** as root to tell the server to re-examine /etc/exports and implement any changes it finds. Many distributions' SysV startup scripts for NFS also do this when you pass the reload option.

For Samba, you should use its SysV startup script; typing **/etc/init.d/smb reload** as root usually does the job, although you may need to change the path to the script or the script name. (Some distributions use samba rather than smb as the script name.)

Once you've made these changes, you should test both the NFS and Samba configurations from appropriate clients. For NFS clients (Linux and Mac OS X systems in this scenario), you should mount both of the NFS exports and test access. Be sure you can read files from both exports (except for any directories to which you have restricted access) and that you can write files to your home directory and the /home/xfers subdirectory on the /home export. For the Samba shares, test your home share, the XFERS share, and the CLIPART share from a Windows system or other SMB/CIFS client. Be sure you can write to the first two shares but not to the third one. If you have problems with any of these operations, review your configurations and try again. Log files can also be very helpful. In most cases, Samba creates a whole host of log files in its own subdirectory of /var/log.

## Criteria for Completion

To complete this task, you should have created matching NFS exports and Samba shares to provide read/write access to users' home directories and to the /home/xfers directory and read-only access to the /opt/clipart directory. The NFS configuration is relatively simple because NFS was designed for Unix-to-Unix file sharing. The Samba configuration is potentially much more complex, but most Linux distributions ship with smb.conf files that come close to most users' needs. Nonetheless, you'll need to set a few Samba options to match your local network.

# Task 6.9: Manage an SSH Server

Unix-like systems have long supported remote access, and Linux is no exception to this rule. Although tools such as Telnet and `rlogin` are available for remote text-mode access, these protocols are insecure and limited. Today, the Secure Shell (SSH) is the preferred method of providing remote text-mode access to a Linux system. In fact, you can even *tunnel* an X session through SSH, meaning that an SSH connection will link your local X server to the remote system, enabling you to run X programs remotely. SSH's greatest feature, though, is its built-in encryption. When you use SSH, the risk of your data being intercepted is slim—or more precisely, anybody snooping on your data will find it useless because of SSH's encryption.

## Scenario

Your mail server, configured in Task 6.6, is located in a physically inconvenient site. To enable easier configuration of this system from your desk, you want to configure the SSH server to accept remote logins. To provide the best security, you want to disable direct SSH logins as `root`, requiring remote users to log in as ordinary users and then, if they require `root` access, to use `su` or some other means to acquire superuser privileges. You also want to use SSH's key generation tools to create and use encryption keys as a substitute for ordinary SSH passwords, simplifying the login process.

## Scope of Task

This task requires configuring an SSH server and creating SSH keys for an ordinary user account. Fortunately, most Linux distributions provide reasonable default SSH server configurations, so the first part of this task is fairly simple. SSH key generation is a bit more obscure, but SSH keys are very powerful tools.

### Duration

This task should take half an hour to an hour to complete. Simple changes to SSH server configuration take very little time. You can generate SSH keys very quickly, too, once you know how.

### Setup

You must have both ordinary user and `root` access to the system you'll be using as an SSH server (`mail.pangaea.edu` in this example). Presumably you'll do this work at the console, although you could do it via another remote login protocol if one is enabled. If this is a text-mode protocol such as Telnet, disabling this protocol after you've got SSH working will greatly improve the computer's security. You'll also need access as an ordinary user to another system to test the configuration.

If the SSH server package isn't already installed on the computer, install it now. In most cases, it's available in a package called `openssh` or `openssh-server`. Major modern Linux distributions invariably ship with SSH (the OpenSSH implementation, to be precise), but you can download it from its Web site, `http://www.openssh.com`, if necessary.

This task assumes you're using OpenSSH, which is the most common SSH implementation in Linux. SSH Tectia (http://www.ssh.com) was the original SSH implementation, but it's uncommon in Linux because it's a commercial package. Various less-common SSH implementations also exist, but most are configured differently from OpenSSH.

## Caveats

Because you must be root to configure OpenSSH, the usual root caveats apply. Because SSH is a server that grants users full shell access to the computer, a misconfiguration of or bug in SSH can quickly lead to security problems. Thus, you should be careful not to make mistakes, and if a system doesn't really need an SSH server, you should disable it or, better yet, uninstall the package when you're done with this task.

# Procedure

This task requires completing two subtasks. First, you must configure the basic SSH server options. This task is fairly straightforward but requires root access. The second part of this task requires setting up SSH keys to enable quicker logins. This part of the task is somewhat more involved but you can do it as an ordinary user.

## Configuring the SSH Server

The SSH server is configured through the /etc/ssh/sshd_config file, and the SSH client is configured through the /etc/ssh/ssh_config file. These filenames are very similar, so be sure not to confuse them! Both files consist of comments (indicated by hash marks, #) and key-word/argument pairs, as in this example:

```
PermitRootLogin no
```

For the most part, both the client and server configurations are reasonable with most distributions. You might want to change a few options, though. Table 6.1 summarizes some additional SSH server options (in sshd_config) that you might want to change. Pay particular attention to the PermitRootLogin server option (it should be set to no to conform with the requirements outlined in this task's scenario) and to the X forwarding options. Using SSH to initiate a connection that supports X-based applications can be a convenient method of remote GUI access, but this configuration requires support in the client and server.

In Linux, the primary SSH client is called, naturally enough, ssh. In its simplest form, you type the program name followed by the system to which you want to connect. Ordinarily, the remote server then prompts you for a password. The first time you connect, the system also informs you that it can't verify the authenticity of the remote site. To test your configuration thus far, you'd do something like this from a second Linux system:

```
alfred@wegener:~$ ssh mail.pangaea.edu
The authenticity of host 'mail.pangaea.edu (192.168.1.6)' can't be established.
```

```
RSA key fingerprint is 4b:68:c1:a8:75:5e:b4:76:7b:a6:a2:0d:3a:8b:5f:48.
Are you sure you want to continue connecting (yes/no)? yes
Warning: Permanently added 'mail.pangaea.edu,192.168.1.6' (RSA) to the list of
➥known hosts.
alfred@mail.pangaea.edu's password:
[alfred@mail alfred]$
```

**TABLE 6.1**    Common SSH Server Configuration Options

| Keyword | Argument Type | Description |
| --- | --- | --- |
| Protocol | Integer | SSH protocol version number. OpenSSH 4 supports versions 1 and 2. To specify both versions, separate them with a comma, as in Protocol 1,2. |
| ListenAddress | Hostname or IP address and optional port number | Binds the server to listen only to the network interface associated with the specified address. If a port number is specified, it follows the address and a colon, as in ListenAddress 172.26.7.3:22. (The default SSH port number is 22.) |
| PermitRootLogin | Boolean, without-password, or forced-commands-only | Whether or not to accept direct logins as root. This option defaults to yes. Changing it to no will improve your system's security by requiring intruders to log in using an ordinary account and then using su, thereby requiring two passwords. The without-password option disables password authentication, meaning that another authentication method must be available. This option does *not* mean that users can log into the root account without any authentication. The forced-commands-only option enables public key authentication only for running commands remotely, which may be useful for performing remote backups or the like. |
| RhostsAuthentication | Boolean | If this option is set to yes, the server accepts authentication based on the rhosts trusted-hosts authentication model for protocol level 1 sessions. This authentication method is inherently dangerous, so I strongly recommend you leave this option at its default value of no. |

**TABLE 6.1**    Common SSH Server Configuration Options *(continued)*

| Keyword | Argument Type | Description |
| --- | --- | --- |
| RsaAuthentication | Boolean | If this option is set to yes (the default), the server accepts *Rivest/Shamir/Adleman (RSA)* authentication for protocol level 1 sessions. This approach can improve security or eliminate the need to type a password, depending on how it's used. |
| PubkeyAuthentication | Boolean | If this option is set to yes (the default), the server accepts public key authentication for protocol level 2 sessions. This approach can improve security or eliminate the need to type a password, depending on how it's used. |
| AuthorizedKeysFile | Filename | Name of the file in which clients' keys for public key authentication are stored. |
| KerberosAuthentication | Boolean | If set to yes, this option enables SSH to accept Kerberos tickets and to authenticate users via a Kerberos server. This option is useful if your network uses Kerberos but is set to no by default. Additional options that begin with Kerberos can fine-tune the configuration; consult the sshd_config man page for details. |
| X11Forwarding | Boolean | If set to yes, this option enables the server to forward X session data. The default value is no. |
| Compression | Boolean | If this option is set to yes (the default), the server accepts requests from the client to enable compression. This option consumes CPU time but reduces network bandwidth use. |

Some configurations automatically add previously unknown sites to the key file, so you may not have to authorize a connection. Either way, subsequent connections to the same system will lack the prompt and need to type **yes** to authorize a connection. You will have to type a password, though, unless you modify the configuration as described shortly. (The password doesn't echo to the screen.)

Linux's ssh client passes the current username as part of the connection protocol. If your username on the server system is different from your username on the client system, you must pass this information. You can do so by preceding the hostname with the username and an at sign (@) or by using the -1 parameter. For instance, both of the following two commands log you onto the al account on mail.pangaea.edu:

```
$ ssh al@mail.pangaea.edu
$ ssh -1 al mail.pangaea.edu
```

## Configuring SSH Keys

In a default configuration, SSH prompts for a password when making a connection. You can use alternative authentication tools, though; several such options are summarized in Table 6.1. When you activate these methods, they're tried before a password prompt. As an example, consider using public key authentication. As described here, this method will enable you to log into the remote system without typing a password. Instead, SSH will use private and public keys stored on the client and server. As a result, an interloper won't be able to masquerade as you without breaking into your computer and stealing your public key. You can use a similar approach, but with some modifications, to require use of an SSH-specific passphrase rather than the client's normal password for logins. To implement a public key system that requires no password, follow these steps:

1.  Log into the SSH client system (say, wegener.pangaea.edu).

2.  Type the following command to generate public and private keys for the client system:

    ```
    $ ssh-keygen -q -t rsa -f ~/.ssh/id_rsa -C '' -N ''
    ```

> Omitting the -N '' parameter from this command causes the program to prompt for a passphrase. You will then need to use the passphrase instead of a password when you connect to the server. If you press the Enter key twice when prompted for the password, the effect is the same as including -N ''.

3.  Copy the ~/.ssh/id_rsa.pub file from the client computer to the server computer. You can transfer this file via floppy disk, using scp (an SSH-based file copy utility), or by any other means you choose. If you use scp, you'll have to enter a password.

4.  Log into the SSH server system (say, mail.pangaea.edu). You may use SSH to do this, but at this point you'll still have to use a password.

5.  Ensure that the ~/.ssh directory exists and has 0700 (-rwx------) permissions. If necessary, type **mkdir** ~/**.ssh** to create the directory or **chmod 0700** ~/**.ssh** to set appropriate permissions on the directory

6.  Add the contents of the id_rsa.pub file you've transferred from the client to the ~/.ssh/authorized_keys file on the server. (This filename may differ; check the AuthorizedKeysFile option in your SSH server configuration.) If this is the first

client you've added, this file may not exist. Whether or not this is the first client, the following command should do the job (you may need to adjust paths or filenames for the public key file):

```
$ cat ~/id_rsa.pub >> ~/.ssh/authorized_keys
```

7. Ensure that the keys file has the correct ownership and permissions. Permissions should be no more than 0600 (-rw-------). If necessary, type **chmod 0600 ~/.ssh/ authorized_keys** to set these permissions.

Once you've completed these steps, you should be able to log in from the client (wegener) to the server (mail) without typing a password. Depending on the order in which the protocols levels are listed in your /etc/ssh/ssh_config file's Protocol line, though, you may have to specify that you want to use level 2 of the SSH protocol:

```
$ ssh -2 mail.pangaea.edu
```

## Criteria for Completion

To complete this task, you should have configured an SSH server to accept connections for ordinary users but not for root. You should also have set up an ordinary user's account to use SSH keys rather than a password for authentication, which can simplify logins from a specific client computer on which you already have an account.

# Task 6.10: Add a Printer Using CUPS

Although you might not think of printing as being particularly network related unless you use a networked printer, in Linux the printing tools are all network enabled. Traditionally, Linux has used the Berkeley Standard Distribution (BSD) Line Printer Daemon (LPD) printing system or compatible tools, such as LPRng. Since 2000, though, most Linux distributions have switched to the Common Unix Printing System (CUPS), which uses entirely different, but still network-enabled, protocols. This task steps you through the process of adding a printer to CUPS. The next task describes the tools you can use to print and manage your CUPS printer queue.

 Unlike most Linux tools, CUPS is best administered through a GUI tool, which in the case of CUPS is a Web-based utility. Some distributions provide their own unique GUI printer configuration tools. You can use such distribution-specific tools if you like, but their details differ from those described here.

## Scenario

You've just obtained a new printer and you want to configure your computer to use it. Your printer is connected directly to your computer via a USB port. (CUPS can also handle printers connected via parallel or RS-232 serial ports and network printers, but a few configuration details differ for these types of printers.)

## Scope of Task

This task requires using the Web-based configuration tool that's part of CUPS. This tool guides you through the setup process, but a few steps provide the opportunity for slipups that can cause problems.

### Duration

This task should take about half an hour to complete, or more if you run into problems. Unfortunately, each printer configuration task is unique, so you're as likely to encounter problems the 10th or 100th time you install a printer as the first time—although if you really do install a hundred unique printers, you'll have seen the most common types of problems and know how to work around them!

### Setup

This task requires that your computer be running CUPS, which most modern distributions do. You'll also need `root` access, both for installing printer drivers and for configuring CUPS via its Web interface. You may also need to restart the CUPS server: After you plug in a USB-based printer, you should turn the printer on and then restart the CUPS server as `root`. In most cases, you can do this via SysV startup scripts, as in **/etc/init.d/cups restart**. You must do this because CUPS looks for USB printers when it starts up, so if you add or turn on a printer after the system has booted, you must restart CUPS so that it can find and use the printer. For this reason, you should also ensure that any USB printer is powered on before you boot the computer. This step isn't necessary for printers that connect via a parallel or RS-232 serial port or for network printers (unless they're USB models that are managed by a computer that runs CUPS).

### Caveats

With the exception of restarting CUPS, as just described, and installing printer definitions, you won't be entering commands as `root`, which reduces the risks associated with this task. You will, however, be using the CUPS Web-based configuration tool as `root`, and you can damage your printer configuration if you make a mistake. In particular, you could delete or make unwanted changes to an existing working printer configuration.

## Procedure

This task requires you to perform two specific subtasks. First, you must obtain and install CUPS printer definitions (aka printer drivers). These may already be installed on your system, though, so perhaps just verifying that they're present will be sufficient. If in doubt, you can move on to the second subtask and go back to the first if you don't see a suitable definition for your printer when you get to that point. The second subtask is actually using the CUPS Web interface to set up and test your printer.

## Obtaining CUPS Printer Definitions

Linux programs that print typically generate one of two types of files: plain text or Post-Script. Linux printer queues typically recognize these two types of files, and perhaps some others such as common graphics file formats, and converts the printed file into a format that the printer can understand. Most commonly, the printer queue first converts non-PostScript to PostScript and then uses Ghostscript (`http://www.cs.wisc.edu/~ghost/`) to convert PostScript to a format that the printer can understand. (Of course, the Linux printing system bypasses Ghostscript when it uses a true PostScript printer.) To do all of this, you must install printer definitions, which tell the printer queue what PostScript options to use to convert PostScript into the desired format for your printer.

The basic version of CUPS ships with support for just a few printers, including raw queues that do no processing and a few models from Hewlett-Packard, Epson, and Okidata. If you use another printer, you should obtain extra CUPS printer definitions. These definitions may consist of PostScript Printer Definition (PPD) files, appropriate behind-the-scenes "glue" to tell CUPS how to use them, and possibly Ghostscript driver files. These printer definitions can be obtained from several sources:

**Your Linux distribution**    Many distributions ship extra printer definitions in a package called `cups-drivers` or something similar, so check your distribution for such a package. In truth, this package is likely to be the Foomatic or Gutenprint package under another name.

**Foomatic**    The Linux Printing Web site hosts a set of utilities and printer definitions known collectively as Foomatic (`http://www.linuxprinting.org/foomatic.html`). These provide many additional printer definitions for CUPS (as well as for other printing systems).

**Gutenprint**    The GNU Image Manipulation Program (GIMP) is a major Linux bitmap graphics program that supports its own printer drivers. These in turn have been spawned off into a package called Gutenprint (formerly GIMP Print), which can be integrated with CUPS to provide additional printer options. Check `http://gutenprint.sourceforge.net` for more information.

**Your printer manufacturer**    A few printer manufacturers make Linux printer definitions available for their printers. Sometimes these are open source definitions that they've repackaged, but sometimes the manufacturers have written their own Ghostscript drivers or definitions. Check your printer manufacturer for details.

**ESP Print Pro**    Easy Software Products (ESP) is the company that first developed CUPS. Although CUPS is open source, ESP offers a variety of printer definitions for CUPS for a price. See `http://www.easysw.com/printpro/` for more details.

If you're printing to one of the basic printers supported by the standard CUPS definitions, you may not need to add anything else. You might also find that your distribution has installed a set of definitions as part of the main CUPS package or in an add-on package, such as `cups-drivers`, without explicit instruction. In either of these cases, you're set and need not do anything else. If you start configuring printers and can't find your model, though, you should look for an additional printer definition set from one of the preceding sources.

## Using the Web-Based CUPS Utilities

CUPS uses a network printing protocol known as the Internet Printing Protocol (IPP), which is closely related to the Hypertext Transfer Protocol (HTTP) used on the Web. The protocol is so similar, in fact, that you can access a CUPS daemon by using a Web browser. You need only specify that you want to access the server on port 631—the normal IPP printer port. To do so, enter `http://localhost:631` in a Web browser on the computer running CUPS. (You may be able to substitute the hostname, or access CUPS from another computer by using the other computer's hostname, depending on settings in the `cupsd.conf` file in `/etc/cups`.) This action brings up a list of administrative tasks you can perform. Click Manage Printers to open the printer management page, shown in Figure 6.4.

**FIGURE 6.4** CUPS provides its own Web-based configuration tool.

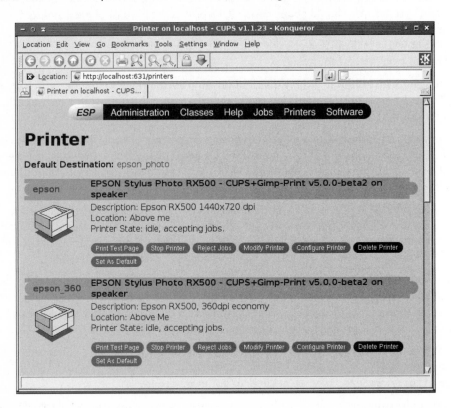

If you're configuring a stand-alone computer or the only one on a network to use CUPS, the printer list will be empty, unlike the one shown in Figure 6.4. If other computers on your network use CUPS, you may see their printers in the printer list, depending on their security settings.

You can add, delete, or modify printer queues using the CUPS Web control system. To add a printer, follow these steps:

1. Scroll to the bottom of the page and click Add Printer. (This option isn't visible in Figure 6.4 because it's too far down the existing printer list.) You're likely to be asked for a username and password.

2. Type **root** as the username and the administrative password as the password, then click OK.

CUPS doesn't normally encrypt its data, so you shouldn't use it to administer printers remotely. Doing so would be a security risk, as the passwords would be exposed to sniffing.

3. The system displays a page asking for the printer's name, location, and description. Enter appropriate information in the Name, Location, and Description fields. These fields are all entirely descriptive, so enter anything you like. (Users will use your entry in the Name field to access the printer, though.) When you click Continue, CUPS asks for the printer device.

4. The printer device may be a local hardware port (such as a parallel printer port or a USB port), a remote LPD printer, a remote SMB/CIFS (Samba) printer, or other devices. The precise options available vary from one distribution to another. This task's scenario specifies a USB printer, and CUPS should have already located and identified your specific USB printer by manufacturer and model number, so you should select that printer. If you're not using a USB printer, select an appropriate option instead.

5. If you entered a network printer, the result is a page in which you enter the complete path to the device. Type the path, such as `lpd://printserv/brother` to print to the `brother` queue on the `printserv` computer. Click Continue when you're done.

6. If you entered a local device in step 4 or after you've entered the complete path in step 5, you'll see a list of driver classes and manufacturers, such as PostScript and HP. Select one and click Continue.

7. CUPS now displays a complete list of printer models within the class you selected in step 6. Select an appropriate model and click Continue.

8. CUPS informs you that the printer has been added.

If you click the Printers item at the top of the page, you should be returned to the printers list (Figure 6.4), but your new printer should be listed among the existing queues. You can print a test page by clicking Print Test Page. If all goes well, a test page will emerge from your printer. If it doesn't, go back and review your configuration by clicking Modify Printer. This action takes you through the steps for adding a printer but with your previous selections already entered as the defaults. Try changing some settings until you get the printer to work.

From the printer queue list, you can also click Configure Printer to set various printer options. What options are available depends on the printer, but common options include the resolution, color dithering options, the paper size, whether or not to enable double-sided printing, and the presence of banner pages.

Linux applications that are designed with CUPS in mind enable you to adjust printer options such as resolution, paper size, and so on. Older programs don't provide access to such options, though. For the benefit of such programs, you can create multiple queues, each of which prints to the same printer. For instance, you could create a low-resolution queue and a high-resolution queue to give users the choice of low- or high-resolution printing. Alternatively, you can use kprinter, the KDE printing tool, instead of lpr to submit print jobs. This option can work well if you're printing directly from the command line in an xterm, but it won't work if you're not using X or if you're using a program that doesn't enable you to alter its printing command.

## Criteria for Completion

To complete this task, you should have installed at least one printer definition package (if one wasn't already installed) and created a new printer definition. You should have a test printout from this configuration, demonstrating the printer's basic features. For a color printer, you should have a color printout, for instance.

# Task 6.11: Manage Printing

Managing printers is a necessary administrative skill, but of course the point of this activity is to enable you to *use* your printers. Linux (via CUPS) supports an array of traditional text-mode printing commands for submitting print jobs and managing those jobs and the printer queues as a whole. You may also need to use GUI programs' idiosyncratic print dialog boxes, so you should have some familiarity with them as well.

## Scenario

You need to print two documents, one of which you already have in PostScript form and the other of which is a plain text file. After you submit them to the print queue, you want to examine the print queue to verify that your file is printing. You recognize one job in the queue as being improper, so you want to delete it. Finally, you want to print a file directly from the KWord word processor.

## Scope of Task

This task investigates the most common Linux printing tools and utilities, including text-mode commands and GUI print dialog boxes.

## Duration

This task should take about half an hour to an hour to complete. Once you're familiar with the commands, you can use them in just a few seconds, although of course print jobs can take anywhere from a few seconds to several hours to complete, depending on the number of pages to be printed, the type of material on the pages (graphics often take longer than text to print), and the speed of the printer.

## Setup

You must have completed Task 6.10 or have an existing working print queue on your system. You can submit print jobs and perform most other parts of this task as an ordinary user, but modifying print jobs that don't belong to you requires root privileges, as does manipulating print queues as a whole.

To complete this task, you'll need PostScript documents. You can generate such documents from many programs. Check GUI programs' print dialog boxes for options to print to disk; such options generally produce PostScript output. Alternatively, you can use sample PostScript documents that ship with Ghostscript. These are usually stored in the /usr/share/doc/ghostscript-*version*/examples or /usr/share/ghostscript/*version*/examples directory, where *version* is the Ghostscript version number. The alphabet.ps and colorcir.ps files should print on most printers. (The latter prints in color on color printers.) Some files don't print correctly on all printers.

## Caveats

If you manipulate your print queue as root, the usual root precautions apply. Other than this caveat, printing is unlikely to cause serious damage to your computer. You could, though, end up printing reams of gibberish. This can happen if your printer is misconfigured—if CUPS sends codes for, say, an Epson inkjet printer to an HP laser printer, the result could get ugly. You can also print reams of paper under some circumstances if you attempt to print a file that's damaged or that's of a type that CUPS's algorithms misidentify. This can sometimes happen with PostScript files that contain stray characters at their starts; CUPS misidentifies the file as plain text and prints it as such, resulting in many pages of PostScript code being printed rather than the formatted document you expected. Such problems may require reconfiguration of the printer queue. Of course, it's also possible to just plain waste a lot of paper and ink or toner by unnecessarily printing documents that really are big.

## Procedure

The lpr program is the most basic Linux printing tool: It's a text-mode program that prints a file you specify to the printer you indicate. Once you've submitted print jobs, you can learn about them with the help of 1pq, control them using 1pc and related utilities, or delete them with 1prm. GUI programs provide their own printing dialog boxes and options. These utilities are increasingly CUPS aware, which provides you with better control over your printing options than was possible in pre-CUPS times.

## Printing Files with *lpr*

Linux uses the 1pr program to submit print jobs. This program accepts many options that you can use to modify the program's action:

**Specify a queue name** The -P*queuename* option enables you to specify a print queue. This is useful if you have several printers or if you've defined several queues for one printer. If you omit this option, the default printer is used.

**Delete original file** Normally, 1pr sends a copy of the file you print into the queue, leaving the original unharmed. Specifying the -r option causes 1pr to delete the original file after printing it.

**Job name specification** Print jobs have names to help identify them, both while they're in the queue and once printed (if the queue is configured to print banner pages). The name is normally the name of the first file in the print job, but you can change it by including the -J *jobname* option. The -C *jobname* and -T *jobname* options have the same effect.

**Raw printing** If you know your print job can be handled by your printer without any filtering, you can use the -1 or -oraw option to bypass the normal CUPS print filters. This is handy if you've got a PostScript printer and CUPS is misidentifying a PostScript file as plain text or if you're printing a plain-text or printer-specific file on a non-PostScript printer.

> Raw printing of text files can result in the last page of the document not emerging from the printer. Most printers have a page eject button that you can use to force the printer to eject the page when the print job is complete.

**Number of copies** You can specify the number of copies of a print job by including the number after a dash, as in -3 to print three copies of a job.

Suppose you have a file called report.txt that you want to print to the printer attached to the 1exmark queue. The printer can handle plain text just fine, so you want to bypass Ghostscript, which consumes CPU time and can result in slower printing:

```
$ lpr -Plexmark -1 report.txt
```

You can print multiple files on one command line, but if they're of different types, you shouldn't ordinarily use -1 to bypass Ghostscript:

```
$ lpr -Plexmark report.txt alphabet.ps
```

The 1pr command is accessible to ordinary users as well as to root, so anybody may print using this command. It's also called from many programs that need to print directly, such as graphics programs and word processors. These programs typically give you some way to adjust the print command so that you can enter parameters such as the printer name. Some programs provide point-and-click methods of adjusting print options, as described shortly, in "Using GUI Printing Tools." Other programs provide a text entry field in which you type some or all of an lpr command instead of selecting from a pop-up list of available queues. Consult the program's documentation if you're not sure how it works.

## Displaying Print Queue Information with *lpq*

The lpq utility displays information on the print queue—how many files it contains, how large they are, who their owners are, and so on. By entering the user's name as an argument, you can also use this command to check on any print jobs owned by a particular user. To use lpq to examine a queue, you might issue a command like the following:

```
$ lpq -Plexmark
lexmark is ready and printing
Rank    Owner   Job    File(s)                    Total Size
active  rodsmit 1048   http://localhost:631/printers  123904 bytes
```

> This example shows the output of CUPS's lpq. Systems that use the original BSD LPD and LPRng display different information, but the most important information (such as the job number, job owner, job name, and job size) are present in all cases.

Of particular interest is the job number—1048 in this example. You can use this number to delete a job from the queue or reorder it so that it prints before other jobs. Any user may use the lpq command.

> If you submit a single small print job with lpr or some other tool, it might vanish from the queue before you can see it appear with lpq. If you believe this is happening, you could try submitting several print jobs. Documents that print slowly, such as graphics files, are likely to stay in the queue longer. Alternatively, you can use lpc or the CUPS Web-based control system to stop the print queue, causing jobs to pile up as they're submitted.

## Removing Print Jobs with *lprm*

The lprm command removes one or more jobs from the print queue. There are several ways to issue this command:

- If it's issued with a number, that number is understood to be the job ID (as shown in lpq's output) that's to be deleted.

- If root runs lprm and passes a username to the program, it removes all the jobs belonging to that user.

- If a user runs the BSD or CUPS lprm and passes a dash (-) to the program, it removes all the jobs belonging to the user. LPRng uses all instead of a dash for this purpose.

- If root runs the BSD or CUPS lprm and passes a dash (-) to the program, it removes all print jobs belonging to all users. Again, LPRng uses all for this purpose.

This program may be run by root or by an ordinary user, but as just noted, its capabilities vary depending on who runs it. Ordinary users may remove only their own jobs from the queue, but root may remove anybody's print jobs.

Suppose the print job you identified earlier with lpq is improper. You could remove it from the queue:

```
$ lprm 1048
```

As shown, this command will work only if you're the owner of the job in question (recall that a leading dollar sign, $, denotes a command issued by an ordinary user). If root issues this command, it will terminate any print job. Of course, if the job has already been sent to the printer, this command will have no effect.

## Controlling the Print Queue with *lpc*

The lpc utility starts, stops, and reorders jobs within print queues. The lpc utility takes commands, some of which require additional parameters. You can pass the printer name with -P, as with other printer utilities, or you can pass this information *without* the -P parameter. In the latter case, the print queue name appears immediately after the command.

**NOTE**   Although lpc is an important part of the BSD LPD and LPRng printing system, its functionality in CUPS is very limited. Instead, CUPS uses its Web-based control system to enable, disable, and otherwise modify printer queues and individual print jobs.

You can use several commands with lpc, including status, abort, start, stop, disable, enable, and topq. Of these commands, only status works with CUPS, so I don't describe lpc in great detail. If you're using a system with the older BSD LPD or LPRng printing systems, though, you might want to peruse the man page for the program to learn more about its capabilities.

If you're using CUPS, you can disable a queue by clicking the Stop Printer link for the printer on the CUPS Web interface (Figure 6.4). When you do so, this link changes to read Start Printer, which reverses the effect. The Jobs link also provides a way to cancel and otherwise manage specific jobs.

Although ordinary users may run lpc, for the most part, they can't do anything with it. Typical lpc operations require superuser privileges.

## Using GUI Printing Tools

The text-mode printing tools are very useful for handling print jobs on the command line, and they're also used behind the scenes by many GUI programs. Some of these programs use elaborate

GUI dialog boxes as interfaces to the traditional text-based tools. Other GUI programs now know how to talk to CUPS using its own protocols, which gives such programs even better printing options. This is true, for instance, of most K Desktop Environment (KDE) programs. Figure 6.5 shows the printing dialog box provided by the KWord word processor. After loading or typing a document, select File ➢ Print to obtain this dialog box.

 If you don't have KWord installed, use any other KDE application that can print to produce a similar dialog box. If you don't have any KDE applications installed, try OpenOffice.org, a GNOME application, or some other GUI program that can print.

In a GUI printing dialog box, you can typically select the printer from a drop-down list, although some programs require you to type a queue name. In the case of the KDE printing dialog box shown in Figure 6.5, you can click the Properties button to set a wide variety of advanced CUPS printing properties, such as the printer's resolution, margins, and so on. Details vary with the printer, so go ahead and explore the options available on your system. If you've configured two or more different printers, try changing the printer and see how your options change.

**FIGURE 6.5**    GUI programs typically present a wide range of printing options in their print dialog boxes.

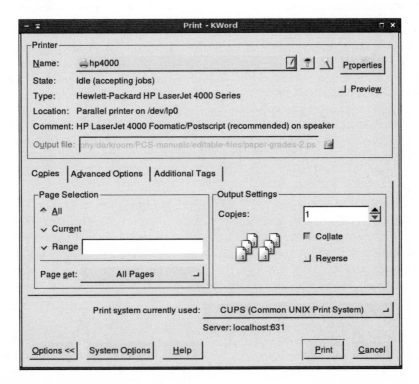

If you want access to advanced CUPS options from non-CUPS programs, you can use kprinter, rather than lpr, to submit print jobs. The kprinter program provides access to KDE's printer options when you submit jobs on the command line or from non-KDE programs; however, it requires that you be running X.

Non-KDE X programs often provide options similar to those shown in Figure 6.5; however, details can vary. Most of these programs provide similar options, so if you're familiar with, say, the KDE printing tool, you shouldn't have too much trouble using an unrelated one, such as OpenOffice.org's tool. If in doubt, explore the options, click the Help button (if one is present), or read any other documentation that came with your program.

## Criteria for Completion

To complete this task, you should have successfully printed a file from the command line using lpr. You should also have used the lpq command to view the contents of a print queue and used lprm to remove a print job. Finally, you should have used a GUI program, such as KWord, to print a document.

# Phase
# 7
# Managing Security

The phrase "last but not least" definitely applies to this phase of the book. Security is covered last because it relies on skills you've learned in previous phases. Security is, though, an extremely important topic—your computer is worse than useless if it's taken over by miscreants intent on spreading spam, attacking other computers, stealing your data, or other things you'd rather not have them do.

This phase begins with a look at ways you can block unwanted network access of your computer. You can then begin setting security restrictions aimed at improper user-level access of the computer. One specific and very important user-level security restriction is to set good passwords, so that topic is given its own task. Finally, despite your best efforts, security breaches could occur, so this phase concludes with a look at ways you can monitor for intruders.

This task maps to portions of the CompTIA Linux+ objective 4 and to portions of the LPIC objective 114.

# Task 7.1: Blocking Unwanted Network Access

The largest phase of this book is Phase 6, which includes 11 tasks. This size is justified and reflects the importance of networking for Linux—or for computers in general, for that matter. Most server computers are necessarily network-accessible at all times, and many business workstations are similarly connected. Even many residential computers have always-up broadband connections. With such constant network access comes constant exposure to network threats. Understanding the basic nature of these threats and knowing how to block them will go a long way toward keeping your computer safe.

Computer security is a matter of degrees, not of absolutes. There's no way to make a computer completely and 100 percent safe from intrusion. Even if you disconnect it from the network, it could be stolen by a burglar. Unfortunately, steps that help keep a computer (relatively) safe from intruders also often make it less convenient to use the computer. You must decide, on a case-by-case basis, whether a particular security measure provides a benefit worthy of its drawbacks.

# Scenario

Your network runs several server computers—mail servers, Web servers, file sharing servers, and so on. You've been given the job of reviewing the network security for these systems and devising a plan to improve that security, with an emphasis on preventing unwanted network access to the computers by unauthorized individuals. (In other words, this task doesn't cover issues such as burglaries or abuse by people who have passwords to the systems in question.)

# Scope of Task

This task's scope is rather broad and covers several security measures you can take. As such, each measure is outlined fairly broadly; you'll need to do more work beyond this task to create working and practical solutions for real-world networks.

## Duration

Most of the network security measures described here can be implemented in a few minutes, but to really tweak them for your specific network requires additional research on your network's configuration and perhaps on the tools you'll be using. Thus, the entire task will take anywhere from an hour to several hours to complete, depending on how thoroughly you implement the solutions described here and how many computers you lock down.

## Setup

This task assumes that your network is functioning in at least a basic way, including having a working Internet connection. You'll need root access to many (perhaps all) of the computers on your network. You may also need access to the network's wiring or wireless infrastructure. If your network includes a router, you'll need root access (or its equivalent) to the router.

## Caveats

The usual root access caveats apply to this task. Furthermore, the types of changes described in this task have the potential to disrupt network access. Thus, it's possible that you'll interfere with some or all users' ability to use the network servers or even to use the clients on their desktop systems. You should always test accessibility after making a change. You should test conditions that both should and should not be blocked.

# Procedure

This task involves examining several aspects of your system's security. Specific subtasks are shutting down unused servers, implementing access rules in the servers you leave running, implementing access control rules in xinetd, implementing access control rules using TCP Wrappers, setting up local firewall rules, and configuring a stand-alone firewall computer. On most computers, you'll implement xinetd or TCP Wrappers rules, but not both. You'll do all of these tasks but the stand-alone firewall configuration on individual client and server computers on your network; the stand-alone firewall is a single computer (typically your existing router) that you configure to protect other computers.

> Security is best applied in layers, even when each layer does a similar job. If one layer fails, the next layer may succeed.

## Shutting Down Unused Servers

The first step to improving network security is to shut down unused servers. Intruders often gain access to victims' computers by exploiting bugs or misconfigurations of servers that run on the computers. If a server isn't running, it can't be exploited in this way. The trick is to identify the servers that are running on your computer.

One approach to identifying servers is to use the netstat program, which was introduced in Phase 6. Its --listening (-1) option provides a listing of the ports to which any server is listening and waiting for external connections. Adding the --program (-p) option causes netstat to display the name and process ID (PID) number of the process that's doing the listening. To get a complete listing, you must issue the command as root:

```
# netstat -lp
Active Internet connections (only servers)
Proto Recv-Q Send-Q Local Address   Foreign Address   State    PID/Program name
tcp      0      0 *:nfs            *:*               LISTEN   -
tcp      0      0 *:netbios-ssn    *:*               LISTEN   10265/smbd
tcp      0      0 *:sunrpc         *:*               LISTEN   10098/portmap
tcp      0      0 *:ftp            *:*               LISTEN   10480/xinetd
tcp      0      0 *:ssh            *:*               LISTEN   10316/sshd
tcp      0      0 *:ipp            *:*               LISTEN   9906/cupsd
```

This example's output has been truncated, but it shows several servers that are listening for connections, including NFS, Samba (smbd), FTP, SSH, and CUPS (ipp). The Sun RPC (portmap process) is required for NFS and certain other servers. You can see the PID numbers and process names for most of these servers; NFS is the only exception, because it's handled by the kernel, which has no PID number.

One limitation of this approach is indicated by the FTP server, which points to the xinetd process: Servers that are launched by a super server show up as being handled by the super server. Thus, you must also refer to the super server configuration to figure out precisely what the server is.

Other methods of identifying running servers exist, too. These include examining SysV startup scripts and your super server configuration and performing a port scan from another computer. You can examine your startup scripts and configuration files, if you like. Port scanning is a moderately complex topic in and of itself, and it's got some major legal drawbacks—performing unauthorized port scans can land you in trouble, so it's best not to do it, even with good intentions, unless you've studied the issues and obtained whatever permissions you need to do such scans.

Once you've identified running servers, you can begin shutting down those that you don't need. Only you (or others at your site) can decide which servers are necessary and which aren't. Once you've made this determination, the best way to shut down an unwanted server is generally to uninstall it, as described in Phase 3. If this isn't possible, you should be able to remove its SysV startup script from your runlevel's configuration (as described in Phase 3) or remove its configuration from your super server configuration (as described in Phase 6). In all of these cases, you should be sure to manually shut down the server (or restart your super server, if the server you've disabled is launched in that way), as described in the relevant phases of this book.

## Using Server Access Rules

Many servers provide their own unique access control methods. The details of these methods vary greatly from one server to another, so I can't do more than describe the rough outline of what you can change in this section.

Some servers provide access rules that enable you to grant access to some computers while denying access to others. For instance, in Samba, you can use the `hosts allow` or `hosts deny` directives, which take hostnames, IP addresses, or network block addresses as options:

```
hosts allow = 192.168.1. goodguy.example.com
```

This example grants access to all computers on the 192.168.1.0/255 network block and to the `goodguy.example.com` computer. You can specify this directive in the `[global]` section, in which case it applies to the server as a whole, or in the section for an individual share, in which case it applies just to that share.

Similar access control rules exist in Apache (the `Allow from` and `Deny from` options in the Apache configuration file), CUPS (which also uses `Allow from` and `Deny from`, but in `/etc/cups/cupsd.conf`), and several other servers. As described in Phase 6, Linux's NFS server relies on IP address trusted hosts authentication exclusively, so setting these options carefully is particularly important with NFS. You should consult the documentation for each of your servers to learn if you can block access by IP address or hostname.

As a general rule, it's best to use IP addresses or network block addresses in options such as these. When you use a hostname or domain name, the server relies on the Domain Name System (DNS) to identify computers. If your—or perhaps even another—DNS server has been compromised or contains inaccurate information, your security rules will be that much less effective.

Many servers use usernames and passwords to control access. Task 7.3 describes how to generate good passwords. You may want to review your server's password access options, if they exist. For instance, as described in Phase 6, Samba supports both encrypted and unencrypted passwords, with the former being preferable. SSH enables you to disable direct `root` logins, which can improve security slightly. You can also use host keys instead of or in addition to passwords with SSH, which can improve convenience—but if a client's key is stolen, the server system can then be compromised.

## Using *xinetd* Access Restrictions

Most Linux distributions use `xinetd` as a super server, and `xinetd` provides some powerful access control features. The distributions that use `xinetd` use a main configuration file called

/etc/xinetd.conf, but this file is largely empty because it calls separate files in the /etc/xinetd.d directory to do the real work. This directory contains separate files for handling individual servers. Phase 6 includes information on basic xinetd configuration. Security is handled on a server-by-server basis through the use of configuration parameters:

**Network interface**   The bind option tells xinetd to listen on only one network interface for the service. For instance, you might specify bind = 192.168.23.7 on a router to have it listen only on the Ethernet card associated with that address. This feature is extremely useful in routers, but it is not as useful in computers with just one network interface. (You can use this option to bind a server only to the loopback interface, 127.0.0.1, if a server should be available only locally. You might do this with a configuration tool like the Samba Web Administration Tool, or SWAT.) A synonym for this option is interface.

**Allowed IP or network addresses**   You can use the only_from option to specify IP addresses, networks (as in 192.168.78.0/24), or computer names on this line, separated by spaces. The result is that xinetd will accept connections only from these addresses.

**Disallowed IP or network addresses**   The no_access option is the opposite of only_from; you list computers or networks here that you want to blacklist.

**Access times**   The access_times option sets times during which users may access the server. The time range is specified in the form *hour:min-hour:min*, using a 24-hour clock. Note that this option only affects the times during which the server will make its *initial* response. If xinetd's access_times option is set to 8:00-17:00 and somebody logs in at 4:59 PM (one minute before the end time), that user may continue using the system well beyond the 5:00 PM cutoff time.

You should enter these options into the files in /etc/xinetd.d that correspond to the servers you want to protect. Place the lines between the opening brace ({) and closing brace (}) for the service. If you want to restrict *all* your xinetd-controlled servers, you can place the entries in the defaults section in /etc/xinetd.conf.

## Using TCP Wrappers

Although the inetd super server doesn't provide xinetd's access control tools, you can use inetd in conjunction with another package, known as TCP Wrappers, to provide similar access controls. This package provides a program known as tcpd. Instead of having inetd call a server directly, inetd calls tcpd, which does two things: It checks whether a client is authorized to access the server, and if the client has this authorization, tcpd calls the server program.

TCP Wrappers is configured through two files: /etc/hosts.allow and /etc/hosts.deny. The first specifies computers that are allowed access to the system in a particular way, the implication being that systems not listed are not permitted access. By contrast, hosts.deny lists computers that are not allowed access; all others are granted access to the system. If a computer is listed in both files, hosts.allow takes precedence.

Both files use the same basic format. The files consist of lines of the following form:

`daemon-list : client-list`

The *daemon-list* is a list of servers, using the names for the servers that appear in `/etc/services`. Wildcards are also available, such as ALL for all servers.

The *client-list* is a list of computers to be granted or denied access to the specified daemons. You can specify computers by name or by IP address, and you can specify a network by using a leading or trailing dot (.) when identifying networks by name or IP address block, respectively. For instance, `.luna.edu` blocks all computers in the `luna.edu` domain, and `192.168.7.` blocks all computers in the 192.168.7.0/24 network. You can also use wildcards in the *client-list*, such as ALL (all computers). EXCEPT causes an exception. For instance, when placed in `hosts.deny`, `192.168.7. EXCEPT 192.168.7.105` blocks all computers in the 192.168.7.0/24 network except for 192.168.7.105.

The `man` pages for `hosts.allow` and `hosts.deny` (they're actually the same document) provide additional information on more advanced features. You should consult them as you build TCP Wrappers rules.

**WARNING**    Remember that not all servers are protected by TCP Wrappers. Normally, only those servers that `inetd` runs via `tcpd` are so protected. Such servers typically include, but are not limited to, Telnet, FTP, TFTP, `rlogin`, `finger`, POP, and IMAP servers. A few servers can independently parse the TCP Wrappers configuration files, though; consult the server's documentation if in doubt.

## Setting Up Local Firewall Rules

The Linux kernel is capable of filtering packets based on various low-level attributes, such as the source and destination IP addresses, the source and destination port numbers, and whether a packet is the first one of a session or a continuation of an existing connection. For it to do so, though, you must use a utility that modifies the kernel's packet filter table. In the 2.4.*x* and later kernels, this utility is known as `iptables`. The 2.2.*x* kernel used a simpler tool, known as `ipchains`, to do this job, and the 2.0.*x* kernel used `ipfwadm` for this task. Each later kernel includes support for the older tools, so you can continue using `ipchains` or even `ipfwadm` with more recent kernels if you like; however, to access the full features of your kernel, you should use the latest packet filtering tool available for it.

To understand packet filter firewall rules, consider Figure 7.1, which shows the configuration of the filter table. In normal packet handling, one or more of three chains is involved: INPUT, OUTPUT, and FORWARD. To protect a computer from unwanted outside access, you'd write INPUT chain rules to block input packets from untrusted sources. You might also write OUTPUT chain rules to prevent abuses by local users or as a secondary line of defense for your local computer. (To gain full control of your computer, an intruder needs to receive data from your system, not just send data to it, so OUTPUT chain blocks can be helpful in protecting the computer.)

**FIGURE 7.1**    Linux uses a series of rules, which are defined in chains that are called at various points during processing, to determine the fate of network packets.

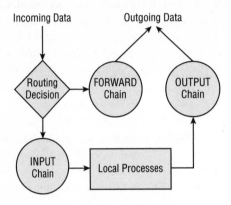

All of the chains implement a default policy. This policy determines what happens to a packet if no rule explicitly matches it. The default for the default policy is ACCEPT, which causes packets to be accepted. This policy is sensible in low-security situations, but for a more secure configuration, you should change the default policy to DROP or REJECT. The former causes packets to be ignored. To the sender, it looks as if a network link was down. The REJECT policy causes the system to actively refuse the packet, which looks to the sender as if no server is running on the targeted port. This option requires explicit kernel support. Both DROP and REJECT have their advantages. DROP reduces network bandwidth use and reduces the system's visibility on the network, whereas REJECT can improve performance for some protocols, such as auth/ident, which may retry a connection in the event a packet is lost. Using either DROP or REJECT as a default policy means that you must explicitly open ports you want to use. This is more secure than using a default policy of ACCEPT and explicitly closing ports because you're less likely to accidentally leave a port open when it should be closed.

To create firewall rules, you use the `iptables` command. You should probably start with the -L option, which lists the current configuration:

```
# iptables -L -t filter
Chain INPUT (policy ACCEPT)
target      prot opt source                destination

Chain FORWARD (policy ACCEPT)
target      prot opt source                destination

Chain OUTPUT (policy ACCEPT)
target      prot opt source                destination
```

The -t filter part of this command specifies that you want to view the filter table. This is actually the default table, so you can omit this part of the command if you like. In any event, the result is a list of the rules that are defined for the specified (or default) table. In this case, no rules are defined and the default policy is set to ACCEPT for all three chains in the table. This is a typical starting point, although depending on your distribution and your installation options, it's possible yours will have rules already defined. If so, you should track down the script that sets these rules and change or disable it. Alternatively, or if you just want to experiment, you can begin by flushing the table of all rules by passing -F *CHAIN* to iptables, where *CHAIN* is the name of the chain. You can also use -P *CHAIN POLICY* to set the default policy:

```
# iptables -t filter -F FORWARD
# iptables -t filter -P FORWARD DROP
```

These two commands flush all rules from the FORWARD chain and change the default policy for that chain to DROP. Generally speaking, this is a good starting point when configuring a firewall, although using REJECT rather than DROP has its advantages, as described earlier. You can then add rules to the chain, each of which matches some selection criterion:

```
# iptables -A INPUT -p tcp --dport 445 -s 172.24.1.0/24 -j ACCEPT
```

In this case, the iptables command implements three rules, all of which apply to the INPUT chain (-A INPUT). First, the packet must be a TCP packet (-p tcp). Second, the destination port number must be 445 (--dport 445). Finally, the source IP address must be on the 172.24.1.0/24 network block (-s 172.24.1.0/24). Packets that match *all* of these rules will be accepted; those that fail to match even a single rule will be dropped (assuming this is the default configuration) unless they match some other rule in the chain.

> The iptables command accepts a large number of rules, some of which are demonstrated shortly. Read the command's man page for more details.

A complete chain is created by issuing multiple iptables commands, each of which defines a single rule. You can then view the result by typing **iptables -L**, as described earlier. Listing 7.1 shows a sample iptables firewall script.

**Listing 7.1:** A Sample Linux Firewall Script for Use on a Workstation

```
#!/bin/bash

iptables -F INPUT
iptables -F FORWARD
iptables -F OUTPUT

iptables -P INPUT DROP
iptables -P FORWARD DROP
iptables -P OUTPUT DROP
```

```
# Let traffic on the loopback interface pass
iptables -A OUTPUT -d 127.0.0.1 -o lo -j ACCEPT
iptables -A INPUT -s 127.0.0.1 -i lo -j ACCEPT

# Let DNS traffic pass
iptables -A OUTPUT -p udp --dport 53 -j ACCEPT
iptables -A INPUT -p udp --sport 53 -j ACCEPT

# Let clients' TCP traffic pass
iptables -A OUTPUT -p tcp --sport 1024:65535 -m state \
        --state NEW,ESTABLISHED,RELATED -j ACCEPT
iptables -A INPUT -p tcp --dport 1024:65535 -m state \
        --state ESTABLISHED,RELATED -j ACCEPT

# Let local connections to local SSH server pass
iptables -A OUTPUT -p tcp --sport 22 -d 172.24.1.0/24 -m state \
        --state ESTABLISHED,RELATED -j ACCEPT
iptables -A INPUT -p tcp --dport 22 -s 172.24.1.0/24 -m state \
        --state NEW,ESTABLISHED,RELATED -j ACCEPT
```

Listing 7.1 consists of three broad parts. The first three calls to iptables clear out all pre-existing firewall rules. This is particularly important in a script that you're creating or debugging because you don't want to simply add new rules to existing ones; the result would likely be a confusing mishmash of old and new rules. The next three calls to iptables set the default policy to DROP on all three chains. This is a good basic starting point for a firewall. The remaining calls to iptables configure Linux to accept specific types of traffic:

**Loopback traffic** The script sets the system to accept traffic to and from the loopback interface (that is, 127.0.0.1). Certain Linux tools expect to be able to use this interface, and because it's purely local, the security risk in accepting such traffic is very slim. Note that the lines that enable this access use both the IP address (via the -d and -s options) and the lo interface name (via the -o and -i options). This configuration protects against someone spoofing the loopback address—an attacker pretending to be 127.0.0.1 from another computer. This configuration, like most iptables configurations, requires two iptables rules: one to enable incoming traffic and one to enable outgoing traffic.

**DNS traffic** The second block of rules enables UDP traffic to and from port 53, which handles DNS traffic. A configuration like this one is necessary on most systems to enable the computer to use its local DNS server. You could strengthen this configuration by specifying only your local DNS server's IP address. (If you have multiple DNS servers, you'd need one pair of rules for each one.)

**Client traffic** Listing 7.1 enables TCP packets to be sent from unprivileged ports (those used by client programs) to any system. This configuration allows new, established, or related outgoing traffic but allows only established or related incoming traffic. (This ability is provided by *stateful* inspection, hence the `-m state` and `--state` options.) This configuration effectively blocks the ability to run servers on unprivileged ports. Thus, an intruder or malicious authorized user won't be able to log into an unauthorized server that runs on such a port—at least not without `root` access to change the configuration.

**SSH server traffic**    The final block of options enables access to the SSH server (TCP port 22). This access, though, is restricted to the 172.24.1.0/24 network (presumably the local network for the computer). This configuration uses stateful packet inspection to outgoing traffic from the SSH server for established and related data but not for new or invalid packets. Incoming packets to the server are permitted for new, existing, or related traffic, but not for invalid packets.

A configuration such as the one in Listing 7.1 is suitable for a workstation that runs an SSH server for remote administration but that otherwise runs no servers. For a computer that runs many servers, you might need to add several additional blocks of rules similar to the SSH block, each one customized to a particular server.

## Setting Up a Stand-Alone Firewall

If your network includes a Linux router, such as the one configured in Phase 6, you can use `iptables` to set up firewall rules on the router system. The emphasis in such a configuration would be on the FORWARD chain rather than the INPUT and OUTPUT chains, although such a system would likely need to perform some INPUT and OUTPUT chain configuration to support its own administration and use. To protect your network using a firewall, you'd typically block outside access to servers that should only be accessible locally, such as your Samba server ports. You might also block certain types of outgoing connections. This configuration can be helpful in preventing abuses by local "bad apple" users or by worms or viruses that have infected your systems. For instance, you might block outgoing email (SMTP) connections except from your local mail server computer; this would prevent local workstations from becoming sources of spam if they're compromised by spambots. Of course, you should also protect the firewall computer itself. The most radical way to do this is to drop all outside access attempts to the server itself. Listing 7.2 shows a firewall script that implements these rules. This script makes heavier use of variables than does Listing 7.1; this type of configuration can make the script easier to change or use on multiple systems.

**Listing 7.2:**  A Sample Firewall Script for a Router

```
#!/bin/bash
# Router firewall rules.

# The local network interface
LOCALNET=192.168.1.0/24

# The interface that links to the Internet
INTERNET=192.168.24.0/24
```

```
# The local mail server
MAILSERV=192.168.1.17

iptables -F INPUT
iptables -F OUTPUT
iptables -F FORWARD

iptables -P INPUT ACCEPT
iptables -P OUTPUT ACCEPT
iptables -P FORWARD ACCEPT

# Block all outside direct access to the firewall
iptables -A INPUT -s $INTERNET -j DROP

# Block outside access to inside Samba ports (137-139 & 445)
iptables -A FORWARD -p udp --dport 137 -s $INTERNET -j DROP
iptables -A FORWARD -p tcp --dport 137 -s $INTERNET -j DROP
iptables -A FORWARD -p udp --dport 138 -s $INTERNET -j DROP
iptables -A FORWARD -p tcp --dport 138 -s $INTERNET -j DROP
iptables -A FORWARD -p udp --dport 139 -s $INTERNET -j DROP
iptables -A FORWARD -p tcp --dport 139 -s $INTERNET -j DROP
iptables -A FORWARD -p udp --dport 445 -s $INTERNET -j DROP
iptables -A FORWARD -p tcp --dport 445 -s $INTERNET -j DROP

# Block outgoing SMTP access except from the mail server
iptables -A FORWARD -p tcp --dport 25 -s $MAILSERV -j ACCEPT
iptables -A FORWARD -p tcp --dport 25 -s $LOCALNET -j DROP
```

**WARNING**   You should consider Listing 7.2 a basic demonstration only; it makes a poor router firewall script. This script uses a default-accept policy for forwarded traffic and blocks *only* the network's incoming Server Message Block/Common Internet File System (SMB/CIFS) and outgoing Simple Mail Transfer Protocol (SMTP) ports, as well as traffic directed at the router from outside systems. A real router's firewall script would most likely be longer and might do well to use a default-reject or default-deny policy.

If your network doesn't use Linux as a router, you should be able to implement similar rules with whatever router type your network uses. Even small broadband routers provide some sort of firewall rules. You'll have to consult your router's documentation to learn precisely how to do the job, though.

## Criteria for Completion

To complete this task, you should have developed a plan for improving your local network's security. You should identify and shut down unused servers, implement server-specific access control rules, examine xinetd or TCP Wrappers access control options, and implement iptables firewall control rules on both individual systems and on your Linux router (if your network uses one). For a small network, this task can take just an hour or two, particularly if you implement only modest improvements. For a large network, or if you intend to perform an extensive security audit, this task can take many hours to complete.

# Task 7.2: Enable User-Level Security Restrictions

Computers exist to help their users; however, sometimes users can become a problem. This can happen because a user is a "bad apple" or because a user does undesirable things through ignorance or sloppiness. For all of these reasons, Linux provides tools to limit the amount of damage that a user can do.

## Scenario

A multi-user Linux system has been experiencing problems every few days because of user processes that consume too much disk space, CPU time, or memory. To head off such problems in the future, you want to configure Linux to place limits on the amount of each of these resources that an individual user can consume.

## Scope of Task

This task involves making changes to two main Linux subsystems: limiting CPU time and memory using Pluggable Authentication Modules (PAM) and limiting disk use via the Linux disk quota system. Each of these tools requires its own configuration, so you'll be working with both systems.

### Duration

This task should take about 1 to 2 hours to complete. Once you've finished the task, you should be able to tweak the configurations in much less time.

### Setup

You must have root access to a Linux workstation to perform this task. The disk quota restrictions require kernel support. As of the 2.6.*x* kernels, the ext2fs, ext3fs, and ReiserFS filesystems support quotas, but you must explicitly enable support via the Quota Support kernel option in the filesystem area when recompiling your kernel. Many distributions ship with this support pre-compiled, so recompiling your kernel may not be necessary, but you should be aware of this option if you do recompile your kernel.

### Caveats

The usual `root` cautions apply to this task. In addition, setting limits that are too restrictive can cause problems for users: They may be unable to create files or their processes may be unceremoniously terminated if they exceed the CPU time and memory limits.

## Procedure

Disk quotas are more difficult to set than CPU time and memory limits. To enable disk quotas, you must both configure various tools (including, perhaps, recompiling your kernel) and enable quota support for various users. CPU time and memory limits, by contrast, are set by PAM options.

### Enabling Quota Support

Quotas require support in both the kernel for the filesystem being used and various user-space utilities. If your kernel lacks quota support, consult Phase 2 for information on recompiling your kernel.

Two general quota support systems are available for Linux. The first was used through the 2.4.*x* kernels and is referred to as the quota v1 support. The second was added with the 2.6.*x* kernel series and is referred to as the quota v2 system. This description applies to the latter system, but the former works in a similar way.

Outside of the kernel, you need support tools to use quotas. For the quota v2 system, this package is usually called `quota`, and it installs a number of utilities, configuration files, SysV startup scripts, and so on.

> You can install the support software from source code, if you like; however, this job is handled most easily using a package for your distribution. This description assumes that you install the software in this way. If you don't, you may need to create SysV or local startup scripts to initialize the quota support when you boot your computer. The Quota Mini-HOWTO, at `http://en.tldp.org/HOWTO/Quota.html`, provides details of how to do this.

You must modify your `/etc/fstab` entries for any partitions on which you want to use the quota support. In particular, you must add the `usrquota` filesystem mount option to employ user quotas and the `grpquota` option to use group quotas. Entries that are so configured resemble the following:

```
/dev/hdc5  /home  ext3  usrquota,grpquota  1  1
```

This line activates both user and group quota support for the /dev/hdc5 partition, which is mounted at /home. Of course, you can add other options if you like.

Depending on your distribution, you may need to configure the quota package's SysV startup scripts to run when the system boots. Phase 3 describes SysV startup script management in detail. Typically, you'll type a command such as **chkconfig quota on**; however, you should check on the SysV scripts installed by your distribution's quota package. Some distributions require use of commands other than chkconfig to do this task, as described in Phase 3. Whatever its details, this startup script runs the quotaon command, which activates the quota support.

After installing software and making configuration file changes, you must activate the systems. The simplest way to do this is to reboot the computer, and this step is necessary if you had to recompile your kernel to add quota support directly into the kernel. If you didn't do this, though, you should be able to get by with less disruptive measures: using modprobe to install the kernel module if necessary, running the SysV startup script for the quota tools, and remounting the filesystems on which you intend to use quotas by typing **mount -o remount /mount-point**, where *mount-point* is the mount point in question.

## Setting Quotas for Users

At this point, quota support should be fully active on your computer but the quotas themselves are not set. You can set the quotas by using edquota, which starts the Vi editor (described in Phase 1) on a temporary configuration file (/etc/quotatab) that controls quotas for the user you specify. When you exit from the utility, edquota uses the temporary configuration file to write the quota information to low-level disk data structures that control the kernel's quota mechanisms. For instance, you might type **edquota sally** to edit sally's quotas. The contents of the editor will show the current quota information:

```
Quotas for user sally:
/dev/hdc5: blocks in use: 3209, limits (soft = 5000, hard = 6500)
           inodes in use: 403, limits (soft = 1000, hard = 1500)
```

The temporary configuration file provides information on both the number of disk blocks in use and the number of inodes in use. (Each file, symbolic link, or directory consumes a single inode, so the inode limits are effectively limits on the number of files a user may own. Disk blocks vary in size depending on the filesystem and filesystem creation options, but they typically range from 512 bytes to 8KB.) Changing the use information has no effect, but you can alter the soft and hard limits for both blocks and inodes. The hard limit is the maximum number of blocks or inodes that the user may consume; the kernel will not permit a user to surpass these limits. Soft limits are somewhat less stringent; users may temporarily exceed soft limit values, but when they do so, the system issues warnings. Soft limits also interact with a grace period; if the soft quota limit is exceeded for longer than the grace period, the kernel begins treating it like a hard limit and refuses to allow the user to create more files. You can set the grace period by using edquota with its -t option, as in **edquota -t**. Grace periods are set on a per-filesystem basis rather than a per-user basis.

A few more quota-related commands are useful. The first is quotacheck, which verifies and updates quota information on quota-enabled disks. This command is normally run as part of the quota package's SysV startup script, but you may want to run it periodically (say, once a week) as a cron job. (Phase 3 describes cron jobs.) Although theoretically not necessary if everything works correctly, quotacheck ensures that quota accounting doesn't become inaccurate. The second useful auxiliary quota command is repquota, which summarizes the quota information on the filesystem you specify or on all filesystems if you pass it the -a option. This tool can be very helpful in keeping track of disk usage. The quota command has a similar effect. The quota tool takes a number of options to have them modify their outputs. For instance, -g displays group quotas, -l omits NFS mounts, and -q limits output to filesystems on which usage is over the limit. Consult quota's man page for still more obscure options.

## Setting CPU and Memory Limits

PAM enables you to set limits on the number of times individuals can log in, how much CPU time they can consume, how much memory they can use, and so on. Specifically, you use a PAM module called pam_limits to do this job. Most major Linux distributions use this module as part of their standard PAM configuration, so chances are you won't need to add it; however, you will still need to configure pam_limits. This is done by editing its configuration file, /etc/security/limits.conf. This file contains comments (denoted by hash marks, #) and limit lines that consist of four fields:

*domain type item value*

Each of these fields specifies a particular type of information:

**The domain**    The *domain* describes the entity to which the limit applies. It can be a username; a group name, which takes the form *@groupname*; or an asterisk (*) wildcard, which matches everybody.

**Hard or soft limits**    The *type* field specifies the limit as hard or soft. A hard limit is imposed by the system administrator and cannot be exceeded under any circumstances, whereas a soft limit may be temporarily exceeded by a user. You can also use a dash (-) to signify a limit is both hard and soft.

**The limited item**    The *item* field specifies what type of item is being limited. Examples include core (the size of core files created in certain types of program crashes), data (the size of a program's data area), fsize (the size of files created by the user), nofile (the number of open data files), rss (the resident set size), stack (the stack size), cpu (the CPU time of a single process in minutes), nproc (the number of concurrent processes), maxlogins (the number of simultaneous logins), and priority (the process priority). The data, rss, and stack items all relate to memory consumed by a program. These and other measures of data capacity are measured in kilobytes.

**The value**    The final field specifies the value that's to be applied to the limit.

As an example, consider the types of limits suggested in this task's Scenario section. If you want to limit CPU time to 30 minutes and memory use per program to 30MB (equally divided between data, RSS, and stack), you might use a configuration like this:

```
@users   hard   cpu     30
@users   hard   data    10240
@users   hard   stack   10240
@users   hard   rss     10240
```

All members of the `users` group are limited in the ways specified: CPU time cannot exceed 30 minutes and memory used by programs may not exceed 10MB for each of the data, stack, and RSS memory. These limits don't apply to users who aren't members of the `users` group, such as `root` and the accounts used to run most servers.

CPU time and total system access time are two entirely different things. CPU time is calculated based on the amount of time that the CPU is actively processing a user's data. Idle time (for instance, when a user's shell is active but no CPU-intensive tasks are running) doesn't count. Thus, a user can log in and remain logged in for hours even with a very low hard CPU time limit. This limit is intended to prevent problems caused by users who run very CPU-intensive programs on systems that should not be used for such purposes.

One particularly radical approach to security is to use the `/etc/nologin` file. If this file is present, only `root` may log into the computer. In many respects, this is like setting critical system limits to 0 for all other users. This file is most likely to be useful on dedicated server systems that have no regular console or remote shell users.

## Criteria for Completion

To complete this task, you should have implemented both disk quotas and limits on CPU time and memory use. Disk quota limits prevent users from consuming excessive amounts of disk space, while CPU and memory limits prevent user processes from running away and consuming ridiculous amounts of CPU time and memory. All three types of limits can be useful on multi-user systems with limited resources, but you'll have to be careful in setting these limits: If they're set too low, they'll interfere with users' legitimate uses of the computer.

# Task 7.3: Set Good User and System Passwords

Passwords are the "keys" to a computer system. Unlike physical keys, though, passwords are chosen by their users, and some passwords are better than others. If your users set poor passwords, the task of crackers who want to break into your system becomes easier. Therefore, you should know how to set passwords that are hard to break. Just as important, your *users* should know how to set good passwords. Thus, you should share the techniques described in this task with your users to improve your overall system security.

> The mainstream media uses the term *hacker* to refer to computer miscreants. This word has an older and more honorable meaning, though: In the Linux world, *hacker* often refers to people who are skilled with computers, and particularly with computer programming, and who use their skills for productive purposes. Many Linux developers consider themselves hackers in this positive sense. Thus, I use another word, *cracker*, to refer to individuals who break into and otherwise disrupt the operation of computers.

The same rules that apply to user passwords apply to the root password, but the root password is even more critical. Thus, you should be particularly diligent about setting a good root password, keeping it secret, and changing it from time to time.

## Scenario

As part of routine security maintenance, you want to change both your user password and your root password. Phase 1 describes the passwd utility, which is used to change your password; but to use this tool most effectively, you need to know how to generate a good password—or *two* good passwords, one for your user account and one for the computer's root account. (Ordinary users without superuser access need only generate one good password for each computer, of course.)

## Scope of Task

This task is basically a mental one; it can be done without access to a computer. Of course, in practice you'll ultimately need to use your Linux system and its passwd utility to change your password.

### Duration

This task should take half an hour or less to complete. Once you're familiar with the techniques of password generation, you should be able to create a new one in under a minute.

### Setup

No special setup is required to complete this task; you can do it using your mind alone (and this book for reference). To actually set your password, of course, you'll need to log into your Linux system and use the passwd utility.

### Caveats

As a purely mental activity, password generation poses no particular risks *per se*. The risks really apply to the consequences of doing this task incorrectly. A poor password might be guessed or otherwise discovered by a cracker, granting full access to your account (or the computer, in the case of the `root` password). Crackers can use network *sniffers* (tools to monitor network activity), *social engineering* (tricking people into revealing their passwords), *dictionary attacks* (encrypting every word in a dictionary and comparing the results to what's stored in a stolen encrypted password file), and other techniques to break into a computer. Even a good password can be a risk if you write it down or store it on a disk file.

# Procedure

Generating a good password requires two main steps: First, you should select a *base* for the password. The base should be relatively easy to remember but hard to guess. Second, you should modify the base in various ways to make it even harder to guess. Once you've selected and implemented your password, you should take various steps to keep it from being compromised.

## Selecting a Solid Base

The password base is a string that's memorable but that shouldn't appear in any language's dictionary as a single word. One reasonable procedure for picking a base is to use an acronym. For instance, you might use *yiwttd*, for *yesterday I went to the dentist*. (Of course, this specific example is a poor one because it's been used as an example in this book. A cracker who reads this book might add *yiwttd* to a dictionary, and it might spread from there.) Another option for a base is to use two short and unrelated words, such as *bunpen*. You won't find *bunpen* in a dictionary, although you will find its constituent words. (Again, this specific example is now a poor base because it's appeared in this book.) A variant on the multiword approach is to use fragments of multiple words, such as *asepho*, derived from *baseball* and *telephone*. As a general rule, an acronym is the safest choice, providing it doesn't happen to spell anything.

 **NOTE**   These examples are all six characters long. Subsequent modifications add characters, and passwords on some OSs are limited to eight characters in length, hence the six-character length. Modern Linux distributions are not so limited, and in fact eight characters is a more reasonable *minimum* safe password length than a maximum. You might need to generate short passwords for some purposes, though, such as for retrieving email from your ISP or logging onto Web pages.

There are many common types of strings you should *never* use as a password, or even as a password's base:

- The name of any relative, friend, co-worker, or pet
- The name of any character in a book, movie, or play or the name of a favorite work of fiction or art
- Your own name or your username
- Any other personally relevant information, such as your Social Security number or street address

- Particularly for the root password, any word signifying great power, such as *deity* or *boss*

- Particularly for workstations, a name or word that appears in plain sight of the terminal, such as the monitor's model number

- Any single word in any language, even if it's spelled backwards

- Any obvious misspelling of a word, such as *r0cket*, where the number *0* replaces the letter *o* in the word

- Any ascending or descending sequence of numbers or letters, such as *54321* or *ghijk*

- Any string of identical characters, such as *mmmmm*

- Any string of characters that appears on the keyboard, such as *qwerty*

The first six prohibitions are designed to protect against targeted attacks—the sort that seem to have a 100 percent chance of working in the movies. The rest of the prohibitions are designed to protect against words that are likely to appear in cracker dictionaries. These dictionaries are larger than ordinary dictionaries; they can include words in many languages, common misspellings, and nonwords that people are likely to try using.

## Modifying the Base

Once you've selected a base by creating an acronym or combining multiple words or word fragments, you should modify that base. These modifications move the base further from the original and make it harder for a cracker to guess the password, even if the base appears in the cracker's dictionary. You can make modifications such as the following:

**Adding random punctuation, numbers, or control characters**   You can add punctuation, numbers, or even control characters to the password. Ideally, you should place these features randomly within the base, as in *yi9wtt}d* or *b#unp0en*. The number of possible additions of even just two characters is so large that password-cracking programs can't check every possibility. One exception: Many people start or end passwords with numbers, so crackers often try the hundred password variants that result from this change, rendering the change ineffective.

**Changing case at random**   Linux's passwords are case sensitive, so randomly altering the case of passwords can be an effective strategy. For instance, your password might become *Yi9wTT}D* or *b#UNp0eN*. This modification isn't effective on all systems or password types, though. For instance, the passwords used by some versions of SMB/CIFS, and hence by Linux's Samba server, are case insensitive.

**Reversing the order of one base word**   If you use a pair of words as the base, you can reverse the order of one of the two words, as in *NU#bp0eN*. By itself, this modification isn't extraordinarily effective, but it does increase the cracker's search space by a modest amount.

As a general rule, adding punctuation, numbers, or control characters is the single most effective modification you can make. Altering the case of random characters can also be an important modification, at least for Linux's primary passwords.

When you're done, the password should resemble gibberish but be memorable to you personally. Automated password-cracking tools will very probably be unable to match your password, which is the goal of the exercise. As an ordinary user, you can then change the password by using the passwd command, as described in Phase 1.

**WARNING** Try not to change your password over an unencrypted link such as a Telnet session. Doing so poses the risk that the password-change transaction will be monitored by a cracker. If some suspicious event compels you to change your password over an insecure link, change it again as soon as possible over a secure link.

## Protecting Passwords from Abuse

Once you've generated a password, you normally use it. Simultaneously, though, you must protect the password from discovery by means other than password cracking. Certain practices put passwords at risk of discovery by others, and other practices can help prevent this discovery, or at least minimize the risk if your password is found out. Steps you can take to improve your password security include:

**Use encryption**   Whenever possible, use encrypted protocols, such as SSH, rather than unencrypted protocols, such as Telnet. This rule is particularly important on the Internet at large; when you send an unencrypted password over the Internet, it probably passes through about a dozen routers, any one of which could be compromised. Unfortunately, it's not always possible to use encryption. For instance, many ISPs support only unencrypted tools for recovering email using the Post Office Protocol (POP).

**Change your password frequently**   If you change your password often, you minimize the time period during which crackers can abuse it should it be discovered. As the system administrator, you can enforce a password-change time by using the `-x` parameter to `passwd`. For instance, typing **`passwd -x 30 ferd`** enforces a 30-day maximum password lifetime on the `ferd` account.

**Use unique passwords for each account**   If you have multiple accounts, don't reuse the same password on each account. Using unique passwords for all your accounts will minimize the risk should the password for one account be discovered. Unfortunately, the proliferation of password-protected Web sites makes this advice practically impossible to follow for Web sites. You may need to categorize your sites according to sensitivity, and assign unique passwords only to sites that are particularly sensitive, such as online banking sites. Alternatively, many Web browsers can now remember passwords for you; however, this approach has its own perils, which are described next.

**Store passwords only in your head**   Writing down passwords is potentially very dangerous; if the paper on which a password is written falls into the wrong hands, your account becomes instantly insecure. Likewise, storing your password in a computer file is risky; if your primary account is compromised, the secondary accounts protected by passwords stored in the primary account's files may also be attacked. Unfortunately, some tools are very awkward or impossible to use without storing passwords on disk; for instance, Fetchmail (`http://catb.org/~esr/fetchmail/`) is virtually worthless if it can't read a password from its configuration file.

**Beware of suspicious notices and activity** If your login failed but you think you typed the password correctly, change your password at once—especially if you logged in using a public terminal. If somebody's lurking nearby when you log in, be careful to shield the terminal as you type the password. Never give your password to anybody else. As a general rule, odd occurrences—both in software and in human behavior—should be treated with suspicion. These events may have perfectly innocent explanations, but if in doubt, take appropriate actions to protect your account. Changing your password is cheap insurance against many types of attack.

Many of these protective measures are essentially defenses against social engineering. Others defend against network sniffing or other dangers. All of them must be practiced by ordinary computer users, which means that you, as a system administrator, must find a way to educate your users. In some cases this is easy; for instance, if you're running Linux on a personal workstation, you may be the only user. In other cases, you may need to include password education in a formal user training program.

One other step you may want to consider as a system administrator is auditing your users' passwords. You can run a password-cracking program, such as Crack (`http://www.crypticide.org/users/alecm/`), to discover weak user passwords. You can then notify users of their weak passwords and give them some time to correct the matter. For the best security, transfer the password file via floppy disk to a computer that's not connected to the network and run the password-cracker on it. This practice will minimize the chance that a miscreant will stumble upon your password cracking.

Although discovering weaknesses in your system security in order to correct problems is an admirable goal, most organizations have strict policies forbidding activities such as password cracking. To avoid running afoul of such policies, even though you're doing it in the service of improving system security, be sure to clear password-cracking activity with somebody who has the proper authority. Obtain this authorization in the form of a written and signed document, not merely a verbal approval. Failure to obtain permission to crack users' passwords may cost you your job or even result in criminal charges being filed against you.

## Criteria for Completion

To complete this task, you should have generated two new passwords: one for your user account and one for **root**. Both passwords should be built from a hard-to-guess base with modifications that make the password even harder to guess. The final part of this task relates to ongoing practices rather than a single objective; you must employ safe and avoid unsafe practices with respect to protecting your password in day-to-day use. Because all users with regular Linux accounts have passwords, all of your users should be made aware of these password generation and protection practices.

# Task 7.4: Monitor for Security Breaches

Many Linux features fall into the "set and forget" category—you can configure them in a way that's reasonable and then leave that configuration in place until new local needs, a software upgrade, or some other factor forces you to make a change. Sadly, this isn't true of security. Because crackers are constantly discovering new vulnerabilities and means of attack, a configuration that was, to the best of your knowledge, perfectly good yesterday may be hopelessly unsafe today. Even if you believe a computer was reasonably secure, it's possible that a cracker could exploit a vulnerability you didn't know about. For these reasons, you should keep on the alert for security breaches and take steps to keep your system secure.

## Scenario

You've configured a computer with what you believe is an adequate level of security. You must now plan how to keep the computer's security level reasonable and monitor it for intrusion in case you've overlooked a vulnerability. To do this, you'll use software update tools, monitor security resources, and monitor your system for signs of intrusion.

## Scope of Task

In some sense, this task is an open-ended one; your security monitoring task is never complete. Creating a basic plan for security monitoring is more bounded, though.

### Duration

Planning your security monitoring regimen should take an hour or two. Actually implementing that plan will require countless hours over the next weeks, months, and years.

### Setup

To plan to monitor your system for security breaches requires little in the way of setup; you'll just need a regular account on an Internet-connected computer to refer to some Internet resources. Actually doing the monitoring, though, requires user access to the computer and occasionally `root` access.

### Caveats

Planning your monitoring activities is fairly risk free; however, implementing them isn't. Some parts of this task require `root` access, for which the usual caveats apply. Aside from those caveats, most security monitoring tasks are fairly innocuous and unlikely to cause harm. One exception is installing updated software, which runs the risk of causing a serious cascade of problems if the new software doesn't work exactly like the old version.

# Procedure

Keeping your system secure can be a full-time job if you do everything that's possible. To keep this task manageable, I focus on just four subtasks: keeping an eye on Internet security information, maintaining your system software, using Tripwire, and using `chkrootkit`.

## Monitoring Internet Security Resources

You should get into the habit of reviewing several security Web sites and other resources to learn about new threats:

**CERT/CC** The Computer Emergency Response Team Coordination Center (`http://www.cert.org`) hosts general security information, including information on the latest threats. Periodically reviewing this site will help you keep up-to-date with security developments.

**US-CERT** The United States Computer Emergency Readiness Team (`http://www.us-cert.gov`) has taken over some of the duties formerly held by CERT/CC. In practice, both sites are worth monitoring.

**CIAC** The Computer Incident Advisory Capability (`http://ciac.llnl.gov/ciac/`), run by the U.S. Department of Energy, is similar to CERT/CC and US-CERT in many respects, but its Web page gives greater emphasis to current threats and less coverage of general security practices.

**CVE** The Computer Vulnerabilities and Exposures (`http://cve.mitre.org`) site is dedicated to maintaining a dictionary of vulnerability names. This information can be useful in facilitating communication about problems. The CVE contains less in the way of descriptions of the vulnerabilities and exploits it names, though.

**SecurityFocus and Bugtraq** The SecurityFocus Web site (`http://www.securityfocus.com`) is yet another general security site. One of its important features is that it hosts the Bugtraq mailing list (`http://www.securityfocus.com/archive/1`), which can be a good way to keep informed—subscribe, and alerts about new threats will be delivered to your email account soon after they're made public.

**Linux Security** The Linux Security site, `http://www.linuxsecurity.com`, is very similar to CERT/CC, US-CERT, CIAC, and SecurityFocus in many ways. Linux Security, though, caters to Linux in particular and so may be more helpful in addressing Linux-specific issues or in pointing to Linux-specific fixes.

**Distributions' Web sites** Most Linux distributions maintain security information on their Web sites. Go to your distribution's main page and look for links relating to security. These sites can provide specific upgrade instructions for your distribution in particular.

**Product Web pages and mailing lists** Many programs have Web pages and mailing lists, and these can be good resources for learning of security problems related to these programs. Of course, regularly perusing all of the pages related to the hundreds of programs that make up a Linux system can be a full-time job. You might want to keep an eye on the Web pages or mailing lists for any high-profile server programs that you run, such as the Apache Web server or the sendmail mail server.

**Security newsgroups**   Several Usenet newsgroups are devoted to security. Of particular interest are the groups in the `comp.security` hierarchy.

I recommend you investigate most or all of these resources and then keep up with a few of them. For instance, you might check the CERT/CC and Linux Security Web sites on a daily basis, subscribe to the Bugtraq mailing list, and check your distribution's security page on a weekly basis. Keeping up with security developments in this way will alert you to new risks quickly—with any luck, quickly enough to avoid problems caused by crackers who might try to exploit weaknesses soon after they're discovered.

> Many of these resources offer RDF Site Summary (RSS) feeds of their content. This protocol enables you to use a news aggregator program, such as AmphetaDesk (`http://www.disobey.com/amphetadesk/`) or BlogBridge (`http://www.blogbridge.com`), to track security problems and learn about them as soon as possible.

## Keeping Your Software Up-to-Date

Phase 3 provided information on using the Yum and Advanced Package Tools (APT) utilities to retrieve data on updated packages and to download and install these packages. Because many security problems are caused by software bugs, you're well advised to keep your software up-to-date. That said, many of the updates offered by your distribution's maintainer are not security related and so can be bypassed if you don't want to bother upgrading them. I recommend you pay particular attention to server updates and to software that's used by `root` or that's installed with the set user ID (SUID) bit enabled. If in doubt, read up on the updated software on your distribution's or the package's Web page; you can learn from these sources what new features and bug fixes a new package includes.

## Using Tripwire

Should somebody manage to break into your computer, Tripwire (`http://www.tripwire.org`) may be your best bet to detect that fact. This utility records a set of information about all the important files on a computer, including various types of *checksums* and *hashes*—short digital "signatures" that enable you to quickly determine whether or not a file has been changed. (These can also be used in other ways; for instance, Linux uses hashes to store passwords.) With this database stored in a secure location, you can check your system periodically for alteration. If an intruder has modified any of your files, Tripwire will alert you to this fact. If you like, you can run a Tripwire verification on a regular basis—say, once a week in a `cron` job.

Many distributions ship with Tripwire, but it may not be installed by default. The utility is controlled through two configuration files: `tw.cfg` and `tw.pol`, which often reside in `/etc/tripwire`. The `tw.cfg` file controls overall configuration options, such as where `tw.pol` resides, how Tripwire sends reports to the system administrator, and so on. The `tw.pol` file includes information on the files Tripwire should monitor, among other things. Both files are binary files created from text-mode files called `twcfg.txt` and `twpol.txt`, respectively. You may need to edit twpol.txt to eliminate references to files that you don't have on your system and to add information on files that you do have but that the default file doesn't reference. Use the twinstall.sh program (which often resides in /etc/tripwire) to generate the binary configuration files and other critical database files. This utility will ask you to set a pair of passphrases, which are like passwords but are typically longer, to control access to the Tripwire utilities. You'll then need to enter these passphrases to have the utility do its encoding work.

Once you've generated the basic setup files, type **tripwire --init** to have Tripwire generate initial checksums and hashes on all the files it's configured to monitor. This process is likely to take a few minutes. Thereafter, typing **tripwire --check** will check the current state of the system against the database, and typing **tripwire --update** will update the database (say, in case you upgrade a package). The --init and --update operations require you to enter the passphrase, but --check doesn't. Therefore, you can include an automated Tripwire check in a cron job. (Phase 3 describes cron jobs in more detail.)

Tripwire is best installed and initialized on a completely fresh system, before connecting the computer to the Internet but after all programs have been configured. Although it's possible to install it on a system that's been up and running for some time, if that computer has already been compromised without your knowledge, Tripwire won't detect that fact.

## Using *chkrootkit*

The chkrootkit program (http://www.chkrootkit.org) is something of a last-resort method of detecting intrusion and is the closest thing in the Linux world to Windows virus scanners. (Linux virus scanning programs also exist, but they're intended mainly to check for Windows viruses on Samba shares. Linux viruses are not a problem in the real world, at least not as of late 2006.)

Many crackers use *root kits,* which are prepackaged intrusion tools. When an intruder runs a root kit against a target, the root kit software probes for known weaknesses (such as servers with known security bugs), breaks in, and installs software to enable simpler access by the intruder. The intruder can then log in using Telnet, SSH, or the like and gain full control of the system.

Intruders who use root kits are often referred to as *script kiddies.* These miscreants have minimal skill; they rely on the root kit to do the real work of the intrusion. Some people prefer to reserve the term *cracker* for more skilled intruders, but others consider script kiddies to be crackers with minimal expertise.

Using chkrootkit is fairly straightforward: Type its name. The result is a series of lines summarizing checks that the software performs. These lines should all end with not infected, no suspect files found, or a similar reassuring message. If any message alerts you to an intrusion, you should take immediate corrective measures.

# Criteria for Completion

To complete this task, you should have a plan in place to keep yourself and your system up-to-date concerning security. You should have reviewed several security Web sites and other Internet resources and be prepared to monitor them regularly. You should plan to use Yum, APT, or another system package tool to keep yourself informed of package updates and to install them when necessary. You should also plan to use Tripwire and `chkrootkit` on a regular basis (perhaps run from `cron`) to monitor your system for intrusion. In reality, this task is never complete; you'll be performing these tasks (and perhaps others) in perpetuity in order to keep your system secure.

# Index

**Note to the Reader:** Throughout this index **boldfaced** page numbers indicate primary discussions of a topic. *Italicized* page numbers indicate illustrations.